Thoughtful foragers

NEW STUDIES IN ARCHAEOLOGY

Series editors

Colin Renfrew, *University of Cambridge*
Jeremy Sabloff, *University of Pittsburgh*

Other titles in the series include

STEVEN J. MITHEN *Trinity Hall, Cambridge*

Thoughtful foragers

A study of prehistoric decision making

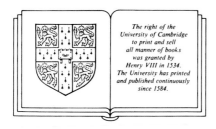

The right of the
University of Cambridge
to print and sell
all manner of books
was granted by
Henry VIII in 1534.
The University has printed
and published continuously
since 1584.

Cambridge University Press

Cambridge

New York   Port Chester   Melbourne   Sydney

Published by the Press Syndicate of the University of Cambridge
The Pitt Building, Trumpington Street, Cambridge CB2 1RP
40 West 20th Street, New York, NY 10011, USA
10 Stamford Road, Oakleigh, Melbourne 3166, Australia

First published 1990

Printed in Great Britain at the University Press, Cambridge

British Library cataloguing in publication data

Mithen, Steven J.
Thoughtful foragers: a study of prehistoric
decision making – (New studies in archaeology)
1. Prehistoric civilization
I. Title   II. Series
930.1

Library of Congress cataloguing in publication data

Mithen, Steven J.
Thoughtful foragers: a study of prehistoric decision makers /
Steven J. Mithen.
    p.   cm. – (New studies in archaeology)
Bibliography.
Includes index.
ISBN 0 521 355702
1. Paleolithic period. 2. Mesolithic period. 3. Hunting,
Prehistoric. 4. Hunting and gathering societies – Decision-making.
I. Title. II. Series.
GN772.M52   1989
930.1′2—dc20   89-1016 CIP

ISBN 0 521 35570 2

For SUSAN

CONTENTS

FIGURES

TABLES

PREFACE

This book has been developed from my Ph.D. thesis which I completed in December 1987. Yet its roots lie earlier and can be pinpointed to two not unrelated events. The first was on a hot and sticky day during the summer of 1978. I sat with my brother in a shady spot near Les Eyzies and pondered the paintings of Font de Gaume after the first of many visits to that cave. How mysterious the prehistoric past appeared. What beauty the hunters must have found in their icy world, and within themselves, to make such art. The second occurred a couple of years later in the midst of a Yorkshire winter – the ice age had returned with a vengeance! Now an undergraduate at Sheffield University, I sat reading in my damp bedsit and was transfixed by *Transformations*, Renfrew and Cooke's book on mathematical approaches to culture change. I understood as little of the mathematics as I did of the French guide's descriptions of the cave paintings. But what an intriguing idea! Can the coldness of equations and computer programmes really help in studying the complexities of culture and the warmth of the human spirit as so perfectly expressed in the smudge of ochre and mark from a burnt stick on the walls of Font de Gaume? Now sitting in my positively post-glacial Cambridge study and with this book before me, I can still confess to ignorance, but also to a continuing fascination with the idea.

For having the chance to explore this idea I must first thank those who taught me archaeology at Sheffield, particularly Robin Dennell, Andrew Fleming, Robin Torrence and Richard Hodges. Similarly to those who taught me a little biology, mathematics and computing at York University, especially Michael Usher and John Lawton. The Ph.D. thesis on which this book is based was written in Cambridge and I must thank the members of the archaeology department for creating such a stimulating atmosphere, notably Colin Renfrew, Todd Whitelaw, Sander Van de Leeuw, Geoff Bailey, Paul Mellars, Ian Hodder and Jamie McGlade. I was also lucky to discuss my work with the American scholars who pass through Cambridge. I particularly thank Jim Bell and Ezra Zubrow. Great encouragement was also gained from Clive Gamble and Rob Foley through the example of their own work and the comments they passed on mine. Others have helped with particular parts of this work. Sander Van de Leeuw, Jamie McGlade and Montserrat Gomendio made useful criticisms of an earlier version of the introductory chapter. S. H. Anderson, H.P. Blankholm, Lars Larsson and Peter Rowley-Conwy have been kind enough to listen to my approach to the Mesolithic and comment upon it. Tony Sinclair made some useful comments on my thoughts about technology. Paul Bahn and Jean Clottes provided me with a series of remarks on my cave art studies which have been particularly useful. When building my red deer simulation model I had the advice of Steve Albon, who kindly allowed me access to the Rhum data. Similarly Nick Tyler helped with my reindeer simulations.

Once the thesis was produced Geoff Bailey and Stephen Shennan made a series of perceptive criticisms, which I hope have now been attended to, and provided great encouragement to develop the work. This book was written while I was a Research Fellow at Trinity Hall, Cambridge. I thank the Master and Fellows for the intellectually stimulating and pleasant atmosphere at Trinity Hall, which enabled me to hit the wordprocessor again so soon after finishing the thesis. I thank Colin Renfrew for inviting me to write this book, and Frances Brown and the editors at Cambridge University Press for their invaluable advice.

I thank the following for permission to reproduce figures: The Smithsonian Institute Press (Fig. 3.2), The University of Washington Press (Fig. 3.3), The Australian Institute of Aboriginal Affairs (Fig. 3.4), Harvard University Press (Fig. 3.5), Lars Larsson (Figs. 4.1 and 4.5). Permission has been sought from C. Hurst and Co. (Publishers Ltd) for permission to reproduce Fig. 3.6, and from Sansoni for Fig. 7.1.

Finally I have three thankyous of a different kind. First to my brother Richard, for sitting and talking with me near Les Eyzies (and all the other places). Secondly to my daughter Hannah, for constantly reminding me, as I was trying to write, that the present is in fact much more interesting than the past! Lastly to my wife Susan, for all her support and interest in my work. I dedicate this book to her.

1

Introduction

In a minute there is time
For decisions and revisions which a minute will reverse

T.S. Eliot, 'The Love Song of J. Alfred Prufrock'

One of the unique characteristics of the human species is the possession of highly developed capacities for learning, decision making and problem solving, as T.S. Eliot reminds us. These result in a behavioural flexibility unparalleled in any other species. Although such capacities often require a social context for their use, they reside in the individual. Quite simply, it is these that constitute the source of cultural behaviour. It is remarkable, therefore, that archaeology, a discipline with the human species as its centre and which claims a pre-eminent role for understanding cultural behaviour, has paid scant attention to the processes of learning and decision making by individuals.

How can we gain an adequate understanding of what happened in the past, and why it happened, without making explicit reference to people taking decisions on the basis of accumulated knowledge between alternative courses of action? Certainly individual decision makers cannot be divorced from their social contexts and are part of natural communities, but it is the individual who perceives, thinks and decides. To make a flint arrowhead in one shape rather than another, to hunt deer rather than to collect molluscs, to paint rather than inscribe upon a pot are all decisions taken by individuals upon which our conception of 'cultures' and trajectories of social and economic change are imposed. Such decisions underlie all processes highlighted in recent archaeological thought, whether they be intensification and population pressure or core-periphery networks and peer-polity interaction. These, and other processes, are insufficiently described and understood when lacking reference to the individuals involved. The great changes in human society recorded in the archaeological record – the development of complex technology, the origin of art and agriculture and the emergence of social complexity – are all ultimately underwritten by people making decisions while going about their daily business.

If our explanation for such culture change is to be improved by reference to individual decision making, then the converse is also true: archaeological data and patterns will contribute to understanding the decision-making process itself. Through archaeological data we can investigate the evolution of decision-making capacities, their characteristics (which are partly defined by the evolutionary context), and the role they play in long-term social and economic change.

These provide, therefore, two complementary challenges for this book. First to develop explanations for problems posed by the archaeological record which make explicit reference to individual decision making. As a subject for this I take the early prehistory of Europe, an archaeological database in which a series of such problems have been clarified by recent syntheses (e.g. Bailey 1983; Dennell 1985; Gamble 1986; Zvelebil 1986b; Rowley-Conway *et al.* 1987; Bonsall 1989. These leave early European prehistory ripe for a new theoretical approach. Hand in hand with this, is an attempt to use the archaeological data to improve our understanding of the decision-making process. These two aims are not easily separated, and it is from their interaction that progress will be most forthcoming – building models of individual decision making, trying these with archaeological data, finding their faults, omissions and strengths, and then revising and developing the model. A learning process of modelling, application and reflection.

The resulting book is both optimistic and audacious. It is optimistic in its intention – to develop explanations which refer to the individual decision maker. The choice of case studies – the Mesolithic of southern Scandinavia in Part 2 and the Upper Palaeolithic of south-west Europe in Part 3 – also require some optimism and a little daring. Both have extensive and complex databases which I hope to simplify without trivialising. It is similarly audacious in that it not only dares to tread into the firing range of archaeological theory, wearing the ready target of an evolutionary approach, but also presumes to offer a new interpretation of Upper Palaeolithic art. Risking the wrath of those hostile to evolutionary theory and those who have devoted themselves to the study of Palaeolithic art is not something I do lightly for I respect their criticisms and knowledge. But I think that such risks are required if archaeological theory and cave art studies are to develop. Those offering symbolic-structuralist approaches have made cogent criticisms of current evolutionary approaches, but offered little of value in their place. If we are to explain the phenomenon of cave art then it must be placed into a wider context of hunter-gatherer behaviour and Upper Palaeolithic subsistence and society. At the 1988 TAG (Theoretical Archaeology Group) conference Richard Bradley warned against the 'loss of nerve' in archaeology. So here, with a deep breath and a steady hand, I set out to try and allay his fears.

Individualistic approaches in archaeology

To focus on the individual decision maker is to adopt the methodological individualism of Watkins (1952a,b) in which explanations for social and economic phenomena must make reference to the dispositions of individuals. I do this cautiously, however, noting the criticisms of Gellner (1987), and in a spirit of enquiry rather than dogma. My position is as much pragmatic as philosophical. I simply want to suggest that part of the reason that archaeologists continue to have difficulty in explaining change is that they have neglected one locus for that change – people making decisions about what to do.

Bailey identified the position I take when in fact arguing against a focus on the individual and the concomitant short time scale: 'since behaviour patterns are mediated through the actions of individuals as members of corporate societies, explanations that leave these factors out of account in an appeal to a different order of scale are somehow incomplete explanations' (1981b: 112). This stance does not result from egocentrism as Bailey claimed. It simply recognises that the biological basis that constitutes the advanced capacities for learning, decision making and problem solving (which I will refer to simply as decision-making capacities) possessed by humans reside in the individual and are exercised in day-to-day activities. These capacities, which along with symboling and self-awareness are central to the capacity for culture (by no means a solely human phenomenon), provide the dynamic for culture change. Consequently my approach to individual decision making is from an explicitly evolutionary ecological position. It might be noted here, however, that other archaeologists have arrived at the same focus from similar (e.g. Earle and Preucel 1987) as well as markedly different persuasions, particularly those which embrace Giddens' (1985) theory of structuration (e.g. Hodder 1985). I believe that there are significant points of contact between evolutionary approaches and those of structuration, as will become evident below. This is also recognised in the recent work of Shennan (1989). Here, therefore, appears to be a subject to return some unity to theoretical archaeology after recent years of fracas. Not surprisingly, that subject is simply people.

Methodological objections to individualistic approaches may be easier to sub-stantiate than those based on theory. Bailey (1981b) stressed that the nature of the archaeological record is such that it is simply not amenable for discussion about individuals. Archaeological assemblages normally result from the corporate ac-tions of many people, accumulating over many years and subject to serious post-depositional change. These are only meaningful in terms of group or 'average' behaviours. This, however, is to miss the point. A concern with individual decision making does not require the identification of particular characters in the past, although in exceptional circumstances this may be possible (Hill and Gunn 1977). Recognising that the actions of particular individuals are inaccessible to us as archaeologists certainly poses a dilemma, but does not invalidate the need for a focus on the individual if that is required for adequate explanations (Shennan 1986: 334). There is a methodological challenge here – to relate the decision-making processes of individuals to the archaeological record. It is a challenge that appears to have been ignored or wished away by others who advocate a concern with individual action in prehistory. Here, however, it is taken seriously and it constitutes a central theme of this book.

A second methodological problem is more serious. People live in symbolically structured worlds, and act in relation to cultural goals which they may, or may not, be aware of possessing. How can we adopt a focus on individuals without access to the minds of prehistoric people and hence to their symbolic worlds and cultural values? Surely, it is only by knowing their thoughts that we can understand why they chose one course of action rather than another? And just as surely, these minds and thoughts are lost to us.

However, decision-making capacities are ultimately of a biological nature; they have evolved by natural selection and to do so have had to confer some benefit of adaptive value. So by adopting this evolutionary ecological perspective, decision-making processes become amenable for study by prehistorians since we can focus on how they enable people to adapt to their social and natural environments. Now, by viewing human decision making and action in this manner we do not deny that people live in a complex symbolic world of their own creation. Huntergatherers, and I suspect people in all types of socio-economic conditions, appear to articulate the natural world (in which I include interactions with other members of their own species) in an ecological and symbolic framework simultaneously and without creating contradictions for themselves (e.g. Blurton-Jones and Konner 1976). As Layton has recently remarked, 'Although the Dorze believe the leopard is a Christian animal they do not leave their goats unattended on fast days' (1985: 451).

The nature of this articulation is not easy to characterise or understand. Gellner (1988) has made a brave attempt. He asks how it is possible that in 'primitive' thought one finds accurate and detailed observation of the world demonstrating an immense empirical sensitivity sitting side by side with what are absurd beliefs about that same world. These beliefs are expressed with the same concepts and language and cannot be explained away as a function of our misunderstanding of their meaning. He argues that one must recognise that primitive thought is multistranded, that it is natural for what we would identify as clearly separate and incompatible activities to be fused and intertwined into one single semantic context. Indeed, he argues that it is our own type of thought today with its inclination to separate and categorise that requires explanation since 'The conflation and confusion of function, of aims and criteria is the normal, original condition of mankind' (1988: 45).

Whether or not this is a valid characterisation of primitive thought, if indeed there is such a thing, it nevertheless emphasises how studies that approach cognition from an ecological perspective with its concern with adaptation and those which focus on symbolism and meaning are neither contradictory nor at loggerheads. They are compatible and require, not preclude, each other. Unfortunately, it is difficult to see how archaeologists can pursue the latter approach when the meanings of prehistoric artefacts are lost except in the most trivial of senses (i.e. those to which Hodder 1987 refers). But the ecological approach is certainly available and can allow us to place the individual decision maker at the centre of our studies and explanations.

For an evolutionary stance the central concept must be adaptation. The implication is not that all actions will play a role in adaptation nor that those which do can in any sense be described as optimal, except again in a rather trivial sense. Adaptation must ultimately refer to reproductive success. When dealing with simple societies I am sympathetic to the position that sees the achievement of cultural goals, such as the possession of wealth, prestige and the attainment of leadership, as being proximate means by which individuals gain reproductive success (Borgerhoff Mulder 1987). This does not imply that there are easy ways to measure reproductive or cultural success, or of coping with the complicated social strategies that people may adopt. As Robert Hinde has recently remarked, those with a biological perspective must come 'armed with humility in the face of the complexity of human cognitive functioning and social systems if their contribution is to be effective' (1987: 174).

Adaptation can also be studied with respect to the achievement of intermediate goals, notably efficient foraging behaviour. This may either confer direct cultural and reproductive success or provide the individual with the means (e.g. time, state of health) to attain these. Consequently my starting point is decision making in foraging strategies though, as will become apparent, this is not easily divorced from social and cognitive activity once a decision-making perspective is adopted. It is another strength of focusing on individual decision making, that the barriers between the social and economic are not so much broken down as non-existent in the first place.

That my archaeological studies start with faunal assemblages and foraging and work towards social and cognitive behaviour is essentially a pragmatic stance. With the current methods and theoretical approaches available, an initial concern with the direct interaction between humans and the natural environment provides us with a window into the complex world of early prehistoric society. Through this window we can find the individual and by focusing on his/her decision making we can relate social, cognitive and ecological aspects of behaviour. By this means we can integrate what initially appear to be disparate elements of the archaeological record relating to these different spheres of activity. Such integration is perhaps the crux of archaeological explanation (Shennan 1986: 336). So let me be clear. In this work I invoke the decision making of individuals and/or the decisions taken to explain patterning and variation in the archaeological record by integrating elements of that record which were previously unconnected. The importance of making such links in terms of constructing explanations has been stressed by Miller and Tilley (1984a: 151). This is not to suggest that this is the only form that explanation may take.

I must make one further point about the approach I adopt. Once we focus on individuals rather than groups, it becomes immediately apparent that even the most egalitarian hunter-gatherer society is immensely heterogeneous. Each individual is different and what may be adaptive for one may be neutral or maladaptive for another. We can of course classify the members by age and sex and then focus on generic individuals of each class. Now, by seeking the individuals through faunal assemblages we do inevitably find only one type of decision maker, i.e. those concerned with the hunting of large terrestrial game. Moreover, I will be focusing on just a small set of the many decisions that those individuals take. Consequently the picture of prehistoric society created will be distorted by this neglect of other individuals and other decisions. A comprehensive picture can only be constructed slowly, by focusing on different classes of individual in society and understanding how they interact. That I do not attempt this is simply because I am not trying to do 'prehistoric ethnography'. Rather I want to tackle specific problems posed by the archaeological record by focusing on the individuals and decisions of principal relevance to these.

Evolutionary approaches in archaeology

Evolutionary perspectives in archaeology have recently been heavily criticised. Here I must refute some of the objections, particularly those of Shanks and Tilley (1987a,b), not because they are damning, but because they are fallacious. I shall also distance my evolutionary approach from the 'cultural selectionism' of Dunnell (1980) and Rindos (1984) and make some brief comments on Ingold's (1986) position concerning the relationship between humans and other animals. First I must make clear what a valid evolutionary ecological perspective entails (see also Mithen 1989a).

The most important feature is a concentration on the individual. The notion that a society may somehow be adapted to its environment cannot be founded on any evolutionary basis, indeed it is not clear at all what this could mean. Here, one must agree with Shanks and Tilley: 'Societies, unlike individual organisms, do not have any clear-cut physical paramaters or boundaries, nor do societies have conscious problems of self-maintenance or a need to adapt. Individuals may have these characteristics but they cannot be validly anthropomorphised in terms of entire social totalities' (1987b: 155).

Palaeoeconomy (Higgs 1972, 1975) which looked to evolutionary theory for justification was inherently flawed in its theoretical base when individuals and short time spans were neglected. A greater error lies with those who have used optimal foraging theory in anthropology and archaeology, and hence have explic-itly adopted an evolutionary stance, but applied the models to groups rather than to individuals (e.g. Belovsky 1987). The sum result of a group of individuals all in some way adapted to their own social and physical environments may be a group extremely out of balance with its natural resources, inefficient in the flows of energy, information and matter through it and generally devoid of any characteris-tics that may be attributed to its members. Consequently it is not legitimate to speak of prehistoric hunter-gatherer populations in terms of adaptive systems (e.g. Binford 1980).

A second element that must be stressed is that the individuals forming the object of an evolutionary ecological approach are not in any sense passive. Hodder describes this position:

The conception of humanity underlying the behaviourism that dominates the social sciences, and archaeology to a greater extent than most, can be described as passive. The key words within this viewpoint are that people react to external stimuli such that their behaviour reflects the rules and goals of the wider society to which the individual is subordinate so their culture serves the function of adaptation within and between systems   (1985: 1–2)

Shanks and Tilley are somewhat more forthright. They argue that an evolutionary approach leaves us with a: 'plastic, malleable cultural dope incapable of altering the conditions of his or her existence and always subject to the vagaries of external non-social forces beyond mediation or any realistic form of active intervention (1987a: 56). This is wrong. A valid evolutionary approach must be founded upon the view of the individual as an active agent, constantly making decisions to alter his/her cognised social and physical environments. When dealing with modern *Homo*, and probably most other species, reference to natural selection must concern the evolution of learning and decision-making capacities resulting in flexible behaviour, with features such as creative thought and action as the driving forces of adaptation. Recent works which have adopted evolutionary approaches to explain cultural behaviour but which concentrate on genetic processes and supposedly analogous cultural ones, such as Lumsden and Wilson (1981), are ultimately flawed. As one reviewer of the Lumsden and Wilson volume was led to comment: 'In the final analysis, behaviour, both human and non-human, is about decision making over more immediate problems of survival and reproduction with more directly measurable proximate consequences, and it is on the details of *these* decision processes and their functional consequences that the new sociobiology will need to concentrate. The genes will look after themselves' (Dunbar 1981: 189).

Consequently the term 'selection' which is frequently invoked by archaeologists when they adopt evolutionary approaches plays little role in this study. It is only when I am dealing with the evolution of decision-making capacities themselves that the concept of selection becomes useful. Arguments which try to use selection to explain the persistence of cultural traits are pushing cultural evolution into a misplaced analogy with biological evolution. We need to deal with people's choices, placing these, not the artefacts, at the centre of our study. This indeed may be construed as artefacts being 'selected' by the choices but such selection is goal-directed and conscious, in direct contrast to the blindness of natural selection. Hence to use the term is not only inappropriate but also confusing.

Rindos (1984) in particular has recently argued for a 'cultural selectionism'. The nub of his argument is that natural selection operates on traits whatever their mode of inheritance, that is, upon the phenotype not the genome (1984: 55). But the error he makes is that while there is a requirement that traits be passed on to offspring for them to be selected, this is simply not the case for cultural (i.e. learnt) behaviour. The offspring of an individual who achieved high reproductive success owing to the possession of a particular set of cultural traits do not necessarily possess that same culture. Genetic traits are passed on, naturally selected by the differential reproductive success of their bearers in the previous generation. General psychological propensities which lead individuals to act in one way rather than another are indeed inherited. It is these, together with a set of unique circumstances, that lead an individual to choose to adopt a particular set of cultural traits. Rindos fails to justify his assertion that 'the fact that human cultural behaviours are not the result of genetic differences does not imply that the traits could not have been the result of selection' (1984: 61). This is exactly what *is* implied unless we distort the meaning of natural selection and we have here a contradiction inherent in a cultural selectionist stance. Consequently Rindos is wrong that we do not have to deal with problem solving and goal-directed behaviour since it is through these processes, which evolved by natural selection, that cultural variability is created and particular traits are chosen, or not chosen, to persist through time. Decision making has a central role to play in explanations of both human (Flannery 1986a: 5) and non-human behaviour (e.g. Dunbar 1984: 3–4).

The failure on the part of social theorists, as well as cultural ecologists, to focus upon these active characteristics of decision-making processes derives partly from the idea that 'adaptation' should be seen as a particular state that can readily be achieved. A more useful viewpoint is to see adaptation as an active process of becoming, rather than an achieved and static state of being. It is indeed a matter of confusion that the term adaptation can refer both to a process and to an end product (Dunbar 1982). When this has been recognised in archaeology the attitude appears to be one of muddling along (e.g. Gamble 1984: 238) so that absolutely everything is subsumed by the term and nothing explained. Archaeologists should focus on the first of these, adaptation as a process, and this will almost incidentally rid us of the optimality issue. The physical environment is in a constant state of flux, as is the social environment in terms of the behaviour of other individuals. People are also severely limited in their knowledge of the possibilities and consequences of different courses of action. It is of little value to suppose that people are engaged in activities which maximise their inclusive fitness since the world simply does not stand still long enough for them to achieve this.

This leads us to one of the principal problems with the use of optimal foraging theory in archaeology, and indeed of optimality models in general, including applications to explain technology (e.g. Torrence 1989b). These approaches explain the static state of individuals or groups (and their material culture) with their environment at one particular point in time by reference to functional relationships (e.g. energy maximising, risk minimising) but cannot address how these states are arrived at and will be maintained as the environment changes. As archaeologists we should be concerned with change and consequently our most useful evolutionary perspective is one thàt emphasises adaptation as a dynamic process rather than a static state. The same critique can be made against other approaches to hunter-gatherer subsistence and settlement patterns outside of the strict optimal foraging framework. For instance Rowley-Conwy (1987) has summarised a common ecological stance in the study of prehistoric foragers in which a series of sites within one region are analysed as to the seasonality and purpose of occupation. These are then pieced together like a jigsaw to reconstruct the socio-economic system – an attempt at prehistoric ethnography. Only then is the question of change addressed from what has now been fossilised as a static system in a harmonious balance with the environment. The studies of site seasonality and function are clearly essential but these must be conducted in a framework which views the system as a continually changing entity composed of dynamic, creative and interacting individuals.

By doing this we avoid the problem of tautology – the fittest survive and those that survive were the fittest – a further criticism levelled by Shanks and Tilley (1987b: 153). By concentrating on the process of adapting we are specifying *how* 'the fittest survive', rather than taking this as a truism (Borgerhoff Mulder 1987). We must agree with Hodder therefore, that 'Any adequate understanding of social change must take into account the knowledgeability of human actors, that is, their monitoring and observation of intended and unintended consequences of their actions' (1985: 3) since this is at the heart of the adaptive process.

Similarly there must be agreement on another issue that Hodder (1985) has recently stressed – that the actions of individuals can only be studied in a historical context. It was a feature of the cultural ecological approach, falsely justified by reference to evolutionary theory, to dismiss or neglect historical factors, as Hodder noted. Yet when adaptation is seen as a process, and actions dependent upon experience and knowledge, the historical context must be essential to any explanation.

If those critical of an evolutionary ecological approach were to accept that this does in fact lead to a concern with active individuals in specific historical contexts, rather than with ill-founded notions of societal adaptation and equilibrium, I fear that they would reject this as trivial. They may argue that even though the biological underpinning of human decision making and symbolic capacities cannot be denied, these have no consequences for the manner in which these capacities are used. This would be Shanks and Tilley's argument: 'a biological evolutionary perspective, when transferred to the activities of human beings, collapses with the redundancy argument, i.e. what people spend most of their time doing is completely redundant in terms of conferring any possible selective benefit,' (1987a: 56).

There are several problems with this position. First it makes an erroneous assumption that evolutionary perspectives necessarily become redundant when people's actions have no selective benefit. Many actions appear to be of this character but these may be the consequences of using capacities in contexts different from those in which they evolved. For instance Humphrey (1984) argues that stamp collecting and listening to Beethoven, which appear to be patently without selective benefit, arise from the exercise of capacities for classification, essential to learning, in new contexts. These are exercised since, like eating and sex, they are essential to survival and hence we have evolved to enjoy using them. As he states, 'Once nature had set up men's brains the way she has, certain unintended consequences followed' (1984: 133). To explain these unintended consequences we must understand and make explicit reference to the evolution of mental capacities.

Similar instances occur when actions that are either neutral or maladaptive arise owing to the expression of propensities that were functional in their evolutionary environment but are no longer so. Hinde (1987: 171) cites the example of irrational childhood fears. Again, understanding comes from examining the context in, and the processes by which, such psychological propensities evolved and the current context in which they are applied.

A further problem with the supposed 'redundancy' argument is that this is an *a priori* dogmatic statement about human actions. It would be more appropriate to recognise the complexities of human actions and to be prepared to engage in serious academic study of these, whether or not one adopts an evolutionary perspective oneself. Whether the activities that people engage in do or do not confer some selective benefit can only be ascertained by study, and cannot be so declared by some form of inspired knowledge on the part of Shanks and Tilley. If it turns out that they are correct, then that is an interesting finding not only for the social but also for the natural, sciences. Whether this is the case, however, remains to be seen.

A further objection that is often made against evolutionary approaches in archaeology, and in the social sciences in general, is that they deny free will by advocating a biological determinism. Related to this is a view that comparisons with other animals are somehow degrading. Such views arise from a belief in fundamental differences between humans and other species. One cannot deny that human beings are unique because of the great complexity of their cognitive processes and possession of language. As such, direct comparisons with other species may be limited in value and misleading (Hinde 1987). Yet these differences do not invalidate an evolutionary approach or create the unbridgeable gulf that Shanks and Tilley suggest: 'we would argue that people do not behave in the sense that animals behave . . . they *act* and the difference between behaviour and action is of fundamental significance. Humans must be conceived as sentient social beings living in a symbolically structured reality which is, essentially, of their own creation' (1987a: 55).

The view that animals are not sentient adopts the position of Descartes – animals are simply automata. Today, little basis can be found for such a stance. A distinction between instinctive (i.e. genetically determined) behaviour and learnt behaviour, or between nature and nurture, is no longer tenable (Bateson 1983; Gould and Marler 1986). Many animals, including insects, are prodigous learners, while the learning process and things learnt are guided by the genetic make-up of that species. In addition, recent work has advanced the case for elements of language, consciousness and culture in other species (e.g. Bonner 1980; Ristau and Robbins 1982; Griffin 1984; Dunbar 1984: 230–5). Moreover, members of other species, particularly primates, often engage in sophisticated social strategies involving the manipulation and deception of others (e.g. Dunbar 1984). None of this work denies the uniqueness of the human species; it simply shows how the unique characteristics are nevertheless on a continuum with those of other animals (Foley 1987a: Midgley 1980). Non-human animals are not automata, though none may have as complex a set of conceptual abilities as humans. But 'conceptual abilities' and 'complexity' have no inherent value in themselves. Other animals have better powers of sight and smell. Are they degraded by comparisons with humans?

Being concerned with the similarities and differences between humans and other animals I must make a brief reference to the recent set of essays by Ingold (1986) since this issue constitutes their principal theme. Ingold provides some of the most stimulating and informed discussion of tool use, storage, mobility and food sharing in hunter-gatherer society. However, I must disagree with his main argument that human *hunter-gatherers* are distinct from non-human *foragers* and that human tool *making* is distinct from non-human tool *construction*, since humans are intentional actors whereas other animals are not. Of course humans do act with intent, are self-conscious and plan tool making and hunting activity ahead of time. But that these characteristics are absent in other species has yet to be demonstrated and Ingold fails to marshall any evidence for this case. Indeed he is correct to write that 'it would be quite wrong to conclude from our inability to penetrate the experience of other species that we are uniquely endowed with subjective will' (1986: 19). Ingold readily concedes that since consciousness is a product of evolution 'it is present with varying degrees of elaboration and complexity at least in all higher animals' (1986: 19) and indeed may be 'poorly developed' in lower animals (1986: 41). And so, too, must be planning, intention and the 'prior representation of an end to be achieved' (1986: 10) which for Ingold constitute the heart of the matter. But when dealing with specific issues of tool use and subsistence, he appears to take the inconsistent position that these are solely human attributes and that other animals behave without intent. In fact he fails to tackle the issue head on since the comparisons he makes are most frequently between humans and 'lower' animals (e.g. insect predators, p. 2,120; spiders, p. 95; ladybirds, p. 103), species which can be most safely assumed to be without conscious intent and planning. But what about chimpanzees, dolphins and cats?

When we turn to these species Ingold's imposition of a threshold in consciousness and intent appears purely arbitrary, serving to maintain a discontinuity in tool use and subsistence between humans and other species for the sake of it. It is the same with the distinction he draws between social and ecological relations. According to Ingold, relations between people are different from those between organisms and their environment since other human individuals are also intentional subjects. But I am not convinced that, for instance, the interactions between Gelada baboons can be described as being between individuals who do not posses their own intentions which are sometimes in conflict and sometimes in agreement, and neither is Dunbar who has spent fifteen years studying them (1984: 4). Griffin (1976, 1984) has championed the arguments for consciousness in non-human species and while the case remains to be proven (how this can be done is obviously an immense methodological and philosophical problem), his arguments are sufficient to reject simple dualistic positions (see also Dunbar 1984: 230–5). Hence I find Ingold's distinction between social and ecological relations unhelpful, and prefer to see those of a social nature as one subset of ecological relations in general.

How about free will? Is this denied when we recognise the biological root of our human characteristics? Of course not. Midgley (1980) has dealt with this issue and moreover argues that our biological nature is in fact essential to claiming our freedom.

The notion that we 'have a nature', far from threatening the concept of freedom, is absolutely essential to it. If we were genuinely plastic and indeterminate at birth, there could be no reason why society should not stamp us into any shape that might suit it. The reason people view suggestions about inborn tendencies with such indiscriminate horror seems to be that they think exclusively of one particular way in which the idea of such tendencies has been misused, namely, that where conservative theorists invoke them uncritically to resist reform. But liberal theorists who combat such resistence need them as much, and indeed usually more. The early architects of our current notion of freedom made human nature their cornerstone. Rousseau's trumpet call 'Man is born free, but everywhere he is in chains' makes sense only as a description of our innate constitution as something positive, already determined, and conflicting with what society does to us. Kant and Mill took similar positions. And Marx, though he officially dropped the notion of human nature and often attacked the term, relied on the idea as much as anyone for his crucial notion of Dehumanization. (1980: xviii)

Noam Chomsky has also addressed this issue but from the perspective of human creativity and his insight also merits quoting. He asks us to consider whether cognitive functions are genetically determined by a rich innate endowment:

If the answer is positive, for some organism, that organism is fortunate indeed. It can then live in a rich and complex world of understanding shared with others similarly endowed, extending far beyond limited and varying experience. Were it not for this endowment, individuals would grow into mental amoeboids, unlike one another, each merely reflecting the limited and impoverished environment in which he or she develops, lacking entirely the finely articulated, diverse and refined cognitive organs that make possible the rich and creative life that is characteristic of all individuals not seriously impaired by individual or social pathology – though once again we must bear in mind that the very same intrinsic factors that permit these achievements also impose severe limits on the states that can be attained; to put it differently, that there is an inseparable connection between the scope and limits of human knowledge. 1980: 45–6

The presence of creative thought in humans has indeed a central role to play in a valid evolutionary approach. If we are to be concerned with adaptation as a process of becoming, with the limited information available to a decision maker and with the inherent irregularity in the environment then creative thought must be recognised as the driving dynamic of cultural change. Every problem that an individual faces is essentially a new problem since its historical, social and ecological context is unique. Each and every possible course of action that may be taken is created in the mind of the decision maker and is not prescribed. And, it is not just solutions that are created. Individuals also address themselves to the creation of problems. Accepted social conventions can be turned into an issue by breaking such conventions either wilfully or mistakenly. Alternatively a new convention might be agreed, but can never become immune from challenge. In these senses creativity in the decision process includes both the 'tinkering' and the 'restructuring' kinds to which Hodder (1988: 100) refers, i.e. innovation within the current domain of problems and solutions and a radical change to a new domain by imaginary leaps. So from an evolutionary perspective we have no choice but to characterise individuals as first and foremost creative beings, free, by virtue of their biological endowment, from the constraints that society and limited experience would otherwise impose.

The second aspect of Chomsky's views concerning the implications of a rich innate endowment of cognitive functionings also requires some elaboration; an evolutionary perspective places limits on human knowledge. That is, people are prone to error and confusion in their decision making. This has two implications for a study of human actions. One consequence is that the process of culture change receives a second boost, to supplement that from human creativity. Some solutions to problems are not initially created in the mind of the decision maker but arise when what is attempted fails as a result of cognitive errors. The result may be the recognition of new types of solutions and/or problems. Indeed, such noise within an adapting organism or system may have a fundamental importance in maintaining variability and allowing adaptation to new environments – it provides 'evolutionary drive' (Allen and McGlade 1987).

The limits on human knowledge also stress the central role that co-operation between individuals must play in a valid evolutionary approach. This is too frequently played down owing to over-emphasis on competition and conflict. It is readily apparent that in the non-human animal world, where learning may play a less significant though still vital role in adaptation, co-operation between individuals to each other's mutual advantage is a pervasive form of social interaction (Wrangham 1982; Packer 1977). Technology may serve to overcome certain human physical and cognitive constraints, as does art and ritual as I will argue below. But of greater importance is the need to co-operate with other individuals in the solution of problems. Game theory models have considered the evolution of co-operative behaviour, and stress three requirements – repeated interactions must occur between the same pairs of individuals, there must be the ability to retaliate against another who switches from co-operation to conflict and there must be the capacity to recognise individuals (Maynard-Smith 1982: 169). These are readily met in both modern and prehistoric human societies, at least from the Upper Palaeolithic onwards. From the decision-making perspective, co-operation allows new solutions to problems to be recognised and achieved, and indeed for new realms of problems to be tackled. The emphasis is on the mutual benefits gained from reciprocal altruism. It is the biological foundation of human behaviour, leading to the weighing up of the costs and benefits of different courses of action, that allows this type of interaction to become pervasive in human society.

Decision-making approaches in hunter-gatherer studies

My call for a concern with decision making may initially be seen as a little tardy. Was not Jochim's (1976) study of hunter-gatherer subsistence and settlement explicitly concerned with decision making? And similarly, cannot optimal foraging models be retitled as 'decision rules for predators' (Krebs 1978)? With the numerous anthropological applications that now exist, such 'decision rule' studies surely must be an established part of hunter-gatherer studies.

Jochim certainly developed a decision-making approach in the theoretical section of his book. He placed concepts drawn from micro-economic theory concerning decision making into an ecological context by viewing the relationship with the natural environment as the most important factor conditioning economic behaviour. In doing this he enlarged on concepts such as decision goals, decision criteria, and information/knowledge constraints in relation to solving problems concerned with subsistence behaviour. As such his work was seminal and set a precedent for later studies which directly employed his methods (e.g. Price 1978; Larsson 1978). It is still hailed as a model study of prehistoric decision making (Earle and Preucel 1987).

However, with the operationalisation of his theoretical framework Jochim's initial explicit concern with decision-making processes became lost in a methodological muddle. When trying to relate his decision-making model to the faunal data in the ethnographic and archaeological records he relied on combinations of six ecological parameters of the hunted animals (weight, density, aggregation, mobility, fat, non-food value) to define which resources would be most suitable for fulfilling the decision goals he attributed to the foragers. There are problems with this approach. For instance the relevance of any parameter will depend upon which resource is being exploited and how it is hunted. The role of factors such as density in defining the utility of a potential resource will vary as to whether we are dealing with fish or red deer, and whether the deer are stalked individually or hunted using drives and corrals. Similarly, characteristics such as mobility have many aspects to them. Is Jochim invoking the size of home ranges, migratory behaviour or running speed? My principal objection, however, is that such methods do not explicitly concern the decision-making process of the hunter-gatherers. For instance, although he discusses information constraints in his theoretical section, these are not applied to foragers, who appear to have the knowledge to take as much or as little of each potential resource as they wish. How did the foragers know which potential resources were available? Which would satisfy their goals? Which goals were the most appropriate to adopt? Were these individual or group choices?

Optimal foraging theory (OFT) is intimately linked to the evolution and assumed characteristics of decision-making processes. While it is now an established part of hunter-gatherer studies, there remains a substantial debate as to the manner in which it should be applied and the implications that it carries (Winterhalder and Smith 1981; Keene 1983; Jochim 1983b; Martin 1983; Smith 1983; Smith and Winterhalder 1985; Foley 1985; Sih and Milton 1985). The basic rationale of OFT is that the 'decision rules' possessed by predators have been shaped by natural selection to perform as efficiently as possible. The aim of an optimal foraging model is to examine the meaning of efficiency and the constraints that act upon it (Krebs *et al.* 1983: 166; Pyke *et al.* 1977; Orians and Pearson 1979). Consequently such models serve, much like Jochim's equations but with a more rigorous theoretical base, to identify how decision makers would act if operating with particular goals (efficiency criteria) and under particular constraints. These serve to build templates against which observed behaviour might be compared (Foley 1985). However, by doing this, optimal foraging models do not address the actual decision mechanisms that hunter-gatherers use to solve foraging problems since they are concerned with ultimate explanations for behaviour.

A brief consideration of optimal foraging applications in hunter-gatherer studies will indicate why a complementary evolutionary approach is required (see also Mithen 1989b). I have already referred to one reason – that as archaeologists we need dynamic models of cultural/behavioural change. When we consider the applications themselves, we are immediately faced with the problem that the majority of optimal foraging studies are methodologically weak, if not in error, and hence their conclusions are ambiguous.

I have already referred to the erroneous application to group behaviour of models developed for individual foragers. In addition, some researchers have not checked that the model is appropriate to their case study. For instance the requirement that prey encounters should be random for the diet breadth model was insufficiently checked in the studies on Amazonian foragers (e.g. Hames and Vickers 1982; Hawkes *et al.* 1982). In some cases it became apparent after the model had been applied that it was in fact totally inappropriate (e.g. Winterhalder 1981). Another related form of methodological weakness concerns knowledge about the environment in terms of the probabilities of prey encounters. For instance Hawkes *et al.* (1982), in their diet breadth model of Áche foraging, had to derive the foraging efficiencies of diets narrower in breadth than that observed by subtracting the calories and the handling time of the low-ranked species from the total in these for the full diet. However, they could not take into account the possibility that ignoring low-ranked species may lead to more encounters with high-ranked species (owing to the availability of more time by not handling the low-ranked species) since they were ignorant of encounter probabilities. In other studies the number of resources or patches used, and the number of foraging events observed, is so small that the significance of any patterns is questionable, such as in the Alyawara plant-gathering diet breadth and patch use studies (O'Connell and Hawkes 1984).

Bearing in mind such methodological weaknesses it is difficult to assess the significance of either agreement or differences between the predicted and observed diets. However, generalising across numerous studies, two points can be made. First, that several studies have claimed significant agreement between predicted and observed diets. Second, when deviations are found these are frequently due either to information constraints on the foragers or to the foragers engaging themselves in activities to acquire information rather than food. Both of these suggest that progress in explaining foraging patterns will be gained by a more explicit concern with proximate decision making.

The models in which agreements between observed and predicted diets are found tend to be diet breadth models and employ the rate of energetic gain as the efficiency criterion (e.g. Hames and Vickers 1982; Hawkes *et al.* 1982; Hill and Hawkes 1983; O'Connell and Hawkes 1984). In light of this finding, however, we still cannot be said to have fully explained the diet choice until we consider how such efficient foraging is achieved – what information is available to the foragers, how is it acquired, how is it used to decide which resources to exploit upon encounter and which to ignore? How do hunter-gatherers manage to be such efficient foragers?

Several studies, particularly those concerning patch use, suggest that deviations are principally due to factors concerning the information flows involved in decision making (e.g. O'Connell and Hawkes 1981, 1984; Winterhalder 1981; Beckerman 1983). This frequent finding suggests that current optimal patch use models are neglecting information availability as a constraint on decision making. The gathering of information could be included into optimality models, along with stochastic factors (which are the principal reason for needing regular information), but the resulting models are complex and the derivation of optimal information gathering and foraging schedules difficult (e.g. Winterhalder 1986; Stephens and Charnov 1982). Rather than developing such models, another approach is to take this as another cue for turning to the proximate decisionmaking process itself.

Information flows are central to decision making. We are led, therefore, into a host of archaeological studies which have argued that variability in information flows and requirements is central to social and cognitive patterns and change in small-scale societies. Moore (1981) has considered the relationship between settlement patterns and information requirements in foraging societies. Johnson (1978) has argued that there is a significant relationship between the size of information flows and the number of hierarchical levels in a society, since as the information increases more levels are required for efficient processing. Similarly Moore has characterised society as an 'information processing organisation in which social process is driven by the dynamic of information flows' (1983: 173). O'Shea and Zvelebil (1984) have proposed that the need to process a lot of information in a complex environment influences the early occurrence of stratified societies in the boreal forests of northern Europe. As I will consider below, Flannery (1986a, b) and Reynolds (1986; Reynolds and Zeigler 1979) have argued that concentrating on information in terms of multi-generational experience improves explanations for the origins of agriculture in Mexico. The art and mythology of huntergatherers have also been discussed in recent years in terms of information storage and decision making in times of crisis (e.g. Minc 1986). Palaeolithic cave art in particular has received a barrage of studies relating it to information flows (e.g. Gamble 1982; Conkey 1978, 1985; Pfeiffer 1982). Even the emergence of the human intellect itself and the form of the earliest human society have been attributed to the demands of information processing (Kurland and Beckerman 1985).

All of these studies argue that information flows and decision making have a prime role to play in the development of prehistoric society, but few are very specific as to what they mean by information and why it is required. Viewing such work from the optimal foraging perspective, however, we can define information as knowledge concerning the location and character of potential resources, and identify the need for it as being to improve foraging efficiency. Consequently by placing the individual decision maker at the centre of our studies and adopting an evolutionary ecological approach the two most important areas of recent hunter-gatherer studies – optimal foraging models and information flows – can be integrated into one coherent framework.

Finally I wish to consider briefly the work of Flannery (1986a, b) and Reynolds (1986). Their model for the origins of agriculture in Oaxaca, Mexico, sets a precedent and charts the path for the models I will develop below. They focus on human decision making and learning as central to the process of adaptation and subsistence change and use computer simulation to link theories to their archaeological data, as I will below. Similarly their rejection of an optimal foraging approach, owing to its inability to deal with change, is one of the grounds that I too adopt. Reynolds' model centres around concepts and components that are similarly central to those I develop in this work: the focusing on individuals in a group context, the concern with the use of experience as the information source for decisions, the inclusion of stochastic factors, the manner in which the efficiency of different strategies is measured (which is also similar to that in optimal foraging models), and perhaps of greatest importance the view that foragers seek to increase, not necessarily maximise, their foraging efficiency. Although these concepts are shared, the actual forms of the models developed in this work and in those by Flannery and Reynolds are in marked contrast. Mine are embedded a little deeper in evolutionary theory, using this as a justification for focusing on these particular model components, but are also rather more accessible, especially to those without a mathematical and computer science background.

That there should be such similarities between the basic concepts is clearly satisfactory. Moreover, the fact that Flannery and Reynolds are concerned with the origins of agriculture, an issue not dealt with in any substantial manner in this book, and with plant gathering rather than with terrestrial hunting, suggests that a truly comprehensive approach to socio-economic change in hunter-gatherer society is emerging.

To conclude this introduction let me clarify my position with respect to individualistic, evolutionary and decision-making approaches in archaeology. I have argued that if we use these as our theoretical building blocks we construct a foundation from which substantial progress can be made in developing explanations for problems posed by the archaeological record. That is, as long as we also pay attention to methodological issues. At the centre of this approach we have people – sentient, creative, emotional people – tackling problems posed by their social and physical environments. Our focus must be on individual action as the result of psychological propensities with which humans are biologically endowed. These are employed in social, ecological and historical contexts that are unique to each individual and that may differ radically from those composing the environment in which such propensities were selected. In this respect the long-term sequences of change recorded by the archaeological record result from a complex of interacting factors concerning individual decisions, the intended and unintended consequences of these, and fluctuations in the external environment. The particular approach I choose is a timely one in light of the current state of theoretical archaeology. The individual decision maker has been woefully neglected and evolutionary approaches misapplied and misrepresented. Both of these need attention, for cultural behaviour is essentially a series of choices and, to quote Robert Hinde once again, 'a view of humankind that neglects the biological perspective is necessarily not only impoverished but also inaccurate' (1987: 1).

PART 1

Learning from the present

2

The eco-psychology of decision making

The more global . . . a cognitive process is,
the less anybody understands it.

> Fodor's first law of the non-existence of cognitive science, 1983: 107

The whole thinking process is still rather mysterious to us, but I
believe that the attempt to make a thinking machine will help us
greatly in finding out how we think ourselves.

> Alan Turing (quoted in Hodges 1983: 442)

We are all experts at decision making. After all, we have been practising the art for most, perhaps all, of our lives. Each of us knows that some decisions are easy to make and some difficult, and also that sometimes we have made the right and sometimes the wrong choice. Occasionally we reflect upon a decision and how we arrived at a particular choice. Most often this occurs when we appear to have been foolish. Why ever did I choose to become an archaeologist? What made me choose to study decision making? Why on earth did I decide to write/read this book? When doing this, we tend to take the decision process apart and look at the information we had available to us, what now appears to have been missing and how we thought that some items carried more weight than others. Often we remain uncertain as to why we made a particular choice. Why did I decide to be an archaeologist? Well, perhaps because I thought that seeking after the roots of human culture would be intellectually fulfilling. Alternatively it may have been the thought of digging for buried treasure in the sun with endless supplies of wine and good food. We are also prone to try and dissect the decisions of others to understand why they chose one course of action rather than another. Often we do not get very far – why did anybody ever vote/not vote for Mrs Thatcher! In engaging in such thoughts we are truly, as Nicholas Humphrey (1984) identified, *Homo psychologicus*.

Now it is this act of dissecting the decision process that I want to engage in here, though in a rather more substantial and less subjective manner than in our own idle moments of reflection. My basic question is, what does making a decision involve? More specifically I look at decisions concerning foraging activity, though I hope that the concepts and model I arrive at override any specific context.

To do this, I will describe an eco-psychological model for decision making in foraging strategies. Building a model here is like Turing building his 'thinking machine'. Decision making is incredibly mysterious and complex, and will always remain so. It is a global cognitive process and as such Fodor suggests it may be inherently unamenable for study. Yet an archaeologist who claims to study individual decision making is nothing if not optimistic (or perhaps foolish) and in that spirit I will try and build a model to help in finding out how decisions are made.

I will draw on material in two fields – studies of decision making by non-human foragers and studies in human psychology and anthropology. The first is relevant since other animals face foraging problems similar to those faced by hunter-gatherers and I am interested in exploring continuities in the ways in which these are solved. The second is needed because unique aspects of human decision making would perhaps be neglected by an over-concentration on ethological and ecological studies. The aim, however, is to locate areas of compatibility and continuity within these fields so that a comprehensive eco-psychological model can be developed. In seeking to draw on both ecology and psychology I am following others who have recognised the need for a greater integration of these fields if an understanding of foraging behaviour is to be achieved (e.g. Kamil 1983).

The essence of the model is illustrated in Fig. 2.1. This is for a choice between discrete alternative courses of action. With respect to foraging these may be different patch or prey types. Such decisions lie at the heart of the wider set of processes I am concerned with. The necessity of making a choice is essentially a problem that requires a solution, while feedback from that choice constitutes learning. Note that I do not specify a time frame for this model. Particular problems may be recognised, information acquired and a course of action chosen within a few minutes or over the course of one or more years. The capacity for forward planning has been much referred to in recent years by those looking for distinguishing characteristics between modern man and early hominids (e.g. Binford 1984) or with other species in general (e.g. Ingold 1986). The consequences (intended or unintended) of the particular choice made may be felt either immediately or after a long elapse of time, or different consequences may be felt over different time periods. Neither do I specify whether these are conscious or unconscious activities. It is clear from our own experience that sometimes we are conscious of making a decision, and at other times do this unconsciously. Most often we are probably conscious of some parts of the decision process and oblivious to others. We might learn to become unconscious about making a decision (e.g. to apply the brakes of a car when approaching a hazard) or conversely to be conscious about others (e.g. breathing when trying to relax). Frequently we appear to slip

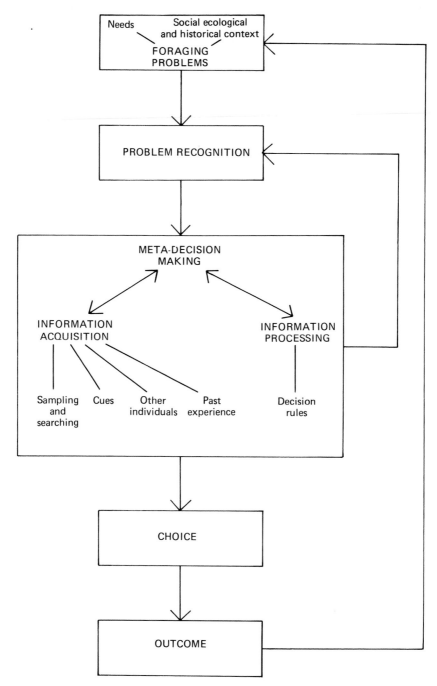

Fig. 2.1. A model for decision making in foraging strategies.

and slide in and out of consciousness about our decision making and in this light I intend to slip away from the thorny issue of consciousness.

This model is obviously, and intentionally, simple. It is a starting point. Further development of it will occur throughout the next chapters as ethnographic and archaeological data are addressed. To use those data, however, requires an initial framework as provided here. Let us start by looking at foraging problems.

Foraging problems

The problems I am concerned with are those concerning the location and exploitation of food as have been defined in optimal foraging theory relating to patch choice, diet breadth, group size and mobility patterns. These arise since foragers need to satisfy basic nutritional needs if they are to survive. Moreover, they need to satisfy these in an efficient manner to be adapting to their environments since the acquisition of food is an intermediate goal towards achieving reproductive success, as discussed above. I will focus on two particular problems – patch choice and prey choice. Both refer to the selection of food items. Patch choice concerns the choice between discrete areas for foraging, or between resources because of heterogeneous prey distributions, and the length of time to remain within each. As such, this decision lies at the heart of my study of Upper Palaeolithic art and economy in Part 3. Prey choice, otherwise referred to as the diet breadth problem, concerns the decision to exploit food items upon encounter or to ignore them and continue searching. This is the central decision I investigate in my study of Mesolithic foraging and society in Part 2. The optimal foraging models for patch and prey choice are summarised by Stephens and Krebs (1986).

It should be noted that breaking the foraging process into a series of discrete problems is a simplification. The character of a problem and the different courses of action available are dependent upon the other problems and past solutions. In particular the problems should be considered as being a hierarchical set and the frequency with which an animal is faced with a problem depends upon its rank in this hierarchy (e.g. Tinbergen 1981). For instance Orians (1980) describes how marsh-nesting blackbirds must first choose a habitat in which to nest, a decision made once a year. The choice constrains the number and types of patches that can be visited, a problem faced on a daily basis. Once in a patch, the type chosen will constrain the prey items available and the blackbird is required to make choices about prey items many times within one day. Choices higher in the hierarchy are expected to influence fitness more than a lower-ranked decision.

Technological problems

Tool use provides a sub-set of foraging problems for humans, as well as for a broad spectrum of other species which use tools. Tools are a means by which choices are carried out, but by their availability or absence they make some courses of action possible, remove others or complicate a choice by requiring a tool to be made.

For instance when the prey choice problem is faced during encounter foraging, a forager may choose to carry certain projectile points, but this choice limits which encountered prey can be exploited. The choice of which to carry may, however, have been made on the basis of the type of prey he expects to encounter. Microlithic technology is particularly interesting from this perspective, as I will discuss in Chapter 4. Hunter-gatherer technology has recently received some interesting studies from a functionalist, problem-solving and optimality perspective (e.g. Torrence 1983, 1989a; Bleed 1986). Yet these repeat the problems with optimal foraging models I discussed above. Static models of tool use are of little value for archaeologists concerned with technological change through time. Issues of information gathering and processing can be equally applied to tool use as to foraging decisions. Some work in this direction will be attempted in Chapter 6.

Being social

A second complicating factor is the thoroughness with which decisions by human foragers are embedded in a social context. The use of other individuals as sources of information, as discussed below and modelled in Part 2, is one aspect of this. Another, is that in some situations certain individuals may decide simply to follow the decisions of others rather than engage in the acquisition and processing of information themselves. In addition, certain courses of action, perhaps the majority, require the co-operation of other individuals. For instance, if one of the patches available is a reindeer herd that can be efficiently exploited only by drives and corrals, then a large number of foragers must agree upon this course of action for it to be available to any one individual.

   The prevalence of food sharing in hunter-gatherer society is a further complicating factor. The nature of food sharing and who 'owns' the food at any one time are controversial issues (see Ingold 1986: 113–17, 229–34) and my concern is simply that one individual may consider another as a 'patch' to exploit for food. In this, I am attracted to the position that sees other individuals as tools for the accomplishment of some task.

   Humphrey (1976, 1984) has emphasised the importance and the complexity of the problems posed to a decision maker by living in a social group. He argues that coping with these problems requires a level of intelligence unmatched in any other sphere of existence. The consequence of following one course of action as opposed to another will depend upon the actions and reactions of other individuals and hence a decision maker must try and anticipate what these may be. This requires 'being sensitive to other people's moods and passions, appreciative of their waywardness and stubbornness, capable of reading signs in their faces and equally the lack of signs, capable of guessing what each person's past experience holds hidden in the present for the future' (Humphrey 1984: 4–5).

Cognition and perception

Foraging problems are solved, and new ones created, by making choices. But just as these problems exist only in a context of technological and social problems so does the making of choices take place only in a web of perceptual and cognitive processes. I wish briefly to outline a model for the mind so that I can place decision making into its context. For this, I use Fodor's *modularity* model (1983, 1985) and Sperber and Wilson's (1986) *relevance* model for cognition, following Carston's (1988) integration of these works.

Fodor argues that the mind is essentially composed of two types of systems – input and central systems. Input systems are those which gain new information from the environment by perceptual mechanisms such as sight, touch and hearing. The critical characteristics of these are that they are *information encapsulated* and *modular*. Information encapsulation refers to the limited access input systems have to the background knowledge of the subject stored in memory. The most telling and simple illustration of this is the persistence of optical illusions even when one knows what one is seeing to be false. The modularity of input systems refers to their independence of each other. They have different and specific neural mechanisms and the limited information available to one (in its own specific database) is not available to another. An understanding of, say, vision has nothing to contribute to how other input systems, such as hearing, work. Two further characteristics of input systems are that they are mandatory (e.g. we cannot help but see or hear when appropriate stimuli are present) and that they work very fast.

By these perceptual mechanisms information is gained about the world and is then processed by the central systems. The physiological character of the input systems will define the type of information that may be acquired and hence may constrain the forager from making 'optimal' choices (e.g. Abrahams 1986). Fodor characterises central systems as being concerned with the fixation of belief but more generally it is here that the processes of thinking, imagination, problem solving and decision making occur. Fixation of belief is a useful term for my decision-making study since we might conceive of a choice as the fixation of belief that one of the alternatives is the 'best' to choose.

The central systems contrast with the input systems by being neither information encapsulated nor modular. That is, they all have access to the background knowledge of the subject which is combined with that delivered by each input system after it has been converted to some common code. Also, central systems, unlike input systems, are essentially under executive control and work slowly in contrast with the speed of perception. Key words for central systems are 'deep', 'global', 'flexible' and 'creative' as opposed to the terms 'local', 'hardwired' and 'fast' appropriate for input systems.

Decision making is found within the central systems, overlapping in its characteristically non-modular way with problem solving and learning. Fodor is not optimistic that we may gain any understanding of how central systems work. However, Sperber and Wilson (1986) present a model for cognition that is useful for my work and compatible with Fodor's thesis (Carston 1988), upon which they draw. Sperber and Wilson argue that cognition is essentially concerned with improving one's knowledge of the world, which amounts to Fodor's term 'the fixation of belief'. For Sperber and Wilson this means 'adding more information, information that is more accurate, more easily retrievable and more developed in areas of greater concern to the individual' (1986: 47).

When considering cognition over the short term (i.e. the way a mind will work in the next few seconds or micro-seconds) Sperber and Wilson emphasise two points. First, perceptual input processes monitor much more information than can be processed by central systems and, second, there is always 'plenty of unfinished business' for the central systems to be concerned with. As a result 'the key problem for efficient short-term information processing is to achieve an optimal allocation of central processing resources' (1986: 48). They suggest that this is achieved by central systems preferentially performing cognitive tasks that are likely to provide *relevant* information. This is defined as being that which improves knowledge of the world through one of several impacts on current assumptions. New information may strengthen, weaken or contradict these, or may combine with existing assumptions to yield something new. However, there is a second principle that is necessary for defining relevance: all other things being equal, the smaller the amount of cognitive effort required, the greater the relevance. Consequently their proposal is that the key to cognition is the goal of maximising relevance, i.e. getting the greatest possible cognitive effects for the least expenditure of effort.

We need one elaboration of this for my decision-making model. 'Knowledge of the world' must also refer to what the world will be like at some time in the future, a belief as to the state of oneself and one's environment. Moreover since decision making is concerned with choosing between alternative courses of action we are concerned with knowledge about several, perhaps many, different possible worlds each resulting from one of the possible choices. It is on the basis of these beliefs about future possible states of the world that a choice is made. In this respect we have characterised the mind as a means for making multiple simulation models of the future. It is this, but of course it is also much more besides.

The evolution of decision-making capacities

One of the attractions of Fodor's model for the mind is that it is plausible when viewed in an evolutionary perspective. As he argues, perception is principally concerned with keeping track of the local environment to cope with the immediate problems of survival. 'It is, no doubt, important to attend to the eternally beautiful and to believe the eternally true. But it is more important not to be eaten' (1985: 4). In this respect the fast, encapsulated and modular characteristics of input systems can be understood. One must quickly sense what is present in the environment, rather than what one wishes there to be, if one is to survive. However, in the long run, to survive and compete successfully one requires reflection upon the world. First impressions may be misleading and regularities in the environment may not be immediately apparent. Wise decisions can only be made by integrating information from the different input systems with that stored in memory and following thought and contemplation. Fodor's position is therefore that 'Nature has contrived to have it both ways, to get the best out of fast dumb systems *and* show contemplative ones, by simply refusing to choose between them' (1985: 4).

Similarly Sperber and Wilson's model of cognition sits comfortably in an evolutionary framework. The types of characteristics they invoke – efficiency of information processing, least effort, relevance – are those to be expected if the mind is a product of natural selection. Similarly the concept of the mind as a simulation device is compatable with an evolutionary approach. This allows one to explore the benefits to be gained from particular choices without actually having to make the investments and take the risks involved. Certainly an individual with such mental capacities would have a selective advantage over one who must rely on actually trying each different course of action.

Now, my particular concern is with the evolution of central systems, notably decision-making processes and I must enlarge upon certain evolutionary arguments since these justify the modelling approach I adopt later in this book. First we can consider the role of irregular flux in natural environments as a pressure for the selection of such capacities. Pulliam and Dunford (1980) have particularly stressed this in their thesis *Programmed to Learn*. Their starting point is the irregular spatial and temporal variability and the sheer complexity of natural and social environments. Consequently it is impossible to have all behavioural 'choices' genetically determined when faced with different courses of action, since novel problems and options continually arise. They argue that organisms have inherited certain criteria that define what are good and what are bad experiences and a predilection to repeat actions that lead to good experiences and avoid those leading to bad, i.e. trial and error learning. They expand this notion with respect to humans by reference to Pugh's (1977) work which characterises emotions as decision criteria.

Trial and error learning is, however, costly in terms of time and energy, risky in that a bad choice may lead to a severe reduction in fitness (i.e. death!) and limiting in what can be learnt during one lifetime. Therefore Pulliam and Dunford argue that certain organisms, and humans in particular, have evolved an ability to bypass trial and error by social learning (though this distinction is not clear cut). They enlarge their discussion to consider how stimuli and events which have no inherent quality, in terms of leading to 'good' or 'bad' sensations, can come to acquire this by association with stimuli that do. Consequently, they argue, even abstract ideas may come to have emotional value.

One of the central concepts in their argument is that of the decision rule. This can be seen as a mechanism that allows the organism to cope with the particular problems it faces in its environment by specifying what information is relevant to a problem and how it should be processed. The suite of decision rules possessed by an organism may be characterised as its 'learning programme'. My use of the decision-rule concept is essentially as a heuristic device to help in the exploration and modelling of the complexities of decision-making processes.

This concept of animal-specific decision rules which evolved by natural selection has been discussed by several evolutionary ecologists (e.g. Gould and Marler 1987). It has led to a criticism of attempts to determine an animal's 'intelligence' by exposing it to laboratory tests which bear no relation to the natural problems faced in its evolutionary environment. Since the decision-making and learning abilities of an animal relate directly to the problems it faced in its evolutionary environment one may expect these to be most developed when the problems require extensive information processing. One measure of the degree of required processing may be the spatial and temporal variability, or patchiness, in food supply. Both Milton (1980) and Ghiglieri (1984) have argued that patchiness in food supply has led to the development of the advanced mental abilities of primates. Supporting such an argument is the finding of a correlation between encephalisation (a morphological index of cognitive capacity) and dietary content, which in turn relates to extent of required information processing (i.e. increased patchiness or size of home range) in several groups of mammals such as bats (Eisenberg and Wilson 1978), primates (Clutton-Brock and Harvey 1980) and rodents (Mace *et al.* 1981).

Several authors, however, have stressed the problem of coping with the social environment as providing the functional advantage for intellectual abilities, particularly those of the creative kind found in human beings. Most notably, Humphrey (1976) has argued that such abilities relate to the need to predict the behaviour of other individuals when living in a social group, and that this further relates to consciousness as a simulation device for the behaviour of others. Kurland and Beckerman (1985) have proposed a related argument that the need to acquire information from other group members, and then the need for information as to the validity of that obtained leading to an information spiral, provides a context in which advanced cognitive skills may be selected. Both of these studies are provocative but suffer from a basic lack of knowledge as to when the human intellect developed and what the form of human society was at that time. Both implicitly assume that fully human mental capacities evolved during the Lower Pleistocene when the form of society was similar to that of modern hunter-gatherers (i.e. home bases, food sharing, hunting). As Binford has vigorously argued (1983, 1985b), such assumptions cannot be held with confidence. Having now considered the context in which the decision-making capacities reside I want to turn to the central elements of my decision-making model.

Problem recognition

It is artificial to separate 'problem recognition' from 'information acquisition' and 'processing', but it is nevertheless useful. This emphasises the differentiation between the 'objective' environment, and hence the spectrum of patch and prey possibilities, which may be simulated using ecological models such as of prey population dynamics (see Chapter 7), and that which is cognised by the decision maker. In referring to an objective environment I am returning to Fodor's concept of information-encapsulated input systems – people do initially perceive a *real world* unaffected by their cultural knowledge, though the conversion of this into a culturally defined reality by cognition is rapid. Consequently, when considering this real environment one may imagine situations in which alternative patches are available but the decision maker is unaware of these, or, vice versa, in which he believes in an option which is in fact unavailable. Similarly when acquiring and processing information with respect to one specific problem another may be recognised, more or less important than that currently being addressed, and which may lead to a dramatic switch in activities. Consequently 'problem recognition' is a useful model component and plays a significant role in my interpretations of

Upper Palaeolithic art in Chapter 8. While problem recognition is integral to information acquisition and processing, it may also be seen as part of 'meta-decision' making.

Meta-decision making

By meta-decision making I mean taking decisions about the decision process itself. This is simply one realm of meta-cognition which has been defined by Flavell (1976: 232):

Meta-cognition refers to one's knowledge concerning one's own cognitive processes and products or anything related to them. . . For example I am engaging in metacognition (metamemory, metalearning, metaattention, metalanguage or whatever) if I notice that I am having more trouble learning A than B; if it strikes me that I should double check C before accepting it as a fact; if it occurs to me that I had better scrutinize each and every alternative in any multiple choice type task situation before deciding which is the best one; if I sense that I had better make a note of D because I may forget it. . . Metacognition refers, among other things, to the active monitoring and consequent regulation and orchestration of these processes in relation to the cognitive objects on which they bear, usually in the service of some concrete objective or goal.

Brown (1978) has provided an extensive discussion of meta-cognition, particularly meta-memory, and has stressed its importance in relation to decision making, emphasizing that knowledge of one's cognitive system is essential if one is to be an effective problem solver.

Johnson and Raye (1981) have also made some particularly interesting comments concerning meta-memory pertinent to this work. They introduce the term 'reality monitoring' to refer to the processes that people use to decide whether a piece of information has been derived from an external source or has been generated internally by cognitive activities such as imagination.

I introduce meta-decision making therefore as an essential part of the decision-making process and the core of my theoretical framework and eco-psychological model. It is meta-decision making that makes the decisions concerning the decision to be taken. Consequently each of the model components I am discussing has it's meta-counterpart. For instance meta-information acquisition is acquiring information as to what types of information are to be acquired when faced with a particular problem. Specifically it is in this realm of the meta-decision-making process that when faced with a decision the actor decides:

1 which alternatives are available;
2 what is the goal aimed for;
3 what is known about the alternatives;
4 what needs to be known;
5 what sources of information are available;

6 what sources of information are relevant;

7 how to acquire this information;

8 what rules of thumb/heuristics are available;

9 which rules of thumb/heuristics should be used.

However, as I will discuss below, a frequent or possibly more usual situation may be that there is not a specific decision in mind, only the knowledge that specific decisions will arise in the future. Human actors may be considered to be constantly engaged in a monitoring of their environment. Consequently the meta-decision-making activity also decides which sources of information shall be attended to, using a general knowledge of what may or may not be important and relevant in future decisions.

As I mentioned above, a decision rule is a useful heuristic concept for investigating how information is acquired and processed with respect to specific problems and goals. To be an efficient forager each specific problem will require a specific decision rule so that the appropriate information is acquired and processed in an appropriate manner. Consequently an equally useful concept is a meta-decision rule which may be conceived as that which chooses which decision rule is to be employed.

Following a choice between alternatives it is the meta-decision-making activity that evaluates whether the appropriate information sources, information gathering and processing mechanisms have been used. This includes, for instance, assessing the validity of a cue or rule of thumb which had been used. More generally, there will be a constant evaluation of whether the continuous information-gathering activity is acquiring relevant information and whether the correct types of decisions have been anticipated.

One, or more, additional levels in a hierarchy of decision-making processes may be considered. Meta-meta-decision making is concerned with, for instance, deciding how to decide which sources of information are relevant. I collapse all the higher level processes into one tier of meta-decision making activities. When considering the benefits that may be gained by having such multi-tiered decision-making apparatus we must not forget the costs. These lie in the greater complexity of neural machinery required for meta-decision-making activity and it must be considered whether the greater flexibility gained is indeed useful for the niche the organism inhabits. There is little evidence to suggest the extent of meta-decision-making activity in non-human animals. Kamil (1984) has referred to experimental studies with blue jays which suggest flexibility in the application of decision rules. Similarly, as I will discuss below, some work on the patch sampling activities of birds suggest they are monitoring not only current spatial and temporal variability in resource distributions but also the change in these measures themselves.

Goal choice

One of the meta-decisions that is taken concerns the nature of the foraging goals and here I wish to consider how we should conceive of these within an eco-psychological model. I have already referred to the position I adopt that the cultural goals of the forager will, to some extent, correlate with those which are of adaptive significance. Consequently, as in optimal foraging studies, I am concerned with issues of foraging efficiency, whether that relates to energy, time or risk. The crux of the question is whether individuals try to optimise? Probably not (outside of a Western capitalist economic framework). Optimality assumptions act as a useful heuristic framework for setting up templates against which to compare what people actually do. But here we are concerned with modelling that behaviour itself and need a replacement for the optimality principle.

Simon's (1979) concept of satisficing has gained much popularity in discussions and models of decision making – all that foragers need to do is to acquire *sufficient* food and raw materials to stay alive. But just to stay alive is not necessarily to be reproductively successful and, owing to the process of natural selection, satisficing would be usurped by an efficiency criterion by which people do not just stay alive, but also have a high inclusive fitness. Dawkins makes this point succinctly: 'evolutionary theory entitles us to be a bit more negative *a priori*. Living things are not selected for their capacity to simply stay alive; they are staying alive in competition with other such living things. The trouble with satisficing as a concept is that it leaves out the competitive element which is fundamental to all life' (1982: 45–6). Consequently I adopt Dawkins' middle ground between optimising and satisficing – that of meliorising. Foragers are attempting to do better, to improve on their own previous performance as well as that of other individuals. When developing models for prehistoric foragers I will refer to meliorising goals, such as utility increasing and risk reducing (rather than maximisation or minimisation criteria). This returns to the position I adopted above, that the appropriate concept for adaptation in archaeology is one of 'becoming', rather than of having attained a static optimal state.

Information acquisition

As should now be apparent, the barriers between any of my model components are fuzzy. This is particularly so between information acquisition and information processing since these often operate in tandem and have no independent existence. However, as with 'problem recognition', it is useful to consider information acquisition as a discrete activity. Four cross-cutting sources of information may be considered – from sampling and searching, cues, other individuals and past experience. The first three of these are contexts in which information is gained by the modular input systems and integrated together and with background knowledge by central cognitive systems to 'improve knowledge of the world'. The fourth refers to the accessing and contents of that background knowledge. These are integral and mutually dependent. For instance cues are received while sampling and searching and are stored in memory; they, or the inferences drawn from them, may be communicated to others. As categories, they are simply useful for organising and discussing a diverse range of material.

Sampling and searching

Since the quality of prey and patches may change in an irregular manner and cues or other sources of information may be unavailable, an animal may need to sample a patch to estimate its quality. This may result in a period of decreased foraging efficiency while information is gathered by sampling different patches, after which efficiency can be increased by commitment to the patch with the highest returns. The extent of the initial decrease and the length of time over which sampling should take place partly depend upon the total time available for foraging and the degree of flux in the relative patch qualities, as will be further discussed below.

To provide a context for examining some of the issues concerning sampling and searching, and the relation of these to efficient foraging, I will discuss bandit problems. These encapsulate a real feature of natural problems animals frequently face – the need to choose between two foraging areas (patches) when there is imperfect information about one or both of these. This is a common problem facing human foragers as optimal patch use studies among the Cree, Alyawara and Bari illustrate (Winterhalder 1981; O'Connell and Hawkes 1981; Beckerman 1983). In my description of the bandit problem I will follow Krebs *et al.* (1978) and Houston *et al.* (1982). The structure of a bandit problem is that there are two sources for reward (i.e. food), each known as an arm. The decision maker has to choose one arm on each trial and the probability of gaining a reward (or the size of that reward) is unknown on either one or both of these. In the former case, called a 'one-armed bandit' the decision maker needs to sample the unknown arm to find its relative value to the known arm in order to forage efficiently. Choosing the unknown arm provides a reward and information, while the known arm provides only a reward. If the decision maker samples too frequently its overall foraging efficiency will fall since it is spending less time on the more profitable arm. Consequently for a specified time period available for foraging and for each set of reward probabilities (or sizes) there is an 'optimal' sampling strategy.

The extent of sampling depends partly on the time available for foraging which is defined simply as the total number of trials available, i.e. the number of choices between the arms. Risking the loss of a reward from the known arm to sample the other, so that information is gained, becomes less valuable as the total foraging time decreases since there will be less opportunity to use that information. In the limiting case of a single trial it is clearly of no value to gather information and the decision maker should simply choose the arm with the greatest expected return. When there is a longer foraging time available the forager can afford to suffer short-term decrease in efficiency to acquire information so that this can be maximised in the longer term.

Each trial on the unknown arm increases the information about that arm's reward. The information can never be perfect since in a finite period there will always remain some uncertainty as to which is the more profitable arm to exploit. The gain of information by sampling can be illustrated with a simple model using a Bayesian approach. The decision maker begins with a guess for the value of the unknown arm, known as the prior, p_{1t}. This prior can be considered to have a beta distribution with parameters a and b. The mean of such a distribution is given by: $a/(a+b)^2(a+b+1)$.

When $a = b = 1$ the distribution is uniform on the interval $(0,1)$. By a suitable choice of a and b prior distributions of p_{1t} can be approximated. In the bandit problem, if n trials have been made on the arm and r successes are gained then a new estimate for the probability of reward can be made, known as the posterior, and which is also beta distributed. This distribution now has the parameters: $(a + r, b + n - r)$. Hence the mean and the variance of the distribution have changed and there will be a new estimate for the value of the unknown arm. Consequently one can model the state of the decision maker's knowledge about the unknown arm as it makes trials and receives rewards from that arm.

The two-armed bandit problem is more complex. In this case the reward rate is unknown for both arms and consequently information as well as rewards are gained on each trial. There are some similarities with the one-armed bandit. A decision maker gains information early on and exploits that information later (i.e. in choosing to fix on one arm). The optimum amount of sampling again depends on the length of foraging time and the values of the rewards. In contrast, the decision maker can never make an irreversible decision to abandon one arm in favour of another since the results of further trials may change the estimate of how good the current arm is.

In a finite time horizon it is theoretically possible to use dynamic programming techniques to determine the optimal sequence of sampling so that rewards are maximised. The absolute optimal pattern is very complex to find although possible in principle. Krebs *et al.* (1978), however, define a constrained optimal. They simplify the two-armed bandit problem by defining that there be an initial 'exploratory' period, during which both arms are sampled equally, followed by an exploitation period when the decision maker, in their case a great tit, fixes on one arm. For a specified time period and set of reward probabilities, there will be an optimal balance between exploration and exploitation. They used simulation methods based on a Bayesian model of information use to determine this optimal balance, the point when their birds should switch from exploration to exploitation for a set of time frame and reward probabilities.

Krebs *et al.* compared such results with the observed behaviour of great tits faced with the actual problems of choosing between two feeding places at the opposite ends of an aviary. The birds followed the assumed pattern of behaviour in spending roughly equal times sampling both feeding places and then fixing on one of them. They found that the behaviour of the birds approximated to the predictions of the model concerning the balance between exploration and exploitation when different lengths of time were available for foraging. The birds behaved as if they were calculating this optimal balance. Krebs *et al.* used sophisticated dynamic programming techniques to discover the optimal sampling strategy, techniques unavailable to the birds. Here, therefore, we return to the use of simple decision rules, mechanisms by which information is acquired and processed that, with time, take the decision maker towards the optimal strategy. I will consider rules appropriate for the bandit problem when considering information processing.

Other studies have also examined the relationship between sampling and efficient foraging. For instance Lima made pioneering studies of sampling behaviour by woodpeckers (1983) and starlings (1985). He found qualitative evidence that the starlings had a patch sampling ability that led to efficient foraging. However, birds tended to over-sample relative to a predicted optimal sampling scheme. It was suggested that such over-sampling may function to detect changes in the patchy environment itself, suggesting some form of meta-decision-making activity. Differences in the sampling patterns between individual birds were also detected. Similarly Orians (1980) discusses the sampling activity of blackbirds when choosing patches and explains how this increases as patches become more variable in their returns.

When foraging in a patchy environment and employing sampling and searching, one of the most important behavioural capacities is mobility. The ability to visit a range of patch types and the cost incurred in doing so are influenced by travel capacities and the nature of the physical environment. If vegetation is very dense, movement may be slow and require considerable effort. However, if the cost of movement is low, an animal may spend considerable time searching and sampling. For instance Milton (1980) describes the foraging strategies of Howler monkeys. She stresses the role of mobility for monitoring a very patchy environment and repeated visits to particular trees, suggesting these were being inspected for food.

In assessing the evidence on such active behaviour Dawkins (1982) discusses the finding that animals appear to search most when they have 'time on their hands'. For instance desert ants, starlings and blackbirds have all been observed to explore when food was abundant so that they might acquire useful information for the future. Drent (1982) interprets such 'exploring for later' as an important risk-buffering mechanism. Similar interpretations have been made for the mobility patterns of human foragers (see Chapter 3) and this takes us on to consider studies of searching and sampling in psychology and anthropology.

Chibnik (1981) argues that a wide set of ethnographic studies indicate that when people first confront an unfamiliar environmental or socio-political problem they conduct a series of low-cost experiments designed to gather information about the probable consequences of alternative actions and that this information gathering must be seen as an integral part of the decision-making process. Sometimes there are two levels of experiments or information-gathering activity. The first is low cost and serves to reduce the options available and the second, more expensive, investigates those remaining options. Chibnik argues that such information gathering is particularly evident in risky situations.

Intuitively one may think that the value of such information gathering will depend upon the increase in the predictability of the outcomes of alternative actions. If this increase is small and the consequences of a 'wrong' choice slight then few resources will be invested in information gathering. Gould (1974) uses formal methods to examine the relationship between the risk or uncertainty faced by a decision maker and the value of information to him which suggests that the relationship between the degree of uncertainty and value of information may be ambiguous. He demonstrates that the value of information to a decision maker does not necessarily increase as the riskiness of a decision increases and argues that this has important implications for the analysis of decision making under uncertainty. For instance resources devoted to information gathering may not be concentrated in those areas where uncertainty is greatest, as one might have thought. This is because there is uncertainty as to the expected payoff from gathering information itself, and risk aversion may apply to the (meta-)decision to acquire information as much as to other decisions.

Estes (1984) suggests there may be an important distinction between the acquisition of information by humans and by other animals. In humans, he argues, it is the rule rather than the exception that the information currently being gathered has little relation to the immediate problems facing the decision maker. He argues that information seems sometimes to be acquired not for a particular purpose but for its own sake. He suggests that this characteristic implies that the acquisition of information may be inherently reinforcing for human beings, without any benefit necessarily arising from its use. This contrast between human and non-human information gathering partly relates to the time frame over which the decision-making process itself stretches. Dawkins (1982) argues that non-human decision making might be thought of as 'tactical' rather than 'strategic' since it relates to a short time frame and is concerned with immediate problems. Human decision making clearly may relate to a very long time frame and information is gathered and decisions taken in relation to events in the distant future and to problems that have not yet arisen. This characteristic of human decision making requires emphasis. When ethnographic or archaeological data are examined we should expect to see evidence of information gathering behaviour unrelated to a specific problem. The problem may not have yet arisen, or may be unknown to the actor himself. Consequently, I need to make an important distinction between directed and non-directed information gathering. The former relates to a specific decision to be taken in the immediate future and for which particular types of information are sought. The latter relates to an anticipated decision(s), although when it it will arise, and what the alternative courses of action will be, are currently unknown.

Cues

Few studies of foraging have paid detailed attention to the use of cues in decision making by animals. Cant and Temerin (1984) comment on how the colour and odour of plant foods indicate their nutritional value to primate foragers. Similarly Elner and Hughes (1978) discuss how shore crabs can distinguish profitable mussels from the rest by lifting them and using their weights as a cue. Barnard and Brown (1981) suggest that shrews use the size of an encountered prey item as a cue to the efficiency of its exploitation.

One study of particular interest is Orians' (1980) study of marsh-nesting blackbirds in which he examines the selection by males and females of habitats in which to breed and hence which must be exploited over a substantial period of time. Orians found that his optimal foraging predictions concerning the distribution and the size of territories had been met by the birds' behaviour. He considered how the birds may have used cues to assess future patch quality when making their territorial decisions. Such cues include the density of larval insects in the shallow waters during the spring which provides information about the density of adult insects in the summer, and the density of stalks of emergent vegetation in the spring which is negatively related to summer patch quality. In general the birds' behaviour closely matched optimal foraging predictions made in light of known summer patch qualities by using cues during the spring to infer the summer environment when choosing between patches.

The habitat structure may impede or facilitate the reception of sensory cues. For instance small-scale topographic relief and foliage density may affect the visual field and cause interference with sound waves (Cant and Temerin 1984). Consequently, which senses are most useful for receiving cues will depend partly upon the structure of the habitat. Climatic variables may also be important. Rainfall may hamper visual, olfactory, auditory and tactile functions, limiting sensory evaluation of the environment.

Turning to human psychology, the use of cues plays a prominent role in social judgement theory (SJT), one of several approaches to the study of human decision making. This approach borders on both human psychology and economics (Hammond *et al.* 1980). SJT is generally compatible with evolutionary perspectives since it lays great stress on the interaction between the environment and cognitive systems. The environment is divided into surface and depth conditions. Surface conditions are considered to be 'cues' to aspects of the environment which cannot be directly measured and are therefore 'depth' conditions or covert variables. Owing to the inherent ambiguity of the environment, depth conditions cannot be wholly predictable from the surface, 'overt' data or cues. Two important and related concepts are the 'ecological validity' of cues and 'cue utilisation' by the subject. The ecological validity of a cue is simply the extent to which a criterion can be predicted by the cue, as measured for instance by the simple product moment correlation between cue and criterion. Cue utilisation is the extent to which a cue is used by a subject in arriving at a judgement, and is similar to the idea of weight in psychological decision theory (Hammond *et al.* 1980). One of the interests of psychologists is the extent to which the validity of a cue is matched by its utilisation. These two concepts provide a useful framework for considering the use of cues in gathering information for decisions.

Alloy and Tabachnik (1984) discuss the assessment of covariation between two events by both humans and animals, i.e. the recognition that one event may act as a cue to another. They stress the adaptive importance of being able to detect such covariations since these lead to explanation, control and prediction of, and in, the environment. They argue that the covariation assessment process can be conceptualized as an interaction between prior expectations about event relationships and currently available situational information. 'Whether an organism detects any particular relationship accurately depends on the relative strength of relevant expectations and the objective situational information as well as on the degree to which these two sources of information converge. . . organisms both assimilate incoming situational information to their preexisting expectations and accommodate their expectations to the objective data of experience. That is, they both make sense of and impose sense upon the world simultaneously' (1984: 142).

Other individuals

Information about patch and prey quality may also be gained from other individuals either by simply observing/listening to their behaviour or by communication with them. In one sense the presence of other individuals, or co-consumers, may be considered to be a source of cues as to patch quality.

Cant and Temerin (1984) discuss how, among primates, co-consumers that have located a patch may signal this to others by their presence, a change in their activity (such as by stopping moving and beginning to feed), by active vocalization or by some form of information transfer as when individuals aggregate between bouts of foraging behaviour.

Certain field and experimental studies have explored such information transfer between members of the same species. For instance DeGroot (1980) examined information transfer in a species of weaver bird which nests in large groups. By laboratory experiments he demonstrated how birds that are naïve as to the location of food and water can learn their whereabouts when in the presence of knowledgeable birds. A further experiment demonstrated that a flock can exploit the more profitable of two food sources of which only some individuals have experience.

Greene (1987) describes how osprey colonies also function as information transfer centres. This increases the foraging efficiency of individual birds by a significant reduction in their search time for fish. Greene recognises that information about different fish species is used differently since its value depends upon the type of spatial distribution that that species adopts. Male ospreys actively pass on information concerning the location of fish by displays.

Clark and Mangel (1984) have made an interesting theoretical study concerning the advantages of living in a group, or 'flocking' as they call it, for the transfer of information when foraging in an uncertain environment. The most basic point is that information can be gained by simply observing the behaviour of other group members; when one individual locates a patch another may intrude. This, however, reduces the intake of both foragers from that possible if they had exploited the patch alone. Clark and Mangel explore a game theory model of this situation examining the costs and benefits for individuals adopting a flocking or nonflocking strategy and show that flocking can be an evolutionarily stable strategy. Their model is extended to describe how this simple advantage gained by flocking leads to equilibrium flock sizes which are larger than the socially optimal flock size, that is the size at which individual feeding rates are maximised. Such socially optimal flock sizes are shown to be evolutionarily unstable.

The advantages of flocking arise only when the information that may be gained about patch location is valuable. If food is abundant then such information is of little consequence since individuals can locate food independently. Similarly when food is scarce but evenly distributed little information will be gained by searching. When food is both scarce and patchy, however, information is at a premium and flocking will be advantageous.

Clark and Mangel argue that a further information advantage of flocking is that it results in a more rapid updating of estimates of patch and environmental quality than does individual searching. First they provide a discussion of how individual foragers may use information to update estimates using Bayesian methods similar to those described above. They then show that if an individual encounters patches only infrequently, although there is plenty to eat when a patch is found, and if as a member of a flock the individual searches independently but communicates its discovery to other flock members, then its variation in feeding rate may be reduced by flocking. However, the rate at which information is generated by co-operative foraging is also greater than that by individual foraging. Using a Bayesian model of information use to update the mean and variance of patch-quality estimates, Clark and Mangel show how the rate at which the coefficient of variation of the patch-quality estimate is updated is positively correlated to the size of the flock.

In more complex animals the use of other individuals as sources of information leads to problems concerning the reliability of information received. This has led to interesting theoretical studies, for example using game theory techniques (e.g. Maynard-Smith 1982). Kurland and Beckerman (1985) suggest that this reliability problem results in an information spiral as further information is needed to validate that which has been acquired from another individual.

So far I have been principally concerned with the acquisition of information from another individual when that person is not purposefully communicating. We must also be concerned with the purposeful, intentional passing on of information. Sperber and Wilson (1986) refer to this as the use of 'ostensive stimuli', that is, the use of stimuli whose source is an intentional organism, rather than an indifferent world, and whose intent is to inform. They develop principally a theory for utterances (i.e. communications via spoken language) but their ideas also apply to other forms of purposeful communication, such as physical gestures and material culture. They emphasise that ostensive stimuli are crucially different from other stimuli since there is a significantly greater expectation that one will receive information relevant to current needs than from one's own self-directed observations of the world.

Past experience
An animal's past experience may be considered as a further source of information and the use of this information is the core of the learning process. There is a fuzzy area between this source and the others I have been discussing since all information must be stored for a short time in memory. To be able to engage in information-gathering behaviour at all depends on stored information. For instance cues can only be used effectively with information as to the relation between a stimulus and a future event.

The simplest form of the use of past experience is in trial and error learning as referred to above. The role of past information will depend partly on the degree of flux in the environment. If conditions are rapidly changing then it may not pay to make a decision based on past experience of the environment. The ability to use past experience will depend partly on the neuro-physiology of the animal, defining the memory capacities. How far back animals retain information and the extent to which it may be considered to be 'memorised' are controversial issues in animal ethology (see Walker 1983) and not immediately relevant to this work. Suffice it to say that information stored in the brain is central to the decision-making process in non-human animals as well as humans.

Garber (1987) reviews literature on primate decision making in foraging strategies to suggest that information regarding the following is retained:

1 the location and distribution of feeding sites;
2 the rate of food capture and resource renewal;
3 the productivity of individual patches;
4 the relationship between the nutritional and energy values of one patch and the time and distance to a second.

A useful concept here is the mental map, built up from past experience of patch and prey distributions. This concept has been used in primate studies (e.g. Menzel 1978) as well as in the human sciences in general (e.g. Gould and White 1974), and archaeology in particular (Renfrew 1987). In the models of learning and decision making I shall develop in Part 2, in which the decision maker constantly updates his estimates of the efficiency of exploiting different prey items, those currently possessed might be considered as the mental map of his environment.

When considering stored information as an information source we are concerned with that stored in long-term memory which can be defined as *encyclopaedic*. Following Carston (1988), this is most appropriately described as being arranged in chunks at conceptual addresses so that the recall of one piece of information will carry with it associated information which one may not immediately require. These chunks are organised in a hierarchical manner, so small ones are grouped into larger chunks. Moreover, information at each conceptual address has multiple cross-references with entries at other addresses. The degree to which any item is accessible depends upon numerous interacting factors. Information tends to be more accessible the more recently it entered memory, the more stereotypical it is and the more strongly it is believed in. Owing to the hierarchical chunking and multiple cross-referencing, it is theoretically possible that any single introduced concept, perhaps from a recent perceptual experience, could lead to the recall of all stored information. In Sperber and Wilson's model for cognition they argue that the order in which information is recalled depends upon its relevance to the new piece of information. The accessing of information stored in long-term memory will be a crucial issue when exploring hunter-gatherer art and ritual in the following chapters.

Stored informaton may also be used to generate new information. Johnson and Raye (1981) describe how information may be self-generated by the manipulation of past experience. There are three types of self-generated information. The first is the re-representation of a perceptual experience, that is, remembering something that had dropped out of conscious or working memory in the absence of the original external stimulus. Secondly, information may be self-generated by 'cotemporal' thoughts. These are the elaborative and associational processes that 'augment, bridge or embellish ongoing experience' but are not part of the true experience itself. Essentially these are the working of imagination on reality. The third type is fantasy, original combinations of information creating imaginary events that take place only in the mind. In this realm we begin to touch upon the creative aspects of human decision making that I have previously argued to be central to an evolutionary approach.

Information processing

What happens to information once it has been acquired? For it to be used to make a decision, it must be processed in some manner. By this I mean different 'bits' evaluated and compared and given a greater or lesser importance when making the choice. A useful starting point is to return to the use of simple decision rules, as models for complex processes, and to consider the problem of when to leave a patch.

Once foraging in a patch, a predator must not remain too long since its foraging efficiency may fall as a result of patch depletion. But equally it must not leave too soon because of the costs and risks of travelling to another patch the quality of which will be unknown. Charnov (1976) provides the optimal solution to this problem in terms of the marginal value theorem: leave when the marginal rate of intake in the current patch has reached the average for the environment as a whole. There are problems with this theorem (Iwasa *et al.* 1981). First, it assumes that food intake is a continuous event when more realistically it must be considered to be a series of discrete events. Secondly, the predator would not know the future capture rate for its current patch and other patches.

Several theoretical ecologists have been provoked by these problems to explore decision rules for leaving patches (e.g. McNamara and Houston 1980; Iwasa *et al.* 1981; McNair 1982; Green 1984; Janetos and Cole 1981). Several of the issues raised in this work are of direct significance to human hunter-gatherers. A frequent subject has been the comparison of an animal's foraging efficiency resulting from the use of different decision rules. Four types of rules have been most widely explored:

1 *Fixed time.* In this rule the forager searches for a fixed period of time in each patch and leaves the patch irrespective of the number of prey that have been found.

2 *Fixed number or assessment.* The forager leaves the patch after a fixed number of food items have been captured.

3 *Fixed GUT.* GUT stands for giving up time. The forager leaves the patch when the time interval since the last capture exceeds a particular value, i.e. the giving up time.

4 *Fixed rate.* The forager leaves the patch when the instantaneous rate of intake has fallen to some critical level.

Each of these rules uses a different type of information deriving from past experience in the patch, but processes it in a similar way by comparing its current value with some predefined threshold. The general conclusion from these studies is that the best rule to use depends upon the particular characteristics of the patch(es) being exploited. Factors such as the shape of the gain function (net energy intake/time) in a single patch and the nature of the differences between patches are significant in defining the best rule. Stephens and Krebs (1986) summarise the results of such studies:

1 when each patch contains the same number of prey (but encounters with prey are stochastic) a number rule does best;
2 when the number of prey per patch has a high variance a GUT rule does best;
3 when the number of prey per patch follows a poisson distribution a time rule does best.

Here we return to the issue of meta-decision making since the flexible forager must acquire and process information, to decide which type of rule is appropriate for the particular problem and circumstances. The over-sampling recorded by Lima (see above) may relate to acquiring such meta-information. Green (1984) makes a similar study but also considers the robustness of different rules. For instance in his model of a stochastic environment he defines the optimal giving up times for the GUT rule, but shows that a slightly different time need not significantly reduce foraging efficiency. Kamil (1983) and Stephens and Krebs (1986) discuss certain experimental studies of patch-leaving behaviour which have bearing on these theoretical studies.

To further the discussion of rules of thumb we can return to the patch-choice problem as modelled by the bandit games. Above, I left that subject with the question of how little birds were managing to adopt such efficient sampling and foraging patterns. To explore this Houston *et al.* (1982) examine a range of different decision rules to determine how the behaviour they lead to compares with this constrained optimal for the two-armed bandit task. They consider five different types of rules. I will briefly describe their models since these indicate how different rules applied to the same problem use different types of information and/or process information in different ways.

1 *WISLOS.* In this rule the first trial is located at random and subsequent trials determined simply by whether or not a reward is obtained. If a trial is rewarded then the same arm is chosen again, otherwise the other arm is chosen on the next trial, hence the name WIn Stay LOose Shift. In this rule there is no learning involved. The decision maker simply remembers the arm which was last chosen and whether or not a reward was obtained.

2 *IMMAX.* In this rule the decision maker uses Bayesian estimates of the reward probabilities for each arm and makes the next trial on the arm with the highest probability. It is therefore a deterministic rule and aims to maximise the immediate returns from foraging, rather than suffer a short-term loss by sampling.

3 *MATCH.* This rule is similar to IMMAX in using Bayesian estimates of reward

probabilities but it allocates the next trial on a stochastic rather than a deterministic basis. The probability of choosing arm 1 on the $t = i$ trial is proportional to the relative size of the estimated reward probability on that arm.

4 *RPS*. The Relative Payoff Sum learning rule was proposed by Harley (1981) to be a widely applicable rule of thumb. It has been discussed by Maynard-Smith (1982, 1984), and subject to some criticism by Houston (1983). The probability of choosing an arm depends upon the relative rewards that have been gained so far from that arm. In computing the payoffs more weight is given to those from recent trials. If there are n alternatives to choose from the probablity of choosing alternative i on trial t, $Pr_{i(t)}$, is given by:

$$Pr_{i(t)} = \frac{r_i + \sum_{d=1}^{t-1} x^{t-d-1} R_{i(d)}}{\sum_{i=1}^{n} [r_i + \sum_{d=1}^{t-1} x^{t-d-1} R_{i(d)}]}$$

where $R_i(d)$ is the payoff that occurred on trial d, and x is the 'memory factor' that determines the relative weight given to the payoffs, and r_i is a residual value associated with each alternative (see Harley 1981). When x is close to zero very little weight is given to early payoffs; as x approaches 1 all rewards become more equally weighted.

As Houston *et al.* (1982) point out, this rule does not require the storage of all previous payoffs. It can be written in alternative notation demonstrating that such information storage is not required. Kacelnik and Krebs (1985) have described applications of the RPS rule to patch-choice experiments involving sticklebacks.

5 *CUMDIF*. Houston *et al.* examine a series of rules which are slight variations on the basic CUMulative DIFference rule. This rule is deterministic and has a sample-then-decide structure. The subject starts by making trials of two bouts on each arm until a decision point is reached. After that the subject makes all remaining trials on the same arm. The decision point is reached when the cumulative difference between the rewards on each arm reaches a critical amount.

Having defined these rules Houston *et al.* compare their performances in the two-armed bandit problem with each other and with the gains from the constrained optimum sampling sequence. By using both analytical and simulation techniques they make a range of comparisons and explore their performances under different time horizons and reward-probability sets. In any one set of comparisons the relative merits of the rules vary. However, an overall performance is derived by comparing them over a range of conditions, ranking their performance in each case and deriving their average rank. By this means the utility of each rule for the two-armed bandit problem is evaluated. The constrained optimum sequence not surprisingly provides the greatest rewards but is closely followed by CUMDIF and IMMAX. RPS rank third and WISLOS and MATCH are the least useful. The first three rules generally perform well and provide returns not substantially less than the constrained optimal sampling sequence. In any one situation it would be difficult to know which would be the best rule.

A study which compares the efficiency of a forager using a simple decision rule and one which uses an optimal strategy has been made by Janetos and Cole (1981). In this case the modelled environment consists of good and bad foraging sites at which a predator receives daily payoffs, those from a good site being larger than those from a poor site. A predator encounters good or bad sites with certain probabilities and also incurs a cost in moving. Janetos and Cole also assume that good sites have a constant life span after which they become bad sites. At the end of each day the predator is assumed to decide whether to stay in its current foraging site or whether to move to a new one. If, after having decided to move, the predator lands in a good site it does not know how much of the site's life span has already expired. This model may be thought to be applicable to human hunter-gatherers with high residential mobility and low people mobility, generally characterised by Binford (1980) as 'foragers' as opposed to 'collectors'.

Janetos and Cole compare the payoffs gained by a predator using a simple decision rule to decide when to move with those of a predator using an optimal strategy and maximising its energetic intake. The simple rule says 'move after having experienced a poor day at the foraging site' and Janetos and Cole derive the average daily payoff from using such a decision rule. The optimal time for leaving patches is calculated and Janetos and Cole derive an equation for the difference between payoffs gained by an optimal and a decision rule predator and use this to examine how these differ as a function of the life-span of good sites.

They find that the optimal behaviour is unsurprisingly always the more profitable. The magnitude of the difference depends on several parameters: the ratio of the cost of moving to the difference between good and bad patches, the probability of encountering a good site and, most importantly, the length of the life-span of a good site. When this last factor is small there is little difference in payoffs derived from an optimal and decision rule strategy. As the life-span increases there is an increase in the benefit of leaving the site at the optimal time and hence decision rule predators, who sometimes stay too long, become less efficient than the optimal predators.

As noted by Boyd and Richerson (1985), considerable experimental data suggest that humans also depend upon simple rules of thumb. Of particular interest is the approach to human decision making known as psychological decision theory (PDT) (Tversky and Kahneman 1971, 1974; Hammond *et al.* 1980). Psychological decision theory is principally concerned with the departure of human decision making from optimality, attempting to explain as well as describe this phenomenon. 'The main interest of these researchers *is* to find the cognitive sources of the departure from the criteria of rationality. Specifically, they seek the manner in which the processes of memory, perception and specific varieties of experience lead decision makers to develop systematic errors in their estimates of the probabilities and utilities that are the key parameters in decision theory' (Hammond *et al.* 1980: 11). We see here a similarity with the interest shown by ethologists and ecologists in the idea of simple decision rules used by animals in allowing the decision maker to approach but not obtain optimality. A significant difference here is that in PDT optimality is purely a descriptive tool, while in optimal foraging theory it is an a priori assumption about behaviour justified by evolution through natural selection.

Uncertainty is a prominent concept in PDT. It refers to uncertainty about whether or not an event will occur and what the outcome of a chosen alternative will be. A decision maker must cope with this uncertainty. Although uncertainty is considered to be a pervasive mental state there is no detailed theoretical analysis offered as to why such uncertainty should exist, unlike in SJT, to which I referred above, where uncertainty arises as a result of the complexity and change in the social and natural environments.

The most important term is 'heuristics', to describe the various rules of thumb used by people when making decisions and it is these heuristics which are the main cause of departure from optimality. Two particularly important heuristics are 'availability' and 'representativeness'. The latter refers to the manner in which people frequently evaluate the subjective probability of an event by assessing how characteristic it is of the process thought to underlie it. For instance, if an event is a sequence of digits which are thought to be generated randomly then the probability of an ascending sequence may be considered low since it is not characteristic of a random number generator. In many cases an event may be erroneously thought to be either representative or non-representative. The availability heuristic simply refers to the manner in which people assess the probability of an event by the number of similar events that they can recall. Consequently the GUT leaving rule discussed above might be described as the use of a representation heuristic, the forager leaving when the time since the last prey capture is thought representative of that in a poor patch.

The efficiency of using simple decision rules is also prominent in the influential work of H.A. Simon (1979). He stresses the modesty of human thinking when compared with the complexity of the environments in which humans live. Faced with such complexity and 'lacking the wits' to optimise, humans must be content to satisfice, find good enough solutions. In relation to this, and following my discussion of goal choice above, I view 'satisficing' behaviour as a description of human suboptimal behaviour rather than as a goal held by the decision maker. He further argues that humans can satisfy their needs and assure a high probability of survival in a complex environment by using simple perceptual and choice mechanisms.

Sherman and Corty (1984) provide a comprehensive description of the use of cognitive heuristics and attempt to provide a general explanatory framework for their use, the biases and errors they create and their persistence. As well as the representative and availability heuristic they describe that of simulation, the ease with which a particular scenario can be constructed, and 'anchoring' (or adjustment) by which one starts with an estimate and gradually adjusts it to reach a final judgement which is biased by being 'anchored' to the starting point. An important point which they stress, and which several authors confuse, is that a distinction must be made between heuristics and algorithms to which I add rules of thumb. Heuristics are applied indiscriminately, without awareness, and lead to systematic errors. These may be thought of as analogous to the 'decision rules' used by animals in foraging decisions which have evolved through natural selection. Algorithms are step by step procedures used for solving a problem and can be considered to be the decision process itself (i.e. acquiring and processing information) which may involve the use of heuristics. Rules of thumb are best characterised as simple algorithms perhaps using one or a few items of information. Most of the anthropological descriptions of the use of heuristics are in fact referring to consciously applied rules of thumb. A further point that Sherman and Corty (1984) emphasise is that there is a contradiction between the fallibility of people's judgements and the confidence they hold in their abilities. This largely accounts for the persistence in the use of heuristics and rules of thumb even though they lead to systematic errors.

Quinn (1978) has invoked the use of heuristics for Fante (Ghanaian) fish sellers. She argues that they do not calculate the possibilities for a given supply of fish at the principal market itself, but instead decide which market to visit by using simple rules of thumb such as the number of lorries leaving for a particular market. Gladwin and Murtaugh (1984) provide another example. They describe a pueblo farmer who ploughs his fields in autumn when 'the volcano is free of clouds'. This works to conserve soil moisture but there is no reason to assume that the farmer is consciously making a probability calculation about the likelihood of rainfall. These heuristics, which should be referred to as rules of thumb, might alternatively be seen as the utilisation of ecologically valid cues about future conditions. Specifically, one might equate the use of a single cue as the source of information with a rule of thumb.

While most studies stress the limited computational power of the human mind one should beware of exaggerating this characteristic. It is apparent that the human mind, without the use of writing or scientific instruments, is capable of complex calculations. This has been stressed by O'Frake (1985) in his study of navigational skills of medieval and Pacific islander sailors. He describes how without the charts or tables used by Western seamen, these sailors achieved remarkable cognitive feats in processing a mass of ever-changing information concerning tides, currents and weather conditions in their seafaring exploits. Although the use of heuristics and rules of thumb are not considered, O'Frake's study does demonstrate that 'correct' decisions can be reached unaided. This relates to certain of the ecological studies I discussed above, showing how simple decision rules can approach optimal behaviour that requires sophisticated mathematics to calculate.

However, I do not wish to reject the idea that humans, and other species, perform sophisticated quantitative calculations about the pros and cons of alternative courses of action in their heads. The central issue is that, given particular contexts, this capacity may be employed; and the important question is, what are those contexts and, when these have arisen, when will rules of thumb as opposed to calculation be invoked?

Culture and cognition

If we now turn to psychological anthropology, which concentrates on cross-cultural studies of perception and cognition, we find further concepts and data compatible with the eco-psychological model so far developed, and which allow it to be extended. These studies suggest that cognitive differences are far reaching, with complex relations between cognition on the one hand and language, ecology, subsistence and social organisation on the other (Bourguignon 1979).

My particular interest is the relationship between cognition and ecology, in terms of how the cognitive strengths and weaknesses are appropriate for the ecological problems that they solve. Here I will be following Fodor in seeing the lowest-level perceptual input systems as being 'hardwired', and not culturally variable.

At a gross level, distinctions have been drawn between hunter-gatherers on the one hand and agriculturalists and craft producers on the other (Barry *et al.* 1959). Cross-cultural comparisons have been made to show how child-rearing practices help develop those cognitive capacities most useful for these economies. In relation to attentive behaviour, child-rearing practices and cultural experiences in general have been identified as being important in determining which of the stimuli constantly bombarding the senses are attended to. Here we can begin to develop Sperber and Wilson's model for cognition by recognising that what is defined as relevant, and hence which cognitive tasks are engaged in, varies with the cultural background and the ecological problems facing the decision maker.

Memory is also a cognitive characteristic which varies among different societies facing different environmental problems – individuals have different abilities to recall past events and different types of information. A contrast that is frequently drawn here is between literate and non-literate societies. In the latter, special practices will be required to transmit information across generations and because information must reside in 'living memory' special mnemonic devices may be required to aid its persistence. As Cole and Scribner (1974: 123) state, even the harshest critic of the mental skills of 'primitives' have united in extolling the superlative quality of primitive memory.

With special reference to hunter-gatherers and to coping with environmental problems, we can consider the environmental-pressures hypothesis as discussed by Kearins (1981). Like ecologists criticising the use of laboratory experiments to determine the 'intelligence' of animals, Kearins argues that experimental tests on humans are unlikely to reveal special skills or insights unless they derive from significant behavioural requirements of the subjects' natural environment. Kearins describes the poor performance of Australian Aborigines in standardised cognitive tests developed in Western culture in this light. She argues that such tests examine cognitive skills which have little value to Aboriginal hunter-gatherers and hence have not been significantly developed. However, an accurate memory for spatial relationships is invaluable in highly mobile life styles and one finds that Aboriginal children constantly perform better in tests of these skills than do Western children. The environmental pressures hypothesis proposes that the cognitive skills which are most highly developed in an individual will be those which are of value in coping with the particular problems posed by the environment of that person. In relation to decision making, flexibility in cognitive skills ensures that the relevant information is acquired and processed in an appropriate manner for the types of problems being faced. As Kearins discusses, the skills developed derive from a complex interplay between learning and inheritance in any one society. Some individuals are naturally endowed with skills in particular cognitive areas and these are naturally employed in situations of greatest value. However, child-rearing practices may strongly emphasise which skills are most highly developed.

Group decision making

It is characteristic of humans that decisions are sometimes taken by groups rather than individuals, or that individuals reach their own decisions by participation within the group. In the ecological studies considered above, groups were seen as a context for information exchange not for communal decision taking. As with all the other issues I have been discussing, group decision making is a complex and controversial subject and I aim only to highlight some of the points relevant to this work. Comprehensive discussions of group decision making is given in the edited volumes by Brandstatter *et al.* (1978, 1982) and the work of Fisher (1980).

There are several differences between group and individual decision making. Within a group there are more minds and hence more information and resources to apply to a decision. There are also more ideas and viewpoints (Fisher 1980). Individuals within a group do not always simply pool or aggregate data in a passive manner but actively combine it (Davies 1982). At the start of a discussion, individuals may be considered to prefer different alternatives and the group task is to map the distribution of individual preferences to reach a collective group decision. A useful concept here is that of a 'social-decision scheme', a model for the underlying group process which guides this mapping (Davis 1973; Laughlin and Adamupoloulas 1982). The form of the social-decision scheme employed is highly variable and relates to both the task and the characteristics of the group members. Davis (1982) suggests that when there is high task uncertainty (i.e. the actors are unaware of the probabilities associated with the outcome of the alternatives) then one tends to find egalitarian social processes. When there is only moderate task uncertainty and consequently grounds about which to disagree and deliberate, the social-decision scheme tends to move away from strict egalitarianism to the formation of sub-groups and the need for a decision rule, such as majority or plurality, arises. This is an idea, therefore, similar to the variability in the use of individual decision rules – different rules being appropriate for particular types of problems.

While it is generally accepted that the quality of a group decision may be better than that of an individual it is also recognised that groups tend to be very slow in reaching a decision. It has been found that the attention span of a group is very short and decisions tend to be made in spurts of activity rather than during a period of sustained effort which characterises individuals (Fisher 1980).

An important phenomenon of group decisions, that is well established but inadequately explained, is 'choice shift' (Davis and Hinsz 1982). This was originally called 'risky shift' and referred to the finding that the average group was more inclined than its average individual member (prior to discussion) to recommend an apparently risky course of action. Since a 'cautious shift' has also been recognised, the best description of this phenomenon is an increase in the extremity of a decision of a group related to an individual response. Choice shift has recently been seen as part of a more general feature of group decision making – group polarisation. It has been found that, following a discussion, members of a group may exhibit more extreme views than before. This was a surprising finding since it had previously been thought that discussion acts as a moderating mechanism (Davis and Hinsz 1982).

A further characteristic of group decision making is identified and discussed by Janis (1972) and termed 'group think'. He developed this concept by examining the decision making of the United States administration during the 1960s. Group think is found among groups which have high cohesiveness, i.e. they have a strong group spirit or sense of identity, and refers to individuals not simply conforming to group pressures but who are seeking agreement and a concurrence of views at all costs. Consequently, critical faculties become suspended so that a consensus can be reached. Typically this leads to poor-quality decisions and defective judgements (Fisher 1980). Group think tends to involve the illusion that the group is invulnerable and rival or opposing groups are discredited.

The actual process of reaching a decision in a group can be thought of as one of emergence, rather than a discrete event. Fisher (1980) has characterised the decision process as consisting of four phases. First, orientation is a phase when interaction patterns are influenced by the early problems of socialisation and the presence of tension among group members. One tends to find a high degree of agreement and only tentative expressions of opinion. Following this is a 'conflict' phase which is characterised by disputes, conflicting opinions about appropriate courses of action, and the expression of these without any ambiguity or tentativeness. One tends to find a polarisation of views and the formation of sub-groups. A phase of 'emergence' follows this during which dispute and conflict dissipate and the views opposing the emerging viewpoint weaken and are expressed ambiguously. Members have become aware in this phase of the eventual outcome of the group interaction. Finally there is a 'reinforcement' phase when consensus about the decision that has emerged is arrived at. Dissent diminishes totally and further support for this viewpoint is given; a spirit of unity returns to the group. Fisher characterises such a process as 'natural' because it is pervasive in group decision making and is found even when members are unaware of its presence and influence.

The identification of a leader in a group is also described by Fisher (1980) as one of emergence resulting from communication patterns. She describes the behaviour associated with an emergent leader as including being verbally active, demonstrating communication skills, constantly introducing themes, seeking opinion and information early on and stating opinions and attempting to persuade others later in the decision process. An interesting study of the emergence of leaders during group decision making and information exchange is reported by Leavitt (1951). By using experiments he demonstrates how the network of communication within a group influences which individual emerges as the leader. This tends to be the individual in a central position, through whom information is channelled to other members.

Choice, outcome and consequences

Once information has been acquired and processed a decision is made to follow one course of action rather than another. The result of this choice may be an intended or unintended consequence, recognised or unrecognised in either the short or/and long term. To consider such effects it is perhaps timely now to return to hunting and gathering and foraging problems. In the diet breadth problem the choice is either to stalk an encountered animal or to pass up that opportunity. Roe deer tracks may be ignored in the hope of finding an elk. For patch choice the hunter will choose to exploit one patch rather than another – move to the coast rather than the hills, go hunting deer rather than fishing for salmon. Now, the outcome from making a choice may be very different from that expected – the simulation models we use in our minds for future worlds often have insufficient or incorrect data or have a bug in the way it is processed. The hunter may not find his elk or it may be impossible to get close enough to strike it. The red deer may be more dispersed than had been thought. It may be that such possibilities have been taken into account and appropriate action planned, or these may arise unexpectedly.

Choices that are made may carry supplementary and unintended consequences. The first of these refer to known costs and benefits which arise from a particular course of action but which were of little concern to the decision maker when reaching his choice. For instance in going to a new patch, information may be indirectly gathered which may or may not be useful in future decisions. Information may also be gained as an unintended consequence of the choice made. When passing up the roe deer tracks in the hope of finding elk the hunter may find those of an auroch. Unintended consequences may also occur over a much longer time span. For instance the choice to hunt a red deer population may have a consequence for the availability of that population in the following year which had not been taken into account. The models in Chapter 7 focus on this feedback from choices made to future problems via the route of unintended consequences.

Unintended consequences also act at the level described by Merton (1936, 1963); he refers to them as the latent as opposed to the manifest consequences of an action. These are the functional benefits gained from what may initially appear irrational behaviour. Rain dances may not bring rain but serve to affirm group solidarity during times of drought. Many of the functional processes I have been describing are most reasonably seen as unintended consequences of actions. My discussion here, however, is beginning to labour under the absence of any data on hunter-gatherers. As my references to hunting red deer and elk illustrate, I am now itching to deal with real people and real problems.

3

The ethnography of hunter-gatherer decision making

Esau was a cunning hunter . . .

Genesis 25:27

Archaeologists studying the Palaeolithic and Mesolithic may use the ethnographic record of historically documented hunter-gatherers in a variety of ways. Some seek cross-cultural generalisations for theory building or hypothesis testing. Others focus on the relationships between behaviour and its material consequences for middle-range research. Alternatively archaeologists may use it simply as a source of analogies for supporting inferences drawn about past behaviour. When we have written and photographic records of hunter-gatherers 'in action' it would indeed be perverse to ignore them. But it would be equally foolish to forget that we are seeing modern and not 'Stone Age' society.

It is readily apparent that historically documented hunter-gatherers provide poor analogies for the 'pristine' hunter-gatherers represented by the archaeological record alone. Often these are dependent upon state societies; they make extensive use of modern technology; hunting and gathering may be pastimes rather than providing essential sustenance and are often pursued only in response to the goading of anthropologists. Some, perhaps many, 'modern' foragers have switched from an agricultural lifestyle. As a result the foraging problems they face, the goals they choose, the information sources exploited, the way such information is processed, and the consequences which may occur, probably bear little if any relationship to those of prehistoric hunter-gatherers.

This is all true but of little consequence for my ends. One of my principal arguments is that the decision-making processes of any group or individual possess unique characteristics whether our subjects are alive today or forgotten in prehistory. I am interested in how the decision-making processes applied in any particular context, and the rich cultural life that arises from their use, are a product both of unique circumstances surrounding that choice and of underlying, uniform biological capacities for decision making. These have been constant since the evolution of modern man; modern or prehistoric foragers remain, like Esau, cunning hunters. So by looking at the ethnographic record I am making further preparations for the challenges presented by the archaeological record. I am not going to try and build theory and method in a rigid, scientific, quantitative framework. Mine is the more humble and less precise art of simply seeking inspiration and ideas prior to the optimistic, some might say foolhardy, task of peering into the darkness of prehistory for the individual decision maker. I want to know if the eco-psychological framework is useful for addressing the way modern hunter-gatherers make foraging decisions. I want to put some flesh onto its bones. If cues are used, then what sort of cues? If information exchange takes place then when and how does this happen? Do modern hunter-gatherers process large quantities of information or rely on individual pieces? And if they switch between the two, what are the criteria that they use to choose between them? I am not pretending that answers to these questions, if indeed they are found, will tell us how prehistoric hunter-gatherers made foraging decisions. But they will help us along that path by allowing us to study, with this particular database, how general and uniform pychological propensities interact with historically, ecologically and socially unique contexts to create a set of foraging choices.

The ethnographic record is a collection of texts varying immensely in the manner of observation and description. At one extreme we have the reports of early explorers, settlers and missionaries, often with imperialist and racist views self-consciously imposed. At the other we have recent anthropological studies going so far as to measure the durations of different activities in their quest for objectivity but nevertheless with paradigmatic or theoretical views subtly embedded in their text.

Few ethnographies have paid specific attention to decision-making processes. However, since these pervade many activities in some form or another, few ethnographies are without relevant material. Often the ethnographer describes activities which to him have no bearing on decision making but, in light of the material discussed in Chapter 2, can now be seen to be relevant to one or more of the model components. Since ethnographies deal principally with observed activities the different model components receive different degrees of attention, some being more manifest in behaviour than others. Consequently there is less material in these works relevant to information processing and meta-decision making than to information acquisition.

The task of this chapter is therefore to examine a sample of ethnographic texts concerning hunter-gatherers in a diverse set of environments (Fig. 3.1) through the eyes of the eco-psychological model. This will serve to 'clothe' that model in a set of data as to how ethnographically described hunter-gatherers make foraging decisions. By doing this it also serves to organise and classify a diverse set of ethnographic data. I am looking for uniformity across cultures, since we are dealing with the same biological species involved in the same activity, as well as variability since each individual has a unique social, natural and historical context. To achieve these ends I will divide the chapter into two principal sections relating to information gathering and information processing. Material relating to meta-decision making will be integrated within these sections at appropriate places.

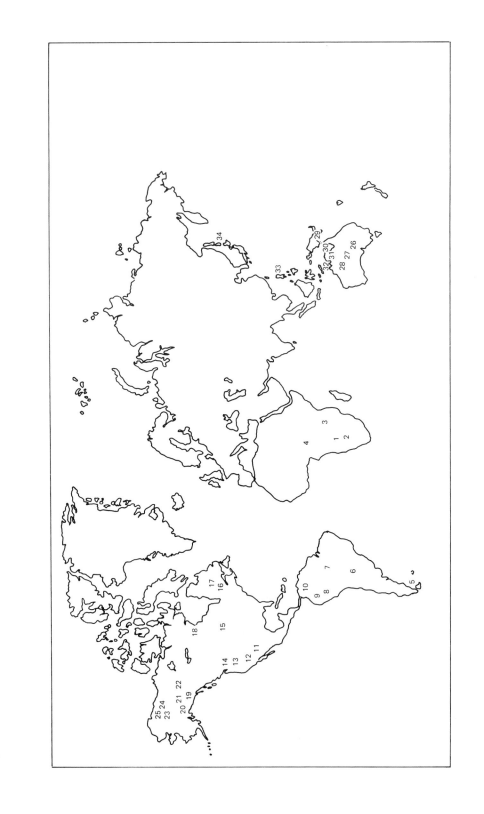

Fig. 3.1. Hunter-gatherers referred to in Chapter 3
   1. !Kung (Yellen 1976; Lee 1976, 1979; Marshall 1976; Blurton-Jones and Konner 1976; Tanaka 1976; Draper 1976)
   2. G/wi (Silberbauer 1981)
   3. Valley Bisa (Marks 1976)
   4. Aka (Hewlett and Cavalli–Sforza 1986)
   5. Selk'nam (Chapman 1982)
   6. Áche (Hill and Hawkes 1983)
   7. Mekranti (Werner 1983)
   8. Waorani (Yost and Kelley 1983)
   9. Siona Secoya (Hames and Vickers 1982)
  10. Bari (Beckerman 1983)
  11. Chiricahua Apache (Opler 1941)
  12. Yumon (Spier 1933)
  13. Modoc (Ray 1963)
  14. Twana (Elmendorf and Kroeber 1960)
  15. Sioux (Hassrick 1964)
  16. Montagnais-Naskapi (Leacock 1969)
  17. Mistassini Cree (Tanner 1978, 1979; Rogers 1972; Jennes 1977; Martin 1978; Winterhalder 1981)
  18. Chipeweyan (Heffley 1981)
  19. Yakutat-Tlingit (De Laguna 1972; Krause 1956)
  20. Eyak (Birket-Smith and De Laguna 1938)
  21. Koyukon (Nelson 1983)
  22. Kutchin (Nelson 1973; Slobodin 1969)
  23. T'ena (Sullivan 1942)
  24. Nunamiut (Gubser 1965; Binford 1978)
  25. Taremiut (Minc 1986)
  26. Wankanguru (Horne and Aiston 1924)
  27. Walbiri (Morphy 1977)
  28. Alyawara (O'Connell and Hawkes 1981)
  29. Kaurareg (Moore 1979)
  30. Groote Eylandt Islanders (Levitt 1981)
  31. Gidjingali (Meehan 1982)
  32. Tiwi (Goodale 1971)
  33. Agta (Bion-Griffen 1984; Estioko-Griffen 1986)
  34. Ainu (Watanabe 1973)

Information acquisition

Sampling and searching

Owing to the high cost of these activities in terms of time and energy these are principally highly directed forms of information-gathering behaviour. Ethnographic examples exist relating to decisions at several different levels of the decision hierarchy. For instance in relation to patch choice, Tanner (1978: 98) describes trapping expeditions by Cree hunters to assess the suitability of an area for settlement. The patch-sampling activities of the Alyawara (O'Connell and Hawkes 1981: 111–12) and the searching for signs of animal movement by the Cree (Winterhalder 1981: 90) so that patch qualities can be assessed have been referred to in optimal foraging studies. Heffley (1981: 134–8) characterises the prime task of Chipewayan hunting groups as to search for caribou so that when the animals prepare for migration the large regional hunter-gatherer groups could come together in an area (i.e. a patch) which anticipated the migration route.

One of the most important examples of searching and sampling within a patch is that of the Bari, as described by Beckerman (1983). The Bari are a group of tropical-forest horticulturalists who depend on hunting and fishing as their principal source of protein. Beckerman explored their hunting and fishing activities using an optimal patch-use model. In direct contrast to his predictions, he found that they spent most of their time hunting, although this had lower returns per hour than either spear or hook and line fishing. His explanation for this is essentially that through their hunting activity the Bari acquire the necessary information to be able to exploit the rich fish patches when they become available.

Two factors define the success of a Bari fishing expedition: the amount of recent rainfall and the knowledge as to which stream fish can be located in. Rainfall is important since when this has been heavy the streams will be deep and opaque, making fishing difficult. Consequently, as Beckerman demonstrates, fishing normally takes place on days following little or no rainfall. Knowledge as to the location of fish is important since the main prey species, the bocachio, is irregular in its movements. One can only predict which river will have a shoal if one has seen fish moving in that direction in the recent past. Information is therefore at a premium and Beckerman argues that this is gained during traditional hunting activity – by moving through the forest and observing the depth and opacity of the water and the movements of fish.

The importance of this information varies with the seasons. Between September and November, when it is wet, the Bari fish as much as possible but the heavy rainfall limits the extent of this. Since hunting returns are poor at this time of year, information is at a premium and is acquired by hunting when fishing is impossible. In the dry season, information is of little consequence since good fishing patches are readily available. The Bari acquire a surplus of fish and hence the need to locate particularly good patches is removed. Consequently, little time is spent in traditional hunting activity. During August, when there is a relatively even balance between time devoted to hunting and to fishing, Beckerman recorded one fishing expedition that stretched over two days and provided returns far in excess of any previous catch. A dam was built across a river during one afternoon. The hunters returned at a precise time the next morning as large catfish began hurling themselves against it and could be easily speared. The success of this catch was dependent upon not only the general knowledge of fish behaviour but also the specific information as to which creek the fish were ascending, their whereabouts in that creek, and when they would return to the main channel. This was acquired during the several days' hunting that preceded the building of the dam.

Such descriptions of information-gathering trips in relation to specific resources are common in the ethnographic literature (e.g. Fig 3.2). A second example is provided by Hassrick (1964: 199) who describes scouting parties going to watch for buffalo. Further down the decision hierarchy, searching and sampling are used to decide where exactly to exploit a chosen resource. For instance, Sullivan (1942: 66) records a T'ena fisherman cutting the ice in several places to test the water depth and the speed of the current before placing his fish traps.

The ethnographic record clearly demonstrates that the intensity of sampling

Fig. 3.2. An Iglulik Eskimo searching for seal (after Damas 1984).

and searching activity is highly variable throughout the year. There are two reasons for this. The first is that a certain day, month or season may present the forager with a particular need to acquire information. This relates partly to the behaviour of specific resources. Searching for caribou by the Nunamiut principally takes place in the spring when their movement and location are most irregular (Binford 1978: 169). Nelson (1983: 175–6) recognises the search for bear dens and moose as principally an autumn activity for the Koyukon. The timing of the arrival of migratory resources may be known in general terms but to exploit such resources most efficiently they may need to be searched for at the start of this period. For instance Nelson (1983: 10) and Watanabe (1973: 26) describe Koyukon and Ainu foragers watching for the arrival of the first migratory fish. These examples relate to specific resources but the time to search for several different resources may coincide. In northern regions, this occurs in the early spring when the condition of many potential resources may need to be inspected following the winter (Nelson 1983: 214; Rogers 1972: 110). As a result, settlements may be located primarily with a view to gathering information, such as the Mask site described by Binford (1978) or the simple piles of stones placed on cliff tops by the Kaurareg to indicate the best location to watch for marine resources (Moore 1979: 272). While the choices of locations for such sites are decisions in themselves they may also be considered as meta-decisions since they are concerned with information gathering for use in future foraging decisions.

In addition to these regular periods of intense searching and sampling, which can be planned for and are highly organised, unexpected events may lead to searching activity. Meehan (1982: 165) describes how sudden storms may dramatically alter the composition and quality of shell beds. Immediately following such storms the Gidjingali shell gatherers make expeditions to inspect the shell beds.

The second principal reason for temporal variability in sampling and searching activity arises from its high cost. Since such activity limits the acquisition of food and the performance of other tasks, periods when time is not required for these is used for searching the environment. This takes place in a less directed manner than the examples I have been describing. Binford (1983: 204–5) describes how the Nunamiut Eskimos and Central Desert Aborigines travel great distances to monitor their environment when they have a secure source of food. Pfeiffer (1982: 157) indicates that Australian Aborigines may also engage in such non-directed information gathering. Similarly the Mekranti Indians of Brazil engage in long treks through the forest at times when hunting and fishing are most productive (Wemer 1983). The same is found among African foragers. For instance Marks (1976) describes how Valley Bisa hunters wander off in search of game when there is no pressing work in their village (Fig. 3.3). Silberbauer (1981: 245–8) relates how the G/wi retreat into their winter ranges before conditions deteriorate so that they can search and sample different areas while food is still plentiful. A further means to cope with the cost of these activities is to embed them. Chapman (1982: 21) describes how in one instance some Selk'nam men took a long travel route between two settlements so that they could search for game on the way. While exploiting one resource others may be searched for. The Apache women often searched for beehives while gathering plant material (Opler 1941: 364). Similarly information gathering about fishing patches by the Bari, as described above, was embedded in hunting activity since some protein could be acquired by hunting.

A further characteristic of searching behaviour is simply that the pattern of movement while searching is chosen to increase the chance of locating the resources. !Kung women often move in a zig-zag pattern when searching for plants (Marshall 1976: 106) and Gould (1980: 70) describes how Western Desert Aborigines may move in a decreasing spiral pattern when locating a water source, the general position of which is known from observation of the rains. The direction in which one looks when moving is also important for efficient searching. Goodale (1971: 161) relates how the Tiwi may look either down at the ground or up in the trees since these are where most cues are seen. Similarly Marks (1976: 116) characterises the Valley Bisa search as a brisk walk interspersed with stops to listen and scan the environment.

It is clear that searching and sampling behaviour is highly related to information exchange. Several of the examples I have described involve individuals or groups searching and then reporting back to other members of the larger group (e.g. Heffley 1981; Tanner 1979). Hill and Hawkes (1983) have described how the Áche

Fig. 3.3. A Valley Bisa hunter searching for game (after Marks 1976).

need to reach a balance between information gathering and exchange when foraging in the Amazonian forest. They need to be sufficiently far apart so that the search is efficient (i.e. reducing the degree of overlap between hunters) but also near enough together so that finds can be communicated and help elicited when required.

Cues

The use of cues is pervasive in all aspects of hunter-gatherer behaviour and my aim here is just to indicate the range of types used in relation to foraging decisions and to identify some general characteristics. I divide cues up into eight classes: tracks, excretions, terrain, vegetation, sounds, smells, animals/plants and weather.

Tracks. The use of tracks as a source of information is the most frequently described cue in the ethnographic literature. In some instances foragers specifically search for tracks of particular species, and when these are found immediate action is normally taken. The Cree foragers searching for moose and caribou tracks (Winterhalder 1981: 90) provide a good example. Sullivan (1942: 93, 95) describes how T'ena trappers search for the tracks of fur-bearing animals such as otter and muskrat, when choosing places to locate traps. In other instances foragers search for tracks, but without particular species in mind; this may sometimes lead to immediate action. When Áche foragers observe the tracks of the paca, which they have not been specifically looking for, they may change their activity and search for more information or engage in pursuit of the animal (Hill and Hawkes 1983: 147). Such a general search for tracks is very frequently referred to in the ethnographic literature (e.g. Estioko-Griffen 1986: 38; Sullivan 1942: 44, 67; Hassrick 1964: 193; Nelson 1983: 46, 164, 175, 176).

In many of these instances it is clear that tracks are being observed and examined without immediate action even if they are fresh and suggest the chance of a kill. In these cases tracks may be being used as a general cue to patch quality, rather than in relation to specific prey. The tracks may be used to estimate general densities of prey and the age structure of prey populations. Such information may be used in high-level decisions such as when to leave the patch. In this light, the absence of tracks will also be important information for the forager.

Ethnographies frequently comment on the immense amount of information that hunter-gatherers can extract from tracks (e.g. Sullivan 1942: 68; Nelson 1973: 200). Lee (1979: 212–13) in particular has documented this in relation to the !Kung bushmen. By considering factors such as the size, shape and depth of the prints, the length of stride and the gait, the amount of material kicked up between footfalls and that collected in the print since it was made, the direction of the prints (especially in relation to the vegetation) and the number of prints, a forager may infer the type, age, sex, weight, state of health and activity (e.g. feeding) of the track-maker, as well as the number of animals in a group, the time of day the tracks were made and the number of minutes that have elapsed since then. To infer such quantity and quality of information requires both learning and skill. Spier (1933: 68–9) has commented that because of the skill required in tracking deer this is limited to particular individuals among the Yumon.

The ability to use tracks also depends on the ground surface, which influences their clarity and survival. Hill and Hawkes (1983) comment on the difficulty of tracking in forests because of the thick ground litter. In northern regions the thickness of snow is crucial in enabling tracks to be found and followed (Sullivan 1942: 77; Jennes 1977: 46).

Human footprints prove no exception to the use of tracks as cues. Gould (1980) describes how Western Desert Aborigines can identify each member of their group from footprints. Similarly Home and Aiston (1924: 26) refer to Aborigines making observations on human footprints.

Excretions. Animal faeces provide a similar type of cue for foragers and are also very widely used (e.g. Blurton Jones and Konner 1976: 342; Lee 1979: 212; Hill and Hawkes 1983: 152). As with tracks, faeces may be specifically searched for and may lead to immediate action or may be more generally observed along with other animal signs. Naturalists like Ernest Seton (1925) have described the immense amount of information that can be derived from an inspection of faeces. Factors such as the shape, size, weight and quantity of faecal pellets are of value, as well as their compactness, composition, and dispersal. Such cues can inform on the type, age, sex and health of the animal, its recent feeding activity and movement patterns. Again this may refer to individual animals which may be pursued or may relate to estimates of patch quality and decisions about patch use. In relation to this latter case, the use made of faeces by modern ecologists (e.g. Bennet *et al.* 1940; Coe and Carr 1983) for estimating population densities and their age structure is simply the application of an age-old skill.

Urine can also provide information. Yost and Kelley (1983: 194–6) describe how the Waorani foragers of Venezuela use urine dripping from the canopy of the rainforest to locate potential prey. Similarly Sullivan (1942: 71) describes how a T'ena forager noted where a moose had urinated when tracking the animal.

A further useful excretory product is blood, particularly from wounds. This may provide an important aid when tracking the animal by giving information about the animal's state (Blurton-Jones and Konner 1976: 343). Hill and Hawkes (1983: 149) relate how the estimation of the initial wound on an animal is important to the Áche. This is partly because the extent of the blood flow will indicate the likely success of tracking the wounded animal.

Terrain. Particular characteristics of the terrain may act as important cues. These may be either permanent features of the landscape or temporary characteristics resulting from animal/plant activity. The presence of natural features such as knolls and streams may serve as cues to the location of game or how game may react if startled by a hunter. For instance Gubser (1965: 121, 221–12, 230; Gould 1980: 14) describes the use of such cues by the Nunamiut when hunting caribou. A homogeneous landscape without a range of natural features may make hunting difficult because of the absence of such cues to animal location and behaviour.

At a more detailed level, the surface of a landscape may be affected by animal and/or plant activity. The most obvious example is the presence of tracks which I have already dealt with above. Related to this, Nelson (1973: 91) describes how extensive disturbance to the ground can occur from the pawing action of moose, and implies that this is used by the Kutchin hunters. In addition, foragers may identify the places where animals have been lying down or sleeping (e.g. Sullivan 1942: 71). The surface of the ground may also indicate the presence of resources or further cues beneath. Tanaka (1976: 107) describes how the !Kung women may locate underground truffles by cracks in the ground surface caused by their growth. When the weather is dry and the truffles do not grow to a sufficient size to crack the ground they cannot be located. Similarly Meehan (1982: 83, 97) describes how shell gatherers may find particular types of molluscs by the patterns they cause in the mud from burrowing and moving, and from the tiny processes resembling small green leaves that are just exposed above the surface of the sand (Fig. 3.4). Nelson (1983: 176) relates how subtle variations in the ground surface may indicate the presence of old bear tracks to Koyukon foragers when they are searching for bear dens.

Vegetation. In this section I refer not to the species of vegetation but to how it has been affected by animal behaviour and hence may provide cues to the location and

Fig. 3.4. A Gidjingali woman collecting shellfish (after Meehan 1982).

state of those animals. Such cues can be divided into three classes. First the leaves or bark may have been nibbled or chewed and hence indicate where and when an animal has been feeding and the type of foodstuff it is currently exploiting. Bion-Griffen (1984: 108) relates how the Agta foragers search for such feeding areas. Alternatively, foragers may recognise places where an animal has been feeding while they are tracking it (e.g. Jennes 1977: 55). Lee (1979: 213) describes how the !Kung may observe which plants have their tips missing in the vicinity of tracks.

A second class of vegetation cues relates to scratch marks on trees. Goodale (1971: 161) describes the exploitation of opossums by the Tiwi as involving an initial search for their scratch marks on tree trunks. Jennes (1977: 55) comments how even the slightest scraping of a tree may provide significant information. Nelson (1983: 91) records that moose scrape bark from short bushes with their antlers.

The third class of such cues are those which arise from the movement of animals. For instance Hill and Hawkes (1983: 150) describe how herds of peccaries are easy to track in the Amazonian forest because of the disturbance they make in the vegetation of the forest floor. Nelson (1983: 175–6) and Jennes (1977: 54) refer to broken twigs and turned leaves, presumably from animals moving, and Nelson (1983: 175–6) and Lee (1979: 213) refer to foliage that has fallen from the mouth while moving, as important cues.

Sound. While visual cues are the most important, some of the information foragers use in decision making comes from sounds, which may also be considered as cues (e.g. Estioko-Griffen 1986: 38; Silberbauer 1981: 209; Blurton-Jones and Konner 1976: 330). Such noise may come from the movement of animals. Marks (1977: 255) describes the Valley Bisa hunters using the sound of moving buffalo herds and Yost and Kelley (1983: 194–6) refer to the Waorani listening to the sounds of animals moving in the forest canopy. The calls of animals are also particularly useful (e.g. Yost and Kelley 1983: 194–6; Tanner 1979: 127). Nelson (1973: 91) records the use of sound by the Kutchin when locating and tracking moose. In this case the sounds include breaking twigs, antlers against vegetation, the raking of antlers in the bush when males are challenging each other and the low calls that males make during the breeding season. Marks refers to the calls of predators following the buffalo herds (1977: 255). Useful sounds may also arise as a result of other animal activities. For instance Blurton-Jones and Konner (1976: 330) record a !Kung bushman's description of how the sounds of kudu fighting can be listened for when stalking that animal for a kill. The sound of dripping urine was apparently important in locating that cue for the Waorani foragers referred to above (Yost and Kelley 1983: 194–6). The importance of audible cues for some hunters can be recognised by the fact that one reason for the fall in hunting efficiency by the Waorani in the wet season is that the noise of rain falling on the leaves masks the sounds of animals (Yost and Kelley 1983: 217).

Smell. The olfactory sense is used by foragers, but is limited because of its poor capacity in humans and there are relatively few ethnographic examples. Blurton-Jones and Konner (1976) particularly emphasise the limitations on information gathering imposed by poor sense of smell, and the need to compensate for this by other cognitive processes. Hill and Hawkes, however, describe how Áche hunter-gatherers smell paca burrows to detect if they are occupied (1983: 147). In addition the droppings of Howler monkeys, to which I referred above, are located partly by their very pungent smell. Nelson (1973: 91) refers to the musky odour of moose which can be used to locate and track it. Certain foragers extend their own olfactory abilities by using dogs to follow scents.

Animals and Plants. In this section I refer to the use of the presence of one or more particular species of animal or plant which provides a cue either about itself in the future, or about other species. These types of cues can be divided into three classes, with the relation between the cue and the inference becoming less direct.

In the first class are observations on plants and animals which provide information about these particular species at that, or later, points in time. Examples of these are legion. The current movement of an animal or herd (including its speed and direction) may indicate where it will be found later. Marks (1977: 255) describes the Valley Bisa making such inferences about buffalo. Similarly, as I described above, the Bari watch the movements of fish. In addition, the composition of a herd in terms of age structure is taken by the Nunamiut to be an important cue concerning the stage the herd has reached in its migration (Binford 1978: 182). The actual number of animals observed/exploited will provide a cue to the productivity of the patch (i.e. the assessment rule referred to in Chapter 3). For instance De Laguna (1972: 384) relates how Yakutat fishermen use the number of fish taken as a cue when deciding whether or not to remove their fish traps. Simple observations on the size of an animal and its characteristics such as antler size may be important cues when selecting which animal from a herd to try and kill (Marks 1976: 208–10; Gubser 9165: 221–2; Jochim 1983b). The Valley Bisa pay particular attention to the presence of fatty tissue (Marks 1976: 105).

Plants provide similar types of cues. One important set is simply the visible parts of a plant providing a cue to the presence of berries or tubers which are more difficult or impossible to observe directly. Lee (1976: 163), Marshall (1976: 95) and Silberbauer (1981: 200) all refer to Kalahari foragers searching for and locating the tiniest wisps of dry plant stem or leaf which indicate the presence of an underground tuber. When there is a bush fire and these are burnt then such tubers may be impossible to find (Marshall 1976: 104). Horne and Aiston (1924: 20) refer to a species of water lily whose flowering on the surface indicates the 'bounteous harvest below'. Similarly Flannery (1986a: 23–5) discusses the manner in which flowering plants help foragers to locate resources from these plants in space and time. For instance the bright flowers of the wild bean enable it to be located within the scrub forest and the spring flowers of plants such as the prickly pear indicate that it will have fruit to harvest in the late summer.

The second class of these cues occur when the presence of one species acts as a cue to another and when there is a direct connection between the two. That foragers are aware of connections between particular animal species and the plant foods or communities which they eat and use for shelter is frequently commented upon in the ethnographic literature (e.g. Yost and Kelley 1983: 194–6; Silberbauer 1981: 94). This knowledge is often used to locate particular animals by travelling to the areas of preferred food (e.g. Winterhalder 1981: 79). Opler (1941: 326) describes how the Chiricahua Apache foragers locate peccary by searching the bushy areas in which they are known to shelter. Marshall (1976: 111) describes how the !Kung may find underground bulbs by observing where guinea fowl have been scratching for them.

Such relationships of ecological significance play an important role when animal species act as cues to other animals. For instance Marks (1976: 116) notes that the Valley Bisa watch the morning flights of cattle egrets and oxpeckers since these act as cues to the location of buffalo, on whose backs the birds forage for bugs (see also Silberbauer 1981: 209). In a similar manner Aborigines who exploited the Bogong moth watched for the aggregation of crows, which also fed upon the moths and hence acted as a cue for their presence (Flood 1980: 66). In certain cases it is evident that the hunter-gatherers are aware of, discuss, and use predator–prey relationships. Gubser (1965: 274) relates how the Nunamiut are aware of relations between foxes and lemmings and how a high density of one of these correlates with that of the other. Similarly Nelson (1983: 211) relates how the Koyukon use the

Table 3.1. *Calendar plants used by the Groote Eylandt islanders (after Levitt 1981)*

Plant	State	Information
White berry bush	Flowering	Mosquitoes appear
White berry bush	Fruiting	Mosquitoes decline
Yellow grass and yellow spear grass	Ripe seeds	Yams ready to dig
Rough-barked gum and bunch spear grass	Flowering	Wet season will end soon
Ball wattle	Flowering	Snapper fish are ready to eat
Cream-flowered wattle	Flowering	Snappers and crabs are ready
Woolly butt and pincushion	Flowering	Honey is plentiful in wild bees nests
Broad-leaved wattle	Flowering	Tern eggs ready for collecting
Bloodwood	Flowering	Salmon will be coming over the reefs
Stringy barks	Flowering	Rains finish and billabongs are unreliable
Stringy barks	Finish	Parrot and venus tusk fish are finished, Burrawong nuts ready and tamarinds ripe
Red kurrajung and wild plum	Flowering	Stingray are ready to be caught
Pandora	Nuts are orange and dropping	Turtles lay their eggs
Cocky apple	Flowering	Time to catch turtles
Sugar grass and giant spear grass	Seeds start falling	Best yams ready to dig
Termite tree	Flowering	Wet season soon begins

density of mouse tracks as a cue to the likely density of fur bearing carnivores and are aware of density relationships between rodents such as voles and lemmings and small carnivores such as weasels, mink and fox. Blurton-Jones and Konner (1976: 341) refer to the practical value the !Kung gain from their detailed knowledge of the hunting behaviour of competing predators.

In the third class of these cues the connection between the species is less direct. They often arise from the fact that the species acting as the cue, and that inferred, are both reacting to a third variable such as air temperature. The 'calender plants' used by the Australian Aborigines provide the most detailed examples of such cues. These were referred to by early ethnographers (e.g. Ainsworth, quoted by Campbell 1978), but Levitt (1981) has been the first to provide a comprehensive description for those used by the Groote Eylandt islanders. Some of these are listed in Table 3.1.

The observation of the presence or behaviour of a species may indicate further cues, rather than relate to a specific resource itself. In particular, future weather conditions may be indicated. For instance Levitt (1981: 12–13) describes how the Groote Eylandt islanders use crabs leaving mangrove swamps and termites building mounds as cues to forthcoming storms. The Koyukon infer the characteristics of the forthcoming winter from the nature of the tracks of the snowshoe hare during the fall. If they are wide, indicating well-furred feet, there are heavy snows ahead (Nelson 1973: 200). Bird behaviour is particularly used to such ends. Nelson (1983: 13, 59, 63, 64, 78) describes the broad range of species which the Koyukon listen to and watch to infer the future weather: the tapping of hawk owls indicates the length of the winter, the sight of grebes running side by side indicates a strong wind coming and the arrival of migratory birds is an eagerly greeted sign of the end of winter. Even the activity of butterflies and fleas is given meaning as to future events. Similarly De Laguna (1972: 804) comments on how the Yakutat take the cheeping of sparrows to be a cue for rain and the flying of bats to indicate bad weather coming. It is difficult to assess whether such cues are valid. Certainly they are utilised, but whether there is a correlation between the cue and the inferred event cannot be determined. Unlikely relationships do exist. For instance Clutton Brock *et al.* (1983) demonstrates how the timing of the arrival of the cuckoo is a very accurate indicator for the weight of deer calves, since both of these are responsive to spring temperatures.

A final example demonstrates the high degree of sophistication in cue use. Gatty (1958) describes an Eskimo group travelling by canoe in thick mist and attempting to find the tributary river down which to turn to find their settlement. Since vision was limited they used the particular dialect of the bird song along the main river to indicate their location in relation to their settlement.

Weather. The weather and climatic and astral phenomena provide an extremely diverse and well-utilised set of cues. For instance the Gidjingali keep a close watch on the moon since that influences the tides and hence the ability to find and exploit shellfish (Meehan 1982: 26). Meehan also notes that a close watch is kept for 'unusual' climatic events. For foragers living in arid environments rainfall is clearly the most important climatic event to be noted and from observing where and how much rain falls inferences can be drawn as to the location and characteristics of resources. Consequently inferences drawn from rainfall provide essential information in mobility decisions and plans are continually revised in light of the rainfall situation (Gould 1980: 69; Lee 1976: 81, 1979: 216; Silberbauer 1981: 245). In general hunter-gatherers are very aware of relations between the characteristics of the weather and their resources and use a variety of cues of this type (e.g. Nelson 1983: 13, 43, 1973: 194–202; De Laguna 1972: 804).

Gubser (1965: 193) describes how in Nunamiut society there is a supposed correlation between the position of the moon and hunting success. He relates how one man watched for this, but he was unable to see any real correlation. This provides an example of meta-decision activity concerning cue use – testing the ecological validity of a cue.

Other individuals
A considerable amount of the information acquisition I have been discussing is directly related to the exchange of information. Individuals within one group may use other individuals from that, or other, groups as sources of information. Such

Fig. 3.5. Information exchange among the !Kung (after Blurton Jones and Konner 1976).

information is of a different type from that acquired by oneself since it is already partly processed by the 'sender'. In discussing this aspect of information acquisition I will make three gross and overlapping distinctions: information from members of one's own group; information from members of another group; and information from an older person in the context of education. Of course the boundaries between groups are fuzzy but these provide appropriate distinctions for organising the ethnographic data.

One of the most frequently remarked features concerning group information exchange is simply the intensity of it; foragers are continually using other individuals as information sources. Marshall (1976: 130, 289) describes how the !Kung talk endlessly about hunting and pass on news of recent events (Fig. 3.5). Transmission of information in a formal context between !Kung males is relatively rare, however (Blurton-Jones and Konner 1976: 344). Similarly Gubser (1965: 230), Nelson (1983: 46), Meehan (1982: 26) and Hill and Hawkes (1983: 153) all comment on the extremely high degrees of information exchange between members of the group. Nelson (1973) draws a contrast, however, between the intensity of communication between members of Eskimo society and the Athapaskan Indians, suggesting that this is significantly higher within the former. Consequently while we might generally characterise the degree of information exchange as high, its intensity appears variable between societies.

Certain anthropologists have been so taken with the extent of information exchange, and its importance in the functioning of the society, that they have characterised the group as an 'information network'. For instance Heffley (1981) has used such terminology for the Chipewayan foragers where sub-groups of the band function to gather information (as discussed above) to channel back to the main band. Similarly Silberbauer (1981) has described the interactions between member of the G/wi bushmen as forming a network of information exchange.

While information exchange may be high, it is not evenly distributed throughout the day owing to the lack of context (i.e. people are engaged in separate tasks) and because an individual's information accumulates and diverges from that possessed by others during the day. Consequently the most important time for exchanging information is the evening so that the day's news is passed on as well as earlier events recounted. Such evening sessions have been described by Ray (1963: 185), Tanner (1978: 98), Jennes (1955: 160), Marshall (1976: 289) and Hames and Vickers (1982: 368). While this is one context for information exchange it is also clear that it occurs as a low-level continuous process throughout the day, simply in terms of 'village gossip' (Ray 1963: 9) and a 'steady dialogue on the turning of environmental events' (Nelson 1983: 46).

A few ethnographies, notably those on North American foragers, suggest that the information exchange may have had a structured pattern so that particular individuals acted as channels for communication. Sullivan (1942: 36–7) describes how the T'ena hunters who were going duck hunting discussed their plans with the chief, whose purpose it was to let all people know of the proposed hunt. Similarly Rogers (1972: 122) discusses how the Cree foragers generally made visits to the leader's lodge, while only on rare occasions did the leader visit other members of the group, implying an asymmetric information exchange network. To what extent these existed as an alternative, rather than as a complement, to less formal networks is difficult to elucidate from such data.

A further important element of an information exchange network is that between the sexes depending upon the frequency with which these are engaged in different activities. Both Draper (1976: 216–17) and Silberbauer (1981: 245) emphasise the importance of women telling men the tracks and animal signs they have seen, and men informing the women of plants they may have located.

The form in which information is passed on between individuals appears to be a highly variable feature of information exchange. It is clear that certain amounts, or types, of information are passed on simply as factual observations, such as the condition of the land or the location of tracks (e.g. Gubser 1965: 230). Past events, however, appear to be most frequently communicated in terms of dramatised personal accounts, often in the form of stories. Blurton-Jones and Konner (1976: 338) particularly comment upon this in relation to the exchange of information about animal behaviour among the !Kung. They remark that this is not directly discussed as a subject in itself but information is passed on in terms of dramatised individual experiences and hunts. These accounts are frequently repeated, a fact also noted by Marshall (1976: 284).

In addition to such a high degree of information exchange between members of one group there is also considerable inter-group information flow. This takes place in what may be termed formal and informal contexts. The aggregations of groups at particular times of the year is perhaps the most important formal context. These occur for many reasons such as feasting, religious observances and marriage and it is clear that at such events much information is exchanged. Binford (1985a) characterises the gatherings of Australian Aborigines in such terms, describing how these occur when economic activities are not successful and serve to allow the groups to re-map themselves onto the landscape following the exchange of information about the state of the environment from members of other groups. While descriptions of such gatherings are common, it is rare for the ethnographer to refer explicitly to the exchange of information, possibly because of the apparently trivial nature of gossip in face of spectacular rituals and ceremonies. However, Sullivan (1942: 54) has referred to the T'ena foragers who 'relish the opportunity to exchange news and to discuss with one another topics of common interest' at annual duck feasts. Similarly Chapman (1982: 59) explains how the Selk'nam foragers 'gather together not only in search of spouses but also to exchange goods, information and knowledge'. In relation to the exchange of information at gatherings Spencer's (1969: 127–8) comment that, among the Tlinglit, people representing a range of ecological settings were present is interesting.

Trade relations between individuals and groups provide another formal context for information exchange. Again some ethnographic descriptions specifically relate to the exchange of information at such occasions. For instance Silberbauer (1981: 281) describes trade goods and information moving simultaneously while Horne and Aiston (1924: 20) relate how Aborigines will travel to trade goods and to 'pass on the news'. Yellen (1976: 96) considers that the trade items themselves are essentially facilitatory devices to maintain the contacts. A further example is provided by Spencer (1969: 169) who describes how, among Tlinglit trading partners, trade only begins after they have greeted each other and 'exchanged gossip'.

In addition to these contexts for information exchange, there is also a continuous communication between groups outside of such formal settings. That individuals from one group regularly make visits to another, partly to 'pass on the news' and also to hear it, is frequently described in the literature (e.g. Meehan 1982; Silberbauer 1981). Individuals from different groups may also meet when engaged in the same activity and then pass on information. Watanabe (1973: 66) describes how women from different Ainu groups may meet when collecting plants and exchange information as to the location of particular species and of the foraging sites they have visited.

An additional feature of information exchange apparent from the ethnographic literature is that, as with the gathering of information, the intensity of it is variable throughout the year. This is partly due to factors such as aggregation being dependent upon a sufficient food supply to feed the large group. Sullivan's (1942) description of the eagerness with which the T'ena assess whether there is to be sufficient duck for a feast may relate to their awareness of this relationship. Among the Ainu the principal meeting time for groups is during the winter (Watanabe 1973). In addition to this constraint, however, there will be particular times of year when between-group information exchange may be of greater importance. Among the G/wi it is during the late summer that territories are searched for and it is at this time that the visiting between bands and the flow of information is at a peak (Silberbauer 1981: 138–40). A similar pattern has been described by Meehan (1982: 36) for the Gidjingali. She relates how the amount of visiting between groups decreases at the start of the wet season.

While the ethnographic record is rich with examples of information exchange within and between groups there has been no detailed study of the type of information that is passed on in terms of whether or not it is 'true'. Studies of modern fishermen (e.g. Anderson 1972) demonstrate that the type of information passed between foragers may be highly variable from 'true' to absolutely false. Passing on information to another may act as a social strategy to manipulate the receiver's behaviour. Consequently information may be required as to the worth of the information received, creating a hierarchy of information about information levels. Kurland and Beckerman (1985) focus on this problem in relation to the evolution of human cognition. There is little comment in the ethnographic literature as to the type of information passed on. Gubser (1965: 227), however, remarks that the Nunamiut are very concerned with the truth of a person's statement implying that both 'true' and 'untrue' information may be flowing within the communication network. Blurton-Jones and Konner (1976: 318) describe how the !Kung are careful to discriminate data from theory, interpretation and hearsay. Moreover the !Kung are very ready to disbelieve each other and to express scepticism over some piece of information (Blurton-Jones and Konner 1976: 331). This evidence relating to the !Kung and the Nunamiut illustrates meta-decision making in relation to using other individuals as information sources.

Information is exchanged by the use of a symboling system. I wish to comment briefly on four such systems: speech, gesture, smoke signals and material culture. The spoken language is the most important communication medium and my only reference to this complex area is in relation to the manner in which language enables categories to be clearly defined and communicated. The most obvious example among hunter-gatherers is that of the Eskimo where many different words exist for describing features such as snow and caribou (Gubser 1965) so that a particular state of these can be communicated quickly and without ambiguity. An interesting example of language change is given by Opler (1941: 331) who describes how amongst the Chiricahua Apache the words for, and the classification of, fish have become elaborated only since fish have become of economic importance.

One of the debated origins for language is body gesture (Lyons 1988) and clearly this still plays an important part in the exchange of information between hunter-gatherers. The most obvious examples are in contexts when there are constraints upon speech. One such example is in hunting game when silence is at a premium.

The use of hand signals in which the position of the fingers and fist mimic the principal characteristics of the species hunted (e.g. pointed fingers for horns) has been described in detail for the !Kung (Marshall 1976: 136) and the G/wi (Silberbauer 1981: 210–11). In other circumstances a person's body gesture and pose may provide important supplementary information to that being communicated by speech.

A third type of communication medium is smoke signals enabling information to be exchanged over large distances. The use of these is most frequently described among Australian Aborigine groups (e.g. Horne and Aiston 1924: 20; Flood 1980: 75, 191; Gould 1980: 70) but there are also references to their use by other groups (e.g. Birket-Smith and De Laguna 1938: 106). The most frequent message is simply to attract attention but it is also apparent that within one group there may be a sophisticated set of signals each used to send a different message. Horne and Aiston (1924) describe how the interpretation put onto an observed smoke signal may depend on previous knowledge about the types of activities those sending the signal were to be engaged in.

A further medium of information exchange that must be referred to is the use of material culture. As Wobst (1977) argues, the style of an object or costume may act to send messages about group affiliation and a considerable amount of hunter-gatherer material culture might be seen in this light. More directly, however, material culture may be specifically designed as an information exchange medium (e.g. Gamble 1982; Weissner 1983). The most notable examples are perhaps the message sticks and the toas of the Australian Aborigines. Horne and Aiston (1924: 22) describe the use of message sticks among the Wonkanguru. Certain of these act as mnemonic aids for the carrier while others possess designs which can be directly 'read' by the receiver, such as the number of people resident in another group. Toas have been described in detail by Morphy (1977) and are essentially elaborated message sticks. They may simply be left in the ground to be found by another group or individual and signify information by their existence, designs and position such as the size and movement of the group leaving the toas. A further form of information exchange occurs in some aspects of rock art. For instance Gardner, writing in the mid-19th century, describes how the Aborigines of New South Wales leave images of particular animals such as emu and opossum engraved on rocks in the areas where the hunting of such animals takes place (McBryde 1978: 239). This probably has functions other than information exchange such as acting as a mnemonic aid to the receiver to recall information about these resources.

The third class of information exchange I wish to focus on is the teaching of young members of the group – passing on information relevant to making decisions concerning foraging behaviour. The amount of data relating to education in hunter-gatherer societies is poor in both quantity and quality, although interesting accounts are provided by Ruddle and Chesterfield (1977: 91–102), Gubser (1965) and Goodale (1971). Hewlett and Cavalli-Sforza (1986) have attempted a quantitative analysis of such information transmission among the Aka Pygmies. One of the most apparent features is that education systems are highly variable between groups. We might consider four types of learning: formal education; education through informal story-telling and song; learning from one's own experience; and education during ritual and initiation periods. These different types of education tend to be found in different proportions within different societies.

Formal training appears to be generally rare among hunter-gatherer societies. When it is reported, it tends to be found within North American groups (e.g. Birkett-Smith and De Laguna 1938: 162; Ray 1963: 106; Tanner 1979: 44; Gubser 1965: 109). More often the reference to formal training is a remark that it is in fact lacking. For instance, Goodale (1971: 37) stresses the minimal instruction given to young Tiwi foragers. That which is found relates to the use of specific tools such as fish spears. Similarly the lack of formal education among the !Kung has been frequently emphasised (e.g. Draper 1976: 211–12; Biesele 1976: 307; Lee 1979: 236; Marshall 1976: 95–6; Blurton-Jones and Konner 1976: 338–9). That which does exist again relates to very specific activities such as stalking and tracking and does not occur until adolescence (Marshall 1976: 130; Lee 1979: 236).

Education via informal teaching using story-telling and song would appear to be much more common. This tends not to be directed towards any specific activity but to be a general account of ways in which foraging problems have been solved and is often done in the context of informal information exchange between adults as all members of the group listen to the stories. Binford (1978: 180) and Gubser (1965: 110) describe such education among the Nunamiut and Blurton-Jones and Konner (1976: 338) describe it in more detail among the !Kung. Hewlett and Cavalli-Sforza's (1986) study of the Aka demonstrates that the parents' contribution to the transmission of information about hunting skills was overwhelming and that of grandparents, other relatives and friends insignificant. Second in importance to the influence of parents was simply watching others. In certain cases this was because the relevant skill was not possessed by the parents, being a recent innovation within the group such as the manufacture of cross-bows.

The importance of learning from one's own experience and experiment is frequently remarked upon (e.g. Gubser 1965: 220; Hassrick 1964: 318–19; Tanner 1979: 44; Lee 1979: 707–8; Goodale 1971: 40). This is closely related to the observation and mimicry of adults (Hassrick 1964: 318–19; Blurton-Jones and Konner 1976: 339). The significance of the prevalence of such self-taught behaviour is that no information is being passed between generations. Societies may, however, have features which allow such learning to take place. Among the Waorani each family has many pets, tame individuals of the species which are hunted, from which the children learn about such animals' behaviour (Yost and Kelley 1983).

A further type of education is the passage of information between generations during ritual occasions. Yost and Kelley (1983) remark that all of the rituals within Waorani society are concerned with producing efficient hunters. Pfeiffer (1982) has particularly stressed the importance of ritual as a context for education among Aboriginal society. He argues that, in the Australian desert environment, survival depends upon the learning of large amounts of information and rules which must be strictly followed. Ritual, with its elements of pain and fear for the initiate, plays the role of imprinting such knowledge on the mind of the child. As he states 'the spirit of free inquiry has no place in education by initiation'.

Stored information and past experience

It is very frequently commented upon in the ethnographic literature that hunter-gatherers have an immense amount of stored information and knowledge concerning their environment and a prodigious memory for detail. Such stored knowledge is of two basic types. First there is that relating to features such as animal behaviour, the dynamics of the climate and the seasonal flowering of plants which allows them to make inferences about the location and state of resources of observed phenomena. This information allows cues to be used as discussed above. The second type of stored information may be termed factual information and relates to the actual location of resources, the density of game and the sequence of resource availability. The second class of knowledge may be derived from the use of the first.

A second cross-cutting classification is also apparent from the material described below. This relates to the frequency with which information needs to be updated. Certain types of information, for instance that about permanent features of the landscape, will not require it since they never or rarely change. Other types, however, such as the availability of game within a patch, may need frequent updating on a daily basis. One can imagine all classes of information as falling on a continuum of this type between two poles which I will characterise as 'stored' and 'acquired' information. This distinction plays an important role in the following study of Mesolithic foraging.

Knowledge concerning animal behaviour is particularly stressed in the ethnographies and, as I have discussed above, this often stretches to knowledge of the interaction between species (e.g. Sullivan 1942: 68; Jennes 1955: 53; Nelson 1983: 73, 205; Silberbauer 1981: 65–6; Yost and Kelly 1983: 194–6; Horne and Aiston 1924: 29). Similarly knowledge concerning plants is often remarked upon (e.g. Chapman 1982: 25; Silberbauer 1981: 94; Marshall 1976: 103). Other ethnologists have stressed the possession of large quantities of geographical and climatic information (e.g. Gould 1980: 84, 87; Marshall 1976: 76; Leacock 1969: 7–8; Gubser 1965: 230). Many ethnologists simply refer to large quantities of stored information about the environment in general (e.g. Leavit 1982: 12–13; Chapman 1982: 21; Nelson 1983: 210–11; Pfeiffer 1982: Blurton-Jones and Konner 1976: 338–9).

With respect to animal resources there are indications that the knowledge possessed is biased towards those of greatest economic value. For instance Silberbauer (1981: 65–6) has made a detailed study of the information about animal behaviour possessed by the G/wi and argues that the classes of species (i.e. mammals, birds, reptiles, etc.) which are known about in most detail are those which are important in the subsistence economy. Similarly Krause (1956: 104) argues that the Tlingit are very knowledgeable about some species in their environment but are unable to recognise and classify others. Silberbauer (1981: 96–7) has described the fall-off in geographical knowledge as one moves away from the area regularly exploited. It is also apparent that within the society different individuals and classes of individual will have different types of stored knowledge. For instance among the G/wi the women have a much more detailed knowledge of the local geography than the men since this is required for plant gathering whereas men only require a rudimentary knowledge for their hunting activities.

In an interesting discussion, Blurton-Jones and Konner (1976: 328) describe how the !Kung will readily admit ignorance and can respond to questions concerning how they know a particular fact with a detailed description. This illustrates meta-decision making with respect to their own information storage and acquisition processes. While there appears to be such an economically orientated bias in knowledge there is clearly not a simple correlation between areas of knowledge and economic importance. First, it is very difficult to investigate this since, as my discussion of cues illustrated, certain species may have a very important role in the economy but not be exploited themselves. Second, it is often stressed that these two factors do not absolutely coincide. For instance Gubser (1965: 242) describes how, for the Nunamiut, interest in their environment goes far beyond that required for efficient economic exploitation. A similar point has been made by Nelson in relation to the Koyukon (1983: 136). Part of this accumulation of information may relate to the risk-buffering strategy of storing information which may be of use in the future without a clear idea of the role that that information will play, i.e. non-directed information gathering and storage.

One aspect of stored information, and one that is important when making decisions, is that it is often maintained within the context of particular episodes and events of the past rather than being abstracted from that context. For instance much of the !Kung knowledge about animal behaviour is maintained in the framework of past hunting episodes (Blurton-Jones and Konner 1976). Gubser (1965: 221–2) describes how when a Nunamiut is faced with a particular situation, such as the tactics to adopt when trying to kill a caribou, he will recall a past situation with similar characteristics rather than draw upon abstracted knowledge concerning caribou behaviour.

One important issue when considering the role of past experience and stored information is the distance into the past from which information is maintained. There are few ethnographic data relating to this question. However, Silberbauer (1981: 110) describes how the G/wi could remember a comet, which he calculates passed in 1965, but no earlier comets. Consequently Halley's Comet of 1910, which would have been highly visible to them, was forgotten. The importance of maintaining information gathered over a lifetime is emphasised in the literature by the frequent references to foragers seeking advice from the elders of their group (e.g. Slodobin 1969: 81; Gubser 1965: 110; Ray 1963; 184; Hassrick 1964: 200; Spencer 1969: 138). As with knowledge about the present, that about the past is inevitably very selective. One type of past event that appears to be frequently remembered is times of starvation and hunger (Nelson 1983: 213–14; Rogers 1972: 104–5).

A further important feature concerning past experience and stored information is its method of retrieval. This would often appear to be a communal event with story-telling and the recounting of experiences helping to spark others' memories and keep stored information accessible. Silberbauer (1981: 195) stresses how the collective memory of twenty to thirty adults in a band is much richer in retrievable knowledge than that of two or three adults. Among the G/wi, and probably other groups, the mention of a single item leads to a chain of discussion. Sufficient information may be stored within the minds of a group which, when used with newly acquired information, may enable the forager to cope with the normal range of environmental fluctuations and the foraging problems they pose. However, severe fluctuations may also occur on a very infrequent basis, after a period of time longer than an individual's lifetime, and consequently there may be insufficient stored information to cope with these. Alternative information storage devices may be used, one of which may be myth and the oral traditions of the group.

This is discussed by Minc (1986) with respect to the Nunamiut and the Taremiut. He distinguishes between secular oral traditions, such as folk-tales, stories and song, and sanctified oral traditions such as ritual. The essential difference is that the former are open to individual error, elaboration and creativity in their telling while the latter must be conducted according to a precise set of rules. I have discussed the secular oral traditions above, with respect to information exchange. Minc considers that the sanctified traditions will be particularly important for the storing and transmission of information concerning the rare and severe fluctuations, because of the high cost (in time and energy) of performing the rituals involved. He claims that an analysis of the traditions of the Nunamiut and Taremiut supports this position. For instance rituals may contain information concerning the resources of different zones, the importance of group cohesion and of economic interdependence between groups, since it is this knowledge and these social mechanisms that allow groups to survive periods of hardship. While his work is interesting, it is also a poor analysis since he fails to consider whether the traditions also contain references to group fission and independence which would militate against his conclusions.

Another example of myth and ritual acting as an information storage and transmission device is given by Goodale (1971: 222–3) in her description of the initiation rites of the Tiwi. In one of these the initiates are meticulously taught how to prepare yams in a ceremony which has remained remarkably stable in its particular sequence of events. The specific variety of yam is not normally eaten by the Tiwi and is poisonous in its unprepared state. The important point that Goodale makes is that this yam, and a toxic cycad the preparation of which is also taught in a ceremony, are used as emergency foods in times of famine. The infrequency of famine and the lack of its normal exploitation (owing to its bitter taste) may prevent human memory acting as an adequate information storage device concerning its preparation. Consequently we find this stored in ritual.

A further example of myth as a storage device is described by Pfeiffer (1982) in relation to the Aborigines' dreamtime stories. He argues that these act as a framework to enable large quantities of information about the geographical environment to be stored and remembered. Knowledge of the dreamtime enables this vital information to be recalled. Consequently they act as both a storage device and as a mnemonic aid.

Another form of information storage may be the use of material culture, such as calendrical devices. These take a range of forms but are found only in rare instances among hunter-gatherer groups. Hassrick (1964: 8) describes the calendar stick used by Sioux Indians as a series of pictures each recording the most important event for each year. De Laguna (1972: 801) describes several types used by the Yakutat. It would appear that such devices act more as cues for the retrieval of mentally stored information than as storage devices in themselves. For instance, recording the most notable event of each year may trigger the recall of associated events. Consequently these devices are probably principally functioning as mnemonic aids.

Other types of material culture may also act in this manner. Pfeiffer (1982) in particular adopts this approach when interpreting the art of the Australian Aborigines. By describing how their apparently abstract art does in fact involve the symbolic representation of geographical features and the locational relationships between these and relates to their dreamtime stories, he explains how it plays a vital role in enabling the recall of stored information about the environment. A further example is the use of certain message sticks which, as I mentioned above, act as mnemonic aids to the person carrying the sticks. Meehan (1982: 26) describes another use of mnemonic aids among the Gidjingali. When the women in that group recall the sequence of ripening of different fruit trees they help themselves by making patterns in the sand with their hands. The production of mnemonic aids in general may therefore be considered as a type of meta-decision activity since they enable information to be recalled and used in decision making.

A further information source to consider is that internal to the forager. By internal information sources I refer to the use of aspects such as imagination, dreams and divination. Of course the distinction that I draw between what is 'internal' as opposed to 'external' information is highly subjective and does not imply that the decision makers themselves employ such categories. However, it would appear from the ethnographic data that hunter-gatherers often do make a clear distinction in their use of information from such internal and external sources, i.e. they engage in 'reality monitoring' (Johnson and Raye 1981). I will focus on three areas of internal information: anthropomorphism, divination and dreaming.

Anthropomorphism is found widely among modern hunter-gatherers living in a wide variety of environments (e.g. Silberbauer 1981; Marks 1976; Gubser 1965). Silberbauer provides a particularly detailed description of the anthropomorphic models used by the G/wi. In this case human attributes are imposed on mammals in particular, and to a lesser extent on other animal classes, such as birds, reptiles and amphibians. Individual animals are classified using terms for human person-alities and character. Silberbauer describes how their typology is apparently exhaustive and serves to predict the animal's behaviour before and after it has been shot. The most important point is that such predictions are usually very accurate. Marks (1976) makes a similar point with respect to the anthropomorphic models used by the Valley Bisa: up to the degree of accuracy required for hunting, attributing animals with human characteristics and personality provides useful predictions for their behaviour. The conflicting cognitive maps of the anthropomorphising hunters and Western scientists are equally effective.

Anthropomorphising has another important characteristic. By using the same set of descriptive and predictive terms for animals as for humans the information load on the hunter-gatherer is reduced. Silberbauer (1981) has stressed how important this is in hunter-gatherer society when knowledge must be maintained without the aid of writing. Consequently anthropomorphism reduces the number of categories which need to be developed and prevents overload of mental capaci-ties, releasing these for other tasks. As I have been discussing, the loss of predictive value is insignificant. The use of anthropomorphic models for animal behaviour as a source of information in decision making thus has functional value on two grounds.

A second type of internal information source is divination, which often involves the use of material culture. As with anthropomorphising, this is widely found among modern hunter-gatherers, for example the use of scapulimancy among the Cree (Tanner 1978) and oracle discs among the !Kung (Lee 1979). In addition, all manner of observed phenomena are regularly endowed with a divinatory signifi-cance. Among the Chiricahua, the sight of a crow before a hunt may indicate good luck (Opler 1941: 317). Some divinations are rather obscure. Among the Cree if a porcupine intestine is found with a peculiar appendage, that appendage is made into the shape of a miniature fat container and filled with fat from the intestine. The sac will have a bend in it and the shape of this will indicate which type of species will be killed (Tanner 1979).

In general divinations are used to acquire information such as whether a hunt will be successful and the direction in which to go to find game. Three important points must be made. First, divination is rarely carried out without empirical information also being sought in relation to the same question (Lee 1979: 210; Tanner 1978: 113). It appears to be rare that decisions are made solely on the results of a divinatory act or omen. Second, individuals are often free to make their own interpretations of an omen; ambiguity in the meaning appears to be an important characteristic. For instance the transformed porcupine appendage is passed around members of the Cree band so that each person can make his/her own interpretation (Tanner 1978). Third, the sight of omens which determined the success or failure of a hunt may be a post-hunt rationalisation for its outcome (Marks 1976).

The most detailed study of divination has been by Tanner (1978, 1979), concerning scapulimancy among the Cree. This basically involves burning a flat

Fig. 3.6. Scapulimancy among the Cree (after Tanner 1979).

bone of an animal, usually the shoulder blade, and interpreting the resulting marks with respect to the location of game or the outcome of a future hunt (Fig. 3.6). He describes and criticises previous interpretations which saw scapulimancy either as a decision-making device acting to randomise hunting locations or as a means of legitimising the decision taken by a hunter to avoid criticism of hunting failure. One of Tanner's principal points is that in this earlier work the anthropologists failed to distinguish between what the divination told the hunters to do, what they said they would do and their actual behaviour. Often these do not coincide. Tanner argues that scapulimancy and other divinations (such as the 'shaking tent') occur at times of important changes in economic activity, such as returning to exploit a species after hunting elsewhere. He proposes that its most important role is as a means of thinking about new hunting activity, a type of mental preparation. It does not replace the use of 'external' information and careful planning about economic activities. In this light, divination would appear to act as a mechanism for aiding the retrieval of information stored in the mind and for thinking creatively about the future.

Elsewhere Tanner (1979: 127) describes how the sight of an omen such as an oddly shaped rock or pike bone sets off a familar round of jokes and comments. This may be interpreted in a similar light as enabling information to be retrieved. Interestingly, Lee (1979: 210) draws a similar conclusion concerning the use of divination and omens by the !Kung. He argues that these give the !Kung a 'feeling of confidence' which again may relate to the possession of appropriate information retrieved from long-term memory. Overall, therefore, an important functional role of divination would appear to be in aiding the recall of information and in the mental preparation for cognitive tasks concerning a set of foraging decisions. Consequently we can consider the use of divination and internal information generally as related to meta-decision making. Ceremonies before hunts for particular species may play a similar meta-decision role. For instance rituals which involve the mimicry of an animal which is to be hunted (such as of deer by the Yumon–Spier 1933: 68–9) may have a role in recalling information about that species and increasing the receptivity of the forager to signs of that animal when foraging. This interpretation may be applied to the various 'increase ceremonies' of the Aborigines which took place to enhance the hunting or gathering of particular resources, as described by Radcliffe-Brown (1929: 399–415; Sabine 1978).

A similar functional significance can be attributed to dreams. Information gained from dreaming is similar to that from omens in relation to when and where to hunt. Dreams appear to influence particularly the decision whether or not to go hunting and in some societies men refuse to hunt unless they have had the appropriate dreams. Use of dreams as an information source is widespread among hunter-gatherers and is also found within modern fishermen crews working in a market economy (e.g. Pálsson and Durrenberger 1982). One of the most interesting studies of dreams is by Marks (1976) in relation to the Valley Bisa. Marks argues that within this group dreams provide the hunters with a feeling of confidence. Moreover he demonstrates a statistically significant relationship between the degree of hunting success and having had a 'good' dream. Three explanations may be made for this. First, dreams may be recalled only after a successful hunt and consequently provide a rationalisation of that success. Second, the feeling of confidence may have prepared the forager mentally so that he was more receptive to external information and took 'better' decisions. Third, the fact of dreaming and hunting success may both be attributable to a further factor such as having taken the decision to hunt and made plans the night before.

Information processing

Since the processing of information has fewer behavioural manifestations than information acquisition, and is also less time-consuming, there is limited reference in the ethnographic literature to this activity. What is present, however, is of considerable interest. The data relating to information processing can be considered in three principal categories: the amount of information that is processed when making decisions, the extent of planning activities for the future and the size of the information processing unit. In all three areas the ethnographic record testifies to great variability both within and between groups.

In relation to the first of these areas it is frequently observed in the literature that information processing involves the integration of data from a wide variety of sources. This is found at all levels in the decision hierarchy. For instance Leacock (1969: 17) and Chapman (1982: 42) refer to the integration of data from many sources when decisions are made about mobility. At a lower level Gubser (1965: 221–2) comments upon the wide range of factors that are taken into account when choosing a particular caribou from a herd to try and kill. The processing of a lot of data has also been referred to by Blurton-Jones and Konner (1976: 343), Silberbauer (1981:248), Martin (1978: 127), Yost and Kelley (1983: 194–6) and Marks (1976: 117; 1977: 255).

In general terms the processing of information appears most often to be hierarchical and sequential. That is, the bits of information available are considered in turn beginning with the most important. Two examples serve to illustrate this. Lee (1979: 213) describes how a !Kung hunter decides whether or not a spoor is worth following. The most important piece of information is the distance ahead the animal is and this is considered first by using cues such as tracks. If the animal is less than 2 km away, the next factor is considered, which is the extent of vegetation cover and the wind direction. If these are such that a stalk is feasible the forager then considers the speed and the activity of the animal. If these are suitable (e.g. resting, feeding or moving slowly) the hunter will choose to follow the spoor. However, if any of these is less than perfect he may be distracted easily by other game. Gubser (1965: 221–2) quotes a Nunamiut Eskimo describing how decisions concerning shooting caribou are taken. This also points to individual variability in decision making.

A man is sitting on a hill and sees two or three caribou in the distance. An intelligent person notes the direction of wind, the relative temperature of the air, the condition of the snow if present, whether it is raining or not, the shape of the terrain, the appearance of the caribou (whether they are feeding, walking or running) and the presence of other animals. After sizing up all these factors in a moment or two, he immediately recalls past situations having similar factors. Then the hunter decides whether to remain where he is or move to another location. If he shoots the caribou, then his decision was based on a knowledgeable use of past experience. If not, he either exercised poor judgement or was unable to observe some critical factor such as a wolf hidden behind a knoll. A few people make little use of their knowledge because of laziness or obstinacy rather than innate ability. Some people simply do not look at a total situation very carefully and decide on a course of action on the basis of only one or two factors; they merely encounter problems as they occur rather than planning ahead and trying to determine what the requirements of a situation will be.

From my previous discussion of information acquisition however, it is apparent that in some instances one piece of information will play a predominant role in decision making. This is more frequently the case for low- rather than high-level decisions. For instance, when tracking an animal the information from a footprint may heavily outweigh that from anthropomorphic predictions of the animal's behaviour. In addition, many of the examples of cues that I discussed above, such as calendar plants, might be considered as 'rules of thumb' since it is upon this single piece of information that decisions are made such as when to move to a new area or to start exploiting a particular resource.

In other instances hunter-gatherers appear to adopt decision-making methods which specifically reject the processing of information. While the above discussion of divination indicated that activities such as scapulimancy are not simple decision-making devices, they still appear to influence decisions. In some cases they might be thought of as activities that avoid information processing although as we have seen they are most frequently used jointly with information-processing methods. However, other examples suggest a total rejection of information processing. Moore (1979: 262) describes the manner in which a member of the Kaurareg is assigned his hunting territory. This is done during a ceremony when the names of the different areas are recited and on each name the youth's front tooth knocked. The name spoken on the knock that removes the tooth is assigned as the youth's hunting territory.

Another variable facet of information processing is the extent to which it is a discrete and well-planned activity. That decision making and hence information processing is of this nature has often been suggested in the literature, particularly for North American groups (e.g. Binford 1978; Sullivan 1942; Tanner 1979). The extent of planning and preparation may be quite considerable. For instance Silberbauer (1981: 112) describes the manner in which the G/wi decide upon their future mobility plans. This involves not only choosing which areas to go to but also a whole set of contingency plans if their expectations about particular locations are not met. Similar contingency planning is described by Gould (1980: 13) for Western Desert Aborigines.

However, while it is often a planned and discrete activity there is also a continuous element to information processing. In many descriptions it is apparent that as soon as information is acquired it is partly processed to assess the immediate situation and options facing the forager (e.g. Winterhalder 1981: 86). Martin (1978: 127) refers to the Cree constantly evaluating the state of their animal populations. Silberbauer (1981: 65) describes how the G/wi are constantly integrating new information into their current picture of the environment. Consequently, as with information gathering, it is useful to think of non-directed information processing. Of course the distinction that I am drawing between information gathering and processing is principally for my own descriptive and analytical purposes. We see in these cases how the separation between them is essentially artificial. Another example of such interdependence would be the period of information exchange at the end of the day when plans for the next day's activities may be simultaneously made.

While the presence of debate and discussion may make it very apparent that information processing is being carried out, in other instances information is apparently processed and decisions and made without this being apparent to an observer. For instance Goodale (1971: 160–1) describes how a group of Tiwi with whom she was living took joint decisions to move in particular directions but the decision process itself was almost unobservable. Similar cases have been described by Meehan (1982: 81).

A further variable of this area of information processing is the distance into the future for which decisions are made. It is clear that this is highly variable, with plans being made for the following day's, season's or even year's activities. It would appear that hunter-gatherers generally do not look further into the future than the coming year. Gubser (1965: 192) has stressed this for the Nunamiut and Silberbauer (1981: 112) for the G/wi. Both these groups appreciate that the irregularity of the weather in their areas prevents them having relevant information on which to base their decisions.

There is, however, an awareness that the same or similar problems will be faced in the future. One controversial area of meta-decision activity relates to resource 'management' or 'conservation' among hunter-gatherers. The extent of resource management has probably been exaggerated in recent hunter-gatherer literature, since behaviour having this effect arises from hunting methods acting to maximise/meliorise short-term gain (Webster and Webster 1984). But clearly some 'management' is practised. Goodale (1971: 173–4) describes how the Tiwi always leave a bit of yam in the ground when they are exploiting it so that they will be able to find it again in the future – anticipating decisions concerning its use and location.

Turning to the size of the information processing unit, it is readily apparent that this is highly variable. In many instances it is constrained by the context of the decision to the individual, such as during a lone hunting trip. In others, however, the fact that individuals are the main decision-making unit appears to be a particular choice (i.e. meta-decision) by the individual. Chapman (1982: 40) describes how among the Selk'nam an individual adult male assumes responsibility for making his own decisions, although he may consult others. Gubser (1965) refers to the importance of the individual as a decision maker within Eskimo societies. Woodburn (1968: 53) reveals how Hadza men decide for themselves when and where to hunt without co-ordinating their activities with other hunters. This is in marked contrast to G/wi hunters who discuss their intentions carefully to avoid mutual interference (Silberbauer 1981: 209).

Decisions may also be made by sub-groups within a society reaching consensus about a particular choice. These sub-groups may be composed of various different classes of individual. Among the G/wi, decisions to leave a particular settlement and move to a new area are made by the individual households, with the women taking the principal role and the shortage of food acting as the principal cue. Another discrete decision-making unit may be the older members of a society. Sullivan (1942: 36) describes the older people among the T'ena deciding upon a course of action to which the chief could only signify his approval. Similarly Gould (1980: 13) describes how older members of the Western Desert Aborigines play an important role in the decision process. A further type of sub-group is referred to by Moore (1979: 265) and consists of the adult males of the Kaurareg who retire each evening to their *kwod* (communal house) to discuss matters affecting the group as a whole. As with the individual as decision maker, sub-groups often play this role simply as a result of the context of their co-operative activities. Spencer (1969: 178) describes whaling crews taking a decision about where to land in which all members of the crew participate on an equal basis.

Certain decisions are, however, reached by the consensus of all adults in the group. This process has been described in greatest detail by Silberbauer (1981: 169–70). He stresses that consensus does not require all participating individuals to agree on the final choice but that there should not be significant opposition. To be a viable form of decision making this requires a shared set of standards and criteria to assess the value of alternatives. In stressing the importance of having agreement on how a decision should be reached, Silberbauer is emphasising the importance of meta-decision making in relation to information processing. Reaching decisions in the sub-groups I have described is also often by consensus (e.g. Altman 1984: 187) and presumably involves similar characteristics.

In direct opposition to consensus decision making and that by individuals for their own activities is the case of a leader in the group who takes decisions for others. Certainly, within consensus decision making one or more individuals may carry more weight than others, but here I am referring to institutionalised leadership in decision making. Examples are infrequent within the hunter-gatherer literature and tend to refer to North American groups. For instance Birket-Smith and De Laguna (1938: 105) describe how, among the Eyak, the hunters in a group had to obey the orders of a leader. Similarly Slobodin (1969: 81) describes how in a Kutchin trapping party there will be a principal leader who is not necessarily under any obligation to discuss decisions concerning the itinerary and trapping locations with other members of the party.

Discussion: individuals, history and evolution

The ethnographic data have shown that at one level there is great unity in the decision processes of modern hunter-gatherers. All foragers share characteristics such as a high degree of information exchange, stored information and the use of a wide variety of cues. Such unity exists, since I have been dealing with the same species involved in the same activity. At a more detailed level there is great variability between individuals and groups in the types of information used, the methods and extent of information exchange and knowledge about their environments. Some of this clearly relates to environmental variability – the hunter-gatherers are adopting decision-making processes which are appropriate to the specific problems they face. To expand on such patterning briefly, I will consider six important environmental parameters and the manner in which decision-making processes should, from a functional perspective, vary with these. Some support for the relationships is found within the material I have presented above although, as I will discuss later, I am not necessarily expecting a perfect fit.

First the nature of the physical environment may be considered. The ground conditions (snow, sand, vegetation) and terrain are important in the types of information that are available to the foragers. Different sets of physical features will provide different constraints and opportunities to the hunter-gatherers in their abilities to infer the locations and characteristics of potential resources. Consequently certain types of information acquisition and processing methods will be most appropriate for certain types of physical environment. A second variable is the types of species present. The particular physical and behavioural characteristics of potential resources and species acting as cues will make certain types of information acquisition and processing methods more appropriate than others. For instance to infer the location of highly mobile resources, information gathering will need to be highly developed, while information storage will be more important for stationary resources. A gross contrast between animals and plants may be drawn, and between species such as fish, about which information is difficult to gather, and large ungulates which may create a lot of visible/audible cues.

As well as the types of species present, the number of species is also important. As this increases, the forager will have a greater amount of information to acquire if his/her knowledge about the environment is to be accurate and he/she hopes to make decisions which achieve the chosen goal. However, as the number of species increase the penalty imposed on the forager by a poor decision, such as the failure to capture a targeted resource, will decrease since there will be other resources to act as backups. From this viewpoint, the amount of information required about the environment will decrease. Therefore in a species-rich environment the appropriate decision process will depend on the goals of the forager. Since these may be flexible it may be those environments that have neither a very high nor a very low number of species that impose the greatest information acquisition task on the forager. A fourth related variable is the structure of the natural community, in terms of predator-prey and competitive relationships. This affects the types of information available, which types are important to acquire and the appropriate processing methods. For instance, if any one predator has many species as its prey then observations on the density of one of those prey species will be a poor cue to the density of the predator. Similarly if the forager and another predator compete for the same prey species then to monitor the availability of that prey species may involve acquiring information about the density of the other predator. In general, as the complexity of the community increases, so will the amount of information required by the forager to monitor its change, with some information sources becoming less useful.

The two final environmental parameters requiring a brief consideration are spatial and temporal variability. As the first of these increases there will be a greater need to acquire information by directed activities, particularly sampling and searching, since when exploiting one resource the forager will not come into contact with others. For the same reason the amount of information exchange between foragers may need to be greater if knowledge about the current environment is to be accurate and comprehensive. The degree of temporal variability, at the scale of the day, season or year (see Whitelaw 1986) will influence the amount of information storage that is appropriate over these different scales. Of course all these parameters themselves may be varying over time and the extent of this will influence the appropriate amount of meta-decision activity to maintain the appropriate decision-making processes.

In the light of this discussion of environmental factors in information gathering and processing, one may characterise any one environment as having an 'information potential' and such potential will clearly vary at both a local and regional level. Similarly, one might characterise different animal and plant species as having information potentials in terms of the amount of cues that they, other animals, or features of the environment create as to their location and characteristics.

While some of the variability in decision-making processes relates to the patterns I have been discussing, it is clearly impossible to evaluate the extent of fit between the decision process adopted and that which may be the most appropriate since the latter cannot be evaluated with current data. In any one case it is difficult to know whether all the available information sources are exploited, the types of information being exchanged and whether the cues used are ecologically valid. This leads to the most important point, that neither is this information or rather meta-information available to the forager. However, one of the main tenets of my theoretical framework is that since (meta-)decision-making processes are the products of natural selection they do lead to choices that are adaptive for the forager in that particular environment. From these two points I can now turn to the importance of the individual and history within an evolutionary ecological framework for understanding the nature and variability of hunter-gatherer decision making.

In any one instance a forager must (meta-)decide which are the appropriate information sources to use, what is the appropriate information and how it should be processed. Such meta-decision will be made on the basis of the effectiveness of the choices taken in the past in relation to these questions, it is essentially a learning process concerning the appropriate methods of decision making. In other words, decision-making processes are 'reflexively monitored' (Giddens 1985). However, the forager faces problems in learning how to take decisions. He/she may not know whether a poor decision in the past resulted, for example, from use of the wrong information or from processing it the wrong way. 'Know' in this sense may relate to either of Giddens' cognitive states of 'discursive' or 'practical' consciousness. In addition any future choice between alternatives will share only certain characteristics with past choices; the exact problem will never be repeated. Even if all the ecological and social parameters of a decision were not significantly different, the actor's experience of the first occurrence of the choice makes the informational aspects of the decision significantly different. There are two further difficulties with learning how to take decisions. First, since only one choice is made the forager will only be able to evaluate the utility of that choice, and hence of the decision process, by an inference about the utility of the unchosen alternative. Second, the time between two similar choices may be substantial, possibly a series of years. Consequently, information about the past decision may have been lost and the characteristics of the decision maker will have changed; this again stresses the uniqueness of each decision.

In light of this general learning process and the problems encountered by the forager I wish to conceptualise the decision-making process of the individual as consisting of one point in a historical trajectory where it is a result of a particular sequence of past problems and decisions. The degree to which the decision process approaches that which is most appropriate for that environment will depend on this sequence. Similarly, the meta-decision-making process of the individual, which is used to learn the decision process, is also at one specific point in a historical trajectory.

In this regard we must see the development of decision-making processes as used in foraging activities as illustrative of the development of cultural activities in general. The model rests upon the simple principle that the forager will repeat the actions that are seen to work, in terms of fulfilling his (or her) goals and aspirations. From my evolutionary perspective, these subjectively defined aims (e.g. 'to please the Gods') will to some extent require activities that increase or maintain the process of continuous adaptation to an ever-changing social and natural environment. This brings us back to the concept of emotions as decision criteria. Subjective goals, and the means to attain them, that lead to feelings of hunger, pain, and misery will be rejected in favour of those that lead to feelings of good health and happiness; these latter sensations arise when the individual is adapting succesfully to his environment. These emotions have evolved as cues to taking decisions about appropriate goals to aim for and methods to use. I must stress here that many, perhaps most, stimuli, actions and their consequences have no inherent relationship with particular emotional sensations. As Pulliam and Dunford (1980) discuss, such relationships may arise through a complex and lengthy process of association with stimuli and actions that do indeed carry such sensations. The capacities for learning with which people are biologically endowed lead individuals to draw upon their own experiences (including, of course, drawing upon those of others which are communicated to them) to create such webs of relationships.

Since the social and natural environments, and the historical context, of the decision maker are always changing, those activities which lead to 'good' and to 'bad' sensations are also in a state of flux. Moreover, since the decision maker has limited information those actions he chooses will not necessarily lead to the 'good' sensations, i.e. he will not necessarily be adapting to his environment. The degree of correlation will depend upon both the rate of change in his environment and context and the rate at which he decides and learns. He may be constrained in the latter by the activities of other individuals. Similarly, since each individual is in a unique environment and context, there will be some variability between individuals as to what they identify as appropriate activities for themselves to engage in, and those activities which they desire for others, and this may lead to conflict.

This process, which explains why we find cultural activities that seem so well fitted to their environments, does not require the individual to make any link between, on the one hand, the activities they engage in and the goals aimed for and, on the other, the good sensations they feel. To return to scapulimancy, I argued above that this can be seen as playing an important meta-decision-making role in enabling the forager to retrieve information into working memory and promoting creative thought. It thus has a functional role and increases the foraging efficiency of the hunter. That scapulimancy is used, however, may be due to the forager's belief that it has magical powers. The fact that foraging efficiency is increased or maintained, or at least not reduced, confirms the belief; scapulimancy will be used again in the future. Similarly aggregations can be seen as contexts for information exchange, but the forager attributes any later hunting success to the ritual and magic conducted at that time. The forager may perceive it as an unwarranted risk to stop performing such rituals. Similarly meta-decisions are made not to engage in an active process of decision making but simply to copy one's own previous, or someone else's current, actions. Indeed, it may well be rare that individuals do actually meta-decide to engage in active processes of acquiring and processing information. Such circumstances may arise when the recognised consequences of chosen actions change, gradually or dramatically. This may act as the cue for meta-decision-making processes to choose active decision making once again. For instance, from my evolutionary perspective, I would see the decision of some Tiwi men no longer to participate in ritual yam preparations as a response to the presence of state aid which acts as a risk-buffering mechanism and removes the need to store such information for use during times of crisis.

An important feature of my argument is simply that an important element in the reproduction and development of cultural activities, of which decision making in foraging strategies is one example, is the unintended consequences of the choices that are made. The analysis of unintended consequences appears to be useful in this context for explaining the role of material culture, art and ritual in terms of information storage and recall devices, these being latent functions. My discussion of scapulimancy is subtly different in that the manifest and the latent functions coincide: the improvement of hunting efficiency. The significant factor is that the discursive knowledge possessed by the forager as to why this function is achieved, e.g. magical powers, contrasts with that of the present writer, i.e. aiding information recall.

The use of cues provides a particularly interesting case. As I have shown, in certain cases the relationship between the stimuli and the criteria is very evident and is discussed by the forager (e.g. a predator-prey relationship). In other instances the relationship is not immediately apparent, but that one exists can be readily believed (e.g. calender plants). In yet other cases, however, it is not apparent or believable (though it cannot be dismissed) that a relationship exists (e.g. omens such as the shape of porcupine intestines as cues to hunting success). The second of these cases is the most important since the question is how the forager comes to recognise that such cues exist. There must be a certain degree of experimentation, an idea that a cue exists and an attempt to use it or to test it. For this behaviour to flourish, the benefit from success must be high and the cost of failure low. We should thus expect to see cues used initially in conjunction with other information and relating to low-level decisions or when risk-buffering mechanisms are available. Since the problems are always changing and the opportunities to use the same cue may be rare, we should expect to see a high degree of experimentation and the use of ecologically invalid cues. The set of cues used will never be the most appropriate set for the environment since they must be learnt and the learning process will be slow in relation to the change in the environment.

To conclude this chapter I wish to summarise the points in my discussion and to outline the areas of decision making requiring further attention by the use of archaeological data. In light of the ethnographic data, I have suggested that the variability in hunter-gatherer decision making arises from three principal factors. First I stress the role of the individual in meta-decision activity, choosing which information sources to use and how to process information. At a higher level, choices are also made about the meta-decision processes to use. Second, the historical context of the individual is important for the particular choices he/she is currently making. The decision process must be thought of as one point on a historical trajectory which has its own unique course. Third, the biological basis of (meta-)decision making indicates that the decision processes employed will be approaching those most appropriate for the environment and the particular problems faced, and this is supported by the patterns in the ethnographic data. This point rests on the principle that foragers are simply repeating the actions that are seen to work in fulfilling their goals. Since the problems will always be changing, and the rate of learning the appropriate decision processes will be relatively slow, a high degree of experiment will be apparent in the types of information gathering and processing in the ethnographic record. Some of this will have little functional value.

With respect to the eco-psychological approach this chapter has served several roles. Most importantly it has clothed that model with a set of data and shown that the theoretical description of the decision process is useful in organising the ethnographic data and interpreting aspects of behaviour in the light of their relevance to decision making. The model has also been expanded through the recognition of the important role of material culture in various aspects of decision making and the similarly important role of myth and story-telling as information storage devices. In addition the complexity and importance of the information acquisition part of the model has been recognised. Certain areas, however, require further attention. Most importantly I need to deal with the goals of the decision maker and the actual choices taken. This will enable this work to be related more directly to optimal foraging studies. Specifically, can the model I am developing be used to explain the choices taken by prehistoric hunter-gatherers, resulting in the particular contents of archaeological assemblages? Further attention will need to be paid to the processing of information, and to do this I will now turn to the first of two archaeological studies – one concerning the Mesolithic of northwest Europe.

PART 2

Mesolithic foraging and society

4

Broken bones and buried bodies: patterns in the archaeological record

Mathematics, rightly viewed, possesses not only truth, but supreme beauty – a beauty cold and austere, like that of sculpture.

Bertrand Russell, *Mysticism and Logic* 1918

And how will your night dances
Lose themselves. In mathematics?

Sylvia Plath, 'The Night Dances'

At this stage in my study it is time to turn away from some of the terminology I have introduced and follow Ingold back to basics: 'the hunter and his spear' (1981, 1986: 1–15). Let us take his advice and consider the simple situation of a lone hunter out in the forest and taking decisions about which game to hunt. It is also time to make life a little more complicated by addressing the archaeological record. Has my polemic as to the need to invoke individual decision making for adequate explanations in archaeology been simply rhetoric and have my lengthy discussions of ecological, psychological and ethnographic data been distractions from my stated aim? Or are we now sufficiently equipped with a qualitative model of decision making to make progress in explaining the variability and patterning in the archaeological record? Now is the time to tell!

It is, of course, the latter. Well, it nearly is. I believe we have an appropriate theoretical framework, but so far lack the methodological tools to operationalise this with the mute stones and bones of the archaeological record. In this case study I am going to use mathematical modelling and computer simulation to play this role. In doing so we must heed Bertrand Russell and view these methods in thier correct guise. I do not pretend that they will provide any magic answers. My view of such techniques in archaeology is that they are simply tools, nothing more and nothing less. Unfortunately, my models lack the elegance of sculpture though they may be able to carve into the past in ways that pick-axes and trowels never can.

Mathematical models are particularly useful when we are thrusting the individual decision maker to the centre of the stage. We can use mathematical models to move from the actions of individuals in the short term, to the aggregate, long-term character of the archaeological record. Now, people have all sorts of thoughts that cannot be captured in a mathematical model. Indeed the intention is not to try and capture the mind in its mysterious entirety; that would get us nowhere. But by using mathematical models as methodological tools we certainly do not deny or lose the emotional and spiritual side of the human mind (Renfrew 1979: 4), the *night dances*. We know that these were present in the past, as they are here today. They pervade our data and demand recognition each time we pull a broken bone or a piece of chipped stone from the earth. How could a few ice-cold numbers and equations possibly compete with, let alone defeat, the human warmth emanating from either the most finely made pressure-flaked tool or the crudest broken pebble. The idea is ridiculous and the contest refused as a mismatch. The scaremongers who attack quantitative methods as somehow dehumanising (e.g. Shanks and Tilley 1987a: 58) appear to feel little of this warmth if they believe that the human spirit can be frozen so easily. Mathematical models are simply tools used with humility in the face of the daunting challenges that archaeologists take upon themselves.

In this section of the book my intention is no less than to demonstrate how a focus on individual decision making can help to develop explanations in archaeology. I will use mathematical modelling as a methodological tool. My subject will be the Mesolithic of north-west Europe. I choose this since, as will become evident below, the 'hunter and his spear' (or more probably with his bow and arrow in this case) conveniently emerges as the principal concern. We also have a nexus of patterns and problems in that archaeological record which desperately await attention. It is with these that I begin.

Problems in Mesolithic archaeology

The Mesolithic archaeological record of the north temperate forest zone presents a set of inter-related problems concerning technological, economic and social change. The issues raised are of relevance to understanding both the nature of human society during the early post-glacial and the process of culture change in general. The premise of this case study, following that of this work as a whole, is that a focus on decision-making processes involved in Mesolithic foraging strategies will aid in tackling these problems. The particular geographical area I will concentrate on is southern Scandinavia.

Detailed syntheses of the Mesolithic period in a wide range of areas are available (e.g. Britain: Mellars 1976; Simmons *et al.* 1981; Ireland: Woodman 1978; France: Rozoy 1978; Cantabrian Spain: Straus 1979; Clark 1983a, b; Denmark: Rowley-Conwy 1983; Scania: Larsson 1975–84; Middle Sweden: Welinder 1977; Finland: Zvelebil 1981). These, with the considerable number of recent publications concerning the Mesolithic (e.g. papers in the recent volumes edited by Bonsall, 1989; Zvelebil 1986b and Rowley-Conwy *et al.* 1987), demonstrate that this period is not now seen as one of little significance, a uniform period lying 'between cave painters and crop planters' (Rowley-Conwy 1986), but as one of dramatic social and economic change with high degrees of innovation and regional variability in cultural trajectories. This recent work identifies new problems concerning the period but fails to answer, often even to address, certain issues that have long

Table 4.1. *Ungulate frequencies in Mesolithic assemblages from Scania and the Upper Danube valley*

	Red deer	Roe deer	Pig	Elk	Auroch
Scanian sites[a]					
Ageröd I:D	76.6	1.1	14.9	4.2	3.2
Ageröd I:B	39.2	14.9	31.4	10.8	3.6
Ageröd I:HC	46.0	11.8	25.6	5.1	11.5
Ageröd V	60.6	17.3	12.6	9.6	0.0
Bredasten	25.2	5.2	69.7	0.0	0.0
Segebro	45.5	25.3	27.5	1.5	0.1
Skateholm	21.2	42.9	35.6	0.3	0.0
German sites[b]					
Jägerhaus	30.8	25.6	43.6	0.0	0.0
Falkenstein	30.0	43.3	20.0	0.0	6.7
Inzigkofen	25.0	40.0	35.0	0.0	0.0
Lautereck	14.3	42.8	42.8	0.0	0.0

Notes:
[a] Based on number of bone fragments from L. Larsson 1978, 1982, 1983; M. Larsson 1986; Jonsson, *in press*. See pages 156–69 for descriptions of sites and fauna. Unfortunately MNI (Minimum Number of Individuals) are unavailable for these assemblages. The site of Segebro is an exception and Larsson (1982: 107) provides the MNI calculated from the number of bone fragments. The ungulate frequencies derived from these (red deer 42.2, roe deer 23.6, pig 23.6, elk 9.4, auroch 0.9) are in close agreement with those based on bone fragments as in the above table. While MNI would be preferable we can have some confidence that the frequencies based on bone fragments are measuring variation in the number of ungulates in the assemblages, rather than being a factor of preservation.
[b] Based on MNI from Jochim 1976. See pages 169–71 for site descriptions.

been matters of contention and concern. Indeed, with the current theoretical framework in which Mesolithic research is conducted, dominated by static models of group adaptation, substantial progress on these problems will remain elusive. I will briefly describe three of the problem areas upon which an individualistic decision-making approach may throw light.

Hunting, fishing and farming

Animal resources have traditionally been seen at the centre of Mesolithic economies (Clarke 1976). There is, at one level, great similarity in the faunal assemblages from the early post-glacial in the temperate zone. Five large ungulate species are present – red deer, roe deer, wild pig, auroch and elk – in what tend to be small assemblages compared with those of the Upper Palaeolithic. The first three of these frequently predominate but the percentages of all five species fluctuate dramatically. Kozlowski and Kozlowski (1986) describe this for sites across north and central Europe; Table 4.1 provides more detailed data from the two areas upon which I shall concentrate in Chapter 6, Scania and south-west Germany.

The basic problem posed by such assemblages is one that archaeologists have not adequately addressed – the meaning of the variability in the proportion of each species within and between assemblages. Several factors can be expected to play a role. These include variation in game densities, selection of game and taphonomic processes.

There must be some gross environmental factors affecting the character of these assemblages. For instance it is generally argued that the changing forest composition from the Pre-Boreal to the Late Atlantic would have led to progressively worse habitats for elk and better ones for pig. In spite of this, no trend of this type can be seen in the proportion of these species in the assemblages (see Larsson 1978, Fig. 117). In some areas, certain species became locally extinct, such as elk and auroch in Zealand (Aaris-Sørensen 1980). Other regions were never colonised by particular species; in Ireland only red deer and pig appear to have been available to the hunters (Woodman 1978).

Gross environmental factors also played a role in defining how important these terrestrial ungulates were in the economy as a whole. A contrast can be drawn between hunters living in coastal and in interior regions of Europe simply because of the availability to the former of sea fish, shellfish, marine mammals and a greater range of bird species. As C^{13} studies have shown, marine resources appear to have played a substantial role in the diet (Price 1985; Tauber 1981). In addition to the coastal resources and forest ungulates, other types of animals were regularly exploited. These included riverine fish, small mammals and birds.

The economic activities in one coastal zone, eastern Denmark, have received particularly detailed attention. Rowley-Conwy (1983) has argued that during the Ertebølle period different types of sites can be identified such as permanent settlements and specialised task sites. It is significant, however, that only in rare circumstances, such as at Ringkloster (Andersen 1973), does any one of the large ungulate species predominate and appear to have been particularly targeted. At other sites, even those specialising in one particular coastal resource (e.g. Aggersund – Møhl 1978b), the range of large ungulates tends to be present though with each species represented only in small numbers. The question of the variability in their numbers remains.

Local variation in game densities will also affect the composition of a faunal assemblage. Detailed environmental reconstructions such as that by Andersen (1984) are required to tackle this issue. While the rarity of such work hinders generalisation it would be surprising if there were not opportunities to hunt a range of large ungulates from each settlement. Larsson (1978) has attempted to reconstruct the distribution of flora and fauna around the site of Ageröd I in Scania at the transition from the Late Boreal to the Atlantic (Fig. 4.1). He suggests that a hunting trip south and south-west of the site would have given occasion to kill red deer, roe deer, wild boar, badger and wild cat, while hunters looking for elk, auroch, bear and marten would have found their prey in the north-west. Such hypothetical reconstructions require a great leap of faith and the assumption of fixed relationships between environmental types and particular resources.

My principal concern in the study that follows will be with a further factor affecting the composition of faunal assemblages – hunters' choice as to which animals to pursue. Yet, as I will demonstrate, such a focus is only useful when

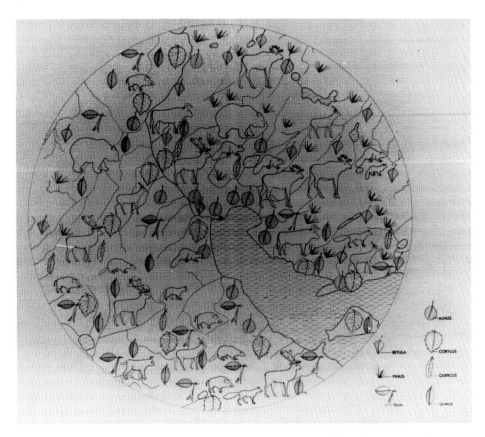

Fig. 4.1. Hypothesised flora and fauna around Ageröd I at the transition from the Late Boreal to the Early Atlantic (after Larsson 1978).

integrated with an understanding of assemblage formation and local environmental variability. Without this it will be impossible to connect theoretical models of hunters' choice with the real archaeological data.

If the variation of game frequencies in assemblages is one problem with regard to Mesolithic economies, a second is the variation in the rate of adoption of agricultural methods. This has received considerable attention from Zvelebil and Rowley-Conwy (1986; Zvelebil 1986c; Rowley-Conwy 1984). They have taken an important step forward by breaking down the adoption of agriculture into three phases – availability, substitution and consolidation – and applying this model to many different areas, but with greatest detail to Finland and Denmark. They affirm the previously recognised pattern that the adoption of agriculture in the coastal zone was markedly delayed in contrast with interior regions (Fig. 4.2). They argue that in the coastal areas the adoption of intensive aquatic resource use strategies played the same role as agriculture elsewhere. As they point out, this finding is in marked contrast with the theoretical arguments of Cohen (1977) and Binford (1968) who argue that the more sedentary and complex coastal communities, such as those in temperate Europe, would have been the most ready to adopt

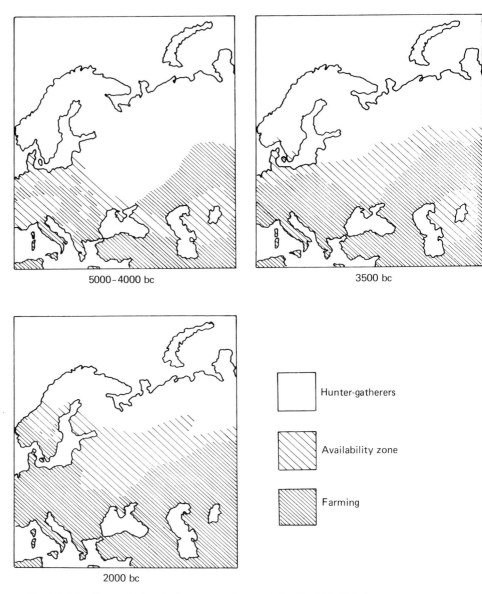

Fig. 4.2. The dispersal of agriculture across Europe (after Zvelebil 1986c).

or innovate agricultural techniques. Blankholm (1987a) presents an 'integrated multicausal' model for the spread of farming into southern Scandinavia but admits to a 'long way to go' before adequate explanations are developed. Part of the journey must be to place people engaged in the process of adaptation back at the centre of the models, ousting the focus on groups and systemic relationships.

The work of Zvelebil and Rowley-Conwy, supplemented by that of Lewthwaite (1986), provides excellent descriptions of the spread of agriculture across Europe and emphasises that there was no one single cause for the transition to farming. It opens up questions concerning the respective roles that terrestrial, coastal and marine resources played in the Mesolithic economies. These roles may have been different, providing, for example, the staple food supply, supplementary but irregular food, 'risk-buffering' resources or a 'prestige' food with social rather than economic significance. There is an underlying assumption that the 'coastal' and 'domestic' came to play an equivalent role, but what that role was remains undefined. This brings us back to the problem of variation in large ungulate frequencies in assemblages prior to the agriculture availability phase in the interior regions. Since at this time marine resources were available and exploited by the coastal groups, we are forced to ask whether this led to different roles for the terrestrial fauna in the economies in the two types of region.

Tools, industries and cultures
At one level there is great homogeneity in the technology of the Mesolithic period – the use of composite tools with microliths set in wooden or bone shafts. Following Clarke (1976), Zvelebil (1986c) argues that the advantage of such a technology over the long blades of the Upper Palaeolithic is that it is more flexible, easier to repair, and more economic in terms of raw materials. These attributes, he suggests, made it an appropriate technology for use when activities are highly time stressed (Torrence 1983; Zvelebil 1984). While such gross generalisations may be useful for crude Upper Palaeolithic/Mesolithic/Neolithic comparisons, they rest upon ill-defined concepts (such as time stress) and conjecture. They cannot tackle the immense variability within the Mesolithic period itself. I wish to highlight the innovation and adoption of new elements within a microlithic technology. This is a neglected problem which a decision-making perspective may illuminate.

Rowley-Conwy (1986) describes how the principal aim of Mesolithic studies since the war has been to classify industries into cultures. This he justly sees as having erected a 'cumbersome and controversial edifice of ever increasing complexity' (1986: 18). The advent of C^{14} dating, together with more sophisticated palaeo-environmental reconstruction and pollen analysis, has put some order and patterning into the industrial groupings. Three principal phases in microlithic technology have been recognised (Jacobi 1976). First were the widespread Maglemosian industries, dominated by obliquely blunted points and large isosceles triangles, which extend from Britain right across the north European plain. The second phase, beginning around 6500 bc, consists of a much more diverse microlith set together with a greater standardisation of types. In general, a range of geometric forms were introduced, made on narrow blades, such as scalene triangles, lancelots and rods. In continental Europe such industries last about a millennium after which they are replaced by ones dominated by rhomboids and trapezes made on broad blades.

Considering the archaeological record at this gross spatial and temporal scale, two related problems are posed, concerning innovation and regional variability. With respect to innovation, we can consider the origin of industries of the second and third phases. Jacobi (1976) considers the earliest known dates for the narrow blade geometric industries, finding them in southern France at the sites of Grotte

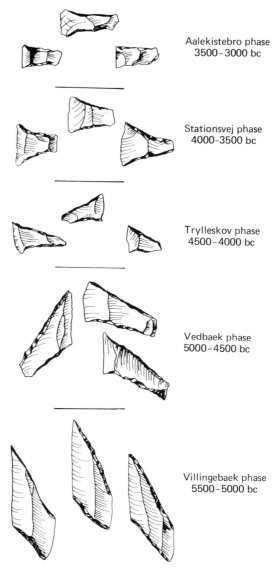

Aalekistebro phase
3500–3000 bc

Stationsvej phase
4000–3500 bc

Trylleskov phase
4500–4000 bc

Vedbaek phase
5000–4500 bc

Villingebaek phase
5500–5000 bc

Fig. 4.3. The succession of projectile point types during the five phases of the Late Mesolithic in north-east Denmark (after Peterson 1984).

des Fieux and Rouffignac during the eighth millennium. In the first half of the seventh millennium they occurred at other French sites and at sites in Holland and Britain. By 6600 bc they were widespread and found, for instance, in all English and Welsh assemblages. Consequently two scenarios are possible. Either these originated in southern France and then slowly diffused northwards, or there were several innovation centres, those in the south having been the earliest.

Whichever of these is correct, there is a marked contrast with the origin of the third phase – broad-blade industries. Jacobi (1976) and Larsson (1978) consider that these appear almost synchronically across Europe. Essentially the same questions concerning local innovation or diffusion arise but the concurrence of these, or the rate of spread, must have been considerably greater.

Regional variability is also a major issue. A contrast between Britain and the continent can be drawn by the absence of third-phase industries in Britain. By 6400 bc Britain had been cut off from Europe by a narrow channel. This is generally taken to be the cause of stasis in British industries but with the substantial canoes known to have existed (e.g. Andersen 1985) it is unlikely that there would have been no contact across the straits. Ireland provides a particularly interesting case (Woodman 1978). While it lacks any evidence for the first-phase Maglemosian industries, it has one of the earliest dates for narrow blades, at Mount Sandel. The later Mesolithic industries in Ireland are characterised by the large-blade Larnian industries, without parallel elsewhere in Europe.

The problems of innovation and regional variability in microlithic sequences are also apparent at a smaller scale, as illustrated by southern Scandinavia. The rich archaeological record here has led to a corresponding increase in the intensity of typological studies. By 1973 E.B. Petersen could identify ten industrial phases grouped into the three cultures – Maglemose, Kongemose and Ertebølle. Such sequences pose problems not only of innovation and adoption but also of the meaning of particular industries in terms of human groups and ethnic identities. Some divisions appear arbitrary. For instance that between the late Maglemose and the Kongemose is simply that the latter has more than half the microliths of the broad type (Larsson 1978: 11). What is totally lacking is a consideration of the formation of these lithic assemblages. A greater appreciation of the accumulation processes and post-depositional modification of a lithic assemblage may make archaeologists more wary of simplistic cultural designations.

With reference to the Kongemose and Ertebølle periods in east Denmark, Vang Petersen (1984) has revised the chronology as based on microlithic forms into five phases (Fig. 4.3). He recognises that the change in the shape of arrowheads is both more common and happens more quickly than has been previously assumed. However, he could only explain this by reference to changes in 'taste and fashion' (1984: 12), which is tantamount to no explanation at all.

I have concentrated on the microlithic technology but this is only one part of a complex and diverse tool kit. Other stone implements include a range of axe and adze types. Sites with good preservation bear witness to a range of tools made from organic materials, including spears, harpoons and fish traps (e.g. Larsson 1977, 1983). Zvelebil (1986a) has characterised such organic tools as specialised, dedicated to particular tasks in contrast to the generalised nature of microlithic tools. From another viewpoint tools such as fish traps (Fig. 4.4) may be described as facilities which operate without constant human presence. Finally I must state here that in my following references to microliths I am assuming that these were used as arrowheads and barbs in the hunting of large game, in spite of Clarke's (1976) warning that this may be simplifying a complex technology. This is

Fig. 4.4. Fragment of a wicker cage, probably a fish trip, from Ageröd V (after Larsson 1983).

essentially a pragmatic stance since by the finds of microliths embedded in bones we can be sure that they were used for hunting, while their use in plant processing remains to be shown.

Cemeteries, stratification and social complexity

During the Mesolithic there appears the first substantial evidence for social differentiation in the form of cemeteries with an uneven distribution of grave goods among the burials. Zvelebil (1986c: 172) summarises the evidence in three points:

1 Cemeteries occur exclusively in coastal areas, in lake districts and along major river courses, as in Fig. 4.5.
2 Settlement patterns in these areas are usually regarded as sedentary or semi-sedentary (i.e. Lepenski Vir in the Danube Gorges, Abora, Sarnate, Sventoji and other sites in the east Baltic, sites on the middle and lower Dnieper and in southern Scandinavia).
3 Most, if not all, the cemeteries revealed variation in mortuary equipment, method of burial and funerary architecture. In most cases this has been interpreted as indicating status differentiation (see Clark and Neeley 1987).

When discussing the appearance of such cemeteries there are two separate issues: first, the fact that individuals within the society were differentiated in terms of wealth and, second, the fact that these individuals were buried in cemeteries. The second probably relates to the delimitation of territories and land rights

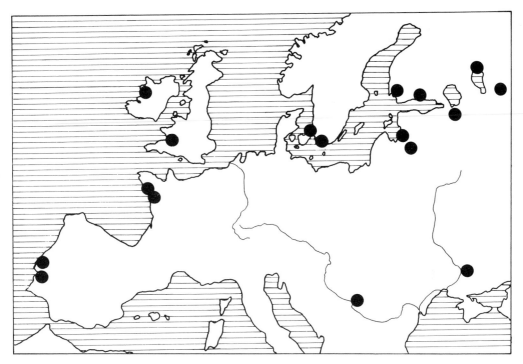

Fig. 4.5. The distribution of Mesolithic cemeteries in Europe (after Zvelebil and Rowley-Conwy 1986).

(Larsson 1984). In the inland areas, where cemeteries are absent, we do not know whether social differentiation existed. My assumption is that it did not, because of the lack of symbols of wealth in the archaeological assemblages and on the basis of modern hunter-gatherers among whom complex societies are principally found in coastal regions. Consequently my interest here is in the apparent variability in social complexity between the Mesolithic societies living in inland and coastal areas. By 'coastal' I include areas adjacent to major lakes or rivers.

The presence of social differentiation in coastal regions has been explicitly related to the richness of coastal resources, the storage and complex technology required to exploit them and the likelihood of resulting surpluses. However, the question of how economic factors articulate with social dynamics has not been sufficiently considered. Similarly the role of terrestrial resources in the equation has been neglected, principally because of the absence of such social complexity in interior regions. This is surprising since a consideration of grave goods indicates some relationship between status and terrestrial hunting. At the cemetery of Oleneostrovski Mogilnik, discussed and analysed in detail by O'Shea and Zvelebil (1984), there is evidence that the individuals who acquired most wealth were the physically strongest and by implication the best hunters. O'Shea and Zvelebil suggest that wealth and prestige derived from being able to procure sufficient quantities of food to permit 'giving it away' within the community. If this is correct it is likely that such food was derived from the killing of large terrestrial mammals since in terms of food quantities such ungulates were very productive in comparison with other resources (Bailey 1978). As Zvelebil and Rowley-Conwy (1986) argue, resources such as shellfish could be collected by women, children and the infirm. Moreover the exploitation of aquatic resources and small game depended on specialised technology rather than on physical strength and endurance, qualities necessary for stalking and slaying large land mammals.

A link between social differentiation and the hunting of large terrestrial game is also indicated by the fact that objects that signify wealth/status relate to terrestrial ungulates rather than coastal resources. At Oleneostrovski Mogilnik wealth was apparently expressed through the possession of pierced elk, beaver and bear teeth. Similarly, in the cemeteries of south Scandinavia, Vedbaek and Skateholm, the teeth of wild pig and red deer are the most frequent goods, other than stone tools, in the graves (Albrethsen and Petersen 1976; Larsson 1984: Fig. 4.6). Some graves also contain teeth from elk, roe deer and auroch but only in one case (grave 8 at Vedbaek) is there a tooth of a marine mammal (seal). The same is found in the burials at Dragsholm, Bottendorf and Plau where the teeth of pig and red deer predominate (Albrethsen and Petersen 1976).

Consequently there appears to be a paradox in the archaeological data. While socially complex hunter-gatherer groups developed in coastal regions, and this social evolution has been explicitly related to the exploitation of aquatic and coastal resources, status appears to have been associated with the large terrestrial ungulates and their exploitation.

Discussion

My discussion of these aspects of the Mesolithic archaeological record has identified four particular problems which require attention:

1 the variation in the proportions of large ungulate species in faunal assemblages;
2 the hiatus in the spread of agriculture to south Scandinavia and the respective roles that aquatic, terrestrial and, in the later period, domestic resources played in the economy;
3 the innovation and adoption of new microlithic forms;
4 the relationship between social differentiation and economic activities, in particular the hunting of terrestrial game.

How are these problems to be tackled? How is this patterning and variability in the archaeological record to be explained? Well, let me first state that the premise of this work demands that we must make explicit reference to decision making by individuals. Since the unifying theme between these four problems is the exploitation of large ungulates I shall concentrate upon decisions concerning this by the hunters within the group. As I discussed in my introduction, we move towards explanation when we have integrated what were isolated features of the archaeological record, as are the issues I have been discussing, into one coherent framework with the individual decision maker at the centre. So my intention is to work through data concerning one of the problem areas, faunal assemblages, to try and gain an understanding of the decision-making process. I will then use this under-

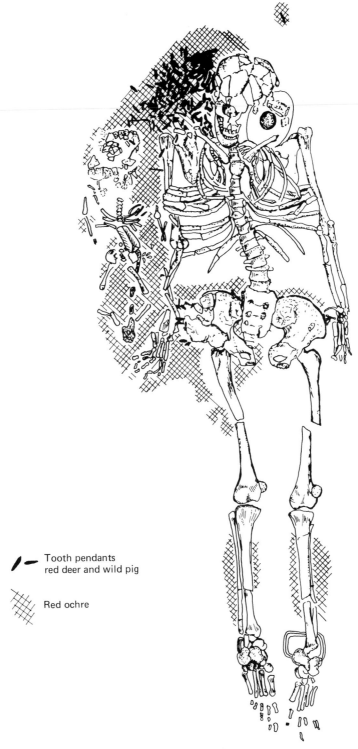

Tooth pendants
red deer and wild pig

Red ochre

Fig. 4.6. A Mesolithic burial from Vedbaek, grave 8, a woman with a new-born baby (after Albrethsen and Peterson 1976).

standing to show how the variability and patterning in the faunal, technological and burial data is in fact related and interdependent.

What do I mean by working through faunal assemblage to locate the decision maker? The first step will be to make some inferences concerning decision making simply by discussing the character of the assemblages in a little more detail. This will make use of the eco-psychological and ethnographic material already presented, and will indicate the types of problems faced, the alternative courses of action and the sources of information available. I shall then build a mathematical model for individual decision making by the Mesolithic hunters and use this as a methodological tool to infer further elements of the decision process, notably goal choice. This will be done by using computer simulation to experiment with different foraging goals and to examine which type of goal produces an archaeological record that is meaningfully similar to those found in two study areas; Scania and south-west Germany. The emphasis here is on a *meaningful* similarity between real and simulated faunal assemblages, as will be discussed below. Once the goal choice(s) has been inferred, I will use this understanding of decision-making processes to swing back from the faunal assemblages to the other problem areas, technology and social differentiation, and show how the patterns within Scania, and the contrasts with south-west Germany can now be explained. By this means, the patterning and variability in the archaeological record will indeed be explained by placing the individual at the centre of the study.

Mesolithic hunting

My concern in this section is to discuss features of the archaeological record which are indicative of the type of hunting behaviour that occurred, and hence the types of problems that were faced, courses of action to choose between and the information sources available. To state my conclusion, we can infer from various characteristics of the archaeological record that the predominant mode by which large game were hunted was of an 'encounter' foraging type, and the foraging problem can be characterised as prey choice. The subsistence-settlement system as a whole was probably logistically organised with specialist task sites (Rowley-Conwy 1983). Hunter-gatherers who predominantly employed encounter foraging methods were termed 'foragers' by Binford (1980) to describe this pole of a continuum of hunter-gatherer systems. In the last few years it has become common terminology in hunter-gatherer studies. Essentially it involves individuals hunting either alone or in small groups, encountering potential resources (most probably their signs) and then choosing whether or not to stalk/pursue that animal or gather that plant. At the base camp, food tends to be shared and very little of it stored. The foragers can be described as having high residential, and low people, mobility. The most frequently described ethnographic groups employing this mode tend to be in equatorial regions, for example the Valley Bisa (Marks 1976), the G/wi (Silberbauer 1981), the Áche (Hawkes *et al.* 1982) and the Agta (Estioko-Griffen 1986), although all hunter-gatherers probably adopt such encounter foraging at certain times (e.g. Binford 1978: 208). Encounter foraging involves one central decision: having encountered a resource should it be ignored or stalked/gathered. The current evolutionary approach to this decision makes use of the diet breadth, optimal foraging model. Before developing my complementary decision-making approach I must outline the evidence for encounter foraging in the Mesolithic.

One of the most important pieces of data is the simplest – the small size and diverse composition of the faunal assemblages. If a 'collector' strategy had been employed, in which the hunters focus for short times on single resources, or techniques of herding and game drives used, we should expect to find larger assemblages more frequently dominated by a single species. Such characteristics of the assemblages has led Noe-Nygaard to propose that 'The Mesolithic hunters probably concentrated on the individual animal, finding, tracking, chasing and killing it' (1974: 242). Support for this type of encounter foraging strategy can be drawn from a detailed consideration of particular faunal assemblages and the Mesolithic technology. An interesting and important faunal study by Legge and Rowley-Conwy (1988) re-analyses the Star Carr fauna. In addition to revising the numbers, ages and sexes of the species present, as well as the seasonality of the site, they analyse the body-part representation to infer the type of site Star Carr represents. Comparisons are drawn between the body-part frequencies of red deer and those of caribou from a variety of site types in the Nunamiut settlement system. They found a very close similarity between the Star Carr data and those from the Kongumuvuk summer hunting camp which had been used by an all-male hunting party between 1951 and 1955. This led them to argue that Star Carr represents a temporary hunting camp playing a similar role in the settlement system as did the Kongumuvuk camp for the Nunamiut. The body-part representation at Kongumuvuk resulted from an encounter foraging strategy, with field butchery and the transfer of selected parts of the carcass back to the site: 'This was strictly a location from which encounter hunting was conducted. The men would go out singly and stay out all day looking for caribou, returning to the camp only when they were tired. Any animals killed would of course be field butchered and sometimes cached. The hunter would return to the camp with some meat from his kill for both humans and dogs' (Binford 1978: 268).

It appears, therefore, that the large terrestrial ungulates at Star Carr had been hunted by an encounter foraging method. While this type of hunting was a small and untypical activity for the Nunamiut, it may have been far more common during the Mesolithic as further body-part frequency studies may demonstrate. An important contrast with the Nunamiut is that in the post-glacial forest the Mesolithic hunters were searching for several, not just one, type of ungulate.

The argument for a predominantly encounter foraging strategy can also be made on technological grounds. Zvelebil (1986a: 89) suggests that the microlithic technology was 'probably employed in situations where hunters set out in search of game without having a specific type of prey in mind. If game was sighted the small stone blades could in a very short time be reshaped for capturing that prey.' This technology, Zvelebil argues, was most suitable when the type and quantity of game were unpredictable. Complementing it, however, is a more specialised technology to be used whenever a game species that may be killed becomes known. Zvelebil appears to be suggesting that at certain times of the year and/or at particular locations the probability of encountering one particular type of game becomes sufficiently high for the hunters to switch to this alternative specialised technology of barbed harpoons and antler spears. He uses the tool assemblages from Star Carr as an example of this strategic use of technology: 'the barbed antler points were used for killing game such as elk or deer at their seasonal peak, and the microlithic weapons were used for hunting expeditions when the prey could not have been predicted easily and any one of a broad range of species may have been encountered' (1986a: 90). These suggestions bear some similarities to Jacobi's (1978) proposition that barbed antler points were linked specifically to the final dispatch of game which had been exhausted by the blood-letting arrows employed in the preliminary stages of the hunt. In that case the specialised character of the spear points still exists but we picture them being chosen for the killing not of a particular type of species but of a wounded animal.

The character of faunal assemblages and technology combine in an important study by Noe-Nygaard (1974) which examines Mesolithic hunting in Denmark from the viewpoint of injuries on the excavated bones caused by the hunters' weapons. She found that the bow and arrow had been used for all species she examined; red deer, roe deer, pig, auroch and swan. Spears and axes had been used for the final killing of auroch and pig respectively. While other killing methods may have been used, this archaeological evidence supports the case for encounter foraging. Noe-Nygaard also found a relatively high frequency of wounds that showed signs of healing. That is, the animal was wounded but escaped only to be killed on another occasion or to collapse after some time into a bog or marsh. The most vivid examples of such hunting failure are provided by the Vig auroch (Noe-Nygaard 1973) and the Poulton le Fylde elk (Hallam *et al.* 1973). Such hunting failure is often recorded among modern 'encounter foragers' (e.g. Marks 1976).

Jacobi (1978) has suggested that early post-glacial hunting in northern Britain was not conducted by individuals stalking particular animals but by groups of hunters using drive methods. He bases his argument on two pieces of evidence. First he uses the Levantine paintings from Cueva de la Caballos of a Mesolithic red deer drive. Second he states that individual stalking only originated with accurate and reliable rifles in the Scottish deer forests. The second point appears to be a remarkable dismissal of much ethnographic data indicating the feasibility of stalking with simple weapons. There is also no reason why the painting from Spain should be generally representative of hunting patterns in northern Europe. It would be unlikely that co-operative drive methods were never used but the weight of technological and faunal data indicates that encounter foraging of the large ungulates by individuals was the norm in Mesolithic northern Europe.

My argument that large game were hunted on an encounter basis by individuals requires one caveat. It is unreasonable to imagine that a single hunter would alone stalk, attempt to kill and (if successful) field butcher, the largest of the forest ungulates, auroch and elk. At some stage in this process help would surely have been elicited from other hunters. This transition from individual to group activity following encounter with a particularly large ungulate is often described in the ethnographic literature (e.g. O'Connell *et al.* 1988). Consequently in the scenario of encounter foraging I will describe below, and when running the simulation in Chapter 6, I restrict my models to red deer, roe deer and pig which were most probably hunted by a 'pure' individualistic encounter method. I am justified in this since the archaeological data sets I deal with are principally from areas and periods when elk and auroch appear to have become very rare, perhaps extinct, and/or played a minor role in the economy (Aaris-Sørensen 1980).

Having established that the predominant mode of large-game hunting was on an encounter basis we have identified the critical decision during the hunting process: whether or not to stalk an encountered animal. The next part of this study will centre on building and exploring a model for this decision and the context in which it is made. Before turning to develop this model I will define an idealised version of encounter foraging which will serve to present the underlying assumptions for the simulation study and from which, in light of my eco-psychological model, the sources of information available to the forager and the processing methods may be inferred. This can be done by listing ten characteristics:

1 There is a constant number of individuals within the group.
2 On days that hunting occurs all the individuals leave the base camp and search the surrounding area for game. They search and hunt individually and there is no contact during the day.
3 The individuals hunt until either there is no more time left in that day, there being a constant number of minutes available, or until they 'wish' to return to the camp.
4 Ungulates (or their signs) are encountered individually, they are immediately recognised and no mis-identifications are made.
5 When encountering ungulates there are only two alternative courses of action to choose from: to stalk it or to ignore it and carry on searching.
6 When pursuing or processing an ungulate no other potential resources are encountered.
7 If an ungulate is successfully killed it may either be field butchered or, if small enough, carried whole. Field-butchered ungulates are collected either after the time available for hunting has elapsed, on days during which no hunting has occurred, or when the stay at the site has expired.
8 All game killed is shared between the group and some or all of the waste from each kill accumulates within the same assemblage. Hence the MNI and the species composition of that assemblage records the kills made by the whole group.
9 Before (or after) foraging all individuals discuss their past experiences and assess the worth of pursuing the potential resources if encountered as soon as they start foraging.
10 After a fixed number of days all members of the group leave the site and move away. If they return at a later date, the new kills are added to the old assemblage.

We have here a simple conceptual model for the manner in which Mesolithic foragers hunted large game. At the centre of this is the decision taken by an individual concerning which game to stalk upon encounter. My contention is that if we can understand the way in which such decisions were made, and their consequences, we will be able to make a significant step towards explaining the variability and patterning in faunal and lithic assemblages and of the burial record. The method required for this is described in the next chapter.

5

Gearing up with methodological tools: building a simulation model

Between my finger and my thumb
The squat pen rests.
I'll dig with it.

Seamus Heaney, 'Digging'

In his poem Seamus Heaney reflects upon his father digging potatoes: By God, the old man could handle a spade. Just like his old man.' He, however, chose to work with the pen. Times had changed for the Heaney family as indeed they have in archaeology. Not long ago, when archaeologists were faced with the types of problems I have outlined in the previous chapter, their reaction would have been to 'dig more sites'. More recently an alternative reaction has been to seek a total immersion in theory. We now realise that more data and theory do not necessarily bring more understanding and explanation by themselves. We need the link between these, new methodology. Tools other than picks and shovels are required. So, with apologies to Heaney: 'Between my finger and my thumb the computer programme rests. I'll dig with it.' Of course I am not implying that there isn't a need for new excavations. Just as poets need potatoes, simulation models need good archaeological data and both must continue to be dug from the ground.

The simulation model, which I see as a methodological tool, will follow the idealised encounter foraging system I proposed above. It can be divided into three components: a model for the hunting process, a model for the post-glacial environment and a model for decision making by the hunters.

Modelling the hunting process

The model for the hunting process provides the structure for the simulation and is described in Fig. 5.1. Quite simply it involves a predefined numbers of hunters leaving a base camp each morning, foraging for a predefined number of minutes and then returning to the camp in the evening at which time they discuss their 'experiences'. This simulation will run for a predefined number of hunting trips, each of which lasts for one day. These are not necessarily consecutive days. We know from the ethnographic literature that hunters do not necessarily hunt every day. Once a large kill is made it may last the group several days before more meat and raw materials are required. These days of inactivity (in terms of hunting) are not modelled since it is assumed that they do not alter the hunter's knowledge of

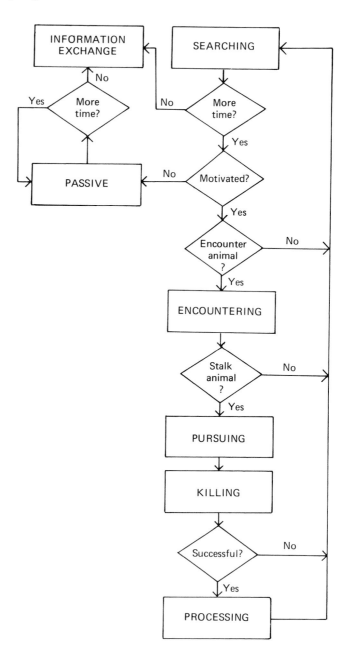

Fig. 5.1. Activity states and transitions for simulated Mesolithic hunters.

the environment (though in reality this is constantly changing – it is a very simple model). In the following text, when I refer to the number of days for which the simulation runs this is the number of hunting trips made. In addition the simulation will model the return of the hunters to the same site for a predefined number of visits. Each visit lasts for the same number of days/hunting trips.

Each hunting trip is modelled in the following manner. Hunting activity is divided up into six separate states and the simulation defines the 'state' of each hunter at each minute of the day. A hunter moves from one state to another according to the encounters with animals, the decisions he takes concerning stalking them, and his success at killing those he stalks. The six states are named 'searching', 'encountering', 'pursuing', 'killing', 'processing' and 'passive'.

At each minute of the day the simulation examines the state of each hunter and takes various actions according to that state. In the first minute each hunter is in a 'searching' state. Using the probabilities for encountering game, which I will model below, the model tests whether the hunter encounters a potential resource (the animal itself, or the sign of one). If so, he enters 'encountering' state for the next minute, otherwise he remains searching. The hunter only remains in the 'encountering' state for one minute during which the decision is taken whether or not to stalk the ungulate. This is taken by using a set of 'stalk probabilities' defined by processing information from past experience, in accordance with a chosen goal, as I will also describe below. If the hunter chooses to ignore the resource he returns to searching state for the next minute. Otherwise he enters 'pursuing' state.

He remains in 'pursuing' state for a time equal to the pursuit time of the ungulate now being hunted. At the end of this time the hunter enters 'killing' state. In this the probability for successfully killing the animal (as defined below) is used to test whether the hunter makes a successful kill. If he does not then the hunter returns to 'searching' state for the next minute. If the ungulate is killed however, the hunter remains 'killing' for a further minute and then enters the fifth state, 'processing', and remains there for the processing time of the ungulate. After that he returns to 'searching'.

If, while 'searching', the hunter's stalk probabilities for deciding whether or not to stalk an encountered animal fall below a predefined value (0.1 was chosen in practice) for all of the game species he may encounter, then the hunter enters the 'passive' state. This is modelling the hunter's loss of interest in taking more game and he remains in this state for the rest of the day. In it, he invests no time in searching and can make no encounters. In effect it models his return to the camp or engagement in other activities.

After the last minute of the day all the hunters are considered to return to the camp, if not already there as a result of being 'passive'. If during the last minute a hunter was engaged in either 'pursuing' or 'processing' then the simulation allows him to spend extra foraging time in finishing these activities. (If the hunter was pursuing and successfully kills the ungulate, the simulation allows him to process it.) At the end of the day, or at the start of the next, the simulation models information exchange and the formation of assessments of the worth of stalking each of the potential resources according to the information the hunters have gained on that and previous days. The manner in which such discussion is modelled is described below.

Each of the simulated hunting trips is modelled in this manner except for the first few (five was the number chosen in practice). The first days at the camp are considered to be different from the others since the hunters will have no information about the area and the availability of resources on which to form their assessments about which ungulates should be pursued if encountered. Consequently the simulation models the first hunting trips in the same way except that no kills are actually made. The hunters search, encounter, pursue in the same manner but do not actually make a kill. The imagined kills are used as their experience of that day on which to base their assessments. This models, therefore, an initial phase of information gathering rather than hunting activity. In the real world such information may be gained from moving to the site or may be carried over from the previous visit.

The collection of field-butchered resources and their consumption are not modelled. I assume that these are collected either at the end of the day, during the inactive days, which are not explicitly modelled, or at the end of the stay at the site – as at the Kongumuvuk Nunamiut site. The simulation assumes, however, that some part of each killed ungulate is returned to the camp and enters one accumulating midden. Consequently the model traces the formation of a faunal assemblage at the site resulting from the hunting activities of the foragers. If the foragers return to the site for another stay, the ungulates killed during this stay are also represented in the same assemblage and similarly for any further visits to the site. It is this simulated faunal assemblage that can be compared in terms of its species and age/sex composition with those from the real archaeological record.

Modelling the post-glacial resources

My model for the environment in which foraging takes place is developed from two main sources: first from the type of hunting process I am modelling, since this indicates the relevant ecological characteristics; Second by using Marks' (1976) material which describes the encounter foraging behaviour and the animal community of the Valley Bisa in quantitative terms. From these sources it is clear that this sub-model must be built by modelling each of the potential resources by five parameters:

1 utility;
2 probability of encounter;
3 pursuit time (minutes);
4 processing time (minutes);
5 probability of a successful kill.

The potential resources I will consider are the large ungulate species: red deer, roe deer, pig, auroch and elk. Smaller terrestrial animals are assumed to have been

Table 5.1. *Ecological characteristics of ungulates exploited by the Valley Bisa*

	Density[a]	Aggregation[b]	Speed[c]	Weight[d]
Impala	1.18	8.7	13	112.5
Zebra	0.89	9.15	14	525.0
Waterbuck	0.6	5.72	12	450.0
Warthog	0.42	2.08	10	153.0
Buffalo	1.29	30.0	7	1171.5

Notes:
[a] Density (animal/km²). From Marks 1976; Leuthold and Leuthold 1976. Laviern and Esser 1979.
[b] Mean aggregation size. From Marks 1976, tables 23, 25, 28, 30).
[c] Maximum running speed (M/Sec⁻¹). From Alexander *et al.* 1977.
[d] Mean adult weight (both sexes). From Marks 1976, appendix B.

Table 5.2. *Exploitation of ungulates by the Valley Bisa (from Marks 1976)*

	Mean stalk time (mins.)	No. of encounters	No. of stalks	No. of kills
Impala	7	197	72	2
Zebra	7	122	11	1
Waterbuck	11	54	29	3
Warthog	8	57	38	7
Buffalo	31	82	73	19

exploited by means other than encounter foraging (e.g. trapping). Each of these five species is separated into three age/sex classes: males, females and juveniles. Consequently there are fifteen separate types that require modelling. To aid in modelling these, I will use data from Marks (1976) and others, concerning the ecology and exploitation of east African ungulates by the Valley Bisa, the relevance of which will become apparent. While data on ungulates in the Boreal forest would be preferable, the east African data are all that are available at present in sufficient detail. To compensate for this I introduce certain parameters into the model which make appropriate adjustments to equations derived from this data for use when considering a forested environment. The east African ungulate and Valley Bisa data are given in Tables 5.1 and 5.2.

Utility
To model the utility of the ungulates I will consider this as a function of two types of materials they provide – meat and raw materials. The form of the function I will use is:

$$U_j = M_j NFV_j \qquad (1)$$

where:

U_j = utility of ungulate j

M_j = meat value of ungulate j

NFV_j = non-food value of ungulate j

M_j (meat value) is a function of body weight. The second term, NFV_j (non-food value) is similar to that used by Jochim (1976) and Keene (1981) and can be estimated by considering the provision of hide, antler and bone by each of the resources. Values of NFV_j just above 1 will increase the utility value, while those below 1 would decrease it. I will make all the NFV values between 1 and 2.

Meat weights can be estimated as a proportion of the total weight of the animal, and I will follow Jochim (1976) and Price (1978) in using 60%. Jochim discusses how the Mesolithic ungulates were substantially larger than their modern counterparts and provides estimates for the mean body weight of red deer, roe deer and pig. Estimates for aurochs and elk have been made by Bay-Petersen (1978). The body and meat weights are given in Table 5.4.

NFV values are more difficult to estimate. My method is to rank the ungulates in terms of each of the three raw materials and then use the equation $1 + (1/R_j)$ to derive NFV_j where R_j is the mean rank for resource j. This provides NFV values between 1 and 2.

Hides can be considered in relation to two variables, size and quality. The mean hide area can be estimated by the surface area of the ungulate which in turn can be estimated by the equation $S = KM_j^{0.67}$, where S equals the surface area, M_j is the body weight and K is a constant (Schmidt-Nielson 1984). A general approximation for mammals, which are of broadly cylindrical shape, is derived with a value of 10.0 for K. As is readily apparent, the ungulates' hide ranks will simply follow their weights, although the smaller ungulates are providing more hide per unit weight. Hide quality could relate to a very broad range of factors including thickness, softness, colour, patterning and suppleness. In the absence of quantitative data, the hide-quality rankings must be made on an intuitive basis. For this I will simply make the hides of auroch and pig as low quality, due to the toughness of the first and the coarseness of the second, and that of elk, red deer and roe deer as high quality. Now taking into account both quality and size the following hide ranking is adopted: male red deer and elk equal first, female red deer and elk equal third and all other equal fifth owing to their small size or poor quality.

Turning now to antler, the problem is slightly easier since it is only the male cervids that need considering. Roe deer antlers are very small and are considered not to have been particularly useful; the lack of roe deer antler tools supports this. Distinguishing between the value of male red deer and male elk antlers can be done with reference to the antler industries from sites with good preservation such as Star Carr (Clark 1954) and Ageröd I:HC (Larsson 1977). These suggest the greater use of red deer antler but there are inevitable problems because of the

Table 5.3. *Bone availability and waste at Ageröd I:HC (after Larsson 1977)*

Humerus	N[a]	W[b]	P[c]	Metacarpal	N	W	P
Auroch	6	0	0.0	Auroch	3	0	0.0
Elk	11	0	0.0	Elk	6	3	50.0
Red deer	71	2	2.8	Red deer	57	3	5.3
Roe deer	31	2	6.4	Roe deer	14	1	7.1
Pig	22	0	0.0	Pig	7	0	0.0
Femur				*Metatarsal*			
Auroch	7	0	0.0	Auroch	2	0	0.0
Elk	1	0	0.0	Elk	7	1	14.3
Red deer	45	1	2.2	Red deer	48	3	6.2
Roe deer	6	0	0.0	Roe deer	37	1	2.7
Pig	9	0	0.0	Pig	31	0	0.0
Tibia				*Cannon*			
Auroch	2	2	100.0	Auroch	3	0	0.0
Elk	7	3	42.0	Elk	13	3	23.0
Red deer	40	22	55.0	Red deer	75	3	4.0
Roe deer	3	0	0.0	Roe deer	5	1	20.0
Pig	44	0	0.0	Pig	3	0	0.0

Notes:
[a] N = Number of pieces on site.
[b] W = Number of pieces of manufacturing waste.
[c] P = W as percentage of N.

greater availability of red deer antler and the acquistion of shed antlers. However, a ranking must be made and I place male red deer first, male elk second, juvenile red deer and elk equal third, male roe deer fifth and all other ungulates in sixth place.

With respect to the value of the bone provided by the ungulates we can make a greater use of archaeological data. Larsson's (1977) detailed description of the bone industry from Ageröd I:HC provides quantitative data on the representation of bone types in the assemblage as well as the number of bone waste pieces from the manufacture of tools from five bone types and for all five ungulates. I will assume that the number of waste pieces measures the intensity of use and the number of bones the number that were available. Consequently we can calculate the percentages used of the different bone types and from these derive the rankings. Table 5.3 reproduces the data and calculates these percentages. This shows several interesting points. First, pig and roe deer bone are not used and are negligibly used respectively. Pig tusks and lower mandibles appear to have been used at other sites, however, which probably puts the value of the bones from these two species on an equal footing. Only the tibia of aurochs were used, but it appears that a high percentage of those available were made use of. In contrast all six bone types for the red deer were used but all of these at a fairly low level. Elk lies between auroch and red deer in that four of the six bone types were used, each at a medium level. Since Larsson's data are not further divided into age/sex classes I assume that the useful bones came from the adult animals only. Consequently the reasonable bone-utility

Table 5.4. *Utility estimates for post-glacial ungulates*

	Weight kg	Meat kg	Hide	Antler	Bone	NFV[a]	U[b]
Red deer							
Male	330	198.0	1	1	1	2.00	396.0
Female	180	108.0	3	1	6	1.30	140.4
Juvenile	100	60.0	5	3	7	1.20	72.0
Roe deer							
Male	43	25.8	5	5	10	1.15	29.7
Female	39	23.4	5	6	10	1.14	26.7
Juvenile	20	12.0	5	6	10	1.14	13.7
Pig							
Male	250	150.0	5	6	10	1.14	171.0
Female	150	90.0	5	6	10	1.14	102.6
Juvenile	50	30.0	5	6	10	1.14	34.2
Auroch							
Male	800	480.0	5	6	5	1.19	571.2
Female	600	360.0	5	6	5	1.19	428.4
Juvenile	150	90.0	5	6	7	1.17	105.3
Elk							
Male	500	300.0	1	2	1	1.75	525.0
Female	346	207.6	3	6	1	1.30	269.9
Juvenile	100	60.0	5	3	7	1.20	72.0

Notes:
[a] NFV = non-food value $(1 + (3/(Hide + Antler + Bone)))$, see pp. 114.
[b] Utility, see equation 1.

rankings appear to be as follows: male and female red deer and elk equal first, male and female auroch equal fifth, juvenile red deer, elk and auroch equal seventh and pigs and roe deer equal tenth.

Table 5.4 lists the rankings for each of the raw materials, derives the averages, then the NFV values and finally, using the meat weights, the utility values for each of the ungulates.

Probability of encounter
It can be proposed that the chance of encountering a species will be related to its population density and aggregation size, the former acting to increase and the latter to decrease this value (Jochim 1976). We can test this using data from Marks' (1976) study of the Valley Bisa since he provides data on all three of these variables. The first is expressed as an absolute number of encounters for each species within the time period of his study. If we regress the numbers of encounters linearly against the population density and the mean aggregation size (see Tables 5.1, 5.2) we derive a very significant relationship:

$$E = -46.4 + 256D - 6.74A$$
$$(r = 0.98, \text{df} = 2, t = 9.4, 0.001 > p > 0.01)$$

where:

E = number of encounters,

D = density, no./km²

A = mean group size

This equation can be used to derive relative encounter frequencies for Mesolithic ungulates, which can then be transformed into encounter probabilities. To do this we must first make estimates for their densities and mean group size. Density estimates have been made by Jochim (1976) and Bay-Petersen (1978) among others. Their approach is simply to draw together as many examples of modern density figures for the same species and then to use the average of these. One of the problems with this method concerns the large size of the early post-glacial animals as compared with their modern counterparts. This would have affected their densities. A better method is to use a quantitative relationship between body size and population density for primary consumers that has been derived from studies of modern populations. Damuth (1981) tested for this relationship using a sample of 307 species and found it to be very significant. For species living in Boreal or Sub-Alpine forest he provides the following equation:

$$\text{LogD} = -0.79(\text{LogW}) + 4.43$$
$$(r = 0.9, \ df = 10, \ t = 95, \ p < 0.001)$$

where:

D = density, no./km²

W = weight, grams

This can be used to predict the population density for the Mesolithic resources using the body weights I provided above, as in Table 5.5.

The mean aggregation sizes are more difficult to estimate. These vary throughout the year and according to the nature of the environment. In this model, I will be making only one estimate and am forced to ignore seasonal variation in group size. This is a pragmatic stance, since we need to start with simple models. It is also one that believes undue emphasis has been put on seasonal fluctuations in ungulate ecology to explain age/sex structure of faunal assemblages in recent work (e.g. see p. 187). Legge and Rowley-Conwy (1988) discuss group size, arguing that Jochim's (1976) estimates are too large because his modern analogies come predominantly from open rather than wooded environments, in which group sizes tend to be small. To amend this situation they provide data from ecological studies of woodland red deer populations. From these data, mean group sizes of 1.3 and 4.95 for stag and hind/juvenile group sizes respectively can be derived. Similarly, in relation to auroch, they provide data for American bison living in forests and refer to studies of European bison in the Bialowieza forest forming female/juvenile groups of 15–18 and male groups of 1–3. From these data I use an estimate of 18 female/juvenile and 1.5 male mean group sizes for auroch. Legge and Rowley-Conwy (1988) suggest that group size for roe deer should be very small, quoting modern estimates for their maximum size. I use estimates of 1 for males and 2 for

Table 5.5. *Probabilities for encountering post-glacial ungulates*

	Density, no./km²	Aggregation	PE[a]
Red deer			
Male	1.17	1.3	0.00231
Female	1.90	4.9	0.00384
Juvenile	3.02	4.9	0.00655
Roe deer			
Male	5.88	1.0	0.0137
Female	6.35	2.0	0.0148
Juvenile	10.77	2.0	0.0255
Pig			
Male	1.46	1.5	0.003
Female	2.19	15.0	0.0039
Juvenile	5.22	15.0	0.0112
Auroch			
Male	0.58	1.5	0.00087
Female	0.73	18.0	0.00018
Juvenile	2.19	18.0	0.00037
Elk			
Male	0.85	2.0	0.00149
Female	1.13	2.0	0.00216
Juvenile	3.02	2.0	0.00674

Note:
[a] PE = Probability of encounter, see equation 2, SF = 0.1, PF = 0.0, Day = 1

females and juveniles. Elk are predominantly solitary or live in small groups and have been discussed with reference to hunting by Zvelebil (1981) in particular. My group size estimates are the same as those for roe deer. Male wild pigs are usually solitary. Females form groups of 2 or more with their young, except during the rut and birth when they are solitary. Since mean litter size is 5 animals I use a mean female/juvenile group size of 15 and a male group size of 1.5.

Using these estimates for density and aggregation, the above equation from Marks' data can be used to derive relative encounter frequencies. However, these must be transformed to encounter probabilities. To do this I make an estimate for the frequency with which any one of the resources may be encountered, e.g. one every 10 minutes, or one every 50 minutes, in which case the probability for encounter in 1 minute will be 0.1 and 0.02. This value is then divided up in proportions according to the relative encounter frequencies derived above. The resulting figures are given in Table 5.5. Consequently one model parameter that must be estimated is the overall frequency of encounter which I will call SF.

These encounter probabilities are for resources in an unexploited environment. As animals are killed densities will be reduced, resulting in a decrease in encounter frequencies. However the killing of animals is not the only reason for their becoming scarcer and hence for a reduction in their encounter probabilities. Even the hunters' presence in the area, and the ensuing noise, smells and disturbance they make, will scare game away. Consequently to model this we need a component in the model to reduce game densities with time. This can be done with a simple algorithm that reduces the encounter probabilities in an exponential manner over time. The complete equation for modelling the encounter probabilities has the form:

$$PE_{jd} = \frac{E_{jd}}{\sum\limits_{j} E_{j1}}(SF)(e^{PF\ D}) \tag{2}$$

where:

PE_{jd} = probability of encountering jth
          ungulate on the dth day
D   = day/hunting-trip number
SF = model constant, $1 > SF > 0$
PF = model constant, $1 > PF > 0$
E_{ji} = $-46.4 + 256D_{ji} - 6.74A_j$
     where:
     D_{ji} = density of jth ungulate on day i,
     A_j = mean aggregation size of ungulate j.

The parameter PF controls the rate of decrease of the probability of encounter with time and is therefore a second one to estimate when making a simulation run. If the hunters return to the site for further hunting, the game densities are assumed to have returned to their initial unexploited and undisturbed values.

Pursuit times
Marks' (1976) data on the stalking times by the Valley Bisa for the five east African ungulates have two features. First, the time for any one species varies very widely, for instance waterbuck varies between 2 and 25 minutes with a mean of 11 and warthog between 2 and 15 with a mean of 8. Secondly there does not appear to be any simple relationship between the mean times and the ecological characteristics of the species. However, the mean stalk time for buffalo, the largest resource by far, is substantially larger than that for the others, at 31 minutes. Consequently there may be a gross relationship with weight affecting the very largest species. Stalk times in the post-glacial forest may have been greater or smaller than these. I assume the former since the lack of visibility and the use of guns by the Valley Bisa allow hunters to strike from further away. I assume a mean stalk time of 30 minutes for all resources, except for the two largest, adult aurochs, which I give a time of 60 minutes (Table 5.6).

We also need to consider the energy cost per minute of pursuit time for a forager stalking an animal. I consider the energy expended to be equivalent to that involved in walking very quickly, which Pyke (1970) estimates at 570 Kcal hr^{-1}, or 9.5 Kcal min^{-1}. In contrast I consider the cost of searching to be equivalent to that of walking, 185 Kcal hr^{-1}, or 3.0 Kcal min^{-1}. This value is also used for the cost of

Table 5.6. *Risk, pursuit and processing values for post-glacial ungulates*

	Speed M/Sec^{-1}	Risk[a]	Pursuit time, mins.	Processing[b] time, mins.
Red deer				
Male	12.00	0.054	30	29
Female	10.82	0.072	30	20
Juvenile	9.80	0.087	30	14
Roe deer				
Male	8.48	0.107	30	9
Female	8.35	0.109	30	8
Juvenile	7.45	0.123	30	6
Pig				
Male	11.45	0.062	30	25
Female	10.49	0.077	30	18
Juvenile	8.71	0.104	30	10
Auroch				
Male	13.95	0.025	60	48
Female	13.28	0.035	60	41
Juvenile	10.49	0.077	30	18
Elk				
Male	12.88	0.041	30	37
Female	12.08	0.053	30	30
Juvenile	9.80	0.087	30	14

Notes:
[a] Probability of making a successful kill following a stalk. $R_j/100$, see equation 3, RF = 0.5.
[b] Field butchering time, see equation 4.

being in the passive state when foraging tasks such as the collection of field-butchered game and the maintenance of equipment may be carried out.

Risk

The chance of a successful kill once a stalk has been initiated may be small. Noe-Nygaard's (1974) data discussed above, suggest a high degree of hunting failure in Mesolithic Denmark. The Valley Bisa data (Table 5.2) suggest that the extent of hunting failure varies markedly between species.

As Torrence (1989c) argues, the chance of successfully killing an animal, which I shall here refer to as its risk, is highly dependent upon the technology used. The general level of risk across all species may be altered by adopting one type of technology as opposed to another, such as shot-guns rather than bows and arrows. As I will expand upon below (p. 190) the risk of one particular type of animal may be reduced by using a specific type of tool, which is only effective for that species. I will focus on deriving relative levels of risk for ungulates when hunted with the same technology.

As before, I turn to the work of Marks (1976). He provides data concerning the number of stalks, and the number which were successful for the five east African ungulates exploited by the Valley Bisa. From these we can calculate the percentage of successful stalks for each species and refer to this as its risk. I have explored the relationship between these risks and the various ecological characteristics of the species such as density and body size. The best predictor of the risk is simply the maximum running speed of the ungulate which provides the linear relationship:

$R_j = 47.0 - 3.01 S_j$
($r = 0.92$, $df = 3$, $t = 19.1$, $p < 0.001$)
where:
R_j = percentage successful stalks of ungulate j
S_j = speed of ungulate j

We can use this to model the risk of the Mesolithic ungulates once estimates for their running speed have been made. These can be derived from a relationship between speed and body weight as described by Schmidt-Nielson (1984). There are problems in such relationships because of different running gaits and the actual attribute of speed that is being measured. However he quotes two independent studies which reach similar conclusions and provides the relationship: Speed = $KM^{0.17}$, where K is a constant and M is body weight. If we assume red deer to have the same running speed as waterbuck, owing to their similar size, of 12 m per second, then we can derive a constant value of 4.477. Using this and the above relationship we can derive the risk for the Mesolithic ungulates. These values would, however, assume use of the same technology and conditions as the Valley Bisa. Success rates in the post-glacial forest may have been generally higher or lower than in the shrubby savanna of Zambia. The forest would have provided more cover, the bows and arrows and spears would have been quieter than shot-guns, stalking may be easier because the vegetation carries more signs. However, the arrows may have had a smaller chance than a bullet of killing when striking the animal, although the Valley Bisa guns were fairly primitive. To resolve this problem I introduce a third parameter, RF, which takes values between 1 and 0 to increase the level of risk of the Mesolithic ungulates. Consequently the final equation has the form:

$$R_j = [47.0 - 3.01(4.477 M_j^{0.17})] \, RF \qquad (3)$$

where:
R_j = percentage successful stalks of ungulate j
M_j = body weight of ungulate j
RF = risk factor, $1 \geqslant R > 0$

Risk values when RF = 0.5 are given in Table 5.6.

Processing time
There are very limited ethnographic and experimental data on processing times for different types of ungulates. The only data available are from Binford (*pers. comm.*), that on average it takes 19 minutes to field butcher a 350 lb (159 kg) animal

without metal knives. In addition he states that there is an exponential relationship between processing time and body weight. The smallest ungulates in this study, roe deer, would not have needed field butchering and could have been carried whole. From this information a relationship can be proposed:

$$\mathrm{Pro_j} = \mathrm{W_j}^{0.58} \tag{4}$$

where:
$\mathrm{Pro_j}$ = processing time of ungulate j
$\mathrm{W_j}$ = bodyweight of ungulate j

This appears to be an appropriate model. It gives processing times ranging from 6 minutes for a young roe deer, sufficient to pick it up, to 48 minutes for field butchering an adult auroch. These processing times, and the values for the risk and pursuit attributes are given in Table 5.6. I consider the cost of processing, of cutting hide, flesh, tendons and possibly bone to be equivalent to that of sawing wood, which Pyke (1970) estimates as 420 Kcal hr^{-1}, or 7 Kcal min^{-1}.

Modelling decision making

Having described models for the post-glacial environment and the hunting process I now turn to the central issue: modelling the decision making itself. Here I draw upon the eco-psychological model and that of the hunting process itself since these define what sources of information are available to the forager. To reiterate, we are concerned with the low-level decision of prey choice among randomly encountered ungulates: should an animal be stalked and an attempt to kill it made, or should it be passed by and searching continued. Specifically I want to define a probability that the hunter will choose to stalk (which I refer to as the stalk probability). This is essentially defined by comparing the estimate of current foraging efficiency with that estimated to be gained from choosing to stalk the encountered animal.

First let us consider the information sources available to the forager. Since we are dealing with prey choice and random encounter, searching and sampling have no role to play (although the prey choices themselves may be thought of as sampling the patch in relation to higher-level decisions of patch choice). The cues that I am concerned with are those that identify that a stalk is possible: the sight of an animal itself, or a sign such as hoof prints. These cues provide the forager with information as to the species of animal encountered, its age and sex. My main interest, however, must be with the use of other individuals and past experience as information sources. The first of these occurs during the 'discussion' and 'story-telling' period at the end of each day. Here each individual acquires information from his colleagues as to their estimates for the worth of stalking each game type if encountered the following day. Different weights are placed upon the information from different hunters according to their past hunting success. The estimates made by each individual are derived from their past experience in foraging in that patch. Here, therefore, I am concerned with 'stored information' in terms of the efficiency of exploiting different game types and 'acquired information' in terms of estimates of current foraging efficiency.

Turning now to the meta-decision of goal choice, I wish to explore a series of goals and investigate their relationship with patterning in the archaeological record. We cannot infer the goals directly from the archaeological record, as we can the information sources used by reference to the hunting process, and hence must use the model and simulation I am building as a methodological tool for this end. Clearly some initial assumptions must be made about the types of goals that may be adopted. Consequently, following my discussion of meliorising in Chapter 2, I will focus on two goals, utility increasing (UI) and risk reducing (RR). I assume that these exist in a hierarchical arrangement with the hunters primarily adopting the UI goal, that is they are attempting to increase their rate of utility gain while foraging in the patch. To this may be added a shorter-term goal of RR operating in relation to a single day. That is, the foragers may (meta-)choose to add a risk-reducing element to their goals to ensure that sufficient food is acquired for one particular day. Hence stalk probabilities for particular game types that were low or zero owing to the UI goal, since those species are inefficient to exploit, may increase in value towards the end of the day. My aim is to investigate whether the Mesolithic foragers used only UI goals, or added an RR element. To construct a reasonable model I need to add a further element of satisficing (S). Once sufficient utility has been gained on a particular day the forager may reduce stalk probabilities since no more hunting is desired. As I discussed above, it is not appropriate to consider satisficing as a goal and I simply adopt it as a constraint upon the hunter. I will refer to these two goals as UIS (utility increasing and satisficing) and UISR (utility increasing, satisficing and risk reducing). I also need to consider one more type of 'goal', or rather what I will refer to as the NULL goal which simply states 'stalk every encountered resource'.

Having defined the information sources and discussed possible goals, I now turn to the information-processing methods. Following the eco-psychological model, these will have a mix of computation and rule of thumb (ROT). During the period of information exchange I model the individual as computing a consensus of the views as to which resources are profitable to stalk from the UI perspective. By this the stalk probabilities are defined for the first minute of the following day. During that day, however, stalk probabilities will be adjusted in relation to the RR goal (if present) and the S constraint. I will assume that simple rules of thumb are used here, since the forager does not have the stimulus of other individuals for information retrieval. If the forager has a risk-reducing element he will increase stalk probabilities towards the end of the day and the ROT for this simply makes use of the time elapsed since hunting began (and hence how much remains). Similarly, the ROT for the satisficing element makes use of the amount of utility gained from kills so far made on that day. These rules involve meta-decisions which concern the rate at which stalk probabilities either increase or decrease, as will be evident below, but I will not model these explicitly.

From this discussion we can begin to develop the mathematical model by formalising these factors relating to the critical decision, whether or not to stalk an encountered ungulate.

First we can define:

$Prob_{ijtd}$ = The probability that the ith individual will stalk the jth ungulate if encountered during the tth minute of the dth day.

$1 \geqslant Prob_{ijtd} \geqslant 0$

This is partly, or totally, determined by the individual's long-term experience. We can therefore define:

F_{ijd} = The probability that the ith individual will stalk the jth ungulate if encountered on the dth day, using information from his own past experience.

$1 \geqslant F_{ijd} \geqslant 0$

The manner in which F_{ijd} is defined, i.e. what information is processed and how this is done, will depend on the goal adopted. Since past experiences are exchanged we can define:

X_{ikjd} = The influence of the long-term experience of the kth individual over the ith individual concerning the jth ungulate on the dth day.

With the constraints that:

$0 \geqslant X_{ikjd} \geqslant 1.0;$

$$\sum_{k=1}^{m} X_{ikjd} = 1.0;$$

where: m = no. of hunters in the group

Consequently the probability for individual i to stalk an encountered ungulate on day d, using his own and others past experience is:

$$Prob_{ijtd} = \sum_{k=1}^{m} X_{ikjd} F_{kjd}$$

It will lie between 0 and 1. This constitutes the model for the UI decision goal.

Turning now to the influence of short-term experience, I wish to model the first factor, the increase in probabilities due to decreasing time (RR goal), as an additive component. I define:

A_{it} = increase in probability that the ith individual will stalk ungulates if encountered due to the value of t

consequently the model now has the form:

$$Prob_{ijtd} = \left(\sum_{k=1}^{m} X_{ikjd} F_{kjd} + A_{it} \right)$$

with the constraint that:

$1.0 \geqslant Prob_{ijtd} \geqslant 0.0$

This constitutes a UIR decision goal model. The second factor of short-term experience, the reduction in probabilities due to the utility already gained will be introduced as a multiplicative component. Hence I define:

E_{it} = proportional decrease in stalk probabilities for the ith individual due to the utility gained up to the tth minute

with the constraint that:

$1.0 \geqslant E_{it} \geqslant 0.0$

consequently the model now has the form:

$$\text{Prob}_{ijtd} = \left(\sum_{k=1}^{m} X_{ikjd} F_{kjd} + A_{it} \right) E_{it} \tag{5}$$

with the constraint that:

$1.0 \geqslant \text{Prob}_{ijtd} \geqslant 0.0$

This constitutes the UISR decision goal model. Removal of the A_{it} parameter reduces this to a UIS goal model. I will now turn to describing how the four elements of this equation can be modelled.

Past experience as an information source

The fundamental character of this component (F_{ijd}) rests upon the idea that to achieve their goals the foragers must make estimates of their expected foraging efficiency, based on their past experience, and the efficiency of stalking the different ungulates. Consequently there is an information component to this rule, the way in which these estimates are arrived at, and a decision aspect, the way they are used to make the decision. The first step is to differentiate between 'stored' and 'acquired' types of information. The estimate of current foraging efficiency will be acquired information since this will change from day to day and hence must be regularly updated. In contrast the mean estimate of the return to be gained from stalking an encountered ungulate may be considered to be stored information, under conditions of stable environment and technology, since this will be approximately the same each time a stalk is made. From this basis I will begin by describing the long-term utility increasing goal (UI).

The payoff from a successful kill of an ungulate can be modelled as in the optimal diet breadth model as:

$P_j = U_j / (C_s \text{Pur}_j + C_b \text{Pro}_j)$

where:

P_j = payoff from killing ungulate j
U_j = utility of ungulate j
Pur_j = pursuit time of ungulate j
Pro_j = processing time of ungulate j
C_s = cost per minute pursuit
C_b = cost per minute processing

However, since not every kill will be successful the expected payoff from choosing to stalk an encountered ungulate will be:

$$AP_j = \frac{U_j PS_j}{C_s Pur_j + (PS_j C_b Pro_j)} \qquad (6)$$

where:

AP_j = expected payoff from stalking ungulate j,
PS_j = probability of killing ungulate j, $(= R_{j/100})$

This reduces the utility gain and the processing time by the proportion of kills that are successful. It leaves the pursuit time alone since all stalked ungulates are by definition pursued, whether successfully or not. I will assume that the hunter stores the AP_j values for each ungulate.

If we now turn to the expected return from foraging in general this consists of acquired information and must be updated each day. I will model this simply as a weighted average of the previous days' foraging efficiency. On one single day the efficiency will be:

$$TP_{id} = TU_{id}/TC_{id}$$

where:

TP_{id} = payoff gained by the ith individual on the dth day
TU_{id} = utility gained by the ith individual on the dth day
TC_{id} = cost of foraging by the ith individual on the dth day

where:

$$TC_{id} = [C_l S_{id} + C_s Pu_{id} + C_b Po_{id}]$$
C_l = cost per minute searching or passive
C_s = cost per minute pursuit
C_b = cost per minute processing
S_{id} = minutes spent searching or passive
Pu_{id} = minutes spent pursuing
Po_{id} = minutes spent processing

Now if the expected foraging efficiency was modelled simply as an average of the previous days' efficiency, this would result in a model of the form:

$$ETP_{id} = \frac{\sum_{c=1}^{d-1} TU_{ic}}{\sum_{c=1}^{d-1} TC_{ic}}$$

The unsatisfactory nature of this can be realised when one appreciates the changing nature of the environment. The general efficiency may be either increasing from day to day, as a result of learning about the environment, or decreasing as a result of depletion of resources. Whatever trend there is, and even if there is no trend, the meliorising hunter will be wanting to improve on the more recent days' efficiency rather than the more distant, that is the more recent days' activity and experience will play a greater role in determining the expected efficiency. In addition there may be biological constraints which prevent the perfect recall of previous days' experience. Consequently a more useful model is one that uses a weighted average of the following form:

$$ETP_{id} = \frac{\sum_{c=1}^{d-1} A^{d-c-1} TU_{ic}}{\sum_{c=1}^{d-1} A^{d-c-1} TC_{ic}} \tag{7}$$

where:

A = Attention factor, $0 > A > 1$

The form of the weighting is taken from Harley's (1981) RPS learning rule (see Chapter 3). 'A' is simply an attention factor which takes a value between 0 and 1. At the extreme value of 1, the equation returns to the non-weighted form and the expected efficiency is derived from all previous days equally. A value less than 1, however, puts greater weight on recent days, and as it approaches 0 the expected efficiency is increasingly a function of the most recent days' experience. Consequently if, for instance, there is a falling rate of returns and the attention factor has a value less than 1, the expected efficiency will be less than the average, whereas if efficiency was increasing that expected will be greater than the average. Note that this does not allow the identification of a trend. If efficiencies were decreasing in a regular fashion then the expectation may in reality be a continuation of this trend and a value less than that of the previous day.

Having now defined the informational components of past-experience component, F_{ijd}, we can turn to the decision part. Since I am assuming a meliorising strategy the model will simply state that if the expected payoff from stalking a resource is greater than the expected payoff from foraging in general, the forager will choose to stalk the resource. Mathematically:

$$F_{ijd} \begin{cases} 1 \text{ IF } AP_j > ETP_{id} \\ 0 \text{ otherwise} \end{cases} \tag{8}$$

We can note here that this rule follows a similar criterion to that in the optimal diet breadth model in which any resource which provides a payoff greater than that from foraging in general should be taken.

Other individuals as information sources

The second component of the UI model concerns the exchange of information; the influence of each individual's past experience upon others. There are, as with the other components, several ways to model this; I will use one of the simplest. This involves the assumption that the influence of one member of the group is the same over all other members, and over himself, and is the same for all resources. Hence rather than considering the parameter, X_{ikjd}, we need only consider the parameter X_{kd}.

My model states that the influence of each individual will depend upon his previous success as a hunter, as compared with that of the other individuals. We can use the relative amount of utility provided by the forager, averaged over the previous days' foraging. Hence:

$$X_{kd} = \frac{\sum\limits_{c=1}^{d-1} TU_{kc}}{\sum\limits_{k=1}^{m} \sum\limits_{c=1}^{d-1} TU_{kc}}$$

m = number of hunters in the group

As before, however, a weighted average may be more appropriate. A hunter who was very successful early on may not necessarily be as rapid a learner as the other hunters and consequently his initial high influence should be weighted against later on. We can thus use the attention factor again and define:

$$X_{kd} = \frac{\sum\limits_{c=1}^{d-1} A^{d-c-1} TU_{kc}}{\sum\limits_{k=1}^{m} \sum\limits_{c=1}^{d-1} A^{d-c-1} TU_{kc}} \tag{9}$$

In this manner all the influences will sum to 1. Since in this model the influence of one hunter does not vary between the other hunters, at the start of the day, that is before the 'particular circumstances' arise, each hunter will have the same probabilities for stalking each of the resources. This is defined by the value:

$$Prob_{ijd} = \sum\limits_{k=1}^{m} X_{kd} F_{kjd}$$

Note, however, that because the F_{kjd} values (1 or 0) for each resource may differ between the individuals, owing to their own personal previous experience, the probabilities for certain species after this 'discussion' has taken place may lie between 0 and 1, not necessarily at one of these extremes. This means that upon encounter the forager may sometimes choose to stalk these ungulates, and sometimes ignore them.

Considerably more sophisticated models of information exchange could be constructed in which the influence of any individual varies for different members of the group. In that case a consensus-reaching model such as described by De Groot (1974) would be appropriate.

The use of 'rules of thumb'
I now move to consider the influence of short-term experience, the gain and processing of information when the individual is by himself during the day. Above, I described two types of circumstances which will affect the forager's assessment of the worth of pursuing different resources.

The first factor relates to the amount of time left for foraging. Since I am assuming there is a limited amount of time available each day, there may be an increase in the probabilities for stalking encountered ungulates as time passes, as a result of the decreased chance of encountering others. This will occur if the forager has a short-term risk-reducing (RR) goal. The role of this factor can be appreciated if we consider the last minute of the day. If an ungulate is encountered in that minute there will be no chance to encounter another if it is passed up and consequently the probability for stalking it will be one, given that no kills have already been made on that day. Early in the day, on the other hand, it would be appropriate that the encounter has little influence over the stalk probabilities. Consequently we can develop the model in the following manner:

$$\text{Prob}_{ijtd} = \sum_{k=1}^{m} X_{kd} F_{kjd} + A_{it}$$

where:

$$A_{it} = \left(1 - \sum_{k=1}^{m} X_{kd} F_{kjd}\right)\left(h^t / h^{tmax}\right) \qquad (10)$$

t $= 1,2 \ldots$ tmax
tmax $=$ total number of minutes available for foraging in day d
h $=$ model constant, $h > 1$

The model now states that at the start of the day, $t = 0$, the probability for taking an encountered resource is solely defined by the long-term experience, since $A_{it} = 0.0$. As t increases, and there is less time to encounter other resources, A_{itd} will increase in an exponential manner. At tmax, the last minute of the day and after which no other resources can be encountered, $A_{it} = 1 - \sum_{k=1}^{m} X_{kd} F_{kjd}$ and consequently $\text{Prob}_{ijtd} = 1.0$. Figure 5.2a illustrates the pattern of increase in probabilities during the day with two different values of the model constant h and with a starting stalk probability of 0.5. Of course if $\sum_{k=1}^{m} X_{kd} F_{kjd} = 1$ when $t = 1$, then A_{it} will always remain at 0.

The second factor of short-term experience is how stalk probabilities decrease in relation to the value of resources already exploited (S). This is required for two reasons. First the hunter will have a constraint on the amount of material that can be carried back to the camp and further processed there, if indeed they are collected in this manner. Second, it must be recognised that foraging is only one of the activities to be accomplished by an individual and consequently there may be a short-term satisficing element interacting with the long-term goals. It is a satisfaction that the meliorising goal has been reached, however, rather than a satisficing goal in itself. Once the long-term goal has been sufficiently achieved on one day the hunter may invest his time in the other essential activities such as tool manufacture and social visiting. Consequently we need a component in the model to decrease the stalk probabilities as kills are made. We can introduce this in the following manner. The model now has the form:

$$\text{Prob}_{ijtd} = \left(\sum_{k=1}^{m} X_{kd} F_{kjd} + A_{it} \right) E_{it} \tag{11}$$

where:

$$E_{it} = \exp \left(-q \sum_{c=1}^{t} TU_{icd} \right)$$

q = Model Constant, $1 > q > 0$

TU_{icd} = utility gained by the individual[ith] at the Cth minute on the dth day

This reduces the stalk probabilities for all ungulates by an equal rate. As with the previous component it uses a model constant, q, to determine the rate of decrease. The hypothetical graphs in Fig. 5.2b show the changes in exploitation probabilities with an initial value of 0.5, an h parameter of 1.02, utility gains of 200 and 500 units at $t = 100$ and $t = 250$ respectively, and two alternative q values of 0.001 and 0.005. As is evident, the larger value of q leads the forager to reduce his exploitation probabilities by a larger amount for the same kill than does a smaller q value. As I discussed above, the simulation model considers that if all exploitation stalk probabilities fall below a critical threshold then the forager is no longer considered to be motivated for hunting and enters a passive state.

The graphs in Fig. 5.2b illustrate the conflict between the role of the two short-term experience components. One works to increase and the other to decrease the stalk probabilities within the same day. In this the model begins to capture the often conflicting pieces of information and the need to reach a compromise between them when decisions are taken.

The simulation model (MESO-SIM)

I have now described the manner in which I model the hunting process, the post-glacial environment and the taking of decisions. These three elements are combined into one simulation model which is summarised in the flow chart, Fig. 5.3.

The input data that the simulation takes are values for three ecological characteristics of the ungulates: their body size, aggregation and NFV. However, values must be assigned to twelve different model parameters, all of which have been referred to in the above text. These are summarised in Table 5.7 along with the values I have used in the majority of runs described in the next chapter. Each time

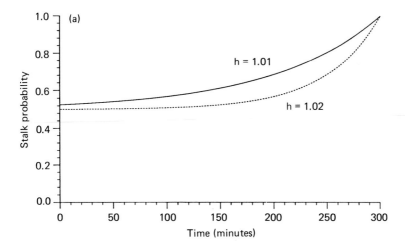

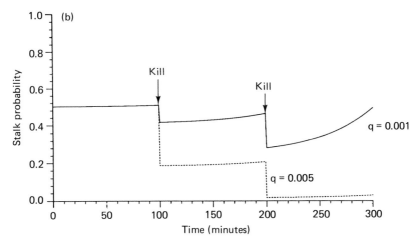

Fig. 5.2 (a) Increase of stalk probabilities with time owing to risk-reducing goal and (b) increase and decrease of stalk probabilities with time owing to interaction between risk-reducing goal and satisficing.

the simulation is run one single faunal assemblage is created, the characteristics of which are defined by the set of values given to these parameters.

A few comments are necessary. The SF, PF and RF parameters have two alternative values assigned to them, a low and a high value. The three low ones together define a relatively 'poor' environment in which game is scarce, easily scared away and difficult to kill. High values define a relatively 'rich' environment with the opposite characteristics. By varying one or more of these between runs we are exploring variability in the local environment as opposed to different global environments which have different sets of animal species inhabiting them. The ability to explore such variability in the local environment is important since we cannot confidently put particular values on game richness, scare rates and ease of

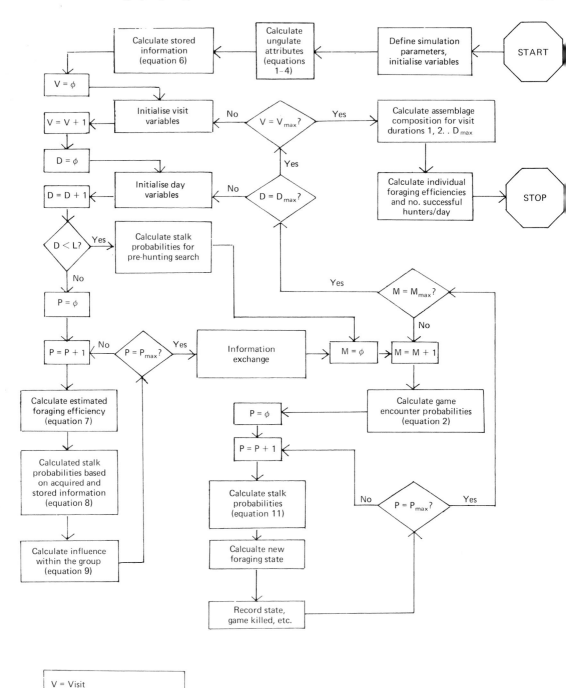

Fig. 5.3. Flow chart for MESO-SIM.

Table 5.7. *Parameters for MESO-SIM*

Parameter	Role	Values used
Goal	The hunting goal used by the hunters	UIS, UISR, NULL
RNG	Seed for the random number generator	Chosen from a 1 . . 1,000 uniform distribution
NoPers	Number of hunters in the group	3, 6, 9
NoVisits	Number of visits made to the same site	5
NoHunts[a]	Number of days spent hunting on each visit	1,2,3 . . . 20
NoMins	Number of minutes available for each hunt	300
SF	Probability of game encounter/minute (see equation 2)	0.1, 0.25
RF	Risk factor (see equation3)	0.5, 1.0
PF	Rate at which game is scared away (see equation 2)	-0.0075, -0.002
A	Attention paid to past experience (see equations 7 and 9)	0.8
h	Rate at which stalk probabilities increase with time (see equation 10)	1.02
q	Rate at which stalk probabilities decrease with utility gain (see equation 11)	0.005

Note:
[a]Plus an additional 5 days of pre-hunting Search.

killing and no doubt these would have varied within the regions we are considering. Hence, when I explore different hunting goals I will pursue this in the total range of different local environments allowed by giving each parameter two values.

The value of 0.8 assigned to the attention parameter also requires a brief comment. This is simply a translation of the qualitative decision-making model in Chapters 2 and 3 into quantitative terms. Since in this foraging problem it is safe to assume that past experience will be used as an information source, we would want to put a relatively high value on this parameter (e.g. >0.7). However, since information recall is imperfect and more recent experience will be of greater relevance for the next day's foraging, a very high value (e.g. >0.9) seems inappropriate. Consequently 0.8 provides a reasonable value. Of course the weighting given to previous days' experience is a meta-decision and individuals may choose to ignore it absolutely (i.e. A = 0.0). Elsewhere (Mithen 1988a) I have explored the effect on foraging efficiency of different A values suggesting that 0.8 is indeed the sort of value which may be chosen by meta-decision processes.

The values assigned to other parameters are done on an *a priori* basis. Of course the different values and combinations are infinite and my choices are made specific to the problems I am exploring.

Let us reflect for one moment upon the nature of this simulation model. At its centre is the simple situation I referred to above; the lone hunter taking decisions about which game to hunt – we have here Ingold's 'hunter and his spear', with which I started this case study. We model the manner in which a hunter acquires and processes information and are to investigate the foraging choices he makes when operating under different decision goals. This hunter is in a social context by his interactions with other hunters, in an ecological context by his interaction with the game and in a historical context by the passage of (simulated) time. With the assumptions about midden formation we move from individuals and a short time frame to the archaeological record – a conglomeration of the results of foraging by all the hunters accumulated over the long term. Hence this simulation model meets the methodological challenge posed in Chapter 1.

To conclude this chapter I want to emphasise the differences between the three hunting goals I will be simulating (NULL, UIS and UISR) and provide a short demonstration of how the simulation runs. For this, we can look in detail at three simulated hunting trips, each by a group of three foragers who all possess one of the three goals. For these demonstration runs I use the parameter set referred to in the next chapter as Test Run A, Table 6.3. Tables 5.8, 5.9 and 5.10 describe the tenth hunting trip made on the first visit to a settlement giving the state of each hunter at each minute, for the NULL, UIS and UISR hunters respectively.

As can be seen from Table 5.8, the NULL goal foragers are stalking every single ungulate that they encounter. Only one of the hunters, no. 1, has any success when the attempted kill is made. He manages to kill a juvenile roe deer almost at the end of the hunting trip.

A very different hunting pattern is apparent from Table 5.9 which describes UIS goal hunters. Here we see great selectivity concerning which ungulates are stalked following encounters. As modelled by the UIS goal, the hunters are choosing only those animals which they believe will maintain or improve their current foraging efficiency. Consequently hunter no. 1 makes a total of sixteen encounters but chooses to stalk none of these since he estimates the returns would not be sufficient. Hunter no. 2 chooses to stalk a female red deer and a female wild boar, though failing to kill either, while the third hunter stalks and successfully kills a male red deer.

Table 5.10 describes hunting by foragers with UISR goal. We see here a pattern that lies between that from the NULL and UIS goals. The UISR hunters start by being selective as to which animals they stalk following an encounter, essentially acting as UIS hunters. For instance hunter no. 3 ignores opportunities to stalk roe deer but does choose to stalk a female red deer and a male wild boar. Under this goal, there is a small chance that low-ranking resources will be stalked early on and

Table 5.8. *Sample day's foraging (test run A, visit 1, day 10) for foragers with NULL goals*

	Hunter 1		Hunter 2		Hunter 3	
Minute	State	Species[a]	State	Species	State	Species
1	searching		searching		searching	
2	searching		encountering	(9)	searching	
3	searching		stalking	(9)	searching	
4	searching		stalking	(9)	searching	
5	searching		stalking	(9)	encountering	(6)
6	searching		stalking	(9)	stalking	(6)
7	searching		stalking	(9)	stalking	(6)
8	searching		stalking	(9)	stalking	(6)
9	searching		stalking	(9)	stalking	(6)
10	searching		stalking	(9)	stalking	(6)
11	searching		stalking	(9)	stalking	(6)
12	searching		stalking	(9)	stalking	(6)
13	searching		stalking	(9)	stalking	(6)
14	searching		stalking	(9)	stalking	(6)
15	searching		stalking	(9)	stalking	(6)
16	searching		stalking	(9)	stalking	(6)
17	searching		stalking	(9)	stalking	(6)
18	searching		stalking	(9)	stalking	(6)
19	searching		stalking	(9)	stalking	(6)
20	searching		stalking	(9)	stalking	(6)
21	searching		stalking	(9)	stalking	(6)
22	searching		stalking	(9)	stalking	(6)
23	searching		stalking	(9)	stalking	(6)
24	searching		stalking	(9)	stalking	(6)
25	searching		stalking	(9)	stalking	(6)
26	searching		stalking	(9)	stalking	(6)
27	searching		stalking	(9)	stalking	(6)
28	searching		stalking	(9)	stalking	(6)
29	searching		stalking	(9)	stalking	(6)
30	searching		stalking	(9)	stalking	(6)
31	searching		stalking	(9)	stalking	(6)
32	searching		stalking	(9)	stalking	(6)
33	searching		killing	(9)	stalking	(6)
34	searching		searching		stalking	(6)
35	searching		searching		stalking	(6)
36	searching		searching		killing	(6)
37	searching		encountering	(5)	searching	
38	searching		stalking	(5)	searching	
39	searching		stalking	(5)	searching	
40	searching		stalking	(5)	searching	
41	searching		stalking	(5)	searching	
42	searching		stalking	(5)	searching	
43	searching		stalking	(5)	searching	
44	searching		stalking	(5)	searching	
45	encountering	(9)	stalking	(5)	searching	
46	stalking	(9)	stalking	(5)	searching	
47	stalking	(9)	stalking	(5)	searching	
48	stalking	(9)	stalking	(5)	searching	
49	stalking	(9)	stalking	(5)	searching	
50	stalking	(9)	stalking	(5)	searching	
51	stalking	(9)	stalking	(5)	searching	
52	stalking	(9)	stalking	(5)	searching	
53	stalking	(9)	stalking	(5)	searching	
54	stalking	(9)	stalking	(5)	searching	
55	stalking	(9)	stalking	(5)	searching	
56	stalking	(9)	stalking	(5)	searching	

Table 5.8. (*cont.*)

	Hunter 1		Hunter 2		Hunter 3	
Minute	State	Species[a]	State	Species	State	Species
57	stalking	(9)	stalking	(5)	searching	
58	stalking	(9)	stalking	(5)	searching	
59	stalking	(9)	stalking	(5)	searching	
60	stalking	(9)	stalking	(5)	searching	
61	stalking	(9)	stalking	(5)	searching	
62	stalking	(9)	stalking	(5)	searching	
63	stalking	(9)	stalking	(5)	searching	
64	stalking	(9)	stalking	(5)	searching	
65	stalking	(9)	stalking	(5)	searching	
66	stalking	(9)	stalking	(5)	searching	
67	stalking	(9)	stalking	(5)	searching	
68	stalking	(9)	killing	(5)	searching	
69	stalking	(9)	searching		searching	
70	stalking	(9)	searching		searching	
71	stalking	(9)	searching		searching	
72	stalking	(9)	encountering	(9)	searching	
73	stalking	(9)	stalking	(9)	encountering	(9)
74	stalking	(9)	stalking	(9)	stalking	(9)
75	stalking	(9)	stalking	(9)	stalking	(9)
76	killing	(9)	stalking	(9)	stalking	(9)
77	searching		stalking	(9)	stalking	(9)
78	searching		stalking	(9)	stalking	(9)
79	searching		stalking	(9)	stalking	(9)
80	searching		stalking	(9)	stalking	(9)
81	searching		stalking	(9)	stalking	(9)
82	searching		stalking	(9)	stalking	(9)
83	searching		stalking	(9)	stalking	(9)
84	searching		stalking	(9)	stalking	(9)
85	searching		stalking	(9)	stalking	(9)
86	searching		stalking	(9)	stalking	(9)
87	searching		stalking	(9)	stalking	(9)
88	searching		stalking	(9)	stalking	(9)
89	searching		stalking	(9)	stalking	(9)
90	searching		stalking	(9)	stalking	(9)
91	searching		stalking	(9)	stalking	(9)
92	searching		stalking	(9)	stalking	(9)
93	searching		stalking	(9)	stalking	(9)
94	searching		stalking	(9)	stalking	(9)
95	searching		stalking	(9)	stalking	(9)
96	searching		stalking	(9)	stalking	(9)
97	searching		stalking	(9)	stalking	(9)
98	searching		stalking	(9)	stalking	(9)
99	searching		stalking	(9)	stalking	(9)
100	searching		stalking	(9)	stalking	(9)
101	searching		stalking	(9)	stalking	(9)
102	searching		stalking	(9)	stalking	(9)
103	searching		killing	(9)	stalking	(9)
104	searching		searching		killing	(9)
105	searching		searching		searching	
106	searching		searching		searching	
107	searching		searching		searching	
108	searching		searching		searching	
109	searching		searching		searching	
110	searching		searching		searching	
111	encountering	(9)	searching		searching	
112	stalking	(9)	searching		searching	
113	stalking	(9)	searching		searching	
114	stalking	(9)	searching		searching	

Table 5.8. (*cont.*)

	Hunter 1		Hunter 2		Hunter 3	
Minute	State	Species[a]	State	Species	State	Species
115	stalking	(9)	searching		searching	
116	stalking	(9)	searching		searching	
117	stalking	(9)	searching		searching	
118	stalking	(9)	searching		searching	
119	stalking	(9)	searching		searching	
120	stalking	(9)	searching		searching	
121	stalking	(9)	searching		searching	
122	stalking	(9)	searching		searching	
123	stalking	(9)	searching		searching	
124	stalking	(9)	searching		searching	
125	stalking	(9)	searching		searching	
126	stalking	(9)	searching		searching	
127	stalking	(9)	searching		searching	
128	stalking	(9)	searching		searching	
129	stalking	(9)	searching		searching	
130	stalking	(9)	searching		searching	
131	stalking	(9)	searching		searching	
132	stalking	(9)	searching		searching	
133	stalking	(9)	searching		searching	
134	stalking	(9)	searching		searching	
135	stalking	(9)	searching		searching	
136	stalking	(9)	searching		searching	
137	stalking	(9)	searching		searching	
138	stalking	(9)	searching		searching	
139	stalking	(9)	searching		searching	
140	stalking	(9)	searching		searching	
141	stalking	(9)	searching		searching	
142	killing	(9)	searching		searching	
143	searching		searching		searching	
144	searching		searching		searching	
145	searching		searching		searching	
146	searching		searching		searching	
147	searching		searching		searching	
148	searching		searching		searching	
149	searching		searching		searching	
150	searching		searching		searching	
151	searching		searching		searching	
152	searching		searching		searching	
153	searching		searching		searching	
154	searching		searching		searching	
155	searching		searching		searching	
156	encountering	(9)	searching		searching	
157	stalking	(9)	searching		searching	
158	stalking	(9)	searching		searching	
159	stalking	(9)	searching		searching	
160	stalking	(9)	searching		searching	
161	stalking	(9)	searching		searching	
162	stalking	(9)	searching		encountering	(5)
163	stalking	(9)	searching		stalking	(5)
164	stalking	(9)	searching		stalking	(5)
165	stalking	(9)	encountering	(7)	stalking	(5)
166	stalking	(9)	stalking	(7)	stalking	(5)
167	stalking	(9)	stalking	(7)	stalking	(5)
168	stalking	(9)	stalking	(7)	stalking	(5)
169	stalking	(9)	stalking	(7)	stalking	(5)
170	stalking	(9)	stalking	(7)	stalking	(5)
171	stalking	(9)	stalking	(7)	stalking	(5)
172	stalking	(9)	stalking	(7)	stalking	(5)

Table 5.8. (*cont.*)

	Hunter 1		Hunter 2		Hunter 3	
Minute	State	Species[a]	State	Species	State	Species
173	stalking	(9)	stalking	(7)	stalking	(5)
174	stalking	(9)	stalking	(7)	stalking	(5)
175	stalking	(9)	stalking	(7)	stalking	(5)
176	stalking	(9)	stalking	(7)	stalking	(5)
177	stalking	(9)	stalking	(7)	stalking	(5)
178	stalking	(9)	stalking	(7)	stalking	(5)
179	stalking	(9)	stalking	(7)	stalking	(5)
180	stalking	(9)	stalking	(7)	stalking	(5)
181	stalking	(9)	stalking	(7)	stalking	(5)
182	stalking	(9)	stalking	(7)	stalking	(5)
183	stalking	(9)	stalking	(7)	stalking	(5)
184	stalking	(9)	stalking	(7)	stalking	(5)
185	stalking	(9)	stalking	(7)	stalking	(5)
186	stalking	(9)	stalking	(7)	stalking	(5)
187	killing	(9)	stalking	(7)	stalking	(5)
188	searching		stalking	(7)	stalking	(5)
189	searching		stalking	(7)	stalking	(5)
190	searching		stalking	(7)	stalking	(5)
191	searching		stalking	(7)	stalking	(5)
192	searching		stalking	(7)	stalking	(5)
193	searching		stalking	(7)	killing	(5)
194	searching		stalking	(7)	searching	
195	searching		stalking	(7)	searching	
196	searching		killing	(7)	searching	
197	searching		searching		searching	
198	searching		searching		searching	
199	searching		searching		searching	
200	searching		searching		searching	
201	searching		searching		searching	
202	searching		searching		searching	
203	searching		searching		searching	
204	searching		searching		searching	
205	searching		searching		searching	
206	searching		searching		searching	
207	searching		searching		searching	
208	searching		searching		searching	
209	searching		searching		searching	
210	searching		searching		searching	
211	searching		searching		searching	
212	searching		encountering	(1)	searching	
213	searching		stalking	(1)	searching	
214	searching		stalking	(1)	searching	
215	searching		stalking	(1)	searching	
216	searching		stalking	(1)	searching	
217	searching		stalking	(1)	encountering	(4)
218	searching		stalking	(1)	stalking	(4)
219	searching		stalking	(1)	stalking	(4)
220	searching		stalking	(1)	stalking	(4)
221	searching		stalking	(1)	stalking	(4)
222	searching		stalking	(1)	stalking	(4)
223	encountering	(7)	stalking	(1)	stalking	(4)
224	stalking	(7)	stalking	(1)	stalking	(4)
225	stalking	(7)	stalking	(1)	stalking	(4)
226	stalking	(7)	stalking	(1)	stalking	(4)
227	stalking	(7)	stalking	(1)	stalking	(4)
228	stalking	(7)	stalking	(1)	stalking	(4)
229	stalking	(7)	stalking	(1)	stalking	(4)
230	stalking	(7)	stalking	(1)	stalking	(4)

Table 5.8. (*cont.*)

	Hunter 1		Hunter 2		Hunter 3	
Minute	State	Species[a]	State	Species	State	Species
231	stalking	(7)	stalking	(1)	stalking	(4)
232	stalking	(7)	stalking	(1)	stalking	(4)
233	stalking	(7)	stalking	(1)	stalking	(4)
234	stalking	(7)	stalking	(1)	stalking	(4)
235	stalking	(7)	stalking	(1)	stalking	(4)
236	stalking	(7)	stalking	(1)	stalking	(4)
237	stalking	(7)	stalking	(1)	stalking	(4)
238	stalking	(7)	stalking	(1)	stalking	(4)
239	stalking	(7)	stalking	(1)	stalking	(4)
240	stalking	(7)	stalking	(1)	stalking	(4)
241	stalking	(7)	stalking	(1)	stalking	(4)
242	stalking	(7)	stalking	(1)	stalking	(4)
243	stalking	(7)	killing	(1)	stalking	(4)
244	stalking	(7)	searching		stalking	(4)
245	stalking	(7)	searching		stalking	(4)
246	stalking	(7)	searching		stalking	(4)
247	stalking	(7)	searching		stalking	(4)
248	stalking	(7)	searching		killing	(4)
249	stalking	(7)	searching		searching	
250	stalking	(7)	searching		searching	
251	stalking	(7)	searching		searching	
252	stalking	(7)	searching		searching	
253	stalking	(7)	searching		searching	
254	killing	(7)	searching		searching	
255	searching		searching		searching	
256	encountering	(9)	searching		searching	
257	stalking	(9)	searching		searching	
258	stalking	(9)	searching		searching	
259	stalking	(9)	searching		searching	
260	stalking	(9)	searching		searching	
261	stalking	(9)	searching		searching	
262	stalking	(9)	searching		encountering	(3)
263	stalking	(9)	searching		stalking	(3)
264	stalking	(9)	searching		stalking	(3)
265	stalking	(9)	searching		stalking	(3)
266	stalking	(9)	searching		stalking	(3)
267	stalking	(9)	searching		stalking	(3)
268	stalking	(9)	searching		stalking	(3)
269	stalking	(9)	searching		stalking	(3)
270	stalking	(9)	encountering	(7)	stalking	(3)
271	stalking	(9)	stalking	(7)	stalking	(3)
272	stalking	(9)	stalking	(7)	stalking	(3)
273	stalking	(9)	stalking	(7)	stalking	(3)
274	stalking	(9)	stalking	(7)	stalking	(3)
275	stalking	(9)	stalking	(7)	stalking	(3)
276	stalking	(9)	stalking	(7)	stalking	(3)
277	stalking	(9)	stalking	(7)	stalking	(3)
278	stalking	(9)	stalking	(7)	stalking	(3)
279	stalking	(9)	stalking	(7)	stalking	(3)
280	stalking	(9)	stalking	(7)	stalking	(3)
281	stalking	(9)	stalking	(7)	stalking	(3)
282	stalking	(9)	stalking	(7)	stalking	(3)
283	stalking	(9)	stalking	(7)	stalking	(3)
284	stalking	(9)	stalking	(7)	stalking	(3)
285	stalking	(9)	stalking	(7)	stalking	(3)
286	stalking	(9)	stalking	(7)	stalking	(3)
287	killing	(9)	stalking	(7)	stalking	(3)
288	killing	(9)	stalking	(7)	stalking	(3)

Table 5.8. (*cont.*)

	Hunter 1		Hunter 2		Hunter 3	
Minute	State	Species[a]	State	Species	State	Species
289	processing	(9)	stalking	(7)	stalking	(3)
290	processing	(9)	stalking	(7)	stalking	(3)
291	processing	(9)	stalking	(7)	stalking	(3)
292	processing	(9)	stalking	(7)	stalking	(3)
293	processing	(9)	stalking	(7)	killing	(3)
294	processing	(9)	stalking	(7)	searching	
295	searching		stalking	(7)	searching	
296	searching		stalking	(7)	searching	
297	searching		stalking	(7)	searching	
298	searching		stalking	(7)	searching	
299	searching		stalking (unsuccessful)	(7)	searching	
300	searching		searching		searching	

Note:
[a](1) male red deer (2) female red deer (3) juvenile red deer (4) male wild pig (5) female wild pig (6) juvenile wild pig (7) male roe deer (8) female roe deer (9) juvenile roe deer

Table 5.9. *Sample day's foraging (test run A, visit 1, day 10) for foragers with UIS goals*

	Hunter 1		Hunter 2		Hunter 3	
Minute	State	Species[a]	State	Species	State	Species
1	searching		searching		searching	
2	searching		searching		searching	
3	searching		searching		searching	
4	searching		encountering	(9)	encountering	(9)
5	searching		searching		searching	
6	searching		searching		searching	
7	searching		encountering	(8)	searching	
8	searching		searching		encountering	(9)
9	searching		searching		searching	
10	encountering	(9)	searching		searching	
11	searching		searching		searching	
12	searching		searching		searching	
13	searching		searching		searching	
14	searching		searching		searching	
15	searching		searching		searching	
16	searching		searching		searching	
17	searching		encountering	(2)	searching	
18	searching		stalking	(2)	searching	
19	searching		stalking	(2)	searching	
20	searching		stalking	(2)	searching	
21	searching		stalking	(2)	searching	
22	searching		stalking	(2)	searching	
23	searching		stalking	(2)	searching	
24	searching		stalking	(2)	searching	
25	searching		stalking	(2)	killing	
26	searching		stalking	(2)	searching	
27	searching		stalking	(2)	searching	
28	searching		stalking	(2)	searching	
29	searching		stalking	(2)	searching	
30	searching		stalking	(2)	searching	

Table 5.9. (*cont.*)

	Hunter 1		Hunter 2		Hunter 3	
Minute	State	Species[a]	State	Species	State	Species
31	searching		stalking	(2)	searching	
32	searching		stalking	(2)	searching	
33	searching		stalking	(2)	searching	
34	encountering	(9)	stalking	(2)	searching	
35	searching		stalking	(2)	searching	
36	searching		stalking	(2)	encountering	(1)
37	searching		stalking	(2)	stalking	(1)
38	searching		stalking	(2)	stalking	(1)
39	searching		stalking	(2)	stalking	(1)
40	encountering	(9)	stalking	(2)	stalking	(1)
41	searching		stalking	(2)	stalking	(1)
42	searching		stalking	(2)	stalking	(1)
43	searching		stalking	(2)	stalking	(1)
44	searching		stalking	(2)	stalking	(1)
45	searching		stalking	(2)	stalking	(1)
46	searching		stalking	(2)	stalking	(1)
47	searching		stalking	(2)	stalking	(1)
48	searching		killing	(2)	stalking	(1)
49	searching		searching		stalking	(1)
50	searching		searching		stalking	(1)
51	searching		searching		stalking	(1)
52	searching		searching		stalking	(1)
53	searching		searching		stalking	(1)
54	searching		searching		stalking	(1)
55	searching		searching		stalking	(1)
56	encountering	(8)	searching		stalking	(1)
57	searching		searching		stalking	(1)
58	searching		searching		stalking	(1)
59	searching		searching		stalking	(1)
60	searching		searching		stalking	(1)
61	searching		searching		stalking	(1)
62	searching		searching		stalking	(1)
63	searching		searching		stalking	(1)
64	searching		searching		stalking	(1)
65	searching		encountering	(9)	stalking	(1)
66	searching		searching		stalking	(1)
67	searching		searching		killing	(1)
68	searching		searching		killing	(1)
69	searching		searching		processing	(1)
70	searching		searching		processing	(1)
71	searching		searching		processing	(1)
72	searching		searching		processing	(1)
73	searching		searching		processing	(1)
74	searching		searching		processing	(1)
75	searching		searching		processing	(1)
76	searching		searching		processing	(1)
77	searching		searching		processing	(1)
78	searching		searching		processing	(1)
79	searching		searching		processing	(1)
80	searching		searching		processing	(1)
81	searching		searching		processing	(1)
82	encountering	(8)	searching		processing	(1)
83	searching		searching		processing	(1)
84	searching		searching		processing	(1)
85	searching		searching		processing	(1)
86	searching		searching		processing	(1)
87	encountering	(5)	searching		processing	(1)
88	searching		encountering	(8)	processing	(1)

Table 5.9. (*cont.*)

	Hunter 1		Hunter 2		Hunter 3	
Minute	State	Species[a]	State	Species	State	Species
89	searching		searching		processing	(1)
90	searching		searching		processing	(1)
91	searching		searching		processing	(1)
92	searching		searching		processing	(1)
93	searching		searching		processing	(1)
94	searching		searching		processing	(1)
95	searching		searching		processing	(1)
96	searching		searching		processing	(1)
97	searching		searching		processing	(1)
98	searching		searching		searching	
99	searching		searching		encountering	(3)
100	encountering	(9)	searching		searching	
101	searching		searching		searching	
102	searching		searching		searching	
103	searching		searching		searching	
104	searching		searching		searching	
105	searching		searching		searching	
106	searching		searching		searching	
107	searching		searching		searching	
108	searching		searching		searching	
109	searching		searching		searching	
110	searching		searching		searching	
111	searching		searching		searching	
112	encountering	(7)	searching		searching	
113	searching		searching		searching	
114	searching		searching		searching	
115	searching		searching		searching	
116	searching		searching		searching	
117	searching		searching		searching	
118	searching		searching		searching	
119	searching		searching		searching	
120	searching		searching		searching	
121	searching		searching		searching	
122	searching		searching		searching	
123	searching		searching		searching	
124	searching		searching		searching	
125	searching		searching		searching	
126	searching		searching		searching	
127	searching		searching		searching	
128	searching		searching		searching	
129	searching		searching		searching	
130	searching		searching		searching	
131	searching		searching		searching	
132	searching		searching		searching	
133	searching		searching		searching	
134	searching		searching		searching	
135	searching		searching		searching	
136	searching		searching		searching	
137	searching		searching		searching	
138	searching		searching		searching	
139	searching		searching		searching	
140	searching		searching		searching	
141	searching		searching		searching	
142	searching		searching		searching	
143	searching		searching		searching	
144	searching		searching		searching	
145	searching		searching		searching	
146	searching		searching		searching	

Table 5.9. (*cont.*)

Minute	Hunter 1 State	Species[a]	Hunter 2 State	Species	Hunter 3 State	Species
147	searching		searching		searching	
148	searching		searching		searching	
149	encountering	(8)	searching		searching	
150	searching		searching		searching	
151	searching		searching		searching	
152	searching		searching		searching	
153	searching		searching		searching	
154	searching		searching		searching	
155	searching		searching		searching	
156	searching		searching		searching	
157	searching		searching		searching	
158	searching		searching		searching	
159	searching		searching		searching	
160	searching		searching		searching	
161	searching		searching		encountering	(8)
162	searching		encountering	(6)	searching	
163	searching		searching		searching	
164	searching		searching		searching	
165	searching		searching		searching	
166	searching		searching		searching	
167	searching		searching		encountering	(9)
168	searching		searching		searching	
169	searching		searching		searching	
170	searching		searching		searching	
171	encountering	(7)	searching		searching	
172	searching		searching		encountering	(7)
173	searching		searching		searching	
174	searching		searching		searching	
175	searching		encountering	(7)	searching	
176	searching		searching		searching	
177	searching		searching		searching	
178	searching		searching		searching	
179	searching		searching		searching	
180	searching		searching		searching	
181	searching		searching		searching	
182	searching		searching		searching	
183	searching		encountering	(7)	searching	
184	searching		searching		searching	
185	searching		searching		searching	
186	searching		searching		encountering	(1)
187	searching		searching		searching	
188	searching		searching		searching	
189	searching		searching		searching	
190	searching		searching		searching	
191	searching		searching		searching	
192	searching		searching		searching	
193	searching		searching		searching	
194	searching		searching		searching	
195	searching		searching		encountering	(6)
196	searching		searching		searching	
197	searching		searching		searching	
198	searching		searching		searching	
199	searching		searching		searching	
200	searching		searching		searching	
201	searching		searching		searching	
202	searching		searching		searching	
203	searching		searching		searching	
204	searching		encountering	(5)	searching	

Table 5.9. (*cont.*)

	Hunter 1		Hunter 2		Hunter 3	
Minute	State	Species[a]	State	Species	State	Species
205	searching		stalking	(5)	searching	
206	searching		stalking	(5)	searching	
207	searching		stalking	(5)	searching	
208	searching		stalking	(5)	searching	
209	encountering	(9)	stalking	(5)	searching	
210	searching		stalking	(5)	searching	
211	searching		stalking	(5)	searching	
212	searching		stalking	(5)	searching	
213	searching		stalking	(5)	searching	
214	searching		stalking	(5)	searching	
215	searching		stalking	(5)	searching	
216	searching		stalking	(5)	searching	
217	searching		stalking	(5)	searching	
218	searching		stalking	(5)	searching	
219	searching		stalking	(5)	searching	
220	searching		stalking	(5)	searching	
221	searching		stalking	(5)	searching	
222	searching		stalking	(5)	searching	
223	searching		stalking	(5)	searching	
224	searching		stalking	(5)	searching	
225	searching		stalking	(5)	searching	
226	searching		stalking	(5)	searching	
227	searching		stalking	(5)	searching	
228	searching		stalking	(5)	searching	
229	searching		stalking	(5)	searching	
230	encountering	(9)	stalking	(5)	searching	
231	searching		stalking	(5)	searching	
232	searching		stalking	(5)	searching	
233	searching		stalking	(5)	searching	
234	searching		stalking	(5)	searching	
235	searching		killing	(5)	searching	
236	searching		searching		encountering	(7)
237	encountering	(7)	searching		searching	
238	searching		searching		searching	
239	searching		searching		searching	
240	searching		searching		searching	
241	searching		searching		searching	
242	searching		searching		searching	
243	searching		searching		searching	
244	searching		searching		searching	
245	searching		searching		searching	
246	searching		searching		searching	
247	searching		searching		searching	
248	searching		searching		searching	
249	searching		searching		searching	
250	searching		searching		searching	
251	searching		searching		searching	
252	searching		searching		searching	
253	searching		searching		searching	
254	searching		searching		searching	
255	searching		searching		searching	
256	searching		searching		searching	
257	searching		searching		searching	
258	searching		searching		encountering	(9)
259	searching		searching		searching	
260	searching		searching		searching	
261	searching		searching		searching	
262	searching		searching		searching	

Table 5.9. (*cont.*)

Minute	Hunter 1		Hunter 2		Hunter 3	
	State	Species[a]	State	Species	State	Species
263	searching		searching		searching	
264	searching		searching		encountering	(7)
265	searching		searching		searching	
266	searching		searching		searching	
267	searching		searching		searching	
268	searching		searching		encountering	(2)
269	searching		searching		searching	
270	searching		searching		searching	
271	searching		searching		searching	
272	searching		encountering	(7)	searching	
273	searching		searching		encountering	(5)
274	searching		searching		searching	
275	searching		searching		searching	
276	searching		searching		searching	
277	encountering	(9)	searching		searching	
278	searching		searching		searching	
279	searching		searching		searching	
280	searching		searching		encountering	(7)
281	searching		searching		searching	
282	searching		searching		searching	
283	searching		searching		searching	
284	encountering	(8)	searching		searching	
285	searching		searching		searching	
286	searching		searching		searching	
287	searching		searching		searching	
288	searching		searching		searching	
289	searching		searching		searching	
290	encountering	(6)	searching		searching	
291	searching		searching		searching	
292	searching		searching		searching	
293	searching		searching		searching	
294	searching		encountering	(9)	searching	
295	searching		searching		searching	
296	searching		searching		searching	
297	searching		searching		searching	
298	searching		searching		searching	
299	searching		searching		searching	
300	searching		searching		searching	

Note:
[a](1) male red deer (2) female red deer (3) juvenile red deer (4) male wild pig (5) female wild pig (6) juvenile wild pig (7) male roe deer (8) female roe deer (9) juvenile roe deer

Table 5.10. *Sample day's foraging (test run A, visit 1, day 10) for foragers with UISR goals*

	Hunter 1		Hunter 2		Hunter 3	
Minute	State	Species[a]	State	Species	State	Species
1	searching		searching		searching	
2	searching		searching		searching	
3	searching		searching		searching	
4	searching		searching		searching	
5	searching		searching		searching	
6	searching		searching		searching	
7	searching		searching		searching	
8	searching		searching		searching	
9	searching		searching		searching	
10	searching		searching		searching	
11	searching		searching		searching	
12	searching		searching		searching	
13	searching		encountering	(7)	searching	
14	searching		searching		searching	
15	searching		searching		searching	
16	searching		searching		searching	
17	searching		searching		searching	
18	searching		searching		searching	
19	searching		searching		searching	
20	searching		searching		searching	
21	searching		searching		searching	
22	searching		searching		searching	
23	searching		searching		searching	
24	searching		searching		searching	
25	searching		searching		searching	
26	searching		searching		searching	
27	searching		searching		searching	
28	searching		searching		encountering	(8)
29	searching		searching		searching	
30	searching		searching		searching	
31	searching		searching		searching	
32	searching		searching		searching	
33	searching		searching		searching	
34	searching		searching		searching	
35	searching		searching		searching	
36	searching		searching		searching	
37	searching		searching		searching	
38	searching		searching		searching	
39	searching		searching		searching	
40	searching		searching		searching	
41	searching		searching		searching	
42	searching		encountering	(6)	searching	
43	searching		searching		searching	
44	searching		searching		searching	
45	searching		searching		searching	
46	searching		searching		searching	
47	searching		searching		searching	
48	searching		searching		searching	
49	searching		searching		searching	
50	searching		searching		searching	
51	searching		searching		encountering	(2)
52	searching		searching		stalking	(2)
53	searching		searching		stalking	(2)
54	searching		searching		stalking	(2)
55	searching		searching		stalking	(2)
56	searching		searching		stalking	(2)
57	searching		encountering	(9)	stalking	(2)

Table 5.10. (*cont.*)

	Hunter 1		Hunter 2		Hunter 3	
Minute	State	Species[a]	State	Species	State	Species
58	searching		searching		stalking	(2)
59	searching		searching		stalking	(2)
60	searching		searching		stalking	(2)
61	searching		searching		stalking	(2)
62	searching		searching		stalking	(2)
63	searching		searching		stalking	(2)
64	searching		searching		stalking	(2)
65	searching		searching		stalking	(2)
66	searching		searching		stalking	(2)
67	searching		encountering	(5)	stalking	(2)
68	searching		searching		stalking	(2)
69	searching		searching		stalking	(2)
70	searching		searching		stalking	(2)
71	searching		searching		stalking	(2)
72	encountering	(8)	searching		stalking	(2)
73	stalking	(8)	searching		stalking	(2)
74	stalking	(8)	searching		stalking	(2)
75	stalking	(8)	searching		stalking	(2)
76	stalking	(8)	searching		stalking	(2)
77	stalking	(8)	searching		stalking	(2)
78	stalking	(8)	searching		stalking	(2)
79	stalking	(8)	searching		stalking	(2)
80	stalking	(8)	searching		stalking	(2)
81	stalking	(8)	searching		stalking	(2)
82	stalking	(8)	encountering	(7)	killing	(2)
83	stalking	(8)	searching		searching	(2)
84	stalking	(8)	searching		searching	(2)
85	stalking	(8)	searching		searching	(2)
86	stalking	(8)	searching		searching	(2)
87	stalking	(8)	searching		searching	(2)
88	stalking	(8)	searching		searching	(2)
89	stalking	(8)	searching		searching	(2)
90	stalking	(8)	searching		searching	(2)
91	stalking	(8)	searching		searching	(2)
92	stalking	(8)	encountering	(7)	searching	
93	stalking	(8)	stalking	(7)	searching	
94	stalking	(8)	stalking	(7)	searching	
95	stalking	(8)	stalking	(7)	searching	
96	stalking	(8)	stalking	(7)	searching	
97	stalking	(8)	stalking	(7)	searching	
98	stalking	(8)	stalking	(7)	searching	
99	stalking	(8)	stalking	(7)	searching	
100	stalking	(8)	stalking	(7)	searching	
101	stalking	(8)	stalking	(7)	searching	
102	stalking	(8)	stalking	(7)	searching	
103	killing	(8)	stalking	(7)	searching	
104	killing	(8)	stalking	(7)	searching	
105	processing	(8)	stalking	(7)	searching	
106	processing	(8)	stalking	(7)	searching	
107	processing	(8)	stalking	(7)	searching	
108	processing	(8)	stalking	(7)	searching	
109	processing	(8)	stalking	(7)	searching	
110	processing	(8)	stalking	(7)	searching	
111	processing	(8)	stalking	(7)	encountering	(9)
112	processing	(8)	stalking	(7)	searching	
113	searching		stalking	(7)	searching	
114	encountering	(2)	stalking	(7)	searching	
115	stalking	(2)	stalking	(7)	searching	

Table 5.10. (*cont.*)

	Hunter 1		Hunter 2		Hunter 3	
Minute	State	Species[a]	State	Species	State	Species
116	stalking	(2)	stalking	(7)	searching	
117	stalking	(2)	stalking	(7)	searching	
118	stalking	(2)	stalking	(7)	searching	
119	stalking	(2)	stalking	(7)	encountering	(9)
120	stalking	(2)	stalking	(7)	searching	
121	stalking	(2)	stalking	(7)	encountering	(9)
122	stalking	(2)	stalking	(7)	searching	
123	stalking	(2)	killing	(7)	searching	
124	stalking	(2)	searching		searching	
125	stalking	(2)	searching		searching	
126	stalking	(2)	searching		searching	
127	stalking	(2)	searching		searching	
128	stalking	(2)	searching		searching	
129	stalking	(2)	searching		searching	
130	stalking	(2)	searching		searching	
131	stalking	(2)	searching		searching	
132	stalking	(2)	searching		searching	
133	stalking	(2)	searching		searching	
134	stalking	(2)	searching		searching	
135	stalking	(2)	searching		searching	
136	stalking	(2)	searching		encountering	(4)
137	stalking	(2)	searching		stalking	(4)
138	stalking	(2)	encountering	(8)	stalking	(4)
139	stalking	(2)	searching		stalking	(4)
140	stalking	(2)	encountering	(9)	stalking	(4)
141	stalking	(2)	searching		stalking	(4)
142	stalking	(2)	searching		stalking	(4)
143	stalking	(2)	searching		stalking	(4)
144	stalking	(2)	searching		stalking	(4)
145	killing	(2)	searching		stalking	(4)
146	searching		searching		stalking	(4)
147	encountering	(2)	searching		stalking	(4)
148	stalking	(2)	searching		stalking	(4)
149	stalking	(2)	searching		stalking	(4)
150	stalking	(2)	searching		stalking	(4)
151	stalking	(2)	searching		stalking	(4)
152	stalking	(2)	searching		stalking	(4)
153	stalking	(2)	searching		stalking	(4)
154	stalking	(2)	searching		stalking	(4)
155	stalking	(2)	searching		stalking	(4)
156	stalking	(2)	searching		stalking	(4)
157	stalking	(2)	searching		stalking	(4)
158	stalking	(2)	searching		stalking	(4)
159	stalking	(2)	searching		stalking	(4)
160	stalking	(2)	searching		stalking	(4)
161	stalking	(2)	searching		stalking	(4)
162	stalking	(2)	searching		stalking	(4)
163	stalking	(2)	searching		stalking	(4)
164	stalking	(2)	searching		stalking	(4)
165	stalking	(2)	searching		stalking	(4)
166	stalking	(2)	searching		stalking	(4)
167	stalking	(2)	searching		killing	(4)
168	stalking	(2)	searching		searching	
169	stalking	(2)	searching		searching	
170	stalking	(2)	searching		searching	
171	stalking	(2)	searching		searching	
172	stalking	(2)	searching		searching	
173	stalking	(2)	searching		searching	

Table 5.10. (*cont.*)

	Hunter 1		Hunter 2		Hunter 3	
Minute	State	Species[a]	State	Species	State	Species
174	stalking	(2)	searching		searching	
175	stalking	(2)	searching		searching	
176	stalking	(2)	searching		searching	
177	stalking	(2)	searching		searching	
178	killing	(2)	searching		searching	
179	searching		searching		searching	
180	encountering	(9)	searching		searching	
181	searching		searching		searching	
182	searching		searching		searching	
183	searching		encountering	(9)	searching	
184	searching		searching		searching	
185	searching		searching		searching	
186	searching		searching		searching	
187	searching		searching		searching	
188	searching		searching		searching	
189	searching		searching		searching	
190	searching		searching		searching	
191	searching		searching		searching	
192	searching		searching		searching	
193	searching		searching		searching	
194	searching		searching		searching	
195	searching		searching		searching	
196	searching		searching		searching	
197	searching		searching		searching	
198	searching		searching		searching	
199	searching		searching		searching	
200	searching		searching		searching	
201	searching		searching		searching	
202	searching		searching		searching	
203	searching		searching		searching	
204	searching		searching		searching	
205	searching		searching		searching	
206	searching		searching		searching	
207	searching		searching		searching	
208	searching		searching		searching	
209	searching		searching		searching	
210	searching		searching		searching	
211	searching		searching		searching	
212	searching		searching		searching	
213	searching		searching		searching	
214	searching		searching		searching	
215	searching		searching		encountering	(9)
216	searching		searching		searching	
217	searching		searching		searching	
218	searching		searching		searching	
219	searching		searching		searching	
220	searching		searching		searching	
221	searching		searching		searching	
222	searching		searching		searching	
223	searching		searching		searching	
224	encountering	(9)	searching		searching	
225	searching		searching		encountering	(6)
226	searching		searching		stalking	(6)
227	searching		searching		stalking	(6)
228	searching		searching		stalking	(6)
229	searching		searching		stalking	(6)
230	searching		searching		stalking	(6)
231	searching		searching		stalking	(6)

Table 5.10. (*cont.*)

	Hunter 1		Hunter 2		Hunter 3	
Minute	State	Species[a]	State	Species	State	Species
232	searching		searching		stalking	(6)
233	searching		searching		stalking	(6)
234	searching		searching		stalking	(6)
235	searching		searching		stalking	(6)
236	searching		searching		stalking	(6)
237	searching		searching		stalking	(6)
238	searching		searching		stalking	(6)
239	encountering	(5)	searching		stalking	(6)
240	searching		searching		stalking	(6)
241	searching		searching		stalking	(6)
242	searching		searching		stalking	(6)
243	searching		searching		stalking	(6)
244	searching		searching		stalking	(6)
245	searching		searching		stalking	(6)
246	searching		searching		stalking	(6)
247	searching		searching		stalking	(6)
248	searching		searching		stalking	(6)
249	searching		encountering	(7)	stalking	(6)
250	searching		stalking	(7)	stalking	(6)
251	searching		stalking	(7)	stalking	(6)
252	searching		stalking	(7)	stalking	(6)
253	searching		stalking	(7)	stalking	(6)
254	searching		stalking	(7)	stalking	(6)
255	searching		stalking	(7)	stalking	(6)
256	searching		stalking	(7)	killing	(6)
257	searching		stalking	(7)	killing	(6)
258	searching		stalking	(7)	processing	(6)
259	searching		stalking	(7)	processing	(6)
260	encountering	(9)	stalking	(7)	processing	(6)
261	searching		stalking	(7)	processing	(6)
262	searching		stalking	(7)	processing	(6)
263	searching		stalking	(7)	processing	(6)
264	searching		stalking	(7)	processing	(6)
265	encountering	(7)	stalking	(7)	processing	(6)
266	stalking	(7)	stalking	(7)	processing	(6)
267	stalking	(7)	stalking	(7)	processing	(6)
268	stalking	(7)	stalking	(7)	searching	
269	stalking	(7)	stalking	(7)	searching	
270	stalking	(7)	stalking	(7)	searching	
271	stalking	(7)	stalking	(7)	searching	
272	stalking	(7)	stalking	(7)	searching	
273	stalking	(7)	stalking	(7)	searching	
274	stalking	(7)	stalking	(7)	searching	
275	stalking	(7)	stalking	(7)	searching	
276	stalking	(7)	stalking	(7)	searching	
277	stalking	(7)	stalking	(7)	searching	
278	stalking	(7)	stalking	(7)	searching	
279	stalking	(7)	stalking	(7)	searching	
280	stalking	(7)	killing	(7)	searching	
281	stalking	(7)	searching		searching	
282	stalking	(7)	searching		encountering	(8)
283	stalking	(7)	searching		searching	
284	stalking	(7)	searching		searching	
285	stalking	(7)	searching		searching	
286	stalking	(7)	searching		searching	
287	stalking	(7)	searching		searching	
288	stalking	(7)	encountering	(5)	searching	
289	stalking	(7)	searching		searching	

Table 5.10. (*cont.*)

Minute	Hunter 1 State	Species[a]	Hunter 2 State	Species	Hunter 3 State	Species
290	stalking	(7)	searching		searching	
291	stalking	(7)	searching		searching	
292	stalking	(7)	searching		searching	
293	stalking	(7)	encountering	(8)	searching	
294	stalking	(7)	stalking	(8)	encountering	(6)
295	stalking	(7)	stalking	(8)	stalking	(6)
296	killing	(7)	stalking	(8)	stalking	(6)
297	searching		stalking	(8)	stalking	(6)
298	searching		stalking	(8)	stalking	(6)
299	searching		stalking	(8)	stalking	(6)
			(unsuccessful)		(unsuccessful)	
300	searching		searching		searching	

Note:
[a](1) male red deer (2) female red deer (3) juvenile red deer (4) male wild pig (5) female wild pig (6) juvenile wild pig (7) male roe deer (8) female roe deer (9) juvenile roe deer

that appears to be the reason why hunter no. 1 chooses to stalk a female roe deer. By the end of the day, however, the RR element in their decision rule has become dominant and we see the frequency of stalks increase. During this hunting trip, hunter no. 1 succeeds in killing a female roe deer and hunter no. 3 a juvenile wild boar.

These three examples illustrate numerous features of the simulation model, although others are not readily apparent. The differences between the goals have been made clear. So too have the varying frequencies with which types of game are encountered, the state transitions during the day and the stochastic factors (i.e. 'luck', from the hunter's perspective) in defining the ungulates which are encountered and which are killed. It must be remembered that these example hunting trips are contained within an ever-changing historical, ecological and social context. With respect to history, the result of the hunting trip, and the fact that it occurred, will affect game encounters and stalk probabilities in the future. With respect to the ecological context, the kills that have been made and the fact that the hunting trip was undertaken will have reduced the future frequencies of game encounters. And in relation to the social context the results of the hunting trip in terms of making successful kills will have affected the influence of each hunter in the group when information is exchanged. For instance among the UIS foragers the distribution of influences changes from (0.26, 0.43, 0.31) for hunters 1, 2 and 3, before the hunt to (0.16, 0.26, 0.59) afterwards since only hunter no. 3 was successful and his kill was substantial. In contrast, among the UISR hunters influences changed from (0.22, 0.74, 0.04) to (0.25, 0.64, 0.11) since both hunters nos. 1 and 3 made kills. That of no. 3 had greater returns although both were small and hence changes in influence were not dramatic.

6

Decision making in the Mesolithic: multiple action replays

Only connect! That was the whole of her sermon.
Only connect the prose and the passion, and both will be exalted,
and human love will be seen at its highest.

E.M. Forster, Howards End

The echo in a Marabar cave . . . is entirely devoid of distinction
. . . Hope, politeness, the blowing of a nose, the squeak of a bat, all
produce 'boum'.

E.M. Forster, A Passage to India

Now comes the crunch – to make a connection between the simulated archaeological record, i.e. the faunal assemblages generated by the computer model, and the real world. I'm not sure which of these might be termed the prose and which the passion but certainly if a connection is made the value of both will be exalted! This connection must, however, be meaningful. To show that the computer model can produce patterning which is similar to that in real assemblages is insufficient in itself. Many very different models may produce patterns which cannot be distinguished between – like the echoes in a Marabar cave – and all of which may bear a resemblance to the real data. This is the problem of equifinality, which haunts those using simulation and has scared some away. Similarly, we can never be absolutely sure that patterns in faunal assemblages are not purely the result of preservation and excavation. My solution to these problems is that we must examine whether the model producing the simulated pattern, and in this case the type of decision making that is implied, is useful for explaining other aspects of the same archaeological record which initially appear unconnected with faunal assemblages. Here I am harking back to my introduction where I referred to what constitutes a good explanation in archaeology – the integration of what would be otherwise disparate components of the archaeological record by invoking the individual decision maker.

Consequently we have two connections to make in this chapter. First that between simulated and real patterning in faunal assemblages. From this we will be able to make an inference about Mesolithic decision goals. The validity of this inference will be demonstrated by whether it can be used to make the second

152

connection, that between the otherwise disparate components of the archaeological record, in this case the three problem areas I discussed in Chapter 4 – faunal assemblages, tool assemblages and burial patterns.

Only connect!

So let us start by considering how the first of these connections can be made. Now the whole premise upon which the computer model has been built is that we can use it to generate patterns in simulated faunal assemblages relating to different types of decision goals. I will refer to these patterns, and the ones that we will recognise in real assemblages from Scania and south-west Germany, as *signatures* (Gamble 1986:22). By a signature I mean a pattern which I hope is unique in the manner in which the composition of the faunal assemblage, which we may consider to be the dependent variable, varies with some other parameter, the independent variable. This latter variable must be one that we can measure for each archaeological site in one particular region and which can be manipulated in the computer model. We can then compare the archaeological signature from our real data set with that from each decision goal and identify which are most similar.

From the characteristics of the computer model and the Mesolithic archaeological record I have in fact chosen two parameters to manipulate in tandem – group size (NoPers) and duration of site occupation (NoHunts). Together these constitute the dependent variable of hunter/days occupation at a site. We cannot directly measure this variable from the archaeological data and need to find a material correlate for it that can be measured so that an inference as to hunter/days occupation can be drawn. Here we can briefly turn for help to some recent ethnoarchaeological studies on site structure.

O'Connell (1987) made a study of the inter/intrasite structure of camp sites of the Alyawara, and made comparisons with that of the !Kung and Nunamiut. Although some degree of variation was apparent between the three groups there were also some invariant features. He succinctly summarised the archaeological implications:

In each case, refuse is concentrated in clusters of various sizes, each representing the former locations of household activity areas, adjacent special activity areas, and in some cases secondary refuse areas. Variation in the size, content and internal organization of these features appears to be the product of at least four factors: (1) the organization of subsistence, especially the relative importance of food storage (2) the degree of seasonal variation in weather, especially as it affects the need for shelter (3) the length of time each area is occupied or in use, and (4) the size of the group occupying or using each area.   1987: 103–4

Note that the last two factors are those which I shall vary in tandem in the computer model. One of the varying features of site structure that O'Connell mentions is the spatial area of household activity – the zone of primary deposition.

Figs. 6.1 and 6.2 reproduce his graphs, showing how this varies with occupation duration and group size. Consequently the work suggests that we can use the spatial area of an archaeological site to measure either the number of hunters occupying the site or the duration of occupation. Of course we cannot easily decide from spatial data alone which of these is the more relevant, or determine absolute figures, but we can make a ranking of sites on an occupation duration/group size axis.

We have a complicating factor in that repeated occupations of a site may influence its size and structure. Blankholm (1987b) has discussed the problems of interpreting spatial data from Maglemosian sites in Denmark and cites the example of Svaerdborg. At that site there are a series of lithic concentrations which have been interpreted as hut floors. It cannot be shown, however, whether these derive from a single occupation by several family/household groups or have accumulated over several occupations each of which produced a single lithic scatter. Other sites, such as Holmegaard IV and Duvensee 5, have stratified hut floors suggesting repeated occupation of the same dwelling. Ethnoarchaeological data to help with this issue are unavailable. To ease matters I will make the assumption that the number of times a site is reoccupied correlates with the length of each stay and hence essentially avoid the problem. This assumption appears reasonable on an intuitive basis. The localities with facilities to allow long stays (e.g. fire wood, drinking water) will be less numerous than those suitable for short-term hunting camps and hence will be more likely to be reoccupied. However, I will not rely on this assumption alone. When discussing the site structure of the archaeological sites below, specific attention will be paid to any evidence for either single or repeated occupation. As it happens, the findings lend support to my assumption and the problem of repeated occupations is shown to be essentially irrelevant for my data set.

Now the wish to infer the relative hunter/days occupation for a set of archaeological sites requires that we use a data set with the highest standards of preservation and excavation, not only of the site structure but also, of course, of the faunal assemblage itself. The region with the most suitable data in this respect is Scania and the rest of the chapter will focus on that data. It is structured as follows.

First I discuss each site in the sample from Scania with respect to the data I have so far identified as being relevant, and to other data that will become so later in this chapter. From this I will derive the archaeological signature of these assemblages in terms of the variation of the faunal assemblage with the measure of relative hunter/days occupation. I will also pay some brief attention to the sites from the Upper Danube in south-west Germany and derive a second signature from this area of post-glacial Europe. Next, I will return to the computer model and derive the simulated archaeological signatures for each decision goal. Then I will make my comparisons between these and the real signatures. If there is a significant similarity between each of the real signatures and one of the decision goal signatures (not necessarily the same one for each region) this will constitute our first connection and provide us with tentative inferences concerning the decision goals

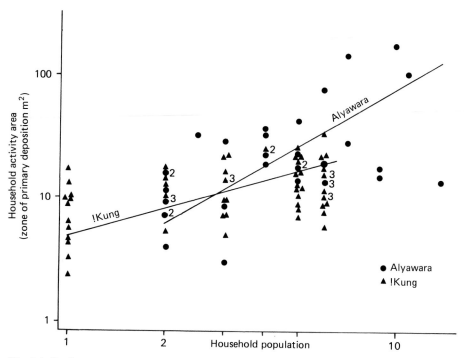

Fig. 6.1. Settlement area against household population for the !Kung and Alyawara (after O'Connell 1987).

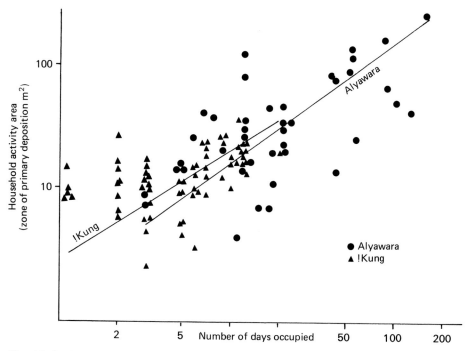

Fig. 6.2. Settlement area against occupation duration for the !Kung and Alyawara (after O'Connell 1987).

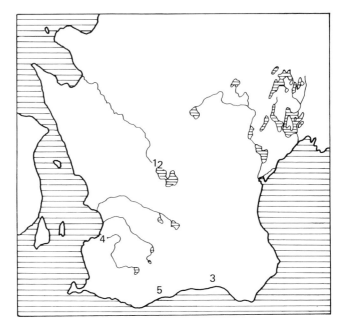

1. Ageröd I
2. Ageröd V
3. Bredasten
4. Segebro
5. Skateholm

Fig. 6.3. Mesolithic sites in Scania referred to in Chapter 6 (after Larsson 1978–84).

of the Scanian and German foragers. We then try and use this to make our second set of connections.

Mesolithic sites in southern Sweden

Southern Sweden provides a set of seven Mesolithic sites, preserved, excavated and published with sufficient quality to make comparison between their faunal assemblages and those from the simulation a useful exercise. As shown in Fig. 6.3 and Table 6.1, these are from both coastal and inland areas and are distributed throughout the Atlantic period. These sites derive principally from the work of Lars Larsson since 1975. His main concern was with establishing settlement patterns and their change through time. It is to the credit of his excellent work that I am able to use his data to look at complementary problems posed by these sites.

The Ageröd I sites

Ageröd I is a complex of sites on the margins of Ageröds Mosse in central Scania. Ageröds Mosse itself is part of a large bog that marks the extent of a prehistoric lake. The sites were investigated in the 1940s by Althin and then by Larsson between 1971–4. Three of the sites have received greatest attention: Ageröd I:D, I:B and I:HC. My summaries are taken from Larsson (1975, 1978).

Table 6.1. *Radiocarbon dates from Mesolithic sites in Scania (from Larsson 1978, 1982, 1983, 1984, M. Larsson 1986)*

	Sample	BP	bc	Material
Ageröd I:D	LU-751	7940 ± 80	5990	charcoal
	LU-991	7780 ± 80	5830	charcoal
	LU-760	7680 ± 80	5680	bone
Ageröd I:B[a]	LU-599	8020 ± 80	6070	charcoal
	LU-873	8000 ± 80	6050	charcoal
	LU-698	7960 ± 80	6010	charcoal
	LU-600	6380 ± 70	4430	peat
	LU-598	6290 ± 70	4340	peat
	LU-598A	6040 ± 70	4090	humus
	LU-601	3930 ± 70	1980	wood
Ageröd I:HC	LU-753	7910 ± 80	5960	hazelnut
(white layer)	LU-993	7870 ± 80	5920	charcoal
	LU-754	7860 ± 80	5910	charcoal
	U-4081	7750 ± 80	5800	bone
	LU-755	7710 ± 80	5760	bone
	U-4082	7415 ± 115	5465	bone
	LU-872	7220 ± 70	5270	bone
Ageröd V	LU-1623	6860 ± 70	4910	bone
	LU-963	6800 ± 90	4850	charcoal
	LU-696	6720 ± 75	4770	hazelnut
	LU-1502	6710 ± 70	4760	bone
	LU-1622	6680 ± 70	4730	hazelnut
	LU-697	6540 ± 75	4560	charcoal
Bredasten[b]	LU-2420		3390 ± 70	
	LU-2422		3220 ± 60	
Segebro	LU-855:2	7140 ± 80	5190	charcoal
(layers 6 and 7)	LU-854	7080 ± 80	5130	bone
	LU-855:1	7030 ± 80	5080	bone
	LU-626	7390 ± 80	5440	charcoal
	LU-759	7320 ± 130	5370	charcoal
	LU-1501	7140 ± 75	5190	charcoal
	LU-758	6970 ± 90	5020	charcoal
Skateholm[c] I	LU-1835		4340 ± 95	
	LU-2109		4320 ± 70	
	LU-1834		4290 ± 85	
	LU-1888		4270 ± 100	
	LU-2116		4040 ± 70	
	LU-1886		3980 ± 125	
	LU-1853		4070 ± 70	
	LU-1849		3850 ± 70	
	LU-1848		3840 ± 70	
Skateholm II	LU-2113		4640 ± 70	
	LU-2115		4430 ± 70	

[a] Larsson (1978: 144) suggests that the difference in the dates derived from charcoal and peat appears to be a function of the material since all samples come from the same level in the site. The peat is probably contaminated by modern humus. The late date derived from the piece of wood (a branch) is also probably the result of contamination since the wood was fragmentary and susceptible to rootlet penetration.
[b] These are taken from features on the site. In light of other dating evidence, principally flint typologies, the excavator rejects these dates as being 'astonishingly late and difficult to verify' (M. Larsson 1986: 39). He suggests a date of *c* 4500–4000 bc.
[c] The first six dates for Skateholm I are taken from graves while the others and those from Skateholm II derive from occupation layers.

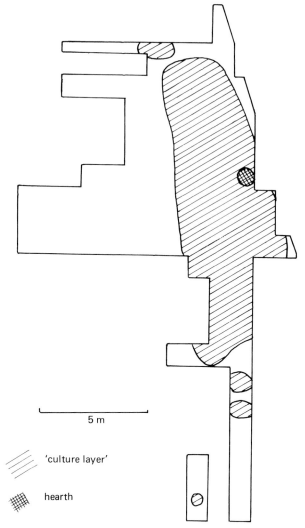

Fig. 6.4. Ageröd I:D showing the extent of the 'culture' layer and the position of a hearth (after Larsson 1978).

Ageröd I:D. Ageröd I:D is the smallest settlement, with cultural debris covering an area of some 38 m² (Fig. 6.4). The boundary of the site to the east, west and north is marked very sharply while to the south the artefactual material gradually tapers out. Larsson suggests that this pattern may have resulted from barriers imposed by hut walls, with the entrance to the hut on the southern side. Central in the area is a small hearth. It is most likely that the site was occupied on only a few occasions and possibly on one occasion alone. Although the peripheral areas of the site suggested more than one finds-producing layer, and one of the wooden artefacts was found buried below the cultural layer, Larsson considers that these are caused by secondary disturbance to the site rather than repeated occupations.

The flint assemblage was not substantial. The largest artefact group was narrow microliths, with 110 examples. These were divided between triangles and narrow trapezes, with the former predominating. A small range of other artefact types was also recovered.

Excellent preservation conditions led to a range of bone and antler artefacts being recovered, including a fish hook, and a diverse faunal assemblage. The faunal material was highly fragmented and only 10% of these could be identified to species. The frequencies in Table 4.1 are taken from the number of bone fragments (auroch 3, elk 4, roe deer 1, red deer 72, pig 14). In addition to these large species there were bones from fur-bearing animals and dog, a single bone from a fish and one from a bird.

Larsson interprets the site as a small summer camp located within a bog. This season is chosen principally because of the position of the site which would have been flooded in any season other than the driest. From the perspective of my work, the small spatial area, the single hearth, lack of structural remains and small size of the faunal and lithic assemblages suggest an occupation of very short duration by a small group.

Ageröd I:B. The distribution of flakes at Ageröd I:B covers a larger area than that of Ageröd I:D. These are concentrated in two distributions, one about 10 m × 3 m and the other about 8 m × 3 m (Fig. 6.5). Larsson notes the similarity in size between these and the area of Ageröd I:D and suggests we may have two huts. The overall distribution of material at Ageröd I:B is more dispersed, however, covering an area of some 200 m². The artefacts were contained in a cultural layer, coloured black by soot and charcoal, which varied from a few millimetres to about 40 cm thick. Where this layer was thickest, the artefacts were found in the lower 5 cm. From this and a consideration of the local topography and formation of the stratigraphy Larsson considers it most probable that there was only one period of settlement on the site.

No structures were present. Some large stones were found which had most probably been introduced by the occupants but no hearths could be identified. The flint assemblage from Ageröd I:B was substantially larger than that from Ageröd I:D. For instance there were 695 cores as opposed to only 20. Of the microliths, 1,502 were narrow and 81 broad types. One notable find was a cluster of 33 microliths, including each type and hence suggesting contemporaneous use, which had apparently been placed in a receptacle and then thrown away. Other artefact groups also had more members than their counterparts from Ageröd I:D and the assemblage was generally more diverse. Larsson has made a thorough typological study and comparison between the Ageröd I:D and I:B flint assemblages.

Conditions of preservation on the site were poor, in comparison with Ageröd I:D, and there were relatively few artefacts made of organic materials. The number of large-ungulate bones identified were: auroch 7, elk 21, roe deer 29, red deer 76 and pig 61. The faunal assemblage also contained a more diverse set of resources than those in Ageröd I:D.

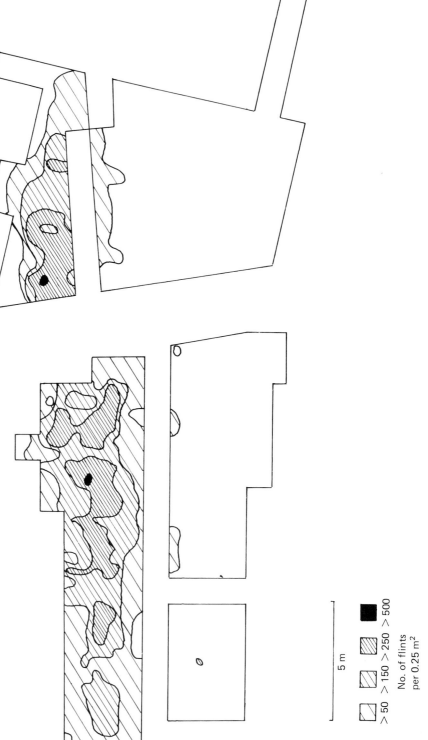

Fig. 6.5. Ageröd I:B showing the distribution of flints (after Larsson 1978).

5 m

No. of flints
per 0.25 m²

> 50   > 150   > 250   > 500

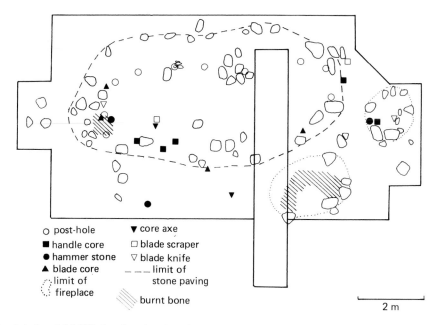

○ post-hole ▼ core axe
■ handle core □ blade scraper
● hammer stone ▽ blade knife
▲ blade core ─ ─ ─ limit of
⸬ limit of   stone paving
fireplace ▨ burnt bone

2 m

Fig. 6.6. Ageröd I:HC showing the plan of the 'hut' (after Larsson 1975).

Ageröd I:B is also interpreted as a summer settlement, lying on the shore of the prehistoric lake. The spatial area and flint and faunal assemblages suggest that we are dealing with a longer period of settlement and/or larger group than at Ageröd I:D.

Ageröd I:HC. Ageröd I:HC is situated on a former lakeshore and the principal feature is a supposed hut (Fig. 6.6). This was built on an artificial layer consisting of sandstone slabs which had been brought from a source 2 km away. These covered an area of 30–40 m² and appear to have been laid so that the settlement could be positioned right next to the lake shore. The area of the site as a whole is around 200 m², similar to Ageröd I:B. The bottom of the hut consisted of a layer of stone covering an area of 8 m × 3 m. Traces of wooden posts were found around the edge of the pavement forming a broad U-shape. There were two hearths close to the hut. High densities of bone and flint were found on the pavement and across the occupation layer.

The hut and occupation layer were excavated within a stratified sequence consisting of a 'bottom layer', a 'lower peat', a 'white layer' and then an 'upper peat'. The white layer consisted essentially of the degraded sandstone slabs and the occupation layer was a burnt horizon covering this. Most of the cultural material was contained within these two layers; a few pieces of bone and chipped stone were found elsewhere. The fauna is classified by Larsson (1978: Fig. 117) and it can be seen that there was little difference in the ungulate frequencies from the lower peat, the white layer and the upper peat. The figures I use in Table 4.1 are the mean values for each ungulate taken from these three layers. The principal occupation layer contained long and narrow triangular microliths and tools made from blades, flakes and bone. Handle cores and a few axes were present, made from both stone and flint. The layer immediately above this contained the same lithic assemblage with the addition of broad trapezes. From this description of the site the most feasible interpretation is of a small, temporary settlement used on few occasions by a small group of hunters. Whether or not the inference of a hut is correct, the site appears to be of a similar ranking in terms of occupation length/group size to that of Ageröd I:B. However, since we have two clusters of material at Ageröd I:B and only one at Ageröd I:HC, I will rank Ageröd I:HC below Ageröd I:B on a group size/ occupation duration axis.

Ageröd V
Ageröd V (Larsson 1983) is located in the southernmost area of the Ageröd bog complex. In the Mesolithic it was situated on an island, about 400 m away from the nearest firm land, and its location appears to have facilitated fishing and fowling rather than the hunting of terrestrial game. As shown in Fig. 6.7, the distribution of flint shows three small adjacent concentrations. Away from this area the finds of flint are sparse. The majority of the artefact-rich area has been excavated. The north-west part of the settlement had been destroyed by peat cutting, which led to the discovery of the site in 1947, but even so the sharp fall-off of flints in this area suggests that the principal part of the site had survived for excavation. The distribution of artefact types followed that of the flakes and waste. The total area of the site is in the region of 125 m². There was no stratigraphic distribution of material.

Larsson describes how the shape and size of each of the flint concentrations is similar to those in the Ageröd I sites and suggests that these may be hut floors. A statistical analysis demonstrated significant differences in the flint assemblages in each concentration which led Larsson to two possible interpretations. The site was occupied either on three separate occasions during which different activities took place (perhaps in different seasons) or on one single occasion with some spatial differentiation in the performance of different tasks. There is some evidence pointing to the second of these. A large hearth was found some 15 m to the south of the flint concentrations which, on the basis of ethnographic analogy, may have been a roasting pit for communal use. Second, a microwear analysis demonstrated a very simple functional distribution pattern, with clustering of artefacts with the same wear pattern (Jensen 1983). This suggests that repeated clearings and tramplings of this site had not occurred since these would have blurred the distribution of functional types. The most reasonable interpretation is that there had been few, perhaps even just one, short-term occupations of the site.

The flint assemblage itself contains a range of artefact types similar to those from the Ageröd I sites. Arrowheads are dominated by trapeze forms, numbering 23. Only 3 narrow microliths are present. To compare it in size with the Ageröd

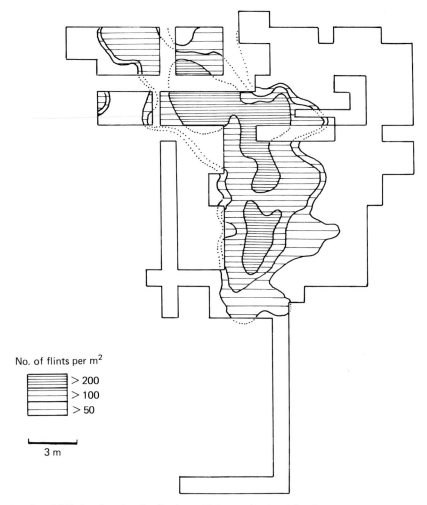

No. of flints per m²

> 200
> 100
> 50

3 m

Fig. 6.7. Ageröd V showing the distribution of flakes and waste (after Larsson 1983).

assemblages we may refer simply to the number of cores, 213, placing it between Ageröd I:D and I:B, as it is in spatial area. The assemblage provides a prime example of the Vedbaek phase of the Ertebølle period, as defined by Petersen (1984).

In spite of good preservation surprisingly few artefacts of bone and antler were found. Those located included slotted bone points, wooden clubs, parts of a long bow and of a smaller bow. Three fragments of a wicker cage, probably the remains of fish or eel traps, were found with two implements described as leister prongs. Thirty-four perforated hazelnut shells were also found, possibly the remains of a necklace.

Of the 1,691 animal bones excavated, 47.5% were of mammals, 2.9% of birds and 49.6% of fish. Fragmentation of the faunal assemblage had been caused by

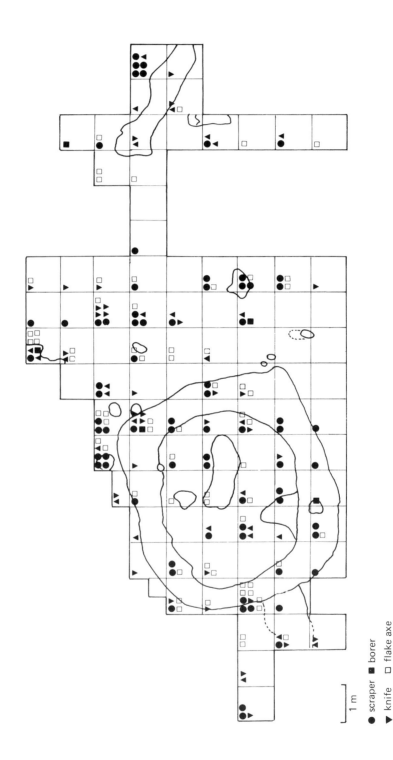

Fig. 6.8. Bredasten showing the 'hut' and distribution of certain artefact types (after Larsson 1986).

1 m

● scraper   ■ borer

▼ knife   □ flake axe

◄ hammer stone

decalcification and gnawing by rodents and dogs. Generally good preservation has allowed the calculation of the minimum number of individuals (MNI), although to maintain comparability the frequencies in Table 4.1 are taken from the number of bone fragments. For the large ungulates MNI were: 2–4 roe deer, 4 elk, 6+ red deer and 3 wild boar. In addition to these there was a sparse representation of fur-bearers and rodents in the assemblage together with six bird species, principally wildfowl, and six fish species. Perch and pike dominated the fish bones. Seasonal indicators at the site were inconclusive. The only available evidence pointed to a limited occupation during the spring and a more intensive period of settlement during the autumn. This too was probably for a short period and the site is interpreted as a small, temporary and seasonal settlement.

Bredasten

Bredasten (M. Larsson 1986) is in the St Herrestad parish of south Scania. It was discovered during the recording of field monuments in that area and excavated in 1984. The stratigraphy of the site is simple; a plough soil 25–30 cm thick lying over an occupation layer of black/grey sand 5–30 cm thick. Cultural material was found in both layers but no chronological distinction could be made. The extent of the site was established in all directions other than to the north. A railway had destroyed it in that area but the scarcity of flints in that direction suggested that the site had not extended far. The total area of the settlement was no more than 500 m².

Twenty-three features were found during the excavation, including post-holes, ditches, hearths and the burial of a puppy. The most important of these was a large ring ditch, 6 m in diameter, 50–100 cm wide and 10–40 cm deep, which dominated the site (Fig. 6.8). This had a hearth in the centre, three large post-holes on a central axis and other smaller associated post-holes. Quite reasonably, it has been interpreted as the remains of a hut, the ditch being either a wall trench or for drainage. As such it is without parallel in southern Scandinavia. An analysis of the distribution of artefacts indicated that tool making had taken place mainly around the hearth, and that the floor of the hut had been kept clear of all food refuse. A small area in the east of the settlement also appeared to have been a locus for activities.

The flint assemblage assigns the settlement to the Ertebølle period and according to Vang Petersen's typology the Vedbaek, Stationsvej and Trylleskov phases were present, with the latter dominant. This may suggest two periods of occupation for the site. However, Larsson points out that the thin occupation layer and the lack of any differentiation in the distribution of different transverse arrowhead types contradicts this. He suggests that Vang Petersen's typology, developed in relation to material from Zealand, is not applicable to Scania. This is strengthened by the presence of artefact types not characteristic of these phases, such as flake axes and scrapers, and the absence of items associated with the Vedbaek phase such as handle cores and soft hammer blades. Consequently the site proved difficult to date on typological grounds. Similarly the C¹⁴ dates were 'astonishingly late and difficult to verify' (Larsson 1986: 39). Taking all the evidence available, Larsson dates the settlement to 4500–4000 bc, between Skateholm I and Skateholm II.

The faunal assemblage (Jonsson 1986) consisted of 699 pieces excavated from 80 m². The majority of these derived from three species – red deer (176), roe deer (36) and wild boar (487). Other species were represented by only one or a few fragments. These included fur-bearers, seals, small ducks, pike, perch and a bird of prey. Blue hare was also found, the first identification since the late glacial period. Jonsson considers the scarce representation of seal and fish at Bredasten in comparison with that at the nearly contemporary Skateholm sites as a real reflection of contrasting activities rather than a factor of preservation or excavation.

Segebro

The Segebro site (Larsson 1980, 1982) is located alongside the west bank of the river Sege in the Spillepengen quarter of the city of Malmö. It was first discovered in 1935 during the laying of pipelines. Small excavations were made in 1960 and 1971 as further developments were made to the pipeline system and in 1973 to recover material for radiometric dating. An extensive excavation was made in 1976 prior to the construction of a large traffic roundabout on the site.

The most important layers of a stratified sequence are numbers 6 and 7 which are interpreted as the occupation and refuse areas of a single settlement. In the occupation layer around thirty features were excavated, principally hearth bottoms, post-holes and pits. Some of these may have been the remains of burials. Since the site was flooded, this being the reason for its abandonment, the original site structure has been lost by water erosion. The north and west areas had been particularly eroded and material from the most elevated part of the settlement redeposited in the northern areas of the refuse layer. Only in the south part of the site did layers 6 and 7 show no signs of erosion. The surviving occupation area was found over 600 m² which provides a minimum for the settlement area.

Larsson (1980) has paid considerable attention to estimating the size of the group occupying the site. He faced the fundamental problem of not knowing whether he was dealing with a single occupation by a large group or many repeated occupations by smaller groups of hunters. He suggests that the site was probably used several times but that these occupations were separated by several years. The minimum number of hearth groups from the surviving deposits is 7 from which he suggested a population size of 35–49 individuals.

The flint assemblage assigns the site to the Kongemose culture, the tool types being dominated by oblique arrowheads. The majority of finds appear to have been deposited in the centuries around 5000 bc. Two decorated antler objects, 73 bone points and 8 slotted bone points were recovered together with a range of shaped wooden logs.

The faunal assemblage from Segebro was substantial and well preserved. Body-part representation of certain species was very uneven, however, some skeletal parts being very under-represented. This probably results either from butchery taking place away from the site or from the effects of differential destruction. However, considering these sources of error, a maximum MNI for each species could be calculated. Red deer dominated at 45 individuals, with 25 roe deer, 25 pig, 10 elk and 2 auroch. Fur-bearing animals and wildfowl were present in substantial quantities and marine mammals also played an important role, with over 35 seals. Of the large assemblage of fish bone the majority belonged to cod (200 individual fish), although perch, pike and dab were also well represented. Seasonal indicators on the site could not rule out the possibility of occupation all year round. The presence of juvenile pig and deer and of migratory bird species suggested that the main occupation had taken place during the spring and early summer.

Skateholm

Skateholm (Larsson 1984, *in press*) is found in Tullstorp parish in the south of Scania. The area had long been known as an area where flints could be found but the importance of the site was only recognised in 1979 and 1980 when small-scale investigations demonstrated the presence of intact Mesolithic occupation deposits over large areas together with an associated graveyard.

In fact three settlement cemetery sites are known in the area, Skateholm I, II and III, of which the first two have received most attention. By 1984 3,000 m² of Skateholm I had been excavated, exposing fifty-seven graves. A preliminary report has been published while a detailed monograph on the site is to be published in the near future.

The occupation areas of Skateholm I and II each cover between 1,500 and 2,000 m² (Larsson, *pers. comm.*). No definite and general stratigraphy at Skateholm I could be identified, although in small local areas of the site some stratified deposits were excavated. The vertical distribution of fish bones is interesting here since these show an increasing frequency of salt-water species, relating to the rise in sea level. Several features have been located in the occupation area of Skateholm I. Some of these have a similar character to the graves while others are pits and post-holes. One feature measured 11 m × 6 m and has been interpreted as a possible hut.

Jonsson (*in press*) has made a detailed study of the fauna from Skateholm I and II. Preservation was poor (by south Scandinavian standards) and less than 100 kg of bones were available for analysis. These were highly fragmented, the median weight being 0.5 gm. The principal destructive agents had been the breaking of bones for marrow, gnawing by dogs and rodents, temperature changes and trampling. Recovery of faunal material had been meticulous with the sieving of all material through a 5 mm mesh, or a 1 mm mesh when concentrations of small bones were excavated. The recovered material was from a sample of one-metre squares made in areas of good preservation and where occupation deposits were thick. About 30 m² from each site has been investigated which, in relation to the large spatial area, provides a small sample. Because of the very similar characteristics of the two sites I will combine the samples when making my comparison with simulated assemblages.

The number of fragments from each of the large ungulates are given in Table 6.2.

Table 6.2. *Bone fragments from Skateholm I and II (after Jonsson, 1986)*

	Skateholm I	Skateholm II	Total
Auroch	—	—	—
Elk	2	5	7
Red deer	182	248	430
Roe deer	174	703	877
Wild boar	447	281	728

In addition to these species a very diverse set of smaller game was derived from the exploitation of three ecological zones: the lagoon, marine and forest biotops. Eighteen other land mammals including fur-bearers and carnivores were present in the assemblage. Grey seal dominated the sea mammals, which included porpoise probably from beached animals. In addition there were thirty-three species of birds, principally wildfowl, and twenty species of fish, mainly perch and pike.

In assessing the evidence for seasonal occupation Jonsson concludes that it was highly probable that the settlement was used throughout the year. This was also suggested by the spatial location of the site which allowed access to an abundance of different resources throughout the year.

At the close of the 1983 season fifty-three graves had been excavated at Skateholm I. Seven of these were of dogs and forty-six were human burials, four of them double graves. Larsson describes the enormous degree of variation in the burial customs 'encompassing the entire gambit of every conceivable method of burial including both inhumation and cremation' (1984: 18). A preliminary analysis suggests that the majority of burials were of men and that children were sparsely represented. The degree of preservation varied markedly between graves. Burial goods were unevenly distributed, appearing to be primarily associated with either older men or younger women. The most frequent finds were the pierced teeth of large ungulates, particularly of red deer and wild boar. Auroch and elk teeth were also present in some graves although these animals appear to have been very rare in the vicinity at the time. Other grave goods included stone, flint and antler artefacts and concentrations of fish bones, amid a discolouration of the soil which was interpreted as the trace of a container made from an organic material and containing fish.

At the time of the preliminary publication eleven graves had been excavated from Skateholm II. This cemetery appears to be very similar to that of Skateholm I although some differences were apparent. For instance the hocker position for the body is absent here while it was the most frequent position at Skateholm I. At Skateholm I dogs received the same burial treatment as humans; at Skateholm II they were found only as secondary burials. In addition the cemetery of Skateholm II had a greater degree of spatial organisation with the majority of burials clustering in a narrow strip above the settlement.

Summary

From my survey of these seven sites it is apparent that we cannot infer the absolute length of time that any one site was occupied or the size of the group involved. Nor can we separate these with any confidence. For instance it is not clear whether Ageröd I:B is larger than Ageröd I:D owing to a larger group size or to occupation for a longer period of time. However I feel confident that these two variables are playing the principal role in determining the spatial area of the sites. Moreover, the most reasonable conclusion to be drawn from the data is that both are operating together. That is, the larger spatial area of a site is reflecting both a larger group size and the length of time a site has been occupied. When discussing the determinants of site structure I referred to the factor of repeated site occupations. Fortunately this appears to play little part in this particular data set. The small sites appear to have been occupied only on very few occasions while the larger sites have additional evidence for longer occupation duration in terms of seasonality data and investment in structures. The largest sites are associated with cemeteries and these are interpreted as reflecting essentially permanent occupation. It is inconceivable that Segebro and Skateholm could result from many short-term occupations by small groups of hunters.

In light of this we can now rank the sites with respect to their spatial area, and the other data which have been discussed, and use this as a ranking for the combined variable of relative group size/occupation duration.

Ageröd I:D
Ageröd V
Ageröd I:HC
Ageröd I:B   Increasing duration of occupation and/or group size
Bredasten
Segebro
Skateholm

We could now plot the composition of the faunal assemblage against this ranking to produce the archaeological signature for this region. Since I am considering the three principal large ungulates, the signature will have three elements relating to pig, red deer and roe deer. These will be given when I make my comparisons with simulated decision goal signatures below.

Mesolithic sites of south-west Germany

Before leaving the archaeological data I want briefly to consider the sites in the Upper Danube valley of south-west Germany (Fig. 6.9) which Jochim (1976) used in his study of Mesolithic subsistence and settlement. Specifically I want to use the faunal data from the sites of Jägerhaus, Falkenstein, Inzigkofen and Lautereck to

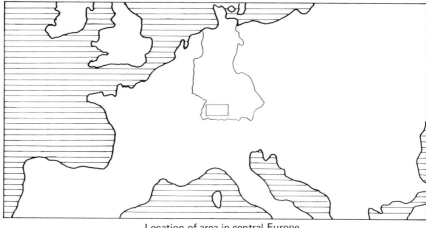

Location of area in central Europe

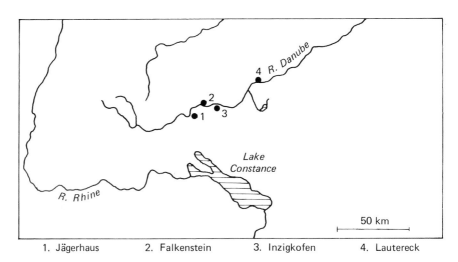

1. Jägerhaus   2. Falkenstein   3. Inzigkofen   4. Lautereck

Fig. 6.9. Mesolithic sites of the Upper Danube Valley referred to in Chapter 6 (after Jochim 1976).

create a second archaeological signature, this time from an inland area of post-glacial Europe. Table 4.1 gives the frequency of red deer, roe deer and pig in these assemblages.

As well as being inland rather than coastal sites, these contrast with the Scanian sites in being either caves or rock shelters. We cannot expect, therefore, the same processes of site formation to operate, because the spatial areas are constant. However, it is still possible to rank the sites along a group size/occupation duration continuum by considering the size, orientation, local topography and probable occupation season of these sites from Jochim's analysis.

Jägerhaus and Falkenstein are large caves, sheltered from prevailing winds by their orientation and local topography. Jochim uses this fact and additional

Table 6.3. *Spatial areas and
population estimates for
Mesolithic sites in the Upper
Danube valley (after Jochim
1976)*

	Area, m²	Population
Jägerhaus	123–156	12–16
Falkenstein	118–150	12–15
Inzigkofen	19–24	2
Lautereck	12–15	1–2

arguments to suggest that these were occupied during the winter and autumn, when group size would have been relatively large, rather than by small hunting groups during the spring. He sees these latter occupations as taking place in the small rock shelters of Inzigkofen and Lautereck, sites with relatively little protection from the weather. He goes on to suggest that the population occupying each site should be proportional to the spatial area below the roof. Table 6.3 gives the areas and resulting group size estimates.

In addition it is a reasonable assumption that periods of longer occupation would take place in sites where there was a larger sheltered living area. Consequently taking all of these factors into account we might rank the sites in the order given above (table 6.3) along the group size/occupation duration axis.

Now we have reached the crux of the matter. Which of the three decision goals (NULL, UIS, UISR), if any, carries a signature which is similar to that from Scania and the Upper Danube valley and can be shown to be meaningful? For this we need to return to the computer model to create the simulated archaeological decision goal signatures.

Re-running the Mesolithic!

As described in Chapter 5, when MESO-SIM runs it creates a faunal assemblage. By varying the parameter values in Table 5.7 we can examine a range of factors which we may believe to cause variability between real assemblages. Since one of the parameters which I intend systematically to vary is NoHunts, I have written the program so that each time it runs not one but NoHunts number of assemblages are created. That is, if, for instance, NoHunts equals 20 then 20 different faunal assemblages are created for lengths of stay at the site for 1 through to 20 hunting trips on each of the NoVisit visits to the site. As a result a graph is produced, as in Fig. 6.10a, which is from the parameter set A in Table 6.4, for just one species, pig, in the assemblage. Writing the program like this is simply a device to maximise the returns from any one run. It will be inefficient if, for instance, we wanted to look at the assemblage resulting from a stay of 20 hunting trips without recording that from all shorter stays up to this value.

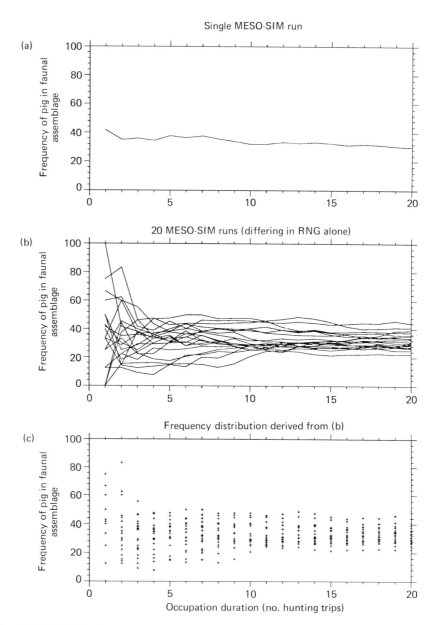

Fig. 6.10. MESO-SIM test runs: A.

Now if we re-run the program with exactly the same parameter set except for the value of RNG, the seed for the random number generator, a different graph will be produced. This is simply the effect of chance on the composition of a faunal assemblage. Two hunters with exactly the same information, goals and hunting ability (not that these can ever be exactly the same in reality) will happen to encounter different animals, in a different sequence and have different degrees of luck in killing those they choose to stalk. Fig. 6.10b shows 20 runs with the A parameter values of Table 6.4 each made with a different RNG value. As can be

Table 6.4. *Parameter values for*
MESO-SIM test runs

	Test run A	Test run B
GOAL	UIS	NULL
RNG	20 values randomly chosen from a uniform distribution between 1 . . . 1000	
NoPers	3	3
NoVisits	5	5
NoHunts	1,2 . . 20[a]	1,2 . . 20
NoMins	300	300
SF	0.1	0.25
RF	1.0	0.5
PF	− 0.0075	− 0.002
A	0.8	0.8
h	1.02	1.02
q	0.005	0.005

Note:
[a] Plus five days of pre-hunting search (see page 112)

seen in this case, there is a wide degree of variation in the frequency of pig in the resulting faunal assemblages. This is particularly so in the assemblages from the shortest length of occupation since in these the MNI is small and the addition of just one or two animals may lead to considerable changes in faunal frequencies. Fig. 6.11a and b shows a single run and twenty runs from a different parameter set, B in Table 6.4 and for roe deer. In this case the degree of variability caused by chance alone is much smaller, i.e. the lines are less dispersed. A more informative representation of these figures is found by replacing the continuous lines with a series of points since the continuity in any one run of the program is simply an artefact of my program to increase the efficiency of its use. Consequently Figs. 6.10c and 6.11c can replace 6.10b and 6.11b and provide us with frequency distributions for the assemblages which derive from the parameter sets in Table 6.4, taking into account the influence of chance. This exercise in exploring stochastic variation indicates that when comparing real and simulated faunal assemblages we must be prepared to recognise that a quite considerable degree of variation in species frequencies may arise from chance alone. The degree of this varies, however, according to the particular parameter set chosen for simulated assemblages, and the particular characteristics of the environment, technology and hunting goals for real assemblages.

Let us now consider two more sources of variation and derive our decision goal signatures. First the local environment (the term 'environment' here including reference to the hunters' technology). As I described above, the character of this is defined by the values given to three parameters, SF, PF and RF. I give two values to each to define a range of eight different local environments. We have to model assemblages created in a variety of local environment types for each of our decision goal signatures. While we might be able to identify the gross environmental

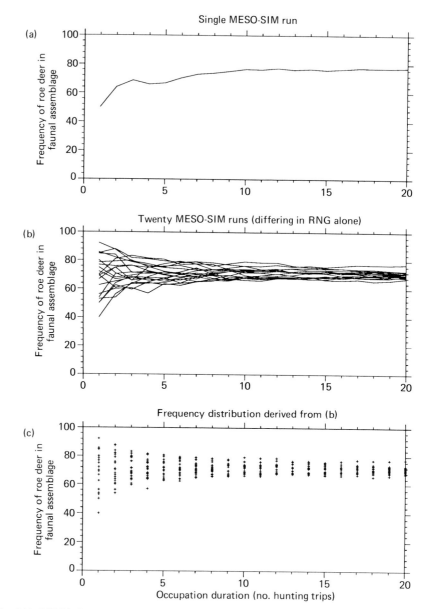

Fig. 6.11. MESO-SIM test runs: B.

characteristics we cannot monitor the local environmental variation across, say, southern Sweden or through a couple of hundred years during which an assemblage may be formed. Hence we need to know the range of variability that may arise in assemblages as a result of differing local conditions and use this as an integral part of the decision goal signature.

The final source of variation I consider is group size. Surely on an *a priori* basis the size of the group occupying a site will affect the composition of the resulting

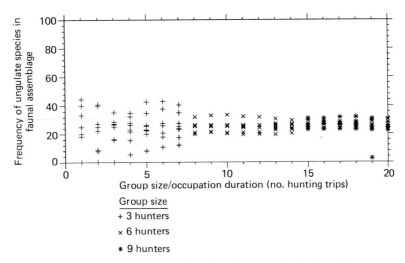

Fig. 6.12. Example frequency distribution of ungulate frequency in simulated faunal assemblages (pig, UISR decision goal).

faunal assemblage. Now, when I discussed the archaeological data from Scania I concluded that the most reasonable interpretation is that group size and occupation duration were positively related. So I now combine these with the 8 different local environments to produce a frequency distribution of assemblages as in Fig. 6.12. In these I have used a group size of 3 for occupation lengths up to 7 trips per visit, 6 hunters up to 14, and 9 hunters up to 20. These may relate to total group sizes of between, say, 9 and 27 people. Now in this plot we have on the x-axis the two variables which I decided to combine for my independent variable for the archaeological signature for the hunting goal and which are positively related to the spatial area of the resulting site. On the y-axis I have the frequency of the species in the faunal assemblage, my independent variable. The vertical displacement of points at each unit on the x-axis (i.e. each group size and occupation duration) arises from the 8 different runs, each made in a unique local environment. Consequently we now have one element of the archaeological signature relating to the hunting goal specified in the parameter set, the other elements being the plots for red deer and roe deer. In light of my discussion of stochastic effects on faunal frequencies we must consider that the frequency distribution may in fact be somewhat more dispersed than that represented. However, it is a plot of this type that I will use as my archaeological signatures for each of the three hunting goals.

The first connection we wish to make is between just one of these decision goal signatures and the real archaeological data. How is that done? Well, quite simply by plotting onto the frequency distributions the real data and seeing whether they fall within or close to the distributions. For this I use the data in Table 4.1, which were discussed in my site summaries above. When elk or auroch are present in the assemblages, the frequencies of red deer and pig have been adjusted to remove these since the simulation has considered only these three species for the reasons outlined above (see pages 106–7). If this frequency of all three ungulates fits one single distribution then we can infer the relevant decision goal as the working hypothesis for the Mesolithic foragers. If it is outside of the distribution then we can reject that decision goal as a viable hypothesis. To plot the real data onto the signatures I simply assume that the x-axis, measuring the occupation duration/ group size, covers the whole spectrum of hunter-gatherer site types. Clearly this is the case near the origin where we have very short occupations, one or two hunting trips by small groups correlating with temporary, possibly overnight, hunting camps. At the other end where we have up to 20 hunting trips, which would correspond to perhaps a two-month occupation if hunting was conducted every third day, we are moving towards semi-permanent sites. We might note here that the changes in the frequency distribution itself along the x-axis have stabilised around a stay of 10 hunting trips in the examples so far given and in all of those I will discuss below. We might therefore extrapolate this pattern further along a now-imaginary x-axis into the area of group sizes larger than 9 hunters and of essentially permanent sites. The archaeological data set from Scania also appears to cover the whole gamut of Mesolithic site sizes ranging from the very small Ageröd I:D to the large and probably semi-permanent sites at Skateholm. Consequently I simply plot the real data from each site and for each ungulate on top of the archaeological signatures for each goal, evenly spacing these on the x-axis in the order of the ranking in terms of occupation duration/group size established above. The data set from south-west Germany contains sites of a relatively small size and it is unlikely that these sites cover the whole continuum of Mesolithic site sizes. It is more probable that the base camps and aggregation sites occupied by large groups for long periods of time are missing. Consequently I plot this data set only into the left-hand half of the signatures referring to the shorter and smaller occupations. Now we can simply inspect each simulated decision goal signature, with the real data imposed, to see in which cases significant overlaps are found. I will deal with the three goals in turn.

The NULL goal – stalking everything encountered

The signatures for the NULL goal, with the real data from Scania and Germany imposed, are given in Fig. 6.13. The simulated pattern in assemblages is a very high dominance of roe deer and about equal frequencies of pig and red deer. In no case do roe deer form less than 50% of the assemblage and red deer more than 20%. For the Scanian data, there is no overlap at all in the real and simulated data for red deer and roe deer. The frequency of pig in the smallest real sites does lie in the distribution and all the others except one fall close to it and are likely to be encompassed by stochastic variation. However, the marked contrast between the real and simulated distributions for red and roe deer means that we have to reject the NULL decision goal as a possibility for the Scanian hunters. They certainly were not stalking every encountered resource. For the German foragers, however, we do have some degree of overlap in that the two smallest sites do appear to fall close to the simulated distributions. But overall the overlap is not particularly marked and we can also reject the NULL decision goal for these inland foragers.

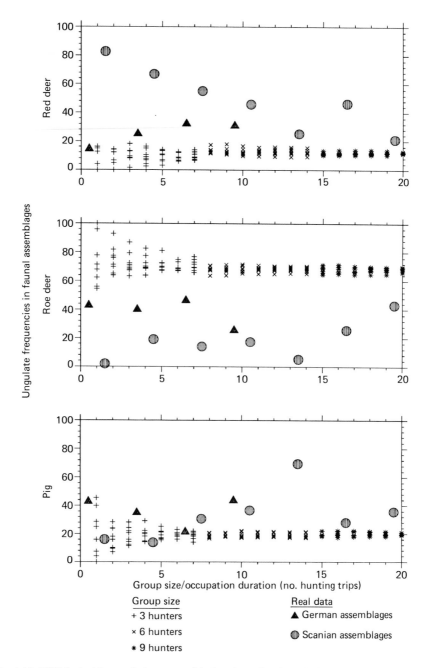

Fig. 6.13. NULL decision goal signature with data from Scania and Upper Danube valley imposed.

UISR goal – try to avoid the risk of returning empty handed

Fig. 6.14 shows the signatures for the UISR goal and as before I have imposed those from Scania and south-west Germany. For the Scanian foragers we have some degree of overlap. All the values for pig fall within the distribution except one, that from Bredasten. Similarly the red deer from the 'larger' sites fall within or sufficiently close to the red deer/UISR signature. However, those from the 'small' sites are a long way off and only a very high degree of stochastic variability might cover them. In addition only one of the roe deer values, that from Skateholm, falls within the distribution with all others lying well below, and probably outside the range of stochastic variation of, the UISR roe deer signature. Our degree of connection is insufficient in this case, therefore, to infer a UISR decision goal for the Mesolithic foragers of Scania. By contrast the overlap between the signature from south-west Germany and the UISR decision goal is substantial. All sites in this case fall within or close to the distributions. We do, then, make a connection here and provisionally infer a UISR goal for the German foragers.

UIS goal – try to meliorise hunting efficiency

The third set of signatures are shown in Fig. 6.15. Here we find a markedly higher degree of overlap between the real and simulated distributions for the Scanian foragers. Only one of the real assemblages falls outside of the signature, that of Bredasten where pig is at a much higher frequency than we would expect for this hunting goal. The fit for all other sites is very significant. Most notable are the two smallest sites, Ageröd I:D and Ageröd V, whose high red deer values now fall within the signature, which has a shape that closely matches the real red deer frequencies – very high (40%–80%) in the small assemblages (though with a small chance that red deer may be infrequent) and then stabilising between 30% and 50% in the larger sites. All the roe deer values lie within the signature and we again find a similar pattern between the real and simulated data, one of a gradual increase in roe deer representation and stabilising at between 10% and 30%. With the exception of Bredasten, the pig values also fall within the signature, although since this has been the case for the other two goals as well this appears to carry little information. Consequently we can infer a UIS decision goal.

The anomalous position of Bredasten might be explained in various ways. We have already seen that it has characteristics different from other southern Scandinavian sites such as the large ring ditch, and this may reflect different types of activities here which may in turn have affected the exploitation of large game. Alternatively, its ranking may have been in error and the faunal assemblage result from a length of occupation and group size which would place it at the far left-hand end of the graph where it would fit the signature – note the very high pig frequencies in some of the smallest assemblages. Of course the anomaly may be due to the faunal assemblage having had considerable post-depositional change so the frequencies from the bone data are a poor reflection of past hunting activity.

Turning to the German data, we again find some degree of overlap between the

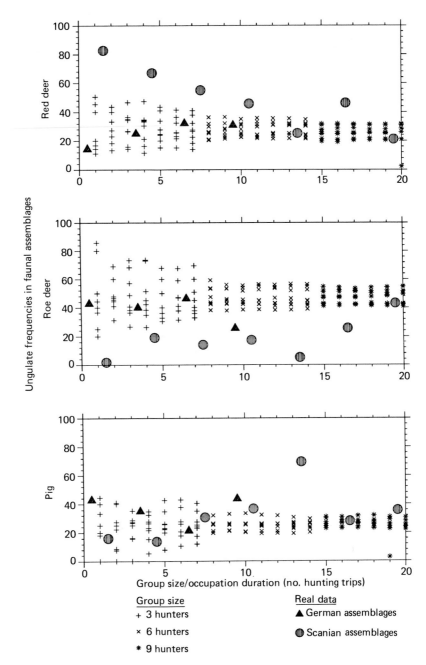

Fig. 6.14. UISR decision goal signature with data from Scania and Upper Danube valley imposed.

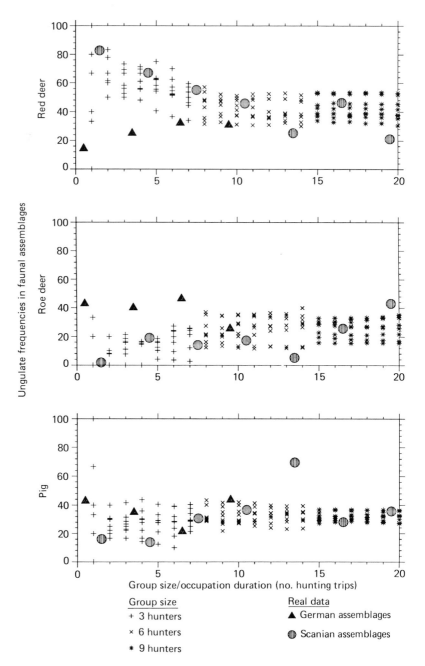

Fig. 6.15. UIS decision goal signature with data from Scania and Upper Danube valley imposed.

real and simulated distributions. This is not, however, as marked as for the UISR decision goal. All the pig frequencies fall in the UIS distribution but, as we have seen, this is not particularly significant. The red and roe deer frequencies are often close to the UIS distributions but overall the UISR signature provides a much better overlap.

To summarise, by comparing the real and simulated signatures I have inferred a UIS decision goal for the Scanian foragers and a UISR decision goal for the foragers from south-west Germany. The former of these inferences can be held with much greater confidence because of the greater integrity of the data set and the distinctiveness of the overlap with the UIS signature. The German data has a little of the 'Echoes from a Marabar Cave' syndrome; it appears to lack a distinctive character. However, the UISR signature did provide the best fit and can be used as a provisional hypothesis. For, as I explained at the start of this chapter, these are only the first of two connections that must be made. Now we turn to the second and see if these inferred decision goals are useful for explaining other aspects of the archaeological record.

Social differentiation in Mesolithic society

Two basic questions were posed in relation to social organisation. Why is social differentiation only found in coastal/lakeside areas and what is the relationship between 'status' and large game, since most of the symbols of wealth relate to large game and the tools used to exploit them? My argument is that the answer to both of these lies in the recognition of different hunting goals for the Scandinavian and Germanic foragers, who we may now adopt as representatives of coastal and inland foragers. The first task is to consider an explanation for the difference in hunting goals.

One of the most important variables differentiating coastal (by which I include areas adjacent to large rivers and lakes) and inland areas is the availability and diversity of resources other than large terrestrial game. Coastal areas have a suite of resources unavailable elsewhere by definition – sea mammals, shellfish and salt-water fish. In addition the diversity and density of bird life are far greater. From five Scanian sites (Ageröd I:B, D, HC; Ageröd V; Segebro) 27 different bird species have been identified, while the MNI from the four German sites is only 7 (the species identities not being published). Plant foods were probably also far more available in the coastal regions than in the inland areas.

My argument is that, owing to the diverse range of foods available and the high biomass of these, large-game hunting in coastal areas became divorced from simply providing food. This was partly made possible by the use of technology such as fish traps, as found on south Scandinavian sites. Such facilities could remain set while terrestrial hunting was in progress, allowing efficient use of time and reducing reliance on large terrestrial game for food. As a result the killing of large game became a mechanism for acquiring wealth and prestige. Such wealth was gained by being an efficient hunter and 'giving food away' from the large kills, thereby building up reciprocal obligations (O'Shea and Zvelebil 1984). I maintain here a strict evolutionary perspective and see the acquisition of wealth and prestige as part of the hunter's process of adaptation. Possessing wealth in these terms would have served to increase reproductive success principally by allowing greater success in the competition for mates (Hill 1984; Kaplan and Hill 1985). In areas where resources such as fish, small game, wildfowl and plants could not be relied upon on a daily basis, and consequently large-game hunting had to maintain a risk-reducing element, such strategies for increasing reproductive success were not feasible. Hunters had first and foremost to provide sufficient food from the large terrestial ungulates that were available.

It is to be expected, therefore, that within the cemeteries of coastal/lakeside regions we should find symbols which appear to signify wealth and which relate to large game species. The reciprocal obligations that these represented could be called in by the wealthy hunters at times of resource failure and consequently acted as a risk-buffering mechanism as well as a source of power. Here I am invoking risk on a larger time scale (i.e. seasonal) than the daily risk of not acquiring game that I have so far considered (see Whitelaw 1986 for a discussion of risk and risk buffering over different time scales). The essence of my argument is quite simple. The availability of resources other than large game removed the need for daily risk-reducing goals in terrestrial hunting and hence the hunters strove to meliorise hunting efficiency in their quest for wealth by adopting a UIS hunting goal. As such, this provided one element, not the totality, of the social dynamics in coastal regions.

In contrast, for hunters in the inland areas such as south-west Germany, these alternative daily risk-buffering resources were not available, or at least could not be relied upon. Consequently large-game hunting could not become divorced from providing food, and hunting goals required a daily risk-reducing element (e.g. UISR). Note that this argument is not falling into the trap of environmental determinism. It simply argues that the character of the environment in coastal regions relaxed a constraint on hunting behaviour and allowed latent social competition and dynamics to become manifest. I am specifying the articulation between hunters and their social and physical environments.

This argument can be strengthened and illustrated by using the results from the simulation runs I have made. In Fig. 6.16a I have plotted the frequency distribution for the percentage of hunters in the group who are successful in killing some game, of whatever utility, on each hunting trip for each of the three goals. Each curve is derived from the 800 simulated hunting trips used in creating the decision goal signatures. As can be seen, that of the UIS goal is spread over low values (few of the hunters in the group are successful on each occasion), while that from NULL spreads over higher values indicating that more hunters are normally successful in making a kill. The UISR curve lies between these two. This pattern is what we should expect from the different goals, with NULL hunters never passing up an opportunity to try and make a kill, UIS hunters being very selective and UISR hunters falling between these extremes.

Fig. 6.16b shows the frequency distributions for the foraging efficiency of the

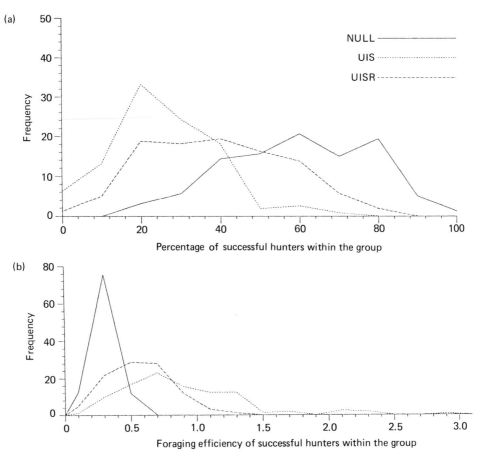

Fig. 6.16. Frequency distributions for (a) percentages of successful hunters in the group, for UISR, UIS and NULL goals and (b) the foraging efficiencies of successful hunters, for UISR, UIS and NULL goals.

hunters in the group who are indeed successful in making some kill. Now we see the NULL hunters tightly clustered over low values – stalking everything is not very efficient but, as we have seen in Fig. 6.16a, has a high chance of resulting in some kill. The UIS curve is much flatter and has a long tail into the values recording a high foraging efficiency. That is, although the chance of being successful in terms of making a kill is small, if one is successful then there is a high likelihood of being a very efficient forager. Again the UISR hunters lie between the UIS and NULL curves, they seek a bit of both worlds but get the best of neither.

These curves might be thought of as the mental map that the foragers carry and use when (meta-)choosing which goal to adopt. I am arguing that the south Scandinavian foragers (meta-)chose the UIS goal since the risk of being unsuccessful in large ungulate terrestrial hunting could be ignored owing to the availability of alternative resources, particularly those caught in unmanned facilities such as fish traps. As a consequence they sought to gain prestige and influence by adopting a UIS goal and trying to be efficient hunters, to fall into the tail of the UIS efficiency curve. In contrast the hunters in Germany chose either the NULL or UISR goal, resulting in low efficiencies, and little variability in this within the group, since the lack of alternative resources meant that the risk of failure when hunting large game had to be reduced.

The analysis of Oleonostrovski Moglinik cemetery by O'Shea and Zvelebil (1984) suggests that one dimension of social differentiation is an association between wealth and age which they interpreted as relating to hunting ability. This may be a general feature of Mesolithic cemeteries in which distinctions according to age, sex and personal achievement are marked (Clark and Neeley 1987). This association is expected from my model of social dynamics and hunting goals. With a slight modification, the simulation model can be used to demonstrate the effect of hunting ability on the build up of wealth since, as I explained above, the influence of an individual in the group relates directly to his past hunting success.

To model the greater ability of one hunter over another we can simply manipulate parameters of the environment or resources when we are modelling behaviour. For instance, the pursuit or processing times of resources may be reduced. Alternatively, the method I adopt is to alter the chances of making a successful kill when the designated hunter is attempting to kill a stalked animal. This may relate to such physical abilities as greater bow-drawing strength. Specifically I make one hunter in the group twice as likely to kill the resource as the other hunters. Having done this we can explore the conditions in which such greater hunting ability does actually lead to greater influence in decision making and hence, in the context of Oleonostrovski Moglinik and Mesolithic Scandinavia, wealth.

To begin exploring this, twelve runs of the program were made with the UIS goal. Half of these related to a 'poor' environment and half to a 'rich' environment, as defined at the end of Chapter 5. The term 'environment' is used here to refer not only to the ecology of the hunted game but also to the technology of the hunters. In each environmental type three runs were made with the abilities of hunters all equal, as in all the previous runs, each run having a different RNG, and the other three runs with hunter no. 3 having a greater ability modelled in the manner I described. All runs were made for only one visit to the site and the influence of each individual on each day was recorded. Fig. 6.17a–1 illustrates the influence of each individual over the hunting trips. While the number of simulation runs made here is too small to provide any substantial conclusions, the patterns they provide are very provocative.

As would be expected, when hunter no. 3 is of superior ability in the rich environment (Fig. 6.17j–1) he may gain considerably more influence in the group than the other members, although, by chance, this did not happen on one occasion. The same runs when the hunters are of equal ability (Fig. 6.17d–f) show that no individual sustains a high influence in the group, although this may be achieved for short periods of time.

The runs concerning foraging in the poor environment show a rather different

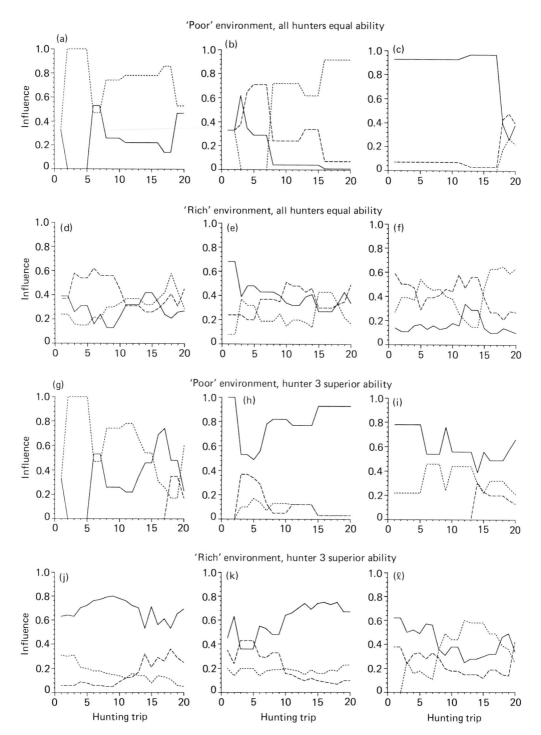

Fig. 6.17. Change in hunters' influence within the group during a visit to the site (dotted line = hunter 1, dashed line = hunter 2, solid line = hunter 3).

pattern. First the changes in hunters' influences are not as smooth but have sudden and dramatic changes either up or down. This is because in the poor environment kills of game (and hence changes of influence) are much less frequent and even a small kill (e.g. a juvenile roe deer) can lead to considerable changes in influence. In two of the runs with no. 3 of superior ability (Fig. 6.17g–i) he attains high influence in the group. However it is apparent that individuals may emerge as having high influence even when they are all of equal ability (Fig. 6.17a–c). This contrast with the rich environment presumably arises because the frequency of kills is so small and 'luck' (i.e. stochasticity) overwhelms any similarities or differences in hunting ability.

This may act as a constraint on the ability of hunters to acquire prestige and wealth from large-game hunting since success is essentially defined by stochastic factors. Even when hunting success in a 'poor' environment is totally or partly due to greater ability (as Fig. 6.17h and i may represent) other members of that group will not be confident that such success has not arisen simply by chance, as in Fig. 6.17a–c. The men and women in a foraging group in a 'rich' environment, however, will be ready to attribute prestige to a successful hunter since sustained hunting success by chance is impossible (Fig. 6.17d–f). This begins to define further the context in which the type of social differentiation we find during the later Mesolithic (Clark and Neeley 1987) may arise. In addition to the availability of a set of daily risk-reducing resources and the technology and organisation to exploit them, the probability of encountering large terrestrial game and/or the rate of success in killing them must be above some critical level. In certain regions during the Mesolithic, and perhaps during the Maglemosian in southern Scandinavia, there may well have been the abundant and diverse coastal/small-game resources to play a daily risk-reducing goal. But the probability of encountering and successfully killing the large terrestrial ungulates may have been so low that stochastic factors were dominant and, while a UIS hunting goal may have been pursued, such hunting could not provide a means of acquiring wealth. 'Lucky' and 'able' hunters could not be differentiated between. Low probabilities of encounter may relate to environmental factors and information flows while high rates of hunting failure may relate primarily to technology rather than the environment. Indeed, there may be some threshold in technological efficiency (in terms of the frequency with which stalks are followed by actual kills) that must be passed before large-game hunting can start to act as a medium for wealth acquisition. Once this is passed, then the competitive hunting may act as a spur to further technological innovation as I will discuss below.

Star Carr and the Early Mesolithic in Britain may represent a situation in which competitive social dynamics were constrained. Legge and Rowley-Conwy (1988) re-analyse the fauna and interpret the site as a hunting camp. The dominance of ungulates with high utility values at the site – red deer, elk and auroch – and the relatively small frequency of roe deer probably reflects a UIS hunting goal. This is supported by the age structure of the red deer and roe deer kills. The first shows an attritional pattern and the second a catastrophic profile (Legge and Rowley-

Conwy 1988: Figs. 14 and 15). Under the UIS goal red deer would have been one of the ungulates initially hunted when foraging efficiencies were high and hence only the more profitable members of that species taken, the young being ignored. By the time that foraging efficiencies had fallen to include roe deer these may have been so low that all age/sex classes of roe deer would be sufficient to meliorise hunting efficiency. Although young red deer would now also be stalked the frequency of encounter with these would have been insufficient to remove the attritional nature of the red deer profile since most time was being invested in stalking the relatively abundant roe deer. (Legge and Rowley-Conwy explain the contrasting profiles by reference to supposed seasonal movements of different age classes in these populations.) Yet while we have evidence for a UIS hunting goal, we do not have any evidence for social ranking and differential wealth in Early Mesolithic society. We may be seeing, therefore, the type of hunting patterns and changes in influence modelled in the 'poor' environments of Fig. 6.17. That is, hunters were seeking to be efficient foragers, and thereby acquire wealth, but the nature of the environment and/or the Maglemosian technology acted as a constraint by allowing stochastic factors to dominate patterns and perceptions of hunting success within the group.

Technological decisions and lithic assemblages
This argument has led us into the second problem area of Mesolithic archaeology that I discussed in Chapter 4: variability in lithic assemblages and in particular the issue of innovation. Can this be integrated into the explanatory framework I am building, centred on the individual decision maker? I have already invoked the role of technology in providing an explanation for the feasibility of possessing a UIS goal in south Scandinavia – daily risk was coped with by the use of facilities such as fish traps and a reliance on small game. Here I am concerned with the large-game hunting weapons and, specifically, microlithic projectile points.

First I want to make a distinction between short-term flexibility in the use of available tool types and the introduction and adoption of brand-new elements into the technological repertoire. In relation to the first of these I will consider technology as essentially a body of knowledge on the basis of which particular tools are chosen to perform the tasks for which they are deemed appropriate. From this perspective, and the totality of the decision processes for the Mesolithic hunters, how may light be shed upon the variability in lithic assemblages in Scania? Let us consider how the microlithic tool kit should vary with the length of occupation at a site in southern Scandinavia. As I have discussed and demonstrated above, these foragers appear to have been using a hunting pattern without daily risk reduction. The resulting hunting pattern was that when hunters first arrived at a site only the animals with high returns were stalked. As time progressed the hunters were forced by falling foraging efficiency to turn to the animals of lower returns, most notably roe deer. We saw how the percentage of this species rose in the assemblages with site size/length of occupation. What decisions would be taken about the microlithic tool kit to cope with such falling efficiency?

Here we can turn for help to the work of Torrence (1983, 1989c). In two related papers she has discussed hunter-gatherer technology as a means of solving subsistence related problems and has made specific predictions for the diversity, complexity and composition of tool kits which were supported by ethnographic data. Her most recent paper centred on the use of tools to prevent the loss of resources. One general proposition is that the more specialised a tool is for a particular task, the greater will be the likelihood of suceeding in that task.

If we apply this to the south Scandinavian foragers we should expect the diversity of their microlith set to increase with site size; there will be an increase in the number of microlith forms. Here I am referring to Zvelebil's characterisation of microlithic tools in which the small stone blades can be quickly shaped to suit killing a specific animal in a particular situation (1986a: 89) since they are not 'purpose made in advance . . . [but] dedicated to their specific tasks in the field in response to the foraging opportunities as they arise' (1986c: 170). The range of targeted prey for the south Scandinavian UIS foragers when they are first at the site is small since they are seeking to kill only the game which provide the largest returns. Others will be ignored. Moreover, once such an opportunity is present (i.e. a stalk initiated, which is rare because of the selectivity of the hunters) the hunter will want the best chances of killing the animal and, according to Torrence's argument, will use a specialised tool. In this context a specialised tool refers to a specifically shaped microlith, or arrangement of these on a shaft, and we must assume that certain forms are 'known' as being most appropriate for killing particular types of game in particular situations. It is not just the diet breadth that is increasing with the length of occupation. As foraging efficiency declines, the opportunities for stalking ungulates with high returns, which had previously been ignored owing to unsuitable factors such as wind direction or lack of cover, will be taken up. The estimated efficiency for hunting a male red deer when there is a particularly low chance of killing it may be equivalent to that of a roe deer with a particularly high chance. Exploiting such unsuitable situations will further increase the diversity of the microlith set. For instance an attempt may be made to strike a red deer from a distance or a peculiar angle and a specifically shaped microlith(s) may be produced. (This dependence of success rates on very local factors is of course something that I did not include in the simulation model.) Consequently as the diet breadth and 'killing' situations increase with the length of occupation, there will be an increase in the number of specialised tools, i.e. microlith forms. This would be particularly marked since as foraging efficiency declines each failed killing attempt would only further decrease this, and hence specialised and dedicated microlith forms would be at a premium.

We can test this prediction by considering the diversity of microlithic projectile points in small (i.e. shorter-stay) and large (i.e. longer-stay) sites: that in the latter should be higher. To do this we must deal with contemporary sites so that we can control for the introduction of brand-new elements into the tool kit. For this the assemblages from the Scanian sites of Ageröd I:HC, I:B and I:D can be examined. They are all dated between 5500 bc and 6000 bc. According to the site rankings

Table 6.5. *Classification of microliths from Ageröd I:D, B and HC (after Larsson 1978)*

Morphological classification				Retouch classification			
Triangles	HC	B	D	*Triangles*	HC	B	D
1	13	1	1	aI	19	154	11
2	3	16	1	aII	30	67	9
3	32	137	4	aIII	21	36	2
4	27	121	10	aIV	19	36	1
5	17	57	7	bII	1	2	0
				dII	2	2	0
				Left	0	35	0
Lancelots							
6a	8	22	0				
6b	6	5	0				
6c	3	3	0				
Narrow trapezes							
7a	10	39	0				
7b	4	11	2				

derived above, we should expect the diversity of microliths at Ageröd I:HC and I:B to be similar, and greater than that at Ageröd I:D. We need a classification of the microliths and a measure of diversity. For the first we can use that of Larsson (1978). He makes two cross-cutting classifications based on morphology and the position of retouch. With respect to the first he divides the microliths into three classes (triangles, lancelots and narrow trapezes) and a total of sixteen types. He also describes the broad trapezes for Ageröd I:B and I:D but does not provide this for Ageröd I:HC. His second classification uses the position of retouch on triangles, dividing these into seven classes. The data are reproduced in Table 6.5.

To measure diversity we can use one of the indices used in ecology to measure the diversity of species in a community. These take into account both the number of species (in this case microlith types) and the number within each type. The most appropriate is the Shannon-Weaver index (Pielou 1969):

$$H = -\sum P_i \mathrm{Log}\, P_i$$

Where P_i is the proportion of tools in the ith class.

H values closer to 1 mean a more diverse assemblage than those nearer to the other extreme of 0. Applying this to the data in Table 6.5 provides the microlith diversity measures shown in Table 6.6.

This meets the expectations and hence we have made some progress towards explaining the complex area of variability of microliths in lithic assemblages. To develop this further, however, we must consider the adoption of brand-new elements into the repertoire of tools, in this case new classes of microliths. To consider this we can return to the eco-pyschological decision-making model and the distinction I drew between acquired and stored information.

Table 6.6. *Microlithic diversity in Ageröd I assemblages*

Classification	Site	Diversity
Morphology	Ageröd I:HC	0.875
	Ageröd I:B	0.741
	Ageröd I:D	0.641
Position of retouch	Ageröd I:HC	0.646
	Ageröd I:B	0.634
	Ageröd I:D	0.464

If we maintain Torrence's proposition that the principal functional role of technology is to cope with risk (here the failure to kill an animal once a stalk has been initiated), then we can think of a particular type of point as affecting the RF value in equation 3. This may be in relation to all resources, but more probably in relation to specific resources, in which case we should consider RF_j. In this case we are stating simply that particular microlith forms are suited to killing particular game, which is the premise on which the investigation of tool kit diversity was based. For tools already in the tool kit, hunters will have stored information for their effect on each RF_j value. That is, they know which forms are best for killing each resource and use this information to make decisions concerning the tool kit in the manner I discussed above.

In the case of a brand-new type of microlith, whose presence may have arisen by accident, by purposeful invention, or from a visiting hunter from another group, the foragers will not have any stored information as to its effect on the RF_j values. Some information may be acquired from 'internal' sources by using the stored knowledge of similar points to imagine how it may perform. However, there will be a period of experimentation to acquire information, which is equivalent to sampling in relation to foraging decisions.

Turning to a concrete example we can consider the introduction of trapeze and rhomboid microliths made on broad blades. Larsson (1978: 175) argues that these make more effective projectile points than narrow microliths since they lead to deeper penetration, have a more effective cutting edge and are more likely to remain within the animal. Consequently their use will increase the RF value(s) – reducing the frequency of hunting failure – and they will be rapidly adopted into the tool kit. This would help to explain their rapid adoption across continental Europe. The important point remains, however, of the need to experiment with the new microlith – the forager must seek a balance between 'exploration' and 'exploitation'. With respect to my above discussion of large-game hunting as a medium for social competition, it is perhaps technical innovation, such as these new microliths, that can sufficiently increase hunting efficiency (in terms of reducing hunting failure) so that the stochastic influences on hunting success are over-ridden by ability (as in stalking and aiming), and strength (as in drawing a bow string). Consequently, in areas such as southern Scandinavia, the adoption of broad-blade microliths, perhaps in conjunction with increasing forest density during the Atlantic, may have created the 'rich' environments as modelled in Fig.

6.17. In this context, sustained hunting success may have arisen from ability alone and hence those individuals would have carried influence and prestige within the group and gained greater success in the competition for mates.

With further reference to southern Scandinavia, the rapid development of new types of microliths during the later Mesolithic is not surprising in light of the UIS hunting goal and the related social dynamics. To maintain and meliorise their current hunting efficiency, particularly in the face of competition from their peers, the hunters will have needed to experiment with and adopt new types of microlith points. In doing this they will have been trying to achieve a high foraging efficiency, i.e. placing themselves into the long tail of the UIS curve in Fig. 6.16. Indeed, we might think of technological change as altering the shape of this curve so that larger frequencies are distributed over the higher values. In doing this we have identified creative thought as an essential element in the process of adaptation. This leads into the important area that has been neglected by archaeologists concerning which individuals within a group will be most ready to experiment with new technology. Economic anthropologists have discussed this question with respect to the innovation of new agricultural methods among farmers (e.g. Dewalt and Dewalt 1984; Cancian 1984). A variety of models have been proposed relating the variables of risk taking and wealth. In the case of the hunters of Southern Scandinavia we can replace the variable of 'wealth' by 'age' (see p. 10 above, O'Shea and Zvelebil 1984) and hence a range of hypotheses could be put forward. It is in this direction that research will need to go to get a grip on the process of technological change.

Economic change: the adoption of agriculture

The variability in decision goals that has been inferred between Scania and south-west Germany may help in understanding the different rate at which agriculture was adopted/dispersed into these areas. In south-west Germany the indigenous population had either adopted agricultural methods or become assimilated into farming societies by 4500 bc, characterised by the LBK culture (Barker 1985). Phases of availability and substitution appear to have been very short. By contrast the first farmers in southern Scandinavia, coinciding with the funnel-necked beaker pottery, are dated to 3300–2700 bc (Barker 1985). This appears to have followed a long period of availability and a gradual process of substitution. While this contrast has been tackled most recently by asking why there was this delay of agricultural dispersal to south Scandinavia (e.g. Rowley-Conwy 1984; Blankholm 1987a), we might take another view and ask why it should have been so rapid in south-west Germany.

I have argued that the Mesolithic foragers in this area used a UISR-type hunting goal for large terrestrial game. Social competition, in terms of acquiring prestige and wealth by selective hunting of the most profitable animals, was constrained by the need to reduce the risk of failing to make a kill. From this viewpoint the availability of agricultural resources/methods may have received two types of responses from the hunters. First they may have chosen readily to engage in farming, or readily to assimilate into farming communities, in order to provide a set of alternative resources to the large game and to fulfil the role played by the diverse and abundant fish, wildfowl and plant resources in coastal areas. In this respect Pryor's (1986) cross-cultural study of simple agricultural societies is interesting. He suggests that one of the reasons that agriculture is pursued is indeed to diminish reliance on wild game and the risks involved.

A second reason why the Mesolithic foragers of south-west Germany may have adopted agriculture, or assimilated into the farming communities, is that the cultivation and domestication of resources may have provided in itself a medium for social competition and the accumulation of wealth that had previously been unavailable. In this scenario we see agricultural resources playing the role not of the fish/wildfowl/small game of the coastal areas but of the large terrestrial ungulates themselves.

To explore this a little further it is useful to consider briefly the hunting of large terrestrial ungulates by the 'farmers' at Hienheim, one of the earliest LBK settlements in the Danube valley. This is situated on the left bank of the Danube on the eastern edge of the loessic plain and dated 4205–3960 bc (Modderman 1977). The faunal remains had a notably high proportion of wild animals for a LBK site, although these were poorly preserved and neither age/sex data nor MNI estimates could be made (Classon 1977). However, in terms of species proportions red deer dominated, followed by wild boar and then roe deer (29, 13 and 7 bone fragments respectively). Of course little can be inferred from such small samples but it is interesting to note that this ranking is in direct contrast to that on the Mesolithic sites of the Upper Danube valley in which roe deer either dominated or were on a par with red deer. Perhaps, if the Hienheim pattern is not simply an artefact of preservation, we see here a change in the decision goals used to hunt large terrestrial game. For while the Mesolithic foragers appear to have used a NULL/UISR-type goal, a dominance of red deer is indicative of a UIS-type goal. This would support the first scenario I suggested. Agriculture was being pursued either by the ex-Mesolithic foragers, by the colonising farmers or by a social mix of the two, to provide risk-buffering resources, and the exploitation of large ungulates provided a medium for social competition as it already had done, and continued to do, in southern Scandinavia. But what is most likely is that the problems created by cultivating and domesticating resources, in terms of their own fluctuations, scheduling work and the change in the individual's social context, would have come to dominate those concerned with hunting. Hence a switch occurs to the second scenario I proposed in which the production of surpluses and trade becomes the dominant medium for social competition and hunting is transformed into the risk-buffering activity.

We might also briefly consider the character of Early Neolithic settlement in Scania. Wyszomirska (1988) has described the site of Nymölla III. This is situated in north-east Scania at the mouth of the Skräbe river on the Baltic coast and is later than 3800 bc. Ertebølle and funnel-necked beaker pottery, much of it decorated, is found on the site and it is possible that both traditions were in contemporary use.

There is no evidence for domesticated resources at the site and the economic base appears similar to the coastal Mesolithic sites I described earlier. Among the large terrestrial ungulates red deer is dominant, followed by pig and then roe deer (77, 31 and 23 bones respectively). Although we again have the problem of a small sample and no MNI calculation, this type of pattern reflects a UIS hunting goal. The faunal assemblage also witnesses the exploitation of a diverse set of sea mammals, small mammals, wild fowl and fish species. These would, as I have argued above, have played the daily risk-reducing role in the economy, allowing terrestrial game to act as a medium for social competition.

Numerous artefacts at the site suggest that its occupants were engaging in an extensive exchange network, perhaps of prestige objects. The flint assemblage includes raw material from south-west Scania while Wyszomirska suggests that the abundant local flint was exploited for a 'conscious control of flint production, distribution, transportation and exchange' (1988: 190). The stone axes at the site were made of dacite and were probably not of Swedish origin. They may have come from Germany or Poland which also appear to be the source of a piece of a Globular Amphora. This evidence for trade agrees with that from other Late Mesolithic/Early Neolithic sites in southern Scandinavia in indicating contacts with the farming communities to the south (Fischer 1982). One engraved axe at Nymölla III has been interpreted as a prestige symbol while an engraved and worn artefact made of wild boar tusk been described as an amulet.

Such combinations of ceramic, faunal and stone material at Nymölla III suggest a reaction of the Scanian foragers to the availability of farming very different from the reaction of those in south-west Germany. Essentially we see here an adoption of new items of material culture, particularly ornate pottery, perhaps in terms of emulation. For instance one finds decorative patterns on Ertebølle pottery similar to those in the Rossen culture (Fischer 1982). In addition we see participation in exchange networks. These reflect an intensification of social competition in the society which had already been established through the UIS exploitation of large game. Domestic resources had no role to play in such social strategies. This contrasts with the situation in south-west Germany where it was the domestic resources, not the material culture, that was initially of most significance and which first allowed, rather than intensified, competitive social interaction.

PART 3

Upper Palaeolithic art and economy

7

Seeking the decision maker: faunal assemblages and hunting behaviour

I saw a jolly hunter
With a jolly gun
Walking in the countryside
In the jolly sun

Charles Causley, 'I Saw a Jolly Hunter'

Over the green pastures there
You shall go hunting the beautiful deer

W.H. Auden with Christopher Isherwood, 'The Ascent of F.6'

My intention in this work is to argue that a focus on the individual decision maker is *the* stance for developing adequate explanations in archaeology. Let me make the tentative assumption that you have found something of value in my study of Mesolithic foraging and society, that you feel my focus on individual decision making has indeed made a contribution to explaining the variability and patterning in that archaeological record, whether or not you agree with my specific arguments. However, I can hear you asking if this was so as a result simply of the particular character of those data rather than of any inherent virtue in my individualistic eco-psychological decision-making approach. Can we find the individual and use our growing understanding of decision-making processes when we have an archaeological record of a markedly different character, for instance when faunal assemblages are large and complex, deriving from 'multiple authors' (Gamble 1984: 239) and co-operative hunting and without the fine chronological resolution of the Mesolithic? And what if our principal problem does not immediately refer to hunting behaviour but to cognition? Does an individual decision-making approach enable us to develop our studies of, say, prehistoric art and ritual? My answer is of course an emphatic yes. To demonstrate this, I will take a step backwards from the Mesolithic to the late glacial and tackle problems posed by Upper Palaeolithic art. Hopefully by taking this step back in time I will be striding forward in persuading you of the general utility of focusing research on the individual decision maker.

Following the general premise of this work, access to the art of prehistoric hunter-gatherers can be made by working through the faunal assemblages and hunting behaviour to locate the decision-making processes. Inferences drawn about these can then help untangle the web of relationships between social, cognitive and ecological aspects of behaviour. By invoking the individual decision maker we can place the art into its ecological context and the hunting into its social and cognitive context. This chapter deals with the first stage of this process – seeking the decision maker by a study of faunal assemblages and hunting behaviour. As with the previous case study, mathematical models and computer simulation will play an important role in this task. I must once again emphasise that these are just *tools*. My focus on the functional aspects of decision making in MESO-SIM did not deny the other facets of the mind of a Mesolithic hunter – the emotional and spiritual feelings for the environment, the symbolic articulation with the natural world that complements the ecological. Similarly, when I build models of Upper Palaeolithic hunting in this chapter which focus on investments, risk and efficiency I am not implying that these constitute the totality of the hunters' relationship with their game. As I discussed in Chapter 1, hunters operate in ecological and symbolic worlds simultaneously and without contradictions. Moreover, I am sure that the Upper Palaeolithic decision makers were often 'jolly hunters in the jolly sun' and, like those of the Mesolithic, didn't spend every moment worrying about foraging problems, the choice of decision goals and their imperfect information. I am equally sure that they thought that the deer were 'beautiful'. My sole, but (for me) incontrovertible, evidence is the stag painted in Niaux (Fig. 7.1). How could anyone create such art without a deep love for the subject? But let me put specific images on ice for the present, as the hunters may have put the flesh from that stag, and make a start with a few brief and general comments as to the problems that the art poses to an enquiring mind.

Palaeolithic art: why there, then, this and that?
The problems posed by Palaeolithic art are numerous and diverse but can be divided into two main camps. On the one hand we have those concerned with its spatial and temporal distribution. At a gross scale we can ask why it is concentrated in south-west Europe and in the Later Upper Palaeolithic (e.g. Jochim 1983a)? Progressively finer distributional problems can be posed as our spatial and temporal scales are reduced. These may concern regional and local variability in the distribution of particular motifs (e.g. Straus 1982a; Sieveking 1980; White 1985), the arrangement of images within one single cave (e.g. Leroi-Gourhan 1968; Sieveking 1984) and changes over time in style and content (e.g. Straus 1982a; Leroi-Gourhan 1968; Lorblanchet 1977). Several explanations, or at least provocative statements, have been put forward concerning such problems. Perhaps the most interesting are those which adopt a functional interpretation of the art (e.g. Jochim 1983a; Gamble 1982; Pfeiffer 1982). However, in doing this the specific imagery in the art has been neglected. The imagery itself has no consequence for the types of explanations proposed other than as evidence that visual symbolism and communication were pervasive and significant for these societies. For instance, Jochim's (1983a) arguments for the gross distributional problems of

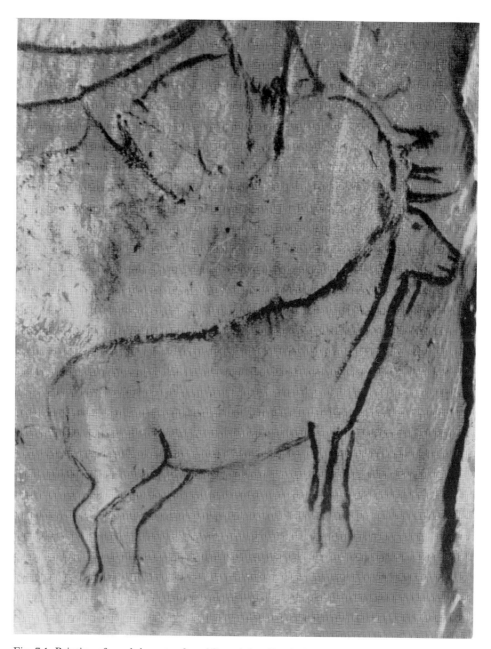

Fig. 7.1. Painting of a red deer stag from Niaux (after Graziosi 1960).

the art would hold if art was dominated by abstract motifs or human figures rather than depictions of large game.

It is indeed the character of the imagery that poses the other cluster of problems presented by the art. These will be my main concern but, as I hope to demonstrate, good explanations integrate these with the distributional patterns. So let me be bold and simply ask the general question: why do we find the particular motifs, at the frequencies and depicted in the manner that we do? The more specific questions are infinite in number. Why is the art dominated by depictions of large game? Why are these almost universally depicted in profile? Why do many animal depictions have parts of their bodies missing? Why are representations of people so sparse? The list is endless.

Now of course such questions have been asked ever since the art was discovered and identified as Palaeolithic, although the recent quantitative studies (Leroi-Gourhan 1968; Rice and Paterson 1985, 1986; Delporte 1984; Altuna 1983; Sieveking 1984) have given them a firmer base and new relevance. The interpretations of the art as 'hunting magic', 'art for art's sake', 'art as education' and so on have long been made and sporadically receive new impetus from further research (e.g. Halverson 1987; Pfeiffer 1982). All of these 'global' interpretations are familiar and it is not my intention to rehearse their arguments once again; these are readily found elsewhere (e.g. Ucko and Rosenfeld 1967; Sieveking 1979; Bahn and Vertut 1988). Rather I want to get straight to work in showing how an understanding of decision-making processes can help in explaining some aspects of the art. So let me turn straight away to seek the decision makers by following the trail of faunal assemblages they have left.

Faunal assemblages and hunting behaviour.

My discussion here will serve to identify the most general characteristics of Upper Palaeolithic hunting and gross patterns of change over time as a preliminary to inferring decision-making processes. Since we are considering over 20,000 years and a large spatial area my discussion will be very selective as to which factors I choose to highlight. I will focus on the three classic areas of the Perigord, the Pyrenees and Cantabrian Spain. For all of these there are excellent syntheses of the palaeo-economic and ecological data upon which I will draw. First, the Perigord.

Views of Upper Palaeolithic subsistence in the Perigord have changed dramatically in recent years. The traditional view consisted of an extreme specialisation on reindeer exploitation in a tundra environment – 'L'Age du Renne'. This has now changed, owing to palaeo-environmental data, particularly pollen (e.g. Paquerceau 1976; Donner 1975), and detailed examination of a large sample of faunal assemblages (Delpech 1983). White (1985) and Mellars (1985) have both made syntheses of these data, remarking on the apparent richness of the environment in terms of plants and animals as compared with the previous views. The palynological work in particular has indicated that the environment should be seen as a varying mixture of steppe and forest communities. Mellars (1985) has highlighted the long growing season and the relatively slight snow cover that the region would have experienced. One of the most important characteristics appears to have been the diversity within plant communities and the small-scale spatial variability with a range of different micro-habitats supporting different plant and animal species.

The floral diversity is matched by that of the animal communities with unique combinations of different species within the same habitat. The work of Delpech (1983) has shown that reindeer is far from being the only ungulate exploited and that it must be seen as one component of a complex economy. As Mellars states, 'The archaeological fauna may well reflect a primary specialisation on the exploitation of reindeer but many assemblages reflect the fact that one or another of the additional species was frequently exploited on an extensive scale when local circumstances either permitted or demanded a different hunting strategy' (1985: 276). The percentage of different ungulates within and between assemblages changes in time and space and the extent to which this reflects purely environmental factors as opposed to hunters' game selection is a moot point.

Consequently while reindeer still remain at the centre of the subsistence economy in this region, their overwhelming dominance as suggested in the Reindeer Age concept is unfounded. Two issues need to be considered – the migratory behaviour of the reindeer and the manner in which they were hunted. The positions put forward by Bahn (1977) and then Gordon (1988) of long-distance migrations between the Perigord and the Pyrenees is untenable. While there is clear evidence for human contacts and movements between these areas, reindeer movements rest on analogy with the north Alaskan caribou migrations. The marked differences in the Late Pleistocene and Alaskan environments show this to be inappropriate. The richer and more diverse plant communities in Dordogne would have made it unnecessary for the reindeer to migrate over such distances. The seasonality data that Gordon (1988) provides to support his argument is open to many different interpretations. Moreover, as Straus (1982a) has emphasised, Depech's analysis of reindeer bones from Perigordian and Pyrenean sites demonstrates marked differences in animal size and consequently separate populations. The studies by Spiess (1979) and Gordon (1988) show that the reindeer were in the Vézère and Dordogne valleys between the autumn and early spring and it is likely that short east–west movements were made to the foothills of the Massif Central during the summer (Mellars 1985; Spiess 1979).

In relation to hunting patterns the most detailed work has been by Spiess (1979) who re-analysed the faunal material from Aurignacian and Perigordian occupations at the Abri Pataud. As a whole these assemblages indicated hunting between the autumn and early spring while an analysis of their age/sex structure indicated that there was no selection for particular age/sex classes, i.e. a 'catastrophic' mortality profile. Spiess used this, and the small MNI from separate levels, to argue that the hunters were not using large-scale drives but either were indiscriminately killing individuals with spears from ambushes or were using self-acting traps like snares, pitfalls and nets. While reindeer were overwhelmingly the most frequent species represented in bone counts and MNI (69%), in terms of meat weight they provided only 29%, with bison at 39%, horse 20% and red deer at 10%.

Later Upper Palaeolithic (LUP) sites in this region, particularly of the Magdalenian period, also tend to be dominated by reindeer in terms of bone counts (Delpech 1983) – MNI and meat weights are generally not available. Slightly to the north of the area in which cave art is concentrated, catastrophic mortality profiles are found for reindeer at Pincevent (Fig. 7.2a – Leroi-Gourhan and Brézillon 1972). In the Perigord itself the dominance of reindeer at certain sites is striking (e.g. La Madeleine). White (1985) has argued that some of these large sites result from mass kills during the movement of reindeer herds during the autumn, probably from the interception of herds at river crossings. The lack of age/sex data and problems with White's analysis (Mithen 1986b) make this interpretation inconclusive, although it is supported by seasonality data. Yet unselective mass slaughter on a substantially larger scale than during the Early Upper Palaeolithic (EUP) at Abri Pataud appears to be the norm. The contrast in the scale of slaughter with the EUP may indicate an intensification of the exploitation of reindeer and a more specialised function for particular sites. This process in the LUP is accompanied by a broadening of the diet base with the inclusion of smaller mammals, birds and fish (Mellars 1985). Population increase may be indicated by the rise in site numbers at the start of the Magdalenian, although the interpretation for this is obviously complicated by settlement system changes to accompany the increase in site specialisation.

The Pyrenean region is the second area that I wish to consider. Bahn (1983, 1984) has summarised the archaeological data and interpreted these in terms of subsistence change through time. The environment in this region has similarities with that of the Perigord although differences in micro-habitats are more marked because of the more varied terrain. Diversity in plant and animal communities across space and time is again a significant feature.

Bahn (1983) argues that the principal economic changes during the Middle and Upper Palaeolithic occur at the EUP/LUP transition. Throughout the Mousterian and EUP the economy appears to have been based principally on bovines and horse with some use of cervids. As would be expected, the use of horse and reindeer increases during the colder periods. The EUP contrasts with the Mousterian in that there appears to be a greater degree of variability between sites, suggesting that hunters concentrated on specific ungulates at particular locations. During the LUP the typical pattern is of a heavy reliance on one species at one particular site, principally horse, reindeer or ibex. For instance La Vache is dominated by ibex, Le Portel by reindeer and the sites around the Arudy basin by horse. Simultaneously with this increased specialisation on particular species, one finds an increase in the use of small and elusive species, one of which is the ibex itself. There is an increase in the presence of hare, birds and fish within the assemblages. It is also during the Magdalenian that bones seem to have been very extensively processed in order that the maximum amount of nourishment could be extracted.

(a)

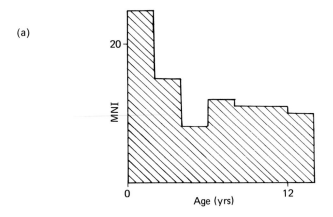

(b)

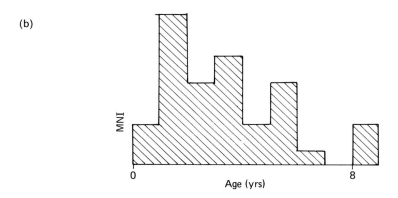

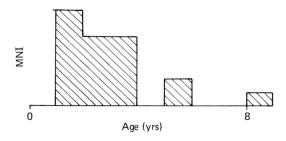

Fig. 7.2. Catastrophic reindeer mortality profile from (a) Mas D'Azil (after Patou 1984) and (b) Pincevent (after Leroi-Gourhan and Brézillon 1972).

In general, therefore, we see a pattern of economic change similar to that in the Perigord, with an increased concentration on particular species at particular locations. This implies that these are being hunted more intensively while the resource base is being diversified. There is also an increase in site numbers at the start of the Magdalenian, as in the Perigord, but Bahn is cautious about using these to imply significant population growth.

The inferred patterns of reindeer migration and hunting are also similar. The most likely reindeer movements are into the high pastures during the summer and to the low foothills and valleys during the winter. Hunting strategies again are most likely to have been of an intercept or driving nature leading to mass kills without any age/sex selection. Evidence for this comes from Mas d'Azil where Patou's (1984) analysis of the age structure of the reindeer bones shows the 'catastrophic' mortality profile, typical of such kills (Fig. 7.2b).

Horse bones from the Magdalenian IV layers of Isturitz represent animals of all ages including some very young animals. These are likely to have resulted from unselective killing. Bahn (1983) has interpreted the abandonment of some sites at the start of the Upper Palaeolithic, such as Le Portel, and the occupation of others, such as Jean de Verges, as being due to the suitability of these for intercept hunting and the control and corralling of herds. Hence the hunters chose sites close to steep-sided valleys or fords rather than in more open locations. The high density of reindeer bones at some sites during the Magdalenian, such as at Gourdon, suggests that large slaughters of deer may have been made in short periods of time.

The third area to consider is Cantabrian Spain and discussion must focus on the site of La Riera excavated and published in detail by Clark and Straus (1983, Straus and Clark 1986, Straus *et al.* 1981). As they have argued, the assemblages and sequence from La Riera are typical for Cantabrian sites.

As in the Pyrenees, the principal economic change appears to occur at the EUP/LUP boundary (*c.* 17,000–20,000 BP) rather than between the Mousterian and the EUP. During the earlier time periods, economies appear to have been based on horse and bovines with some small-scale exploitation of red deer. Straus and Clark (1986) characterise this as 'unspecialised and opportunistic hunting' possibly involving scavenging of the largest ungulates together with the killing of individual red deer. The age distributions of horse from the pre-Solutrean layers at La Riera support this by showing that only very young or very old animals were exploited. The Solutrean and Magdalenian economies, in contrast, are dominated by red deer and ibex, although horse and bovines continue to be present throughout the sequence. Straus and Clark (1986) consider whether this economic change may have been caused by environmental change, as Bailey (1983) argues, but reject this in favour of contrasting hunting strategies.

Since horse and bovine are present in the LUP assemblages, Straus and Clark argue that the large-scale exploitation of red deer and ibex were essentialy additions to the suite of foraging strategies employed. They use two pieces of evidence to argue that red deer and ibex were exploited by large-scale drives, the use of corrals or by intercept hunting. First, as for reindeer in France, the mortality profiles are of a 'catastrophic' type, demonstrating that age/sex classes were taken in the same proportion as in the living herd. Fig. 7.3a illustrates this for La Riera and Fig. 7.3b for El Juyo.

At the latter site, Klein *et al.* (1981, 1983) argue that red deer were driven into corrals, deep snow or some other traps where all individuals in a group could be dispatched at once (1983: 55). Such profiles are also found at Altamira, Tito Bustillo and Ekain (Straus and Clark 1986). These could have resulted from individual stalking but Straus and Clark point to the large number of individual animals found in thin and discrete layers at La Riera and elsewhere. These derive, they argue, from mass kills at specific times, and they point to the restricted seasonality of some of these assemblages to support this interpretation. This specialised herd hunting appears to be characteristic of the whole Cantabrian region during the LUP and can be recognised at Tito Bustillo, Bolinkoba, El Juyo, El Rascãno, El Castillo, El Pendo, El Cierro, and Las Caldas, in addition to La Riera (Straus and Clark 1986). Moreover, the increase in the number of juveniles in the profiles in the Late Magdalenian is used by Straus and Clark to argue that the red deer herds may have been over-exploited at this time.

A second similarity with the EUP/LUP economic change in France is that this increased specialisation is accompanied by diversification of the resource base. At La Riera this is demonstrated by the addition of ibex to the diet and then, increasingly from the Solutrean onwards, shellfish, small game and birds. Evidence for this diversification is also found at other sites such as El Pendo (Clark and Straus 1983).

Taken together, this increase in specialisation and diversification is used to argue for substantial subsistence intensification during the LUP. Having rejected environmental explanations, Straus and Clark argue that human population growth was the principal cause. The marked increase in site numbers at the start of the LUP is used as evidence for this. The extreme fragmentation of many of the ungulate bones is interpreted as arising from extracting marrow which is again taken to indicate stress on the resource base.

Some general points concerning Upper Palaeolithic economies and hunting behaviour can be extracted from these three brief summaries. First, while the multifaceted nature of these economies must be recognised, reindeer and red deer can still be seen to have played central roles during the LUP. During the LUP individual species appear to have been targeted in a much more systematic manner from particular locations and in particular seasons. Specialised red deer, reindeer and ibex sites are apparent. This can be seen in all areas, as can a process of diversification of the resource base to include small mammals, fish, birds and shellfish. While sites often have just one large ungulate in substantial quantities, along with these smaller species other large ungulates are also frequently present in small numbers. To explain these changes population pressure has been invoked by specialists working in all three areas.

In addition to such economic trends, the hunting patterns in the LUP also appear similar. In all areas assemblages of reindeer or red deer show catastrophic

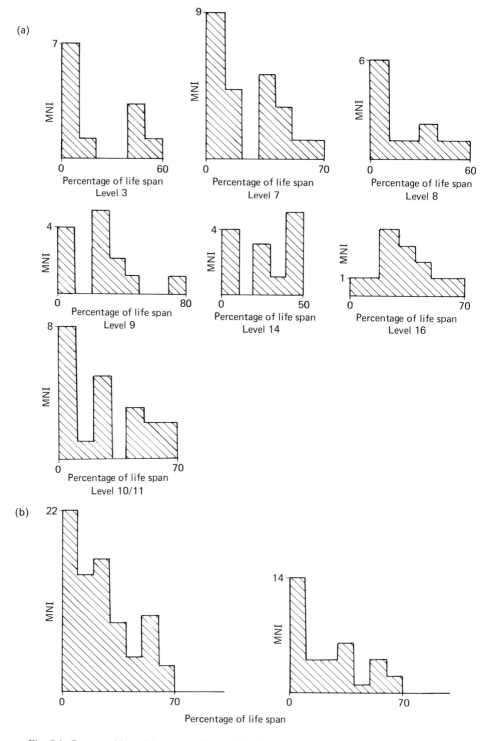

Fig. 7.3. Catastrophic red deer mortality profiles from (a) La Riera (after Clark and Straus 1983) and (b) El Juyo (after Klein *et al.* 1981).

mortality profiles and together with large MNI/bone densities this suggests mass unselective kills probably from driving, traps or intercept hunting. High fragmentation of the long bones is also frequently found, suggesting that the hunters were extracting maximum food value from their kills and consequently that they may have been suffering stress on resource base. The most likely scenario for the exploitation of red deer and reindeer (as well as ibex and horse) is that large slaughters were made on an annual basis at particular locations. In this light we might describe the hunters as 'harvesting' these resources, without implying any degree of management but just to refer to a regular cull. From this basis we can gain further insights into Upper Palaeolithic hunting behaviour by the use of mathematical models for large-game exploitation.

Modelling Upper Palaeolithic economies

In this section I will describe two simulation models which are designed to gain a greater understanding of red deer and reindeer hunting in the late glacial as a further step towards understanding the decision-making processes. They achieve this by translating patterns in the archaeological record (catastrophic mortality profiles, intensification through time) into alternative patterns of investments, risk and benefits, which are relevant to decision-making processes. That is, they act as methodological tools to elucidate the context in which the later Upper Palaeolithic hunter decision makers operated.

The structure of these models is essentially the same. Both are built around the equation:

$$(M_{(N_t)}N_t) \; D \; W = Y_{t+1}$$

In this M, D and W are $n \times n$ matrices and N and Y are n dimensional vectors. The first part, $(M_{(N_t)}N_t)$, is a Leslie matrix model with density–dependent factors (Lewis 1942; Leslie 1945; Usher 1972, 1976). A Leslie matrix is a powerful tool for predicting the future size and age/sex structure of a population from its present state by using estimates for the fecundity and survival of each age class. Elsewhere (Mithen 1986a) I have considered the role that such models might play in archaeology. To build a Leslie matrix model, the animal population is divided into $n/2$ age classes (e.g. calves, yearlings, $2,3 \ldots n/2$) so that the oldest class is that in which animals remain until they die. Estimates for the fecundity of each age/sex class are placed in the first row of the matrix and for survival in the subdiagonal. These estimates may be mean values, mathematical functions or include random elements for a stochastic rather than a deterministic model. When the resulting matrix pre-multiplies a vector containing the size of each age/sex class at time t, then a new vector will be created for the population at time $t+1$. Further pre-multiplications trace the growth and fluctuation in the population over subsequent years.

The matrix D relates to the manner in which the population is exploited. The only non-zero elements are those on the diagonal which specify the proportion of each age class remaining after the population has been hunted at time t. By

Table 7.1. *Leslie matrix for Norwegian wild reindeer*

0.00	0.00	0.00	Y/2	0.00	M/2	0.00	0.45
0.00	0.00	0.00	Y/2	0.00	M/2	0.00	0.45
CS	0.00	0.00	0.00	0.00	0.00	0.00	0.00
0.00	CS	0.00	0.00	0.00	0.00	0.00	0.00
0.00	0.00	0.88	0.00	0.00	0.00	0.00	0.00
0.00	0.00	0.00	0.94	0.00	0.00	0.00	0.00
0.00	0.00	0.00	0.00	0.88	0.00	0.88	0.00
0.00	0.00	0.00	0.00	0.00	0.94	0.00	0.94

Where: $Y = 70.4 + 44.0d - 16.7d^2 =$ fecundity of 1–2 yr olds
$M = 87.3 + 18.0d - 7.0d^2 =$ fecundity of 2–3 yr olds
$CS = 1.08 - 0.186d =$ calf survival
$d =$ herd density

manipulating these values, hunting which is random or selective, light or intense, can be modelled. If all the values are the same then a catastrophic mortality profile will result while if some are higher than others the profile may have an attritional nature. If more than one predator is exploiting the population then additional D matrices may be introduced, possibly with a different set of values for a different hunting pattern. W is a matrix whose diagonal elements contain the yield from each age/sex class. I have concentrated on meat yields but the yield may be hides, antler or bone. Again several matrices may be used for different types of products. Consequently the vector Y (or vectors if several products or predators are considered) contains the yield gained from the population at time t when exploited with the hunting pattern described in the matrix(ces) D.

The manner in which this model is used is essentially the same as that in Part 2 for investigating Mesolithic decision making. We place it into a simulation program and then make experiments. By manipulating different parameter values we can investigate the effect of variation in the environment, in hunting patterns and in predator competition, on human yields and on the age/sex structure of the resulting faunal assemblage. My particular concern has been with different intensities of hunting and how these affect yields in terms of their mean values and their variability. In contrast to the model in Part 2, however, I will not be using these to infer aspects of the decision-making process directly. Rather, they are designed to investigate the feedback between the types of decisions that were taken in the past, which we have already inferred from the archaeological record (unselective killing, intensification in the LUP), and the foraging problems that the hunters faced as a result of those decisions. From this basis we will be able to address the decision-making process and its change over time. First I will explore reindeer exploitation.

A simulation of reindeer exploitation

To construct a model of a reindeer population we must rely on data from modern herds in environments similar to the Late Pleistocene in south-west France. The most suitable is that from wild reindeer populations in Norway as described by Skogland (1983, 1985). Using this, reindeer population dynamics can be modelled

Table 7.2. *Utility of reindeer carcasses (after Spiess 1979)*

Meat and fat content

Age/Sex	Live weight Kg	Meat yield Kg	Winter fat content Kg
Calf	40.0	22.0	0.80
Yearling	60.0	33.0	3.00
Adult male	120.0	66.0	2.40
Adult female	75.0	41.0	7.50

Human food requirements
0.33 kg fat and 0.25 kg meat for protein/person/day
3.25 kg meat for energy and protein/person/day

in terms of four age classes; calves, 1–2 years, 2–3 years and > 3 years, giving eight age/sex classes. If we analyse Skogland's data (Mithen 1988a) a Leslie matrix model can be built (Table 7.1) which has density-dependent functions for certain of the elements. It is apparent from the matrix that I assume a 50:50 male:female birth ratio. As illustrated in Fig. 7.4 this model shows a close similarity between the real and simulated reindeer populations. When I explore the degree of fluctuation in yields that hunters may experience I include a stochastic element in the matrix by making calf survival a normally distributed variable using the constant in the matrix as the mean and a standard deviation of 0.1. Consequently each year a different proportion of calves survive, reflecting the vagaries of the environment.

In addition to the Leslie matrix some additional data is required for the simulation. We need an estimate for the range over which the reindeer moved, since we have density-dependent functions in the matrix. For this I use a value of 840 km² which is based on the area in the Perigord in which assemblages with the highest frequencies of reindeer are found (see Delpech 1983: Fig. 32). I must stress however that this figure is not significant for the types of results I will be describing. These would equally arise if this area was either smaller or larger. It is simply a value to allow the model to 'run'. In this simulation I want to convert sustainable yields from reindeer into estimates for human population densities since there has been interesting speculation as to the role of population in the problem of explaining the art (e.g. Jochim 1983a). For this I use Spiess' (1979) estimates for the meat and fat value of a reindeer carcass and for that which people require, as reproduced in Table 7.2. His values do, however, appear to be on the high side for food requirements and those of Binford (1978), based on ethnographic data, appear to reduce this by up to six times. Consequently I will use estimates based on Spiess' figures as the maximum and a six-fold decrease of these as the minimum.

I also want to include wolf predation in the model (wolf being a representative of non-human carnivores in general) since this will create a more realistic model of Late Pleistocene predator-prey interactions. The role of carnivores in assemblage

(a)

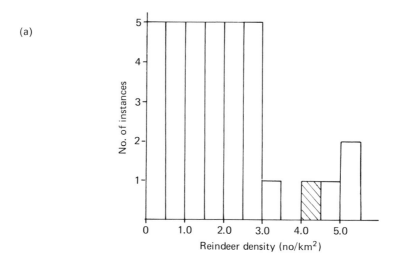

(b)

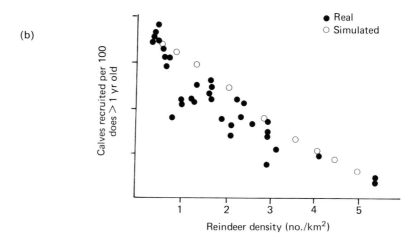

(c)

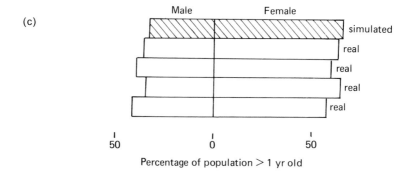

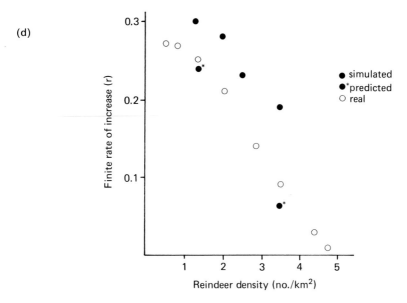

Fig. 7.4. Comparison between simulated and real reindeer populations (real data from Skogland 1985): (a) simulated and real reindeer herd densities (simulated value (dashed) is for an unexploited herd at equilibrium); (b) simulated and real calf recruitment for herds at varying densities; (c) simulated and real adult sex structure (simulated value if for an unexploited herd at equilibrium); (d) simulated and real finite rates of growth for herds at different densities.

formation is now widely recognised (e.g. Straus 1982b; Gamble 1983). However, little attention has been paid to their role in the community ecology of the Late Pleistocene and their competitive interactions with the human hunters for grazing herbivores. Wolves would have survived partly by scavanging the dead carcasses of the reindeer. But they would have also hunted the population and, on the basis of modern wolf behaviour, predominantly taken the oldest and the youngest of the herd (Mech 1974; Pimlott 1967; Bergerud 1980). Consequently we model this selective predation with a D matrix in which only the elements relating to the calves and the >3 years age classes are positive, the others being zero.

This joins a D matrix for the human population. Their predominant hunting strategy appears to have been intercepting herds at fords or forcing them off crags and to have taken place during the autumn when all the members of the herd were together. This would have resulted in all age/sex classes being killed indiscriminately to produce the catastrophic profiles that we find in the archaeological record. Consequently this second D matrix has elements all of which are positive and equal.

The simulation
We combine all of these elements into one simulation model which is described in the flow chart of Fig. 7.5. Now, I wish to use this model to examine the relationship between hunting intensities, mean yields – which I convert to human population densities – and the fluctuations in those yields. Human hunting intensities are

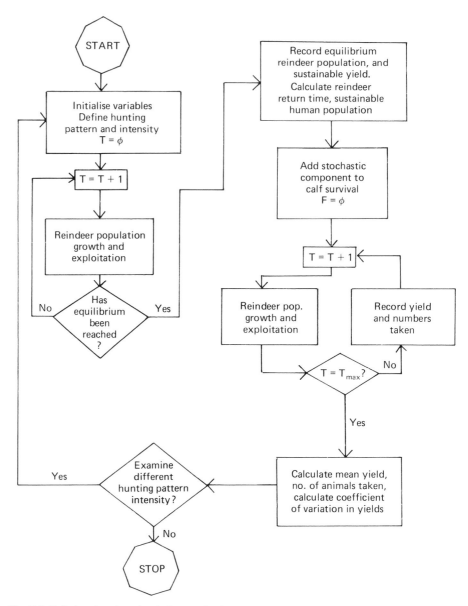

Fig. 7.5. Reindeer hunting simulation model flow chart.

varied from 1% (i.e. 1% of each age/sex class is taken each year) to that which pushes the reindeer population into extinction. This range of human hunting intensities is explored three times. On each occasion a different intensity of wolf selective predation is also imposed on the reindeer – levels of 0%, 5% and 15%.

The degree of fluctuation in the hunters' yields is measured in two ways, following Beddington and May (1977). First the return time of the population is calculated. This is the time the population takes to return to its equilibrium value after a perturbation away from that and hence measures the sensitivity of the population to environmental disturbances. High values mean that the population returns more slowly and hence will be more susceptible to fluctuations. This is calculated by running a deterministic model (i.e. without the stochastic component in the Leslie matrix) until the population reaches an equilibrium. Then I record how long the population takes to return to that value after having been reduced by 20%. As Beddington and May (1977) discuss, a more realistic measure of the fluctuation in a population is derived when it is subject to a continuous spectrum of disturbances. Consequently, when the reindeer population is again at equilibrium I introduce the stochastic element into the Leslie matrix and simply run the simulation for 500 years, recording the annual reindeer population and the hunters' yield. I then use the coefficient of variation in hunters' yields as a second measure of yield fluctuation and use the mean yield to derive the sustainable human population.

The results

The results are summarised in Fig. 7.6a–c. Fig. 7.6a shows the effect of increasing human hunting intensity on the mean sustainable population and the yield fluctuation when wolf selective predation is absent. We see here the characteristic parabola of the mean yield/sustainable population which reaches its apex – the maximum sustainable yield (MSY) – at a 15% cull. On the basis of Spiess' figures, this supports 21.5 individuals for a year, or a population density of 0.026 per/km². As I mentioned above, however, Binford's figures suggest this may be an underestimate and that the top range may be as high as 0.156 pers/km². Moreover, since reindeer appear to have supplied only one third of the food (Spiess 1979) we can treble this to a maximum population density of 0.47 pers/km². The second variable we are concerned with is the fluctuation of yields and this shows an interesting pattern. Whether measured by the return time or the coefficient of variation in yields, it falls slightly until intensities of 8–9% are reached and then increases exponentially, resulting in high levels once the MSY level is passed. Then even small degrees of intensification, which may cause only slight decreases in annual yields, may lead to substantial rises in the fluctuations of the yields. This agrees with more general models of the relationship between yields and harvesting in fluctuating environments (Beddington and May 1977; May *et al.* 1978).

The fundamental features of these relationships remain when the model is made more realistic by including wolf predation. Fig. 7.6b shows the sustainable human population and yield fluctuation when wolves take 5% of the youngest and oldest age classes. As would be expected, the sustainable human population falls but there is also a significant increase in the extent of fluctuations in the yields. These changes are further exaggerated if wolf predation is more intense. For instance if wolves (or a combination of carnivores) take 15% of the youngest and oldest age classes of the reindeer, then sustainable human populations are considerably reduced (0.0106–0.0636 pers/km² on reindeer alone), but the human hunters also experience very significant increases in the extent to which their yields fluctuate (Fig. 7.6c). Since we know that there were numerous carnivore species competing for herbivores during the Upper Palaeolithic it is this sort of pattern between human intensification and yield fluctuation that appears to have occurred. That is,

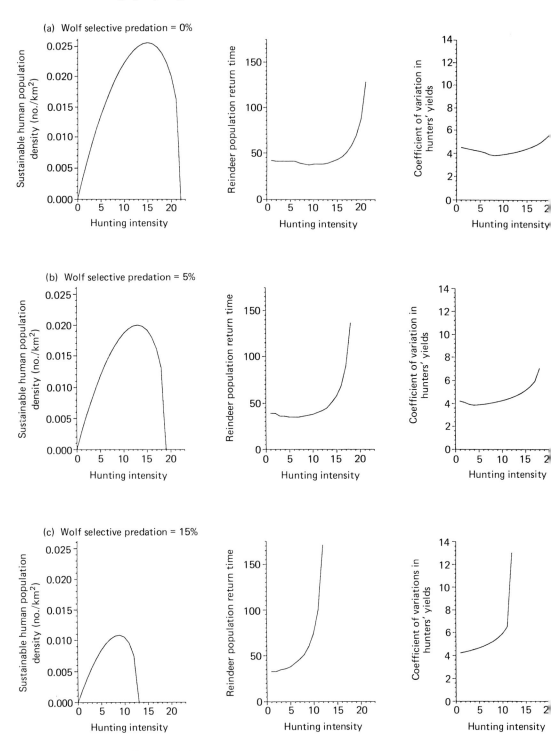

Fig. 7.6. Sustainable human population, reindeer population return time, and coefficient of variation in yields against hunting intensity for reindeer exploitation.

as the hunters intensified on reindeer, they experienced a significant increase in their yield fluctuations and hence were in a context of increasing uncertainty.

The population estimates are interesting since they cover a range similar to those found among 'modern' hunters who exploit caribou. These vary from 0.01 pers/km² among the Asiaqmiut, who have a primary dependence upon reindeer, to 0.178 among the Tikiraqmiut for whom caribou is a relatively minor resource (Burch 1972; David 1973). Since these are similar to the estimates I have derived for the Upper Palaeolithic arguments which invoke particularly high population densities, and the social problems which result, as a means to explain the phenomenon of cave art (e.g. Jochim 1983a) are rather weakened.

This model has attempted to investigate the consequences of hunting intensification on reindeer populations for human population densities and the amount of fluctuation the hunters would have experienced in their yields particularly in a multi-predator environment. The process of intensification has been inferred from the archaeological record, and the task will now be to feed these results back into further interpretations we make of that data, so that inferences can be drawn concerning decision-making processes. Before that, however, I need to make a similar study of the other principal ungulate, red deer.

A simulation of red deer exploitation

The model will be similar to that for reindeer hunting just described except that I will not investigate the effects of carnivore predation nor attempt to convert the yields into human population densities. Alternatively I will investigate a range of different human hunting patterns.

To develop such a model of red deer exploitation I will use data concerning the red deer population from the island of Rhum (Clutton-Brock *et al.* 1983, 1986; Albon *et al.* 1987). These data have been collected by ecologists over a period of fifteen years and are the most appropriate for three reasons. First the quality of the environment of the island for the red deer is poor, with the herds living at the extent of their range. This provides, therefore, an appropriate analogy for the herds living on the largely treeless landscapes of the late glacial in northern Spain. Second, the quantity and quality of the data are unique for a large ungulate herd and a detailed model can be constructed. Third, there has already been some analysis of the population data which provides a secure foundation for the model I will develop. These data contrast with those for the reindeer model in that they are from only one herd, the density of which changes over time.

Elsewhere (Mithen 1987) I have developed a Leslie matrix model for this red deer population, showing that a very close fit between the simulated and real population growth can be made. Here I use a slightly different set of density-dependent functions and population parameter estimates using more recently available data, as listed in Table 7.3. I also include density-independent factors to make a more realistic model. This follows the work of Albon *et al.* (1987) who show that for individuals born in any one year (i.e. a cohort) their lifetime reproductive success and survival, as well as that of their offspring, were related to the environ-

Table 7.3. *Density-dependent and constant values for red deer Leslie matrix*

Age	Intercept	Slope	Significance[a]	Mean
Hind Survival				
Calves	1.13	− 0.0032	★★	
1 yr			NS	0.901
2 yr			NS	0.972
3 yr			NS	0.972
4 yr			NS	0.98
5–12 yr	1.04	− 0.00075	★★★	
> = 13 yr	1.1	− 0.00273	★	
Stag Survival				
Calves	1.155	− 0.003371	★★	
1 yr	1.191	− 0.002836	★	
2–7 yr	1.015	− 0.000277	★	
8–10 yr	1.163	− 0.002580	★	
> = 11 yr	0.985	− 0.00399	★	
Fecundity				
Calves				0.00
1 yr				0.00
2 yr				0.00
3 yr	0.904	− 0.0048	★★	
4 yr			NS	0.742
5–12 yr	1.081	− 0.0024	★★	
> = 13 yr	1.185	− 0.0039	★★	

Note:
[a]NS = not significant, ★ = p < 0.05, ★★ = p < 0.01, ★★★ = p < 0.001

ment at the time immediately preceding their birth. If the April/May temperatures of that year were high, then the cohort was generally more successful than if they were low.

To model such density-independent effects, each simulated year was attributed with one of three classes of temperature – good, average or poor. These were assigned at random and with equal frequency using a 3 × 3 Markov matrix with an equal probability that any one type of year would follow any other. Once the type of year a cohort was born in had been determined, this was referred to throughout the life of that cohort (except when it entered the final 13+ grouping). Its fecundity and survival parameters, as derived from the equations in Table 7.3, altered accordingly: born in a good year these were incremented, in a poor year decremented and in an average year unchanged. The survival of the cohorts of calves and yearlings was similarly increased and decreased, since hinds who had been born in good years gave birth to strong calves, whatever the type of that particular year. Since the offspring in any one year were derived from a set of hinds born in a mixture of year types, the degree of adjustment to calf and yearling survival was based on the relative 'good', 'average' and 'poor' proportions. The increments and decrements added to the population parameters are listed in Table 7.4.

Table 7.4. *Density-independent increments to red deer population parameters*

Cohort type	Adult survival		Fecundity		offspring viability	
	Male	Female	3 yr	Adult	Calves	Yearlings
Good	0.04	0.025	0.18	0.11	0.124	0.109
Poor	−0.04	−0.025	−0.18	−0.11	−0.155	−0.187

For the first thirteen years of the simulation the recorded birth ratios were used. An analysis of these showed that they had a normal distribution with a mean of 0.478 and standard deviation of 0.045. Consequently for all following years a random value from this distribution was chosen. The area for the red deer population was arbitrarily set at 78.5km². This is based on a 5km diameter exploitation area. Again, as with the reindeer model, this value has no influence over the results. Meat yields were estimated using larder weights, approximately 75% of live weight (Clutton-Brock *et al.* 1983: Fig. 2.4).

As I described above, the mortality profiles from northern Spain suggest a 'random' hunting pattern without selection as to age. It appears that certain sites have mortality profiles which suggest that hunters may have specifically targeted herds of hinds with their calves (Clark and Straus 1983). At such time the stags may have been dispersed and a mass slaughter technique less viable for them than the hinds and calves. However, there are few quantitative data on the sex structure of the assemblages. Consequently three slightly different hunting strategies will be explored. For all of these the female component of the population will be exploited with the set of integer hunting intensities until the exploitation is unfeasible (i.e. 1%, 2% . . .). The male population will be exploited at a certain proportion of this intensity, these being 0.1, 0.5 and 1.0 for the three strategies. For instance under the second strategy when the hunting intensity of the females is 12% that of the males will be 6%. The hunting intensities will not vary as to age so that the catastrophic mortality profiles are created.

The simulation

As with the reindeer, simulation was used to explore this model. It was similar to that of the reindeer model, the principal differences being the inclusion of the density-independent effects and the simulation of year 'types'. The simulation modelled red deer population growth and exploitation under a particular hunting intensity without stochastic effects until an equilibrium value was attained (using a 0.478 birth ratio), if that intensity proved to be feasible. If so, the age/sex structure of the red deer now being exploited (and which is now constant) was recorded. This provides the age/sex structure for the red deer faunal assemblages in the catastrophic mortality profile. Comparisons can then be made with the age structure of the assemblage from La Riera. Following this the simulation was run for a further 500 years with a varying birth ratio and the inclusion of the density-independent elements. These 500 years of data were used to estimate the mean yield and the coefficient of variation of that yield.

Results

Fig. 7.7 provides the results from this simulation concerning relationships between hunting intensity, mean sustainable yield and the coefficient of variation of that yield. As is apparent, these are similar to those from the reindeer simulation. However, the coefficient of variation remains more stable and only rapidly increases at the most extreme hunting intensities, there being only a gradual increase in this at lower intensities.

The fact that the coefficient of variation in yields is either stable or slightly increasing as hunting intensifies and mean yields increase, indicates that the absolute degree of fluctuation in the yields is significantly increasing. This can be illustrated by inspecting the annual yields over a 500-year period resulting from the same hunting pattern, and with the same sequence of good average poor years, but at different hunting intensities. Fig. 7.8 illustrates a set of these, showing substantial increases in the amplitudes of fluctuations of the yields with increased hunting intensity, even before the maximum sustainable-yield hunting intensity is reached.

The argument developed above is that such results are relevant to the Upper Palaeolithic in Cantabrian Spain since the exploitation of red deer was intensified during the Later Upper Palaeolithic, as Straus and Clark have argued. We can use the simulated faunal assemblages to verify that such intensification took place since these show a slight increase in the proportion of juveniles with increased hunting intensity. This is due to the red deer population being pushed to a lower density with a resulting increase in the fecundity of the hinds. Fig. 7.9 illustrates the age structure of the La Riera assemblages from the Upper Solutrean, Lower Magdalenian and Upper Magdalenian and compares this with the age structure in the simulated assemblages at a 1%, 8% and 16% hunting intensity. There is a close similarity clearly supporting the inference of intensification during the LUP. We can reject the possibility that the pattern in the real assemblages arises as a result of differential preservation through time. Altuna has shown that there is no significant change in the ratio of identifiable to non-identifiable pieces of bone through the La Riera sequence (Altuna 1986: table B3). This is in effect a measure of fragmentation and hence of preservation.

Decision making by Upper Palaeolithic hunters

In discussing my simulation results I want finally to attain the aim of this chapter and make some inferences about decision making by Upper Palaeolithic hunters. So I will first discuss this in general terms and then turn to decisions concerning red deer and reindeer hunting using the simulation results.

At an admittedly crude level of generalisation there can be little doubt that the Upper Palaeolithic settlement-subsistence system, and particularly that of the LUP, was logistically organised with high degrees of scheduling and forward

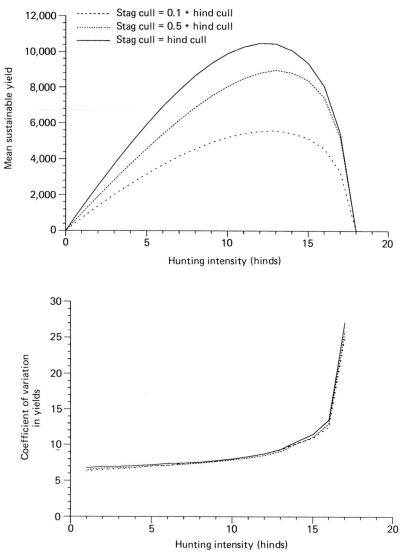

Fig. 7.7. Mean sustainable yields and coefficient of variation of yields against hunting intensity for red deer exploitation.

planning. The archaeological record has a range of classic indicators that economic activity was so organised. For instance, the Upper Palaeolithic technology includes a range of highly specialised and complex tools suggesting concentration on particular resources at particular times and places and a heavy investment in gearing up and manufacture. Many sites appear to be functionally specific, as expected in this type of settlement-subsistence organisation. Specialised red deer, ibex and reindeer hunting sites have already been noted (e.g. La Riera, Rascano, La Vache), and small temporary hunting camps are present such as Fontanet as well as large aggregation sites such as Altamira and Isturitz. The evidence for long-

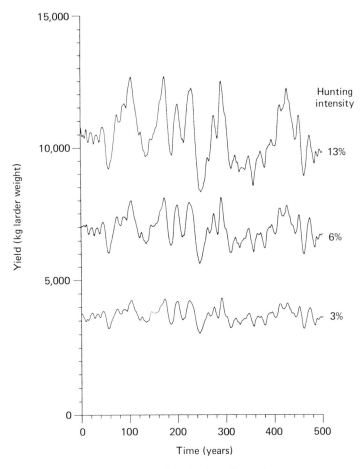

Fig. 7.8. Yields against time for red deer exploitation in a fluctuating environment and with a random killing strategy.

distance contacts, or perhaps movement of people (Bahn 1982), is a further indication of a logistical organisation. Moreover, the intercept/herd hunting of large ungulates suggests high degrees of co-operation and planning. Simek (1987) argues that a logistical form of subsistence and settlement can also be inferred from site structure by analysing artefact distribution patterns at Le Flageolet. This type of settlement-subsistence organisation is what should be expected in the spatially and temporally patchy environments of the Late Pleistocene. It may be argued that the degree of logistical organisation increased in the LUP owing to the increased specialisation and diversification of the resource base. Of course, this is a crude generalisation and considerable variability is likely in the form of logistical organisation across Europe.

The conception of the subsistence-settlement system that is required is one that is an ever-changing entity. This gross designation of logistical organisation is simply to identify the principal foraging problem that the hunters faced, i.e. patch choice. We may see this either as the choice of a particular biome (e.g. coastal

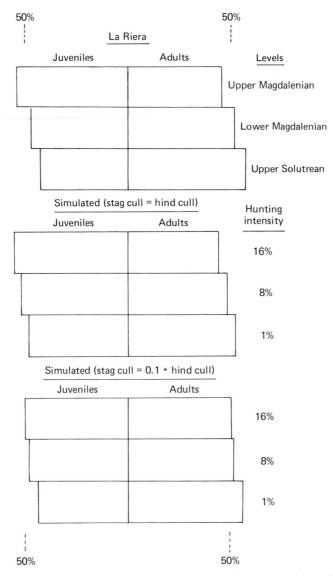

Fig. 7.9. Red deer age structure in simulated assemblages and in real assemblages from La Riera (data from Straus *et al.* 1981).

rather than mountainous) or, since resources would have been highly segregated in space, as the choice of a particular species to exploit. That is, we might consider red deer, ibex, salmon and shellfish as different patches for the hunters in Cantabrian Spain amongst which choices must be made at particular times of the year. We might also consider the option to engage in the individual stalking of ungulates as another patch choice.

At this stage in the work, we can be confident as to how such patch choices were made by the Upper Palaeolithic foragers. In particular seasons of the year individuals, families or larger groups would have taken decisions as to which patch to exploit in the coming season, or for a shorter period of time, geared up their technology and moved to the relevant locations. Such decisions will, as discussed above, form a hierarchical set. For instance in the Pyrenees the hunters at La Vache chose to exploit an ibex patch but while doing so took daily decisions to hunt or set traps for hare and game birds, species well represented in the faunal assemblage (Bahn 1984). This can be thought of as a choice at a lower level of the hierarchy since its existence is partly determined by the original choice of the ibex patch. Since exploitation of some patches would have required co-operation between individuals and groups (e.g. a reindeer drive), and any choices will depend upon information about which patches have been exploited by others in the recent past, processes of group decision making will have been of considerable importance, no doubt at the aggregation sites such as Altamira.

At any one time several alternative foraging patches may have been available to the foragers – red deer or ibex, reindeer or salmon – and the choice made by acquiring and processing information in accordance with particular foraging goals. In light of the eco-psychological model and by analogy with the ethnographic data, information may have been acquired from four different and interrelated activities. Patches may have been searched and sampled possibly during short exploratory hunting trips, such as to see if a migratory resource had arrived. The late glacial environment would also have provided a rich set of cues, for example from the tracks and trails of potential prey. In this sense we should characterise it as having a high information potential though this would have fluctuated with the seasons and environmental change. Information was also no doubt passed on from group to group, and between individuals. Past experience would have been a valuable source of information for the hunters particularly if there was a periodic or irregular repeat of particular combinations of environmental events so that the hunters could remember how they coped with these on previous occasions.

According to my eco-psychological model, information gained from these sources will have been processed and choices made according to goals (meta-) chosen by the hunters and using a mix of computation and rules of thumb. In Chapter 6 I explored a range of goals that hunters may adopt. Elsewhere (Mithen 1987) I have argued that those of the Upper Palaeolithic hunters were of a risk-minimising type, though I would now prefer to use the meliorising terminology and refer to these as risk-reducing. We can see this by considering the size and fluctuations in yields that other hunting strategies would return. Specifically, we might consider a selective strategy in which the hunters would be focusing on particular age/sex classes rather than making a random kill. This is modelled by making the values in the D matrix unequal. Fig. 7.10 shows the types of returns that are found when hunters concentrate on the adult age classes of a red deer population. The pattern of increasing yield fluctuation with intensification remains. However, a second dimension of resource fluctuation has now been imposed, operating over a shorter interannual time scale. Overall, there is a

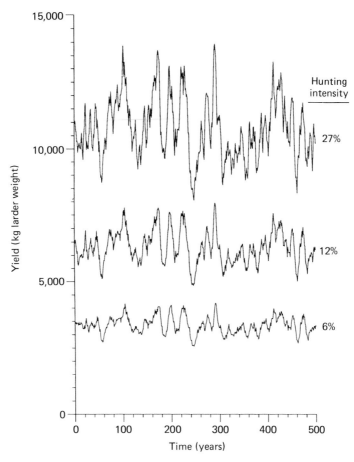

Fig. 7.10. Yields against time for red deer exploitation in a fluctuating environment and with a selective (adult-biased) killing strategy.

substantial increase in the degree of yield uncertainty over that resulting from a random cull. While a selective cull results in a greater degree of yield fluctuation (i.e. risk) to achieve the same mean yield as under a random killing pattern, the cost of achieving this, in terms of the number of animals that must be slaughtered and processed, is less (Mithen 1987: Fig. 8.7). Quite simply, a random hunting strategy involves taking the young and the old animals which have a relatively low meat yield/butchery time (i.e. benefit/cost) ratio and hence this strategy has a higher cost per unit yield than a selective strategy which takes only prime adults. Selective killing appears to increase the utility returns (benefit/cost ratio) but at the expense of yield predictability while a random killing pattern reduces (though it does not remove) risk at the expense of greater effort. In these regards, therefore, the Upper Palaeolithic hunters adopted risk-reducing hunting patterns. As we have seen, in spite of this, the yield fluctuations did increase dramatically as a result of intensification during the LUP.

There are two important points to note here. The first concerns the times scales over which yield fluctuation, and hence risk, is being measured (Whitelaw 1986). The random hunting pattern appears to be effective at reducing risk over the short interannual time scale. Whether at low or high hunting intensities, this is less than that from a selective killing pattern, as Figs. 7.9 and 7.11 demonstrate. However, neither a random nor a selective hunting strategy is effective at coping with the longer-term yield fluctuations, the amplitude of which increase markedly with intensification under both strategies. The second point, however, is that this time-scale distinction probably had no consequence for the Upper Palaeolithic decision makers. As we saw in Chapter 3, hunter-gatherers do not appear to plan subsistence activities over time scales longer than one year (p. 82). During the Later Upper Palaeolithic, therefore, the long-term fluctuation would have simply fed back into the interannual fluctuation, with the hunters experiencing greater troughs and peaks in their yields, and hence the failure of their risk-reducing goal. In any one year (and hence for the mass co-operative hunts during that year) the hunters would have had greater uncertainty about their yields, not knowing if these were to fall even lower, and possibly pass below some threshold of sufficiency, than those of the previous year or would begin to climb again. Certain information to reduce this uncertainty may have been gained from observing the age/sex structure of the red deer and reindeer populations and noting the state of relevant climatic variables. Yet as the model for red deer population dynamics demonstrated, having both density-dependent and independent components, there are complex and inherently unpredictable relationships between these variables and the annual growth/decline in the population. In particular, there are feedback relationships with the state of the environment over many years that affect the current reproductivity of the population. In other words, such observations on the current age/sex structure of the population and the environment, and even the combination of these with those from the previous year, would have provided a set of ecologically invalid cues. Of course, the hunters may have been unaware of this and utilised such cues, creating poor models of the future in their minds.

The evidence for intensification on red deer and reindeer appears incontrovertible. Whether this was an intended action or an unintended consequence of the foraging decisions that were taken is debatable. The argument that it results from an increase in human population densities remains the most convincing. We have seen that, up to a point, the yield increases as greater percentages of the population are culled each year, this no doubt being an intended consequence of the foraging decisions. However, what is most probably an unintended consequence is the concomitant increase in the amplitude of the fluctuations in those yields and we might ask what consequence this would have had for the decision-making process. In general by pushing the hunters into ever greater degrees of uncertainty concerning their yields it will have placed a greater premium on acquiring information. The yields gained in past years, and the knowledge of the size of peaks and troughs of yields, would have been increasingly redundant as sources of information for the hunters and hence past experience of red deer and reindeer hunting would have been reduced in value as an information source.

Now in characterising the Upper Palaeolithic decision makers in this respect I have tried to develop a model that meets the criteria I laid down in my introductory chapter. Rather than creating a static subsistence-settlement system and decision process, my aim has been to see these as dynamic and changing entities from the start. I have tried to situate the decision makers of the LUP into their historical context by focusing on the process of intensification and its consequences, into an ecological context by building sophisticated models of red deer and reindeer exploitation (taking into account competing carnivores) and into their social context by exploring human population densities. I have then referred to a general model for the manner in which human hunter-gatherers take foraging decisions, owing to a common biological endowment, and asked how this would be manifest in this particular situation.

In reaching these proposals I have seen individuals in a group context. The catastrophic age/sex profiles of red deer and reindeer are most likely to have resulted from co-operative hunting. Hence the processes of group decision making discussed in Chapter 2 are relevant here. But while we have not focused on the individual directly, as in the Mesolithic case study, we must maintain him/her at the core of this study. For otherwise the concept of adaptation becomes meaningless and attempts at explanation will founder. So let me be clear that group hunting results from the decisions of individuals to participate and co-operate. And the escalation in yield uncertainty that occurs in the Late Upper Palaeolithic is perceived by individuals, although perhaps only through the use of numerous other individuals as information sources. This in turn plays a role in the decision making by individuals, which may be to continue co-operating in group activities or to switch to an alternative form of hunting behaviour.

The most significant issue appears to be the knowledge that the hunters would have possessed that red deer and reindeer yields may be low, i.e. the possible failure of their risk-reducing hunting strategy, but not knowing if this would occur on any particular game drive or cull. If these were low, then a rapid switch to another type of patch and hunting method would have been necessary. It is in this context of increasing uncertainty and the need for rapid patch switching that information about alternative resources becomes essential. It is here that we can turn to the art created by these Upper Palaeolithic decision makers.

8

Through a hunter's eyes . . . and into his mind?

After we have responded to a work of art, we leave it, carrying away in our consciousness something which we didn't have before. This something amounts to more than our memory of the incident represented, and also more than our memory of the shapes and colours and spaces which the artist has used and arranged. What we take away with us – on the most profound level – is the memory of the artist's way of looking at the world. The representation of a recognizable incident (an incident here can simply mean a tree or a head) offers us the chance of relating the artist's way of looking to our own. The forms he uses are the means by which he expresses his way of looking. The truth of this is confirmed by the fact that we can often recall the experience of a work, having forgotten both its precise subject and formal arrangement.

Yet why should an artist's way of looking at the world have any meaning for us? Why does it give us pleasure? Because, I believe, it increases our awareness of our own potentiality. Not of course our awareness of our potentiality as artists ourselves. But a way of looking at the world implies a certain relationship with the world, and every relationship implies action. The kind of actions implied vary a great deal. A classical Greek sculpture increases our awareness of our own potential physical dignity; a Rembrandt of our potential moral courage; a Matisse of our potential sensual awareness. Yet each of these examples is too narrow to contain the whole truth of the matter. A work can, to some extent, increase an awareness of different potentialities in different people. The important point is that a valid work of art promises in some way or another an increase, an improvement. Nor need the work be optimistic to achieve this; indeed, its subject may be tragic. For it is not the subject that makes the promise, it is the artist's way of viewing his subject. Goya's way of looking amounts to the contention that we ought be able to do without massacres.

John Berger, *Permanent Red*, 1960

In the previous chapter I worked from hard archaeological data to soft, though hopefully not mushy, inferences concerning decision-making processes by Upper

226

Palaeolithic hunters. Now I wish to work back again from those inferences to archaeological data, but to paintings, engravings and sculpture rather than to faunal assemblages. As in Chapter 6, I want to pivot on these decision-making processes to connect the otherwise disparate elements of the archaeological record and move towards explanation.

I have characterised the Late Upper Palaeolithic hunters as being in high states of uncertainty concerning patch choice, particularly those of the beautiful deer. Their ecological context appears to be one of marked fluctuations in red deer and reindeer populations/yields and their historical one of a failure of risk-reducing hunting strategies owing to unintended consequences of past decisions concerning intensification. Through the eco-psychological model and the study of modern hunter-gatherers we can infer, or rather have a jolly good guess, at the types of information the hunters would have sought and where they may have found it. Now much of the recent work on Upper Palaeolithic art, particularly that which takes a functional perspective, characterises it as something to do with information, though that term is often poorly defined. I will show in this chapter that one of the information sources, the use of cues from the natural environment, is represented in the art and accounts for the form and frequency of certain motifs. Moreover, in considering why this should be so, we are led to another information source – the recall of past experience – and the explanation of further features of the art, notably the pattern of large-game representation. Finally we will identify the principal means by which the Late Upper Palaeolithic hunters sought adaptation to their ever-changing environment: creative thought.

Overall, I think that Berger's insight quoted above comes closest to describing my interpretation of the art. For Upper Palaeolithic hunters I believe that the art promised an increase in their knowledge about their environment, and indeed, their meta-knowledge about that knowledge itself – what they already knew and what they needed to know. For us today, viewing the art promises an increase not only of our understanding of the lost lives of these ancient men and women but also of the roots of culture itself. It reassures us that the life of a prehistoric hunter was not short and nasty, but one of great sensitivity to the world, the changing seasons and the animals of the chase. So let me get straight to the heart of the matter and describe this information gathering theme in the art.

Information-gathering imagery in Upper Palaeolithc art

I want to start by summarising the arguments that I have made in greater detail elsewhere (Mithen 1988b) concerning information-gathering imagery in Upper Palaeolithic art. In Chapter 3 I described the range of natural cues that modern hunter-gatherers use to acquire information about their environment. Before that I had considered cue use with particular reference to the concepts of ecological validity and utilisation of cues. Here I will follow the classification of cues used there and make reference to a set of specific images which relate to such information-gathering behaviour. These show us the cues which the hunters had identified as being ecologically valid, and which they utilised.

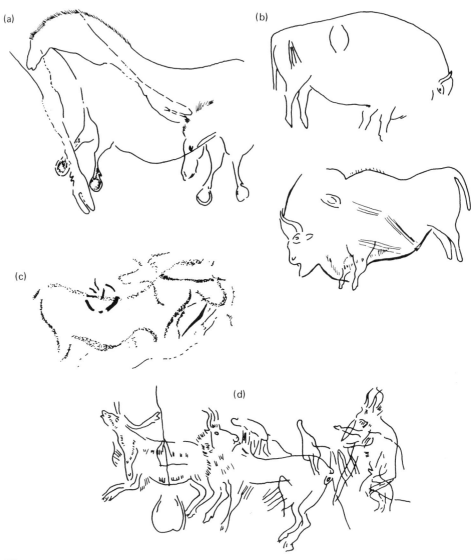

Fig. 8.1. Track and hoofprint imagery in Upper Palaeolithic art: animal depictions (not to scale): (a) detail of engraved cow and horses from Lascaux (after Vouve *et al.* 1982); (b) engraved bison from Font de Gaume (after Capitan *et al.* 1910); (c) detail from a painted panel in La Pileta (after Dams 1978); (d) detail from an engraving in Les Trois Frères (after Laming-Emperaire 1962).

Tracks and hoofprints

As described in Chapter 3, pp. 59–60 hunters acquire an immense amount of information concerning specific resources and the state of the environment in general by inspecting tracks and hoofprints. Reference is made to this in the art in three principal ways. First the feet of many animals are depicted as one would see them in tracks, rather than in profile as is the rest of the animal (Guthrie 1984: 58). This constitutes one aspect of the 'twisted perspective' stylistic trait that is pervasive in the art. Fig. 8.1a illustrates an engraving from Lascaux which shows

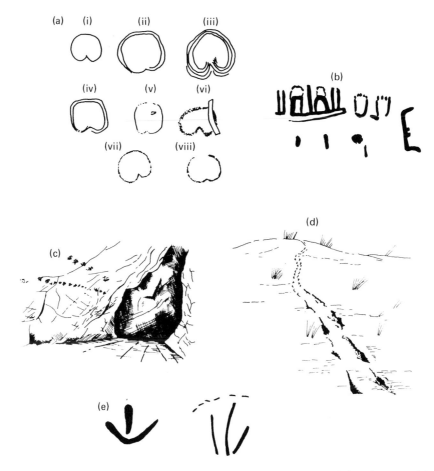

Fig. 8.2. Track and hoofprint imagery in Upper Palaeolithic art: 'abstract' signs (not to scale): (a) i–vii circular signs with indent; i–iii Roucadour, iv, v Pech Merle, vi Castillo, vii Tito Bustillo (after Lorblanchet 1977); viii track of reindeer on hard snow (after Murie 1954) (b) the 'inscription' from La Pasiega (after Sieveking 1979) (c) lines of dots on a gallery wall at Castillo (after Graziosi 1960); (d) cervid tracks in the snow (after Bang and Dahlstrom 1974); (e) signs from Comarque (after Delluc and Delluc 1984).

the feet of both horse and cow depicted in this manner. A second reference to tracks is found when we have an abstract sign which bears a significant resemblance to the footprint of an animal depicted either next to, or upon that same animal. Fig. 8.1b–d provides examples of this for bison, horse and reindeer (see Mithen 1988b: Fig. 1 for comparative hoofprints). The third manner of reference is one step away from this, by the depiction of abstract signs with similarities to hoofprints but without the support of the animal itself. Fig. 8.2a (i–vii) illustrates this, reproducing a type of abstract sign that is found in numerous instances in the art and showing that it bears considerable similarity to the hoofprint of a reindeer shown in Fig. 8.2a (viii). Another example is one of the elements composing the 'inscription' from La Pasiega (Fig. 8.2b). This interpretion may also apply to the long lines of dots that are found on the walls of certain caves. Fig. 8.2c and d demonstrates the similarity between those from Castillo and a line of deer tracks in the snow. Certain signs which have traditionally been interpreted as vulvas could equally be the depiction of hoof prints and track (Bahn 1986). These include the tracks of birds, as in those from Comarque (Fig. 8.2e).

Excretions

As with tracks, excretions provide valuable sources of information (see pp. 60–1). The most important of these are faeces. We can again make a three-fold classi-fication for references to this in the art. First, there are images of animals in the process of defecating in which both animal and faeces are shown. The most important, and least controversial, of these are the spear-throwers depicting defecating ibex from several Pyrenean sites (Fig. 8.3a–c). In terms of paintings, the rhino from Lascaux (Fig. 8.3d) and deer from Levanzo (Fig. 8.3e) might be cited while further examples are described by Camps (1984). In the second type of image we have only the animal itself depicted in the posture of defecation. The tail is raised but no faeces are depicted. This tail-up posture is very common in the art (Fig. 8.3f). A third type of image is when a person is depicted in association with such defecation imagery, possibly in the act of acquiring information. The most intriguing example of this is the engraved bone from Laugerie-Basse seemingly depicting a defecating bison and a little man inspecting the faeces (Fig. 8.3g). This may also be the case in the engraving from Les Trois Frères (Fig. 8.1d), in which the bison's anus appears to be exaggerated. It may be defecating, and a shaman/ hunter is associated with the scene which, as we have seen, also includes references to hoofprints. Certain mammoths in Pech Merle also have very detailed and accurately drawn anuses and anal flaps, while the rest of their bodies are either omitted or stylised (Lorblanchet 1977) which may again refer to the hunters'/ artists' interest in defecation.

Terrain

Here I refer to the information contained in marks left on the ground by animals which have been either rolling or sleeping (see p. 61). In this case, reference is made in the art simply through the depiction of rolling or lying animals. The classic examples are the bison from Altamira (Figs. 8.4a and 8.7) and Castillo (Fig. 8.4b). Similar images are found elsewhere such as on the reindeer bone from Laugerie-Basse (Fig. 8.4d). All these cases probably relate simply to bisons wallowing and leaving marks on the ground (Fig. 8.4c), rather than the more dramatic interpretations of bison giving birth, dying or marking territory. Prior to wallowing, bison may tear up the ground with their horns (Fig. 8.4e), and this may be a more appropriate interpretation for the engraving from Pech Merle (Fig. 8.4f) rather than that the bison is about to charge. Lascaux carries several images which may be interpreted as animals lying or rolling on the ground (Fig. 8.4g–i), while the 'cervid mourant' from Gourdan shows a very striking similarity to wallowing red deer (Fig. 8.4j–k).

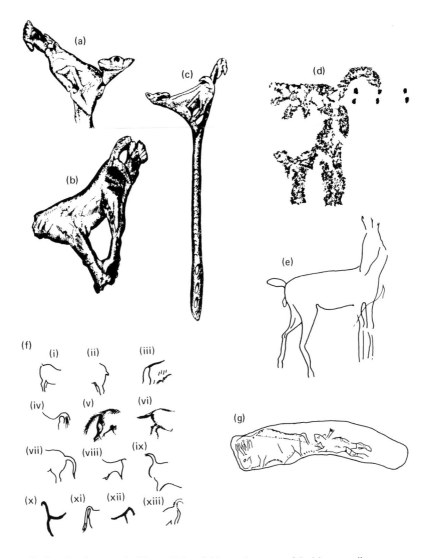

Fig. 8.3. Defecation imagery in Upper Palaeolithic art (not to scale): (a) young ibex on a spearthrower from Bédeilhac (after Graziosi 1960); (b) young ibex on a spearthrower from Arudy (after Graziosi 1960); (c) young ibex on a spearthrower from Mas d'Azil (after Graziosi 1960); (d) rear quarters of a rhino from Lascaux (after Leroi-Gourhan 1968); (e) engraved deer from Levanzo (after Graziosi 1969); (f) tail-up display in cave paintings (after Guthrie 1984): i reindeer, Les Combarelles, ii red deer, La Marié à Teyjat, iii, mammoth, Pech Merle, iv mammoth, La Madeleine, v horse, Font de Gaume, vi horse, Lascaux, vii horse, Les Combarelles, viii bison, La Pasiega, ix bison, Gabillou, x bison, Lascaux, xi bison, Lascaux, xii bison, Le Portel, xiii bison, Altamira; (g) Engraved bone from Laugerie-Basse (after Graziosi 1960).

Fig. 8.4. Terrain cues imagery in Upper Palaeolithic art (not to scale): (a) bison from Altamira ceiling (after Breuil 1952); (b) bison from Castillo (after Breuil and Obermaier 1935); (c) bison wallow (after Murie 1954); (d) bison on a reindeer bone from Laugerie-Basse (after Capitan *et al*. 1910); (e) bison tearing up the ground with its horn (after Murie 1954); (f) 'charging' bison from Pech Merle (after Dams 1980); (g) 'jumping' cow from Lascaux (after Leroi-Gourhan 1968); (h) 'falling' horse from Lascaux (after Leroi-Gourhan 1968); (i) 'rolling' horse from Lascaux (after Leroi-Gourhan 1984); (j) red deer wallow (after Bouchner 1982); (k) 'cervid mourant' from Gourdan (Piette 1907).

Vegetation

As described in Chapter 3 pp. 61–2, hunter-gatherers make use of the marks that animals leave on vegetation or the disturbance they cause to it by their activities. In the art, reference is made to this in two ways. First, animals are depicted actually feeding, such as the reindeer on the baton from Kesslerloch and on the plaque from Limeuil (Fig. 8.5a–b). Bison and deer also may be feeding in the images on the bone polisher from La Vache and the baton from Raymonden (Fig. 8.5c–d). The second manner of reference is the juxtaposition of an animal with an 'abstract' mark which bears resemblance to a plant or to marks which may be left on plants. For instance in Lascaux bovids and horse are depicted next to what look like plants and may be images of the animals disturbing these by their activities (Fig. 8.5e–f). A further example may be the engraved bear's head and signs on the baton from Massat (Fig. 8.5g). As shown in Fig. 8.5h, bears leave a variety of marks on trees.

Sound

Listening to noises and the calls of animals is a further important means by which information is acquired by hunter-gatherers (see p. 63). Here I note simply that there are numerous depictions of animals bellowing or calling in the art. Several images exist of red deer calling, as from Altamira, El Buxú and Les Horteaux (Fig. 8.6a–c). Altamira also has two depictions of bellowing bison, one within the main panorama (Fig. 8.7) and one some distance from this (Fig. 8.6d). Similarly, images of calling animals are found in the mobiliary art, such as the horse's head from Mas d'Azil (Fig. 8.6e).

Body cues

By this I refer to the cues found on the body of the animal which refer back to other parts of the body and which are of interest to the hunter, for example indicating likely yields (see p. 64). These are principally used when a hunter is watching a herd and selecting an animal to try and kill. Reference to such cue use is made in the art by the use of distortion and omission, that is, those parts of the body to which a hunter directs his/her attention are exaggerated in size or generally made dominant in the image, while the unimportant features are neglected. Secondary sexual characteristics are often treated in this way. The size and form of an animal's antlers or horns provide considerable information to a hunter concerning that animal's age (Fig. 8.8a) and state of health (Guthrie 1984). We see in the red deer painted in Lascaux that the antlers are often exaggerated in size and/or twisted into full view while the animal remains in profile. Alternatively, this may constitute the principal aspect of the image, the rest of the animal being omitted (Fig. 8.8b–d). Ibex receive similar treatment (Fig. 8.8e). Images from Le Portel, Pech Merle and La Marie à Teyjat take this stylistic trait to an extreme (Fig. 8.8f–i).

The body of the animal itself is also significant in that a hunter may evaluate the amount of meat or fat that an animal carries. Exaggeration and omission are also used here to refer to such information gathering. For instance the fatty tissues of

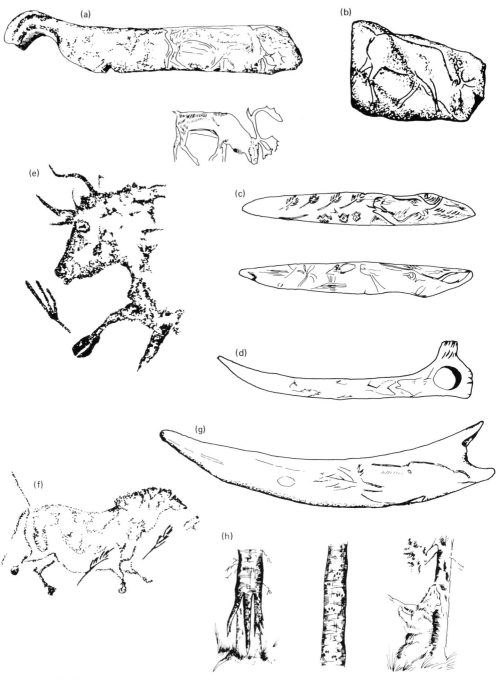

Fig. 8.5. Vegetation cues imagery in Upper Palaeolithic art (not to scale): (a) engraved reindeer on a baton from Kesslerloch (after Graziosi 1960); (b) engraved reindeer on a baton from Limeuil (after Graziosi 1960); (c) engraved bone polisher from La Vache (after Graziosi 1960); (d) engraved baton from Raymonden (after Marshack 1972); (e) bovid and sign from Lascaux (after Vouve *et al.* 1982); (f) 'chinese' horse and signs from Lascaux (after Vouve *et al.* 1982); (g) engraved bear's head and signs on a baton from Massat (after Graziosi 1960); (h) bear marks on trees (after Murie 1954).

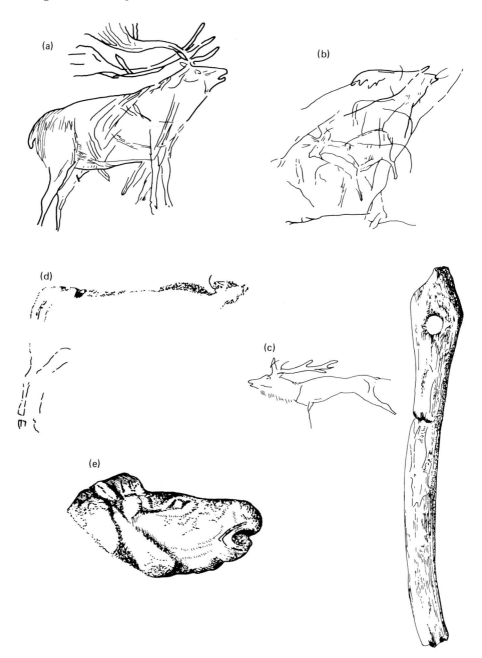

Fig. 8.6. Audible cues imagery in Upper Palaeolithic art (not to scale): (a) roaring red deer from Altamira (after Graziosi 1960); (b) roaring red deer from El Buxú (after Graziosi 1960); (c) roaring red deer on a baton from Les Horteaux (after Graziosi 1960); (d) bellowing bison from Altamira (after Breuil and Obermaier 1935); (e) carved horse's head from Mas d'Azil (after Graziosi 1960).

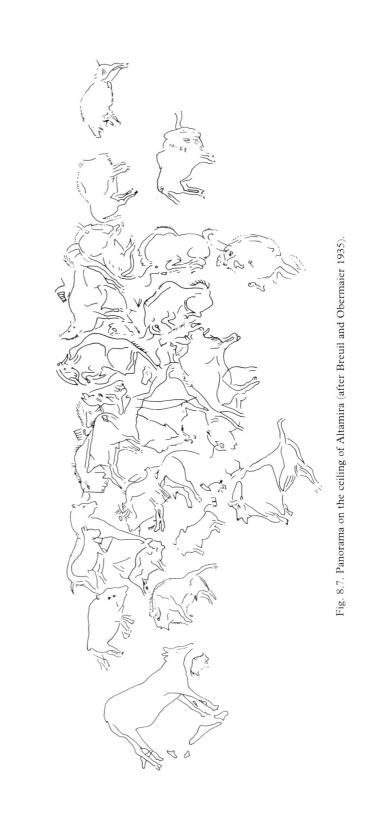

Fig. 8.7. Panorama on the ceiling of Altamira (after Breuil and Obermaier 1935).

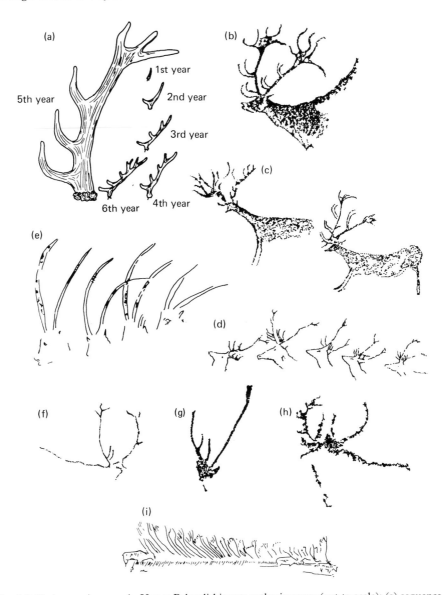

Fig. 8.8. Body cues imagery in Upper Palaeolithic art: antler imagery (not to scale): (a) sequence of red deer antler growth (after Lawrence and Brown 1967); (b) painted red deer from Lascaux (after Graziosi 1960); (c) painted red deer from Lascaux (after Graziosi (1960); (d) red deer from Lascaux (after Graziosi 1960); (e) engraved and painted ibex heads from Lascaux (after Graziosi 1960); (f) antler imagery from Le Portel (after Graziosi 1960); (g) antler imagery from Le Portel (after Graziosi 1960); (h) antler imagery from Pech Merle (after Graziosi 1960); (i) antler imagery from La Mairie à Teyjat (after Graziosi 1960).

many animals often appear very large and distorted (Baffier 1984), as in the bison from Font de Gaume (Fig. 8.9a), and it is unlikely that these are accurate depictions considering the environmental conditions of the late glacial. In general the depiction of animals in profile and the frequent omission or reduction in size of the legs and heads (Fig. 8.9b–g) may be a reference to the information-laden parts of an animal. Figures which are highly schematised into just a line for the head and back are frequently found. As Bahn and Vertut comment, 'it is possible that the figures simply depict a part of the animal, since the shape of the back and head would be fundamental in recognition at a distance' (1988: 117). Only the informationally laden parts of the animal are depicted. These allow the hunters to identify the type of animal (species, age, sex, size, etc.) with the same ability as the Kutchin, 'by fleeting glimpses of their shape' (Nelson 1973: 91). A similar use of exaggeration is found in the fish depicted in Pindal (Fig. 8.8h). As Leroi-Gourhan (1968) explains, the body of the fish is strikingly similar to either a trout or a salmon but the very large forked tail is an anomaly. However, the tails of sea trout and salmon do differ slightly, the former being convex and the latter concave (Fig. 8.9 i–j), and this is useful for identifying the fish (Falkus 1987). The highly exaggerated concave tail of the Pindal fish may be a reference to the information that is gained by inspecting the tail.

Animals as direct cues

By direct cues I mean the manner in which the sight of one species of animal (or its signs) may provide information about another with which it is directly associated (see pp. 64–5). This information may concern either the simple existence of the cued animal in the environment or its specific location/current behaviour. The principal nature of such an association is a predator-prey relationship. This is indicated in the art simply by the depiction of predators and prey in association with each other. These are images which depict the carnivore either upon or over the herbivore (Fig. 8.10a–c), or in an active process of hunting (Fig. 8.10d–j). An image of a wolf menacing a deer appears as a theme on engraved pebbles from Lortet (Fig. 8.10i), Mas d'Azil, Pendo and Les Eyzies (Bahn and Vertut 1988: 120). This theme of carnivore-herbivore association is particularly interesting in light of the reindeer simulation model which I described in Chapter 7. We saw there how the presence of carnivores exploiting the reindeer population, and by implication other herbivores, would not only decrease the yields that the hunters may acquire but also make these yields subject to greater fluctuation. Hence while knowledge of the whereabouts and behaviour of carnivores will act as a cue to the location of herbivore populations it also indicates the size and character of that population. The simulation model suggested that the hunters may have had cause to be concerned with the density and behaviour of competing carnivores and this theme in the art appears to reflect such interest. The majority of predator-prey associations refer to terrestrial animals but Fig. 8.10j shows that such imagery extends to aquatic communities. A second type of direct association is when one animal uses another as a 'patch' for foraging. The most notable example of this is

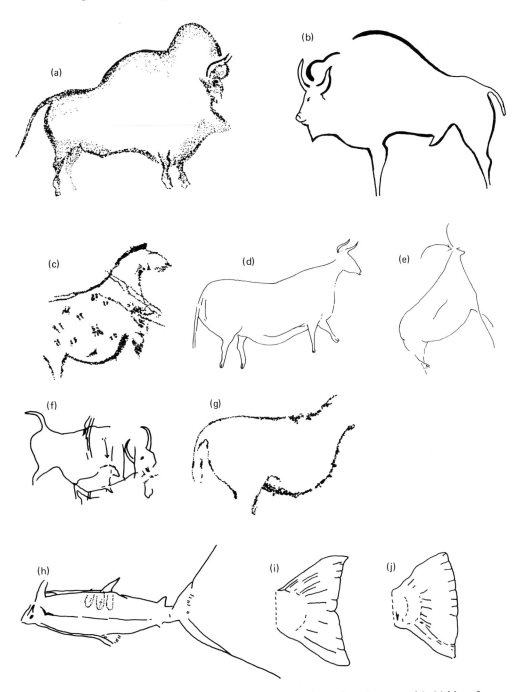

Fig. 8.9. Body cues imagery in Upper Palaeolithic art: body shape (not to scale): (a) bison from Font de Gaume (after Graziosi 1960); (b) engraved bison from La Grèze (after Graziosi 1960); (c) horse and signs from La Pileta (after Leroi-Gourhan 1968); (d) engraved and painted cow from Lascaux (after Leroi-Gourhan 1968); (e) engraved ibex from Ebbou (after Graziosi 1960); (f) engraved bison from Gabillou (after Graziosi 1960); (g) 'horse' from Bédeilhac (after Leroi-Gourhan 1968); (h) engraved fish from Pindal (after Graziosi 1960); (i) tail of a salmon (after Falkus 1979); (j) tail of a sea trout (after Falkus 1979).

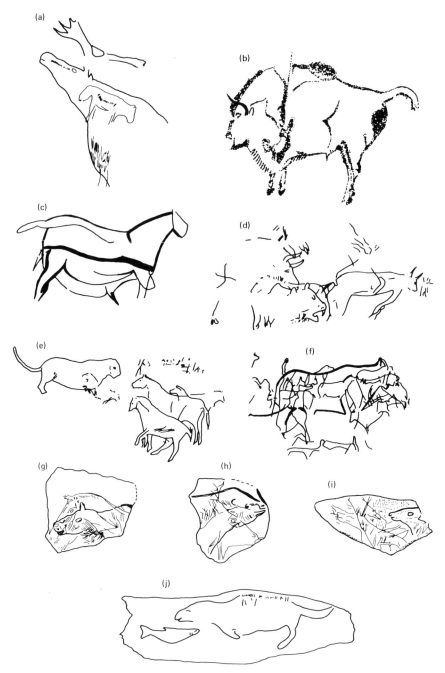

Fig. 8.10. Direct animal cues imagery in Upper Palaeolithic art: predator-prey imagery (not to scale): (a) reindeer and wolf/fox from Altxerri (after Sieveking 1979); (b) bison and wolf from Altamira (after Breuil and Obermaier 1935); (c) feline and horse from Niaux (after Leroi-Gourhan 1968); (d) feline and bovines from Gabillou (after Nougier and Robert 1965); (e) lion and horses from Font de Gaume (after Leroi-Gourhan 1968); (f) felines, horses and anthropomorph from Casares (after Nougier and Robert 1965); (g) wolf and horse from Lourdes (after Clot 1973); (h) glutton (?) and reindeer from Lourdes (after Clot 1973); (i) wolf and cervids from Lortet (after Clot 1973); (j) otter and salmon from Laugerie-Basse (after Reinach 1913).

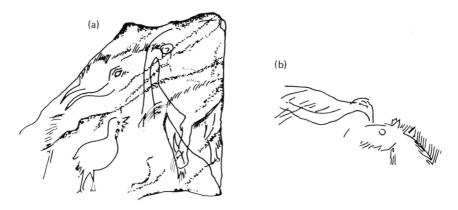

Fig. 8.11. Direct animal cues imagery in Upper Palaeolithic art: bird-herbivore imagery (not to scale): (a) bison and birds from Puy de Lacan (after Leroi-Bourhan 1968); (b) horse's head and bird from Lourdes (after Clot 1973). (b) horse's head and bird from Lourdes (after Clot 1973).

when birds forage on the backs of large ungulates for fleas and grubs. In this respect the association found between birds and large ungulates in certain images (Fig. 8.11a–b) is intriguing. Engravings from Les Ezyies and Raymonden, which had previously been seen as depicting humanoids and bison, have now been re-interpreted by Eastham as being birds, probably swallows, with bison (Bahn and Vertut 1988: 132).

Animals as indirect cues

The sight of an animal may also provide information about another species because of an indirect association between them (see pp. 65–6). They are both related to a third species or environmental event that is not itself observed. The use of animals as information sources in this respect appears in the art as the depiction of a set of animals or images which all either relate to one season or are engaged in specific seasonal activities and hence may provide a cue to each other. The Montgaudier baton (Fig. 8.12a) provides a good example in which all the images appear to relate to early spring (Marshack 1972). The fish is identified as a male salmon at the time of spawning because of the 'kype' or hook on its lower jaw. The seals (which are predators of salmon) may be following the salmon up the river or be gathering at estuaries or coasts as they do at this time of year. The eels, one of which is clearly a male, emerge from hibernation in the spring and form breeding pairs. Marshack also claims that the minor images on the baton such as flower buds also refer to early spring. From the information-gathering perspective this repre-sents the association of animals each of which may act as a cue to the other since they are all reacting to the same environmental changes. A second example is equally interesting, the baton from Lortet (Fig. 8.12b). On this, three deer and leaping salmon are depicted, along with some other diamond-shaped marks. Marshack suggests that this is an image either of autumn, when the salmon runs are the largest and the stags collect their harems, or of summer when the stags

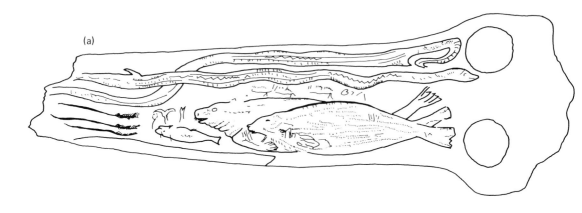

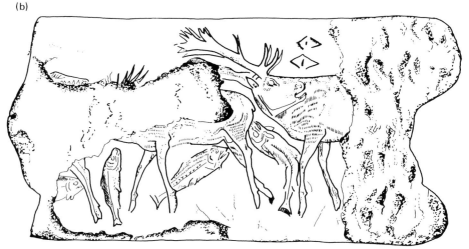

Fig. 8.12. Indirect animal cues imagery in Upper Palaeolithic art: seasonal imagery (not to scale):
(a) the Montgaudier baton (after Marshack 1972); (b) engraved baton from Lortet (after Graziosi
1960).

depart from the hinds. Whichever it may be, this is an association between the
movement of deer and the jumping of salmon. Observation of one may act as an
indirect cue to the other.

A further aspect of imagery which may relate to indirect cue use is the representation of birds in general. Lorblanchet (1974) and Hooper (1977) have described
how the majority of bird images which can be identified are of waterfowl, such as
ducks and geese (Fig. 8.13a–j). In contrast the predominant species in the faunal
assemblages are game birds. The depiction of waterfowl may be a further example
of this information-gathering theme since it is these species, particularly those
which migrate, that provide the hunter-gatherers with indicators of forthcoming
environmental events. As I described in Chapter 3, p. 66, modern hunter-
gatherers keenly monitor the arrival and departure of waterfowl, as for instance

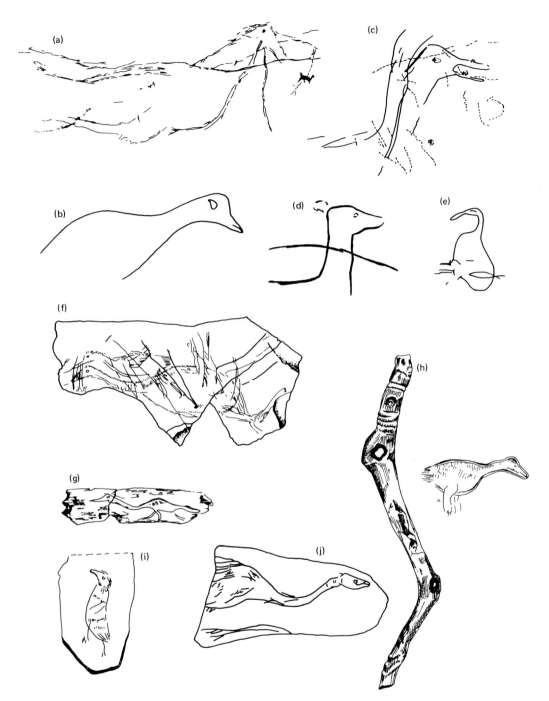

Fig. 8.13. Indirect animal cues imagery in Upper Palaeolithic art: waterfowl imagery (not to scale): (a) from Ganties-Montespan (after Rivenq 1984); (b) from Roc de Saint Cirq (after Dams 1980); (c) from Escabasser (after Lorblanchet 1974); (d) from Labastide (after Leroi-Gourhan 1968); (e) from Gargas (after Clot 1973); (f) from Labastide (after Graziosi 1960); (g) from Bevis (after Saachi 1972); (h) from Gourdan (after Piette 1904); (i) from Lourdes (after Clot 1973); (j) from Gourdan (after Piette 1904).

among the Kutchin: 'The arrival of migratory birds, particularly waterfowl, is watched carefully as an indicator of the beginning of warm spring weather. Around late April, ducks and geese will fail to show up during warm spells if there is another period of cold weather. And when they do arrive in large numbers, the Indians say that the weather will remain warm' (Nelson 1973: 200).

Information-gathering imagery: problems and proposals

In identifying this theme in the art I am partly drawing on patterns and interpretations that others have made and partly proposing new ideas myself. The essence of my argument is to show how all of these previously separated and isolated ideas are compatible and relate to the single information-gathering theme. That tracks and hoofprints are represented in the art has previously been suggested (Bahn 1986), though I have added further possible candidates and made the case more robust. Similarly Camps (1984) has pointed to the presence of defecation imagery in the art. Marshack (1972) has made the excellent case for seasonal imagery in the art. My role here has been to identify the common theme behind such characteristic features of the art.

Now several of these identifications of cue-use imagery involve putting a subjective interpretation onto an image: 'I think that this is a picture of . . .'. Doing this is of course fraught with problems and critics are quick to pounce. A single image may bear a similarity to many different things, so how can we choose between them? How can we possibly infer what the artist intended to depict? How do we know if two juxtaposed images are associated? Interpretations can only reflect the prejudices and interests of he/she who is making them! I am not going to deny that these are problems but will find myself a few criteria by which they may be tackled or which show them to be of little importance. First, what the artist intended to depict is not really of any great relevance. I am interested in the interpretations put onto the pictures by the hunters viewing the art and these may no more coincide with the intention of the artist than my own. Also, this indicates that there can never be one single correct interpretation. The artist may have intended to draw an arrow, a contemporary hunter may have seen it as a blade of grass while another may have seen a phallus. Similarly the artist may not have intended to associate two images he painted side by side, or one image with another painted previously. But this does not prevent the hunter viewing the art from making an association.

The interpretation placed on any single image may be strengthened if it is compatible with interpretations for other images and hence relate to a common theme. For instance some of the raised-tail imagery may be depicting animals inviting copulation, but this does not fit the information-gathering theme (and some of the animals with raised tails are clearly males). The curled-up bison from Altamira may be dead or giving birth but the idea that they are simply rolling on the ground and leaving signs of their presence which the hunters may use is compatible with interpretations of the way their hooves and horns are painted. Similarly the Kesslerloch reindeer has been seen as a male in rut rather than a grazing animal, but since grazing fits the information-gathering theme I have preferred that interpretation. Generally, many images appear ambiguous to us, and this may have also been the case for the Palaeolithic hunters (Clottes 1986; Delluc and Delluc 1985; Bahn 1986: 117). Indeed I will refer to this when speculating on the art's role in decision-making processes.

Because so many images are ambiguous, we should work from the less controversial ideas e.g. that the ibex spearthrowers do depict defecation, to those which are more ambiguous such as the raised-tail posture. The bison from Altamira illustrate another feature of my argument. When I have been placing interpretations on certain ambiguous images I have frequently chosen those which are the most simple and straightforward. For instance many different interpretations have been placed on the set of red deer heads from Lascaux (Fig. 8.8d), such as swimming animals or a herd lying in long grass (Hooper 1980). I simply take these at face value, the depiction of a set of heads and antlers, since these are informationally laden for the hunters. Finally to those who suggest that we should not attempt to place an interpretation on paintings and abstract marks since we are trapped by our own prejudices, I disagree. It is part of our character as inquiring human beings to do this. To suggest it is out of bounds is to deny our own nature. What we do need, however, is to make such interpretations in a robust framework as provided here by my focus on the individual decision maker and the ground work I have laid throughout this book.

I believe that the information-gathering theme helps explain, at one level, numerous elements of the art – problems posed by the imagery that have for too long been explained away simply as stylistic traits and no more. For instance the twisted-perspective convention can now be seen as a means to point out the most informationally laden views of an animal. The picture says, 'Look at the body in profile, the antlers/horns straight on and the hoofprints rather than the hooves themselves.' Similarly the use of exaggeration and omission of body parts serves to emphasise the areas of the body which are useful when acquiring information. Animals are depicted lying on the ground, calling, defecating and feeding since all of these leave signs for the hunter as to the whereabouts and the character of potential prey. Similarly the presence of seasonal imagery, the predominance of migratory wildfowl over other bird species, the association between carnivores and herbivores, can be seen as further aspects of this theme rather than as isolated stylistic traits with no relevance beyond themselves. I might also draw in 'negative' evidence here and refer to what is 'missing' from the art. A range of features of animal populations and behaviour which the hunters would have observed and known about are not depicted. For instance there are few images of young animals or overt sexual behaviour. These are, I would suggest, of little relevance for information gathering about the environment and resources.

However, if I have identified a theme of information gathering in the art this hardly explains the imagery, it simply remoulds the problem into another form. Rather than having many little questions to ask (e.g. why twisted perspective, why seasonal imagery, why migratory wildfowl?) we now have one big question – why information gathering? So now let me ask what functional explanation might be found for this cue-use imagery.

One provocative area is the role of art in education as has been described by Pfeiffer (1982). He summarises the arguments for this but the idea remains very controversial. This is partly because it is unclear what could be taught via the art when explicit hunting scenes are so rare and the art/fauna species frequencies often disagree (as will be discussed below). But now these difficulties may be overcome. In a general sense, the information-gathering theme acts to specify which cues, from the infinite number available in the natural environment, are the most important. Consequently the art may be related to the development of selective attention in young children.

This is a crucial component of cognitive development in young children which modifies their mode of obtaining information from the environment. Wright and Vlietstra (1975) have discussed this in most detail, distinguishing between 'exploratory' and 'search' behaviour. The former is essentially spontaneous and motivated by curiosity, while search behaviour is goal orientated and organised, serving to fulfil a plan by attending to stimuli which are relevant and possibly informative for the task at hand. Children use only exploratory behaviour while adults supplement this by searching – selectively attending to particular stimuli in preference to others. Upper Palaeolithic art may be related to the cognitive development of 'search' behaviour. Together with the song, dance and myth discussed by Pfeiffer (1982), the art channels the development of selective attention and searching by specifying which particular types of animals, and which aspects of their behaviour and form, should be attended to if relevant information is to be gathered.

Consequently if the art did indeed play a functional role in education this is in marked contrast to the one proposed by Pfeiffer. The imagery itself may be seen as mnemonic aids to the 'teachers' concerning the material that requires to be taught during the ritual, initiation ceremonies or story-telling. Rather than providing the children with a store of information this process serves to teach them how to acquire it. We might characterise this as learning how to learn about the environment and its resources.

This explanation for cue-use imagery does not exclude others since in a functional sense the art may be benefiting different sections of the population in different ways. As I quoted from Berger at the start of this chapter: 'A work can, to some extent, increase an awareness of different potentialities in different people.' So let me take a look at a second role that the art may have played, that of a mental preparation for the hunt.

In Chapter 2 I described how past experience is an essential source of information in decision making. Encyclopaedic memory contains a vast amount of knowledge, as the study of modern hunter-gatherers demonstrates. But this information has to be accessed and it is my contention that the art may have facilitated the recall of information relevant to the task in hand. I am drawing a direct analogy with the use of scapulimancy among the Cree and oracle discs among the !Kung. In proposing this I appear to be creating a contradiction. In Chapter 7 I argued that red deer and reindeer were principally hunted by game drives and large-scale co-operative hunting. However, the cue-use imagery in the art relates to hunters working alone or in small groups and exploiting individual animals. The recall of information about previously seen tracks, trails and signs (through either directed or non-directed information gathering) is of little consequence for game drives.

To resolve this paradox I refer back to my simulation studies of red deer and reindeer hunting. These suggest that in the Later Upper Palaeolithic the fluctuations in the yields from these increased markedly. My proposal is that at times of particularly low yields the hunters turned from co-operative game drives to the tracking and stalking of individual animals and the art facilitated the rapid recall of information that had become relevant but which had not been foremost in the mind owing to the co-operative drives. This was the principal mechanism by which the large fluctuations in yields were coped with. But the faunal assemblages also bear witness to another method – the diversification of the resource base to include smaller, low-return species. As I described earlier, the processes of intensification and diversification appear to go hand in hand and we can now understand why. Intensification leads to increased fluctuations in yields and one method of meeting the occasional shortfall is to exploit a greater range of species such as fish, small mammals and birds. But when the shortfalls were substantial such resources may have been insufficient and the hunters had to remain with the large game by switching to the stalking of individual animals. To support my case I will invoke a second theme in the art, one of 'information required'. This can help explain the frequency with which large species are represented in the art. Let me first briefly outline the problem that large-game representations present.

Animal frequencies in the art and fauna

It has long been recognised that there is a discrepancy between the frequency of large game depicted in the art and in the faunal assemblages. Recent quantitative studies have emphasised this finding. Rice and Paterson (1985, 1986) examine the relationship between species representation in the art and in faunal assemblages. They analyse the faunal assemblages by creating a prevalence index for each of five large ungulate species (reindeer, red deer, horse, bovines and ibex) in the assemblages from discrete regions of France and Spain, having to base their measures on qualitative reporting (such as 'rare' or 'abundant'). They then consider the percentage contribution of each species to the total index for each of these regions (ten regions in south-west France and four in Cantabrian Spain). The species representation in the art is measured simply by the number of images of each species in that region and then as the percentage of the total. They then compare the relative contribution of each species in the faunal assemblages and in the cave paintings.

Before considering their results, a few comments on this method are required. First, one must question whether their species-prevalence index bears any relationship either to the representation of the species in the assemblages or to their role in the economy. There is no guarantee that different excavators are using the descriptive terms (e.g. 'rare', 'common', etc.) in the same way, and these refer to bone counts rather than MNI or some measure which is meaningful in terms of subsistence. A second problem is whether it is justifiable to lump data from the whole duration of the Upper Palaeolithic together. For instance if a correlation is found between a particular species in the art and in the assemblages, we do not know if this arises because it was painted and hunted together for 20,000 years, or if it was only hunted for 10,000 years and then only painted for the following 10,000. Leroi-Gourhan (1968) has indeed suggested that there is temporal variability in the frequencies with which different species are represented. Bahn is wrong, however, to describe the analysis by Rice and Paterson as a 'waste of effort' suggesting that it only makes sense to compare an individual cave's figures with the bones from the same site or locality (Bahn and Vertut 1988: 157). If we adopt a proper economic, as opposed to a site diet, approach to Upper Palaeolithic subsistence, then our analyses must include studies at the regional scale. A better chonological resolution of cave art/faunal assemblage relationships is certainly necessary but there is a need for the gross art/fauna approach of Rice and Paterson, as well as for studies concerning individual sites.

Bearing in mind these methodological problems, Rice and Paterson's analysis and results are very interesting. The most important result is that the frequency of species in the art is very different from that in the faunal assemblages, as had been previously recognised on a less formal basis. In the art, bovines are most common, followed by horses, reindeer, ibex, red deer and mammoth. By contrast, reindeer has the greatest prevalence, followed by horse, bovines, red deer, ibex and mammoth. Table 8.1 summarises this lack of correlation.

One problem with this work is its gross temporal extent and it must be supplemented with a consideration of particular sites and periods. But for individual sites in which the art and fauna are approximately contemporary the most frequent pattern remains a lack of correlation between species represented in the art and in the fauna, although this is not always the case. This is well known at Lascaux, where 'les hommes tuaient des rennes et représentaient d'autres espèces' (Leroi-Gourhan, quoted in Delporte 1984), and at Altamira where bison are most frequently represented but are rare in the fauna. Sieveking (1984) considers this relationship for a range of Magdalenian sites (Balmori, Les Eglises, La Vache) and finds a lack of correlation. For instance at Ekain the fauna consists of 66.4% ibex, 26.7% deer and 1.6% horse but the paintings are predominantly of horse (33 horses, 10 bison, 14 caprids, 2 stages, 2 bears and 2 fish). Many French sites which have a marked discrepancy between the frequency of species in the fauna and in the art such as Grotte des Eyzies, Abri Morin, Comarque, Villars, the Ardèche caves and Gargas. All of these have fauna dominated by reindeer which is either absent or minimally represented in the parietal or portable art at the site. Similarly Gönnersdorf in Germany has a large collection of portable art objects on which the mammoth dominates, but this species is rare in the fauna (Bahn and Vertut 1988: 156–7). Altuna (1983) reaches a similar conclusion of a significant

Table 8.1. *Percentage of species prevalence in cave art minus percentage prevalence in fauna (after Rice and Paterson 1985)*

Reindeer	− 19.0	Horse	7.0
Red deer	− 8.5	Ibex	1.5
Bison	14.6	Mammoth	4.2

discrepancy between species frequencies in the art and in the fauna for Cantabrian cave sites. Some sites, however, do show a similarity between the art and faunal representations (Sieveking 1984; Bahn and Vertut 1988). For instance at Covalanus and La Pasiega deer is most frequent both in the paintings and in the bone assemblages. Sieveking notes that these are earlier and further inland than those caves which lack this correlation and suggests that in general it is during the Magdalenian that the discrepancies between faunal and artistic representations are greatest.

This discussion has so far focused mainly on the parietal art. Delporte (1984) considers art/fauna frequencies in relation to mobiliary art and arrives at similar results. He examines the mobiliary art of La Madeleine, La Vache and Gargas and finds substantial discrepancies between the animals illustrated and those in the fauna. For instance at La Madeleine reindeer contribute 91.9% of the fauna and only 20.8% of the images, while horse has the figures of 4.2% and 43.0% respectively. Splitting the site into three levels (lower, middle and upper), it is only in the latter that reindeer is the most frequently represented species in both the art (42.5%) and the fauna (96.1%) while horse remains far more heavily illustrated (21.3%) than its faunal contribution (0.4%). La Vache shows a similar pattern with the role of reindeer replaced by ibex. In this case horse is practically absent from the assemblage but provides 25.6% of the representations while ibex has values of 88.2% and 17.9% for the fauna and art respectively.

To explain this pattern I suggest that the frequencies of species representation in the art relate to the frequencies with which species were tracked as individuals. The faunal assemblages, on the other hand, combine the results of this tracking with the mass kills of red deer and reindeer, and are hence dominated by the latter. And, of course, this does not require that disagreements between species frequencies in faunal assemblages and in the art are always to be found. The co-operative mass hunting would have been feasible only from certain locations since its success is dependent upon particular topographic features (e.g. river fords, natural corrals) and the aggregation sites of the red deer and reindeer. In contrast, hunters stalking individual animals, either alone or in small groups, would have had a far greater flexibility as to the sites from which they could operate. Consequently some sites may have the results of the latter hunting method alone, and we should expect a correlation between species frequencies in the art and fauna at such sites.

My argument is, therefore, that the frequency with which different species are depicted constitutes an 'information-required' theme. Information is required either from encyclopaedic memory or from new tracks, trails and signs in the environment. The frequencies for each species in the art might be further explored by developing encounter-foraging models of the type I built in Part 2 for the late-glacial environment. At a rather simpler level, the correlation that Rice and Paterson (1986) describe between species frequencies in the art and their individual meat yield gives some support to my proposal.

Upper Palaeolithic art, creative thought and adaptation

In recalling stored information about the animals they may wish to hunt, and about the cues that may help them, hunters are not necessarily using this information in any straightforward manner. As I discussed in Chapter 2, stored information may itself generate new information through its use for imagination and fantasy. The art itself acts as a cue to creative thought about the future. Hence we are not solely concerned here with a mechanical process of recalling information. As I explained in my introduction, the future courses of action available to a decision maker must be first created in the mind and this creative thought is the driving force of the process of adaptation. By surrounding themselves with the images of the animals about which they require information, and by depicting these in manners which refer to the way that information is acquired, the hunters are creating in their minds many possible and different future worlds. And of course, each individual will be creating a unique set of future worlds for him/herself, overlapping with those of other hunters but dependent upon that individual's unique historical, social and ecological context in terms of age, sex and experience. He/she may then attempt to create one of these future worlds through action. It is in dealing with this issue of creative thought that we return to one aspect of the art which was only briefly mentioned but which has caused many disputes in the study of Palaeolithic art. What is actually depicted in many images is, or may be, ambiguous (Clottes 1986: 107; Bahn 1986: 117). Do the Altamira paintings depict a bison dying, rolling in the dirt or giving birth? Is the reindeer on the bone from Kesslerloch simply grazing or in rut? Are 'penniforms' depictions of vegetation, arrows or phalluses? Are 'vulva'-like signs actually vulvas, or perhaps hoofprints, or something else (Bahn 1986), or indeed are they intentionally ambiguous (Delluc and Delluc 1985)? It may be that they are ambiguous to us because we do not have the eyes and mind of a Late Pleistocene hunter. But perhaps this ambiguity is indeed a real feature of the art as Clottes (1986: 107) suggests. This would indeed make sense from the interpretation I am putting forward here. On the one hand an ambiguous image makes one look more closely, try to derive as much information as possible from the image. This may be precisely what was required for the hunters when tracking their prey and finding initially ambiguous signs. On the other hand, if ambiguity in an image does anything it generates some creative thinking about it and what it represents. So, if the art is indeed playing the functional role I am proposing, we might recognise ambiguous images as a real and significant feature of the art.

Before concluding, it is useful to look briefly at one area of south-west Europe in a little more detail to illustrate how my proposals can be applied in a specific context, and how the ideas may be developed. Let us consider the Tarascon Basin in the Ariège, an area whose Magdalenian art and economy has been well studied (e.g. Clottes and Simonnet 1979; Bahn 1979, 1984; Delpech and LeGall 1983). Within an area of a few square kilometres there is a cluster of sites which include the magnificent 'sanctuary' of Niaux, the painted caves of Bédeilhac and Fontanet, and sites with substantial habitation debris such as La Vache and Les Eglises. Ibex dominates the faunal assemblages at both of these sites, particularly at Les Eglises, and a specialised winter exploitation of ibex has been inferred (Delpech and LeGall 1983; Bahn 1984: 272; Straus 1987b). Some form of mass killing appears likely – Bahn refers to 'heavy seasonal culls' being made from La Vache (1984: 272). We must assume here that ibex populations react in the same manner as red deer and reindeer when exploitation is intense, i.e. a substantial rise in the degree to which their numbers fluctuate. A second element of the economy appears to have been the slaughter of reindeer herds. Bahn describes how the 'outer salle' at La Vache appears to have been dominated by reindeer bones, as are certain locations within Bédeilhac, and suggests that 'reindeer were culled at strategic points as they passed through the area, no doubt in late spring and early autumn' (1984: 276). Together with this focus on ibex and reindeer, we find evidence for the exploitation of small, 'low return' resources such as fish, birds, hare and rabbit in the assemblages from Les Eglises, La Vache, Fontanet and Bédeilhac (Bahn 1984: tables 35, 36). According to my models in Chapter 6, we must envisage the 'specialised' ibex and reindeer hunters in the Tarascon Basin as being in high-risk situations, facing large fluctuations in the ibex and reindeer populations.

Turning to the art, it is first necessary to assume that the cave paintings are contemporary with the intense exploitation of reindeer and ibex. To be more specific, I assume that the ibex and reindeer hunters engaged in rituals and ceremonies which involved the parietal art, not necessarily that they actually produced the paintings themselves. The majority of parietal art in the area is currently attributed to the Middle Magdalenian on rather dubious stylistic grounds. This is earlier than the widespread intensification and diversification in the Pyrenees. However, stylistic affinities between the paintings in Niaux and the mobiliary art from La Vache may indicate contemporaneity in this case (Bahn 1984: 263).

The paintings in Niaux, Les Eglises, Fontanet and Bédeilhac are dominated by bison, followed by horse and then by red deer and ibex at lower frequencies and sparse representations of small animals including the unique weasel from the René Clastres gallery of Niaux (Galli *et al.* 1984; Clottes 1984; Clottes and Simonnet 1984; Clottes and Rouzard 1984; Clottes *et al.* 1984). According to my proposals the frequency with which the large ungulate species are depicted relates to the frequency with which they were stalked as individuals when either the ibex or reindeer mass kills failed to supply sufficient returns. In support of this we find bison, horse and red deer at low frequencies in the ibex and reindeer dominated assemblages from La Vache and Bédeilhac (Bahn 1984: table 35).

The sites of Fontanet and Les Eglises provide a particularly interesting contrast. The faunal assemblage from Les Eglises is totally dominated by ibex (Delpech and Le Gall 1983), while bison predominate in its parietal art (Clottes and Rouzard 1984). Similarly bison and horse are dominant in the art at Fontanet (Clottes *et al.* 1984) but, in contrast to Les Eglises, the available faunal assemblage has rather even proportions of bison, horse and ibex (Bahn 1984: table 36). In light of my arguments, the Fontanet fauna is probably the result of individual stalking of ungulates, and hence there is a broad agreement between the art/fauna species frequencies, while there is no correlation at Les Eglises since the assemblage there derives from co-operative group hunting of ibex. This may be examined further by an analysis of body-part representation in the two assemblages. Les Eglises has marginal-utility parts, reflecting the close vicinity of a kill site (Straus 1987b). We should expect the Fontanet fauna to be represented by high-utility parts following the field-butchery of kills at some distance from the cave.

A second contrast can be drawn between the 'sanctuary' of Niaux (in terms of its size, the extensive parietal art and the lack of habitation remains) and the sites of Fontanet and Les Eglises in which occupation debris and parietal art are found together. This contrast may reflect the two complementary functional roles that I have been proposing for the art. The character of Niaux suggests a context in which the art played the 'educational' role described by Pfeiffer (1982) and which I have developed as 'learning how to learn' about the environment. The art in the occupied sites however may have principally related to the mental preparation of hunters at times of switching from group to individual hunting. Certainly the deep location of much of the art in Niaux is what we should expect if the art is playing an educational role in the context of initiation ceremonies (Pfeiffer 1982). It is perhaps useful to look at the black outline figures in Niaux, (e.g. Fig. 7.1) and particularly at those in the René Clastres gallery (Fig. 8.14), with two bison just represented by an evocative dorsal line, with the statement by Nelson in mind as to how a skilled hunter can pick out the best animals at a glance by *the curve of their back and their general fullness* (1983: 165). The depictions in Niaux appear to be concerned with creating such skilled hunters.

We have seen in this example how further features of the archaeological record are now being connected with the patterning in the art. With respect to the faunal assemblages which are dominated by red deer, reindeer or ibex, the ungulate species which are at low frequencies such as horse and bison now acquire significance. It is indeed a characteristic of the classic mass kill sites such as La Madeleine, Gare de Couze and La Riera that there are low frequencies of ungulates other than that being specially targeted within the assemblage (Delpech 1983; Altuna 1986). These probably resulted from the stalking of individual animals. The smaller sites with more balanced ungulate frequencies (e.g. White 1985: 159–60), which may correlate with the species frequencies in the art of the region, are also linked into the explanation in that these relate to the stalking of individual ungulates alone. In addition, the pattern of body-part representation in the faunal assemblages is now significant since, along with mortality profiles, this

Fig. 8.14. Three 'bison' and a horse from the réseau René Clastres, Niaux (after Clottes and Simonnet 1984).

may inform on hunting patterns. Generally, when we find sites with similar ungulate frequencies in the art and fauna we should expect the mortality profiles to be of an attritional nature reflecting the stalking of individual animals.

The Tarascon Basin example has also shown how a further dimension of variability in the archaeological record can be linked in with my proposals. Specifically, the degree to which the parietal art is associated with occupation debris may relate to which of the two alternative, but complementary, functional roles of the art is of principal significance at that site. Niaux and Les Eglises appear to be specifically orientated to just one of the functional roles, education and mental preparation respectively. Other sites, such as Altamira, which have a sanctuary-like appearance as well as important occupation debris may have fulfilled both roles.

To conclude let me emphasise how on the one hand my proposals are very modest, while on the other they are rather ambitious. Their modesty lies in that I am not trying to explain every single image in the art. I am ready to concede that only a small proportion of images may be directly related to an information-gathering theme – though if one had the eyes and mind of an Upper Palaeolithic hunter, this proportion might be considerably greater. Similarly while the information required theme may have some value in understanding species frequencies in the art, no doubt other factors are also important. Information gathering and information required are just two of perhaps many themes in this complex and diverse artistic tradition. Patterns in the art not considered here, such as the localised distribution of particular motifs, may relate to the art functioning as territorial markers and in consolidating group identity (Straus 1982a; Sieveking 1980).

The audacious side of my proposals is to specify how the patterns in the art I have considered relate to certain patterns in the faunal assemblages. My goal has been to make connections via an understanding of decision-making processes since this is a path to explanation. I have suggested a very specific context in the LUP when hunters acquired functional benefit from their artistic traditions and associated ritual – the failure of co-operative mass hunting and the switch to the stalking of individual animals. This complemented a more general educational role of the art. In essence, the art with its information gathering and information required themes facilitated the recall of information from encyclopaedic memory and creative thought about the future at the transition between these hunting activities. Whether this role was restricted to 'crisis' situations, when it would have had greatest functional significance, or also occurred under more normal circumstances (such as at seasonal changes in subsistence activity) is a moot point. In proposing this mental preparation role, I am drawing a direct analogy with that of scapulimancy among the Cree. This was also used at the juncture between economic activities, though predominatly at the switch from individual to group hunting (Tanner 1978: 100). Similarly, in proposing a switch from group co-operative hunting of red deer/reindeer to the stalking of individuals when herd densities were low, an analogy is drawn with the responses of Greenland caribou hunters to caribou densities (Meldgaard 1983: 267). These analogies, however, simply support my argument since I have built it from a consideration of the archaeological data alone.

During the earlier Upper Palaeolithic, prior to the occurrence of intensification and diversification, the art may have played similar roles in education and mental preparation for the hunt. But the degree of functional benefit so gained increased dramatically during the Later Upper Palaeolithic as ungulate populations begun to experience large fluctuations. Consequently there occurred the great expansion in artistic activity. Indeed, when elucidating the historical context of the LUP decision makers the established existence of an artistic tradition must be stressed. In essence the art was co-opted to help with the required information flows, perhaps being pre-adapted to this by its existing character. In doing this the hunters of the Later Upper Palaeolithic were engaging in the process of adaptation to their ever-changing environment.

9

Conclusion

Cultural behaviour derives from capacities for learning, decision making and problem solving. As biological endowments these reside in the individual. Consequently, explanations for cultural behaviour require explicit reference to decision making by individuals. Bold statements indeed. Perhaps safe in a purely theoretical paper or at the end of a book, but I foolishly made these in my introduction! Did the archaeological studies live up to such extravagant claims? It is not for me to judge.

To conclude this work I want briefly to review my two archaeological studies and draw out the type of prehistoric world I am envisaging. I also wish to emphasise certain elements of the archaeological approach I have advocated.

I have suggested that explanations in archaeology can be improved by explicit reference to the individual decision maker. However, I have not stipulated that this should take any particular form. Indeed, I myself have been rather flexible. In my study of Mesolithic foraging I built a model for decision making by an individual and used that as a methodological tool. This is perhaps the most explicit reference. In the Upper Palaeolithic study, however, I concentrated on understanding the ecological and historical context in which the decision makers would have been operating and then, using a conceptual rather than a quantitative model for decision making, made reference to individuals tackling patch-choice problems. We might also note that each study focused on rather different elements of the decision-making process. When studying Mesolithic foraging, I concentrated on information acquisition from past experience and other individuals. But in the Upper Palaeolithic study greatest attention was paid to cue use and the creative manipulation of past experience.

I tried to use this reference to the individual decision maker to allow previously isolated features of the archaeological record to be integrated into a single coherent framework. It is a case of showing how all the bits and pieces fit together and can only be understood in terms of each other. This might be done in several different ways but I want the individual to be at the centre and his/her cognitive processes to be the hub around which everything revolves. It was a case of moving from some archaeological data to inferences concerning the individual decision maker, and then pivoting back to other features of the archaeological record. In both cases I moved from patterns in the faunal record to inferences about individual decision making and then swung back to data concerning technology, social organisation or art. One might equally begin with archaeological data that immediately refer to art or social organisation, work towards the decision maker and then return to patterns in faunal assemblages. By doing this we recognise that these separate categories of activity (e.g. hunting, tool making, social interaction) are intimately linked but that we can only make progress by imposing artificial divisions to find what is at the core and then use this to erode the divisions.

The study of Mesolithic foraging and society demonstrated how several patterns in the archaeological record of southern Scandinavia are related and can be understood only in terms of each other. The variability in large ungulate frequencies within and between assemblages, the occurrence of socially complex societies, the rapid changes in technology and the late adoption of farming were all shown to rely on each other once the decision-making process of the individual, particularly goal choice, had been identified and placed at the centre of cultural change. And in a wider field the contrasts between southern Scandinavia and south-west Germany made sense once variability in decision goals was recognised. Looking at Upper Palaeolithic art and economy I again tried to show how several features of the archaeological record make sense once we have identified the characteristics of the decision-making process. In this case the important elements were the failure of risk-reducing goals in the Later Upper Palaeolithic and a reliance on information to allow a rapid switch between patch types and from group to individual hunting. By this I could relate the catastrophic mortality profiles of red deer and reindeer, the phenomena of intensification and diversification, the temporal distribution of the art, the disparity in faunal frequencies between the art and the assemblages and a range of stylistic features found in the art.

Now I must stress here that I am not for a moment suggesting that this is all that needs to be said about any of the archaeological problems I have tackled. I have only been pinpointing particular features of the archaeological record, not reaching for global explanations. For instance an understanding of social dynamics in Mesolithic society must require far more than a focus on the competition for prestige by those hunting large terrestrial game. I have tried simply to make some connections between patterns in the faunal and burial records, which help explain such patterns but which can only be a small part of a much larger picture. Similarly, Upper Palaeolithic art is an extremely complex and diverse artistic tradition. I have not been trying to provide *the* explanation but to address particular features of it. As I made clear in my introduction, these global explanations can be arrived at only when we have considered decision making by many different types of individuals in the society, the many different types of decisions that each individual must take, and how all of these interact with each other.

I have addressed only a small number of questions that, say, Mesolithic faunal assemblages or Upper Palaeolithic art present, and I have had to neglect whole areas of problems posed by the archaeological record. So in this respect, too, I am only aspiring to make a small contribution to an understanding of Mesolithic and Upper Palaeolithic society. For instance, in relation to the Mesolithic, no reference has been made to storage, territoriality, population growth and environmental change. Similarly the Upper Palaeolithic study glossed over or ignored issues concerning technology and social interaction as well as the multitude of further questions posed by the art and fauna. As with the problem areas I did tackle, all of these are artificially separated from each other and our aim must be to integrate them by a focus on the individual decision maker, or rather multiple individual decision makers.

In both of my archaeological studies my first move was away from faunal assemblages to the decision-making processes, and in both cases I used mathematical modelling and computer simulation as methodological tools. I must make it clear that I have not been advocating this as the only available type of methodology, or any one particular way in which it can be employed. In fact in my case studies I have used simulation in rather different ways. In the Upper Palaeolithic study I used models for red deer and reindeer hunting to examine the implications for the problems that the hunters faced partly arising from their own past decisions. That is, I worked from patterns in the archaeological record (the catastrophic mortality profiles and intensification through time) to create patterns in a field that is relevant to decision making – yields and the fluctuations in those yields. Inferences about hunting patterns were developed by using a knowledge of processes that can be assumed to have remained constant, i.e. large-ungulate population dynamics. This contrasts with my use of modelling in the Mesolithic study. In that case I had made some initial inferences about the decision-making process from the archaeological record and asked what archaeological patterns (in a different data set, i.e. species composition of faunal assemblages) would result under different foraging goals – an aspect of decision making that could not be directly inferred. Simulated faunal patterns were then created to compare with those in the archaeological record.

In both of these studies I have referred to the use of mathematical modelling and simulation as methodological tools. An alternative view is to see the running of simulation models simply as experiments. We might make a comparison with an ecologist studying predator-prey interactions by building a model pond in an aquarium and introducing or removing different species, or manipulating different variables such as temperature and light. In both cases we are working with simple models of the real world and in both cases there is no easy translation of results to the real world. We are simply working at difficult problems, whether in the archaeological record or in ecological communities, by a process of modelling, application, reflection, modelling, application, reflection . . . and so on.

I was careful when making comparisons between simulated and real archaeological records not to lay too much weight on any similarity found. Similar patterns were seen as insufficient in themselves. I had to show that this similarity, and hence the inference drawn about decision goals, was meaningful by allowing those disparate elements of the archaeological record to be drawn together – to be connected. In this respect two birds are being killed with one stone. For as we find support for the inference about decision making we are also integrating the previously isolated patterns in the archaeological record. In doing this I was emphasising how mathematical models and simulation are just tools, to be used certainly with caution but also with confidence, as an experienced excavator may wield a trowel. Neither excavations or simulation models provide any magic answers and the value, as well as the constraints, of both must be recognised.

When two very different mathematical models allow the same inference to be drawn then we might have some confidence in their value. This has happened here. The Mesolithic study, using a model for human decision making, concluded that the hunters of southern Scandinavia ignored risk reduction by looking at the frequencies of different species in the assemblages. The same conclusion is derived from the simulation of red deer exploitation used in the Upper Palaeolithic study when selective killing patterns, of the type found in southern Scandinavia (Bay-Peterson 1978: Fig. 3), are employed. Hence these two very different models, using different aspects of the Mesolithic assemblages, converge in their results – a pincer movement on prehistoric society.

While I have clearly set out one form in which explanation in archaeology may take (though not necessarily the only or the best form), I have not prescribed any set rules for reaching this, nor followed any myself. I have not built theories, derived hypotheses and then attempted to test them. Nor have I relied on ethnographic analogy. Nor have I simply tried to read off the past from the archaeological data. I have not set up a model for the world, or decision making, and then tried to accommodate the data into that, but neither have I let the archaeological data play the dominant role. All of these have played some part when they seemed appropriate. I tested the hypothesis that some lithic assemblages in Scania would be more diverse than others. My interpretation of Upper Palaeolithic art has some elements of analogy with that of scapulimancy among the Cree, but does not rely on this. In general, I let my theory and my model building weave in and out of the archaeological data.

This is perhaps clearest in the Mesolithic study. I began with ideas about the way decisions are made from the eco-psychological model, looked at the archaeological data to infer the foraging problem and important information sources, returned to model building, then back again to further archaeological data concerning settlement size, returned again to the model to run the simulation and then back once again to further data concerning cemeteries and tools. The approach was similar in the Upper Palaeolithic study. Theoretical issues, such as those concerning the importance of creativity, only became important after discussion of the data, although that discussion had been prompted by model building which in turn was a response to problems posed by the archaeological record. In these regards I am recognising that archaeology is difficult. We do injustice to the subject, and to ourselves, when any one method is totally rejected or embraced. Am I advocating an extreme wishy-washy eclecticism? Perhaps. Or perhaps I am simply putting weight on the final product – the connections that are made between an otherwise disparate set of data by reference to the individual – and recognising the diversity and creativity in archaeologists to find their own way there (or wherever else they wish to go).

Now in working in this framework of dialogue between the data, models and ideas, I hope that the models I have built and the explanations I have forwarded can be seen as signposts for further work rather than as blind alleys. Certainly the simulation models I have constructed demand further development for a better understanding of the issues I tackled. There are two essential ways in which the Mesolithic simulation must be expanded. First an element of meta-decision making must be introduced. An immense problem with the model as it stands is that each individual within the group is attributed with the same decision goal. They are all UIS, UISR or NULL foragers. A far more realistic model would allow variability within the group as to which goal is adopted. A hunter's age, sex, health, knowledge will affect which goal he/she adopts when seeking to adapt to his/her unique environment. What must be done, therefore, is to develop the model so that a hunter can choose which goal to adopt on any one day. Such (meta-) choices would in turn be based on knowledge as to the likely merits of different goals and according to some meta-decision goal. Other meta-decisions also need to be modelled. For instance the degree to which past experience is used (the A parameter) was kept as a constant, its value based on an *a priori* basis. But this should be modelled as a variable so that an individual can meta-choose the amount of experience he/she wishes to use (again on the basis of knowledge about the likely returns to be gained from that) on any one hunting trip. The resulting model will have, therefore, a group of individuals who vary in their goals, in their use of past experience and in other parameters of the decision process. Perhaps we will find that in particular historical and ecological contexts all individuals, when given the capacity to meta-choose, will converge on the same types of goals and parameter values (a society of conformists), while in others diversity will reign supreme.

To build this model it will also be necessary to expand the hunting-process part of the simulation so that the encounter foraging of large terrestrial game is modelled as one element of the foraging strategies used. The simulation will need to model choices higher in the decision hierarchy, for example a patch-choice decision to engage in encounter foraging, prior to the prey-choice decisions that have been modelled.

It is also easy to speculate how the models used in the Upper Palaeolithic study should be developed. In these we had sophisticated models for the population dynamics of large ungulates, but no explicit modelling of human decision making. This needs to be included so that the actual decisions to exploit reindeer or red deer, arrived at through group decision-making processes as described in Chapter 2, are modelled. As with the developed Mesolithic study, we would need to broaden the model so that the alternative individual stalk strategy would be an option for hunters in choosing whether to participate in some communal game drive or in coping with their failure. In this respect we would need to monitor the knowledge that individuals possess about game and the value of different hunting strategies, as we did in the Mesolithic simulation model. Again, we will be modelling unique historical, ecological and social contexts for each individual.

In fact the developed Mesolithic model and the developed Palaeolithic model will gradually begin to converge. Meta-decision making, hierarchical decision problems, decision making, global and local environments all need to be incorporated into the same model. Clearly developing either one, or both, of the simulations in these manners is a substantial enterprise. However, I would suggest that this investment would be worthwhile since we have already made some contact with hard archaeological data, have shown these models to be useful for *doing* archaeology, and consequently can justify some more sophisticated and complex modelling.

Just as the studies I have presented appear to be a launching pad for a more developed study of Mesolithic and Upper Palaeolithic society, so equally do they provide a platform for striking into other periods and areas. Most notably, the study of pre-*Homo sapiens sapiens* could benefit. One of the great problems with such work is the biological difference that would have existed in cognitive capacities. Hence any use of modern ethnographic material is very questionable. However, if the model for encounter-foraging decision making that I have developed is indeed recognised as useful for modern man then we can use this to make some progress with early man. For we can impose constraints upon the decision-making process and conduct experiments to examine the relationship between hypothetical hominid behaviour and the character of the archaeological record. For instance the attention parameter models the amount of past experience used when making decisions. I have modelled this as a constant with high value but suggested that a better model will treat this as a variable – a biologically modern hunter can choose whether to use much or just a little of his/her past experience. But we could explore the idea that early man was inherently limited in the amount of past experience that could be used, because of constrained memory capacities, and treat the A parameter as a constant but with a low value. What type of foraging patterns would then have existed? How do these compare with those inferred from the Lower or Middle Palaeolithic? Alternatively, we might suggest that the exchange of information between individuals was limited or absent, perhaps in combination with limited memory, and remove these elements from the decision model. How would this change foraging behaviour?

Two suitable contexts spring to mind for the application of such an approach. The first is hunting and/or carcass scavenging during the Early Pleistocene of East Africa. Studies of scavenging opportunities are sufficiently developed (e.g. Blumenschine 1986) as to make such modelling feasible and interesting. Could a hominid with limited memory and communication skills have been a successful forager in those environments? What sort of decisions about carcass utilisation would have been made under different decision goals?

A second alternative context in which to apply such models would be the Middle Palaeolithic in western Europe. Again we could run experiments which explore different types of mental/communicative capacities for Neanderthal man and the types of archaeological records that are created. What sort of constraints need to be imposed onto the model (or rather a more developed form of it with meta-decision-making elements) to create the apparently inflexible behaviour that we infer from the Middle Palaeolithic record (Dennell 1983: 199–200; Bahn 1984: 73–4; Chase

1986: 147; Foley 1987b: 391)? Once these constraints are present, is it possible to distinguish between different foraging goals? Or, indeed, is it a case of the inflexible restriction to a single goal, perhaps of a NULL or UISR type, that creates the static character of the archaeological record and the apparent inflexibility to adapt to minor environmental fluctuations. In addition, we might ask if some minor change can be made to such a model, perhaps in allowing greater meta-decision-making activity, that leads to dramatic behavioural change as we see in the archaeological record at the start of the Upper Palaeolithic.

While progress may be made by developing the types of quantitative models I am proposing, I hope that this work has also introduced some concepts useful outside of a mathematical/simulation framework. The distinctions I have made between stored and acquired information as the two poles of a continuum and between direct and indirect information gathering may be of general utility when studying information flows in hunter-gatherer society. Similarly the characterisation of environments, and particular resources, as having 'information potentials' may help provide a more comprehensive understanding of forager–environment interactions than that from a concentration on energy alone. Cue use by hunter-gatherers has been neglected previously, and the emphasis placed upon it in this work, with the concepts of cue viability and utilisation, may help to fill the gap. More generally, the importance attached to creativity and error making when adopting an evolutionary perspective may help to guard against slipping into 'economic man' type arguments. As with the quantitative models, the framework provided by these concepts may be useful when tackling issues concerning pre-*Homo sapiens sapiens*. Again we might contrast the flexibility and detailed environmental tracking by modern man with the apparently stable and repetitive behaviour of early man. Is this contrast due to a change in emphasis between stored and acquired information, between direct and indirect information gathering and/or the degree to which information potentials of environments are exploited by the use of cues?

Let me return again to modern man. What sort of prehistoric world have I tried to discover in this work? It is one in which people are very thoroughly part of the natural world. This is inevitable, of course, since I deal with hunter-gatherers. I hope to have argued, however, that this derives not from the nature of their way of life, but from human nature itself – we are products of biological evolution and this has consequences for our behaviour. We today are just as much part of nature as Palaeolithic or Mesolithic man. The prehistoric world in these pages has been first and foremost one inhabited by individuals unconstrained by social convention and ideology. These individuals interact, and compose a society which is not just the sum of these individuals, though what it is remains unclear in this work. But my conception of the individual is rather clearer. He (she) is not just the 'economic man' of optimal foraging studies. He has imperfect knowledge and often makes erroneous choices (in terms of adaptation). But what knowledge he possesses is used creatively and he engages in co-operation as well as competition with other individuals. Emotions, characterised in an evolutionary framework as decision criteria, are at the centre of his/her existence. The behaviour of these prehistoric foragers results from a complex mix of conscious and unconscious choices, with intended and unintended, recognised and unrecognised consequences. They live in an uncertain world in which neither the physical nor the social environment is constant. And most of all, they themselves are not constant but ever changing. The very essence of their behaviour is that it is in a constant state of change, always in the process of adapting to changing circumstances. From this milieu of individuals arise the long-term cultural patterns that we recognise in the archaeological record and wish to explain. As I remarked in my introduction, more than anything these result from people going about their daily business.

What is the overriding feature of this prehistoric world? It is individuals exercising universally held psychological propensities to think and behave in one way rather than another in contexts which are historically, ecologically and socially unique. On the one hand it is the universality that must be stressed. It is because there is a common biological endowment that individuals who developed in markedly different environments can interact and create a rich cultural life. Without this, people would be swamped by limited experience and lack entirely the behavioural flexibility that is so characteristically human. The universality has another role. It gives us an anchor in the past. Not an anchor that has trapped our ship in the middle of an ocean so that all we see around is a blank and uninteresting sameness. Empty horizons tend to be seen by archaeologists bobbing about on shaky theoretical rafts which cannot be secured to any archaeological data. The anchor here might be compared to that which moored the Beagle in the Galapagos so that Darwin could study the diversity, not uniformity, he found there. Our diversity is provided by human cultures, not finches, and we must put down some anchors before we can get to work. Then, once we feel secure, we might navigate carefully rather than drift randomly into the uncharted waters of early man. But this anchor, the universality, is insufficient in itself. We must recognise the second of the pervading features of this prehistoric world – the unique and ever-changing contexts in which these universal psychological propensities are employed. We can have no understanding or explanations until we start to elucidate the historical, ecological and social contexts in which the individual is operating. It is from the interplay between the universal and the unique that cultural life develops. Neither is sufficient in itself.

Some may wish to see my reliance on universal properties of the human mind as a reliance on 'laws' of cultural behaviour. To this I have three replies. First, I probably agree with them. Second, if this is the case then I must emphasise a fundamental error made by Hodder with respect to such laws. He states that: 'To discuss humanity in terms of general laws, is ultimately to deny people their freedom' (1986: 102). It should be apparent from this work that the reverse holds when these laws refer to a biological endowment. To recognise that there is a biological foundation to human thought is to assert people's inherent freedom from any social ideology and their own limited experience. It demands that creativity is seen at the core of the human condition. Third, as Binford (1988) has pointed out in relation to Hodder's writing, those who have been most damning of the idea of law-like generalisation and evolutionary approaches, may employ precisely the same ideas within their own work. Hence Hodder wishes 'to argue that there are some very simple rules underlying all languages – or at least underlying the ways in which *Homo sapiens sapiens* at all times and in all places gives meaning to things' (1986: 123). Similarly Miller and Tilley, in a passage that otherwise criticises law-like approaches, find they need to 'grant to all *Homo sapiens sapiens*, those abilities and characteristics we would wish granted to ourselves' (1984: 2). My reliance on universals and law-like generalisations is no greater and no less than that of Hodder, Miller and Tilley.

It is inevitable, and proper, that we see our present world and possible futures through the knowledge of our past. After all, I have stressed throughout this work that this applies to prehistoric foragers who use their own and others' past experience as information sources when making decisions. And so too must this apply to us today. The prehistoric worlds that archaeologists create have a significance beyond academic study. These are used in the present either by seeping into and moulding our understanding of society or for overt political ends. Shanks and Tilley (1987a, 1987b) have been most forthright about the implications of this. They want to place it at the centre of archaeological practice: 'The point of archaeology is not merely to interpret the past but to change the manner in which the past is interpreted in the service of social reconstruction in the present' (1987b: 195).

From this basis they reject any value in evolutionary approaches, claiming that these simply naturalise and legitimise concepts such as optimisation and efficiency as universal features of humankind, while in their view these are simply features of capitalist thought. That is, archaeologists who adopt evolutionary approaches are simply re-writing the past as the present and denying the possibility of change. I hope that this work has shown the error in their argument. As I explained in my introductory chapter their characterisation of evolutionary approaches is mistaken. I have argued that, from an evolutionary perspective, optimality modelling and cultural ecology are inappropriate for archaeology. Efficiency is indeed a central concept, as is the focus on the individual. But complementing these are concepts such as creative thought, freedom from the constraints that society may impose, and the pervasive recognition of the value of co-operative behaviour. These provide another side of the evolutionary coin. If, as Shanks and Tilley argue, efficient behaviour is naturalised by the adoption of an evolutionary approach, then these complementary concepts must be viewed in the same light. And it is these very features of human thought and behaviour that are central to challenging the present.

Evolutionary approaches stress that humankind is part of the natural world and on a continuum with other species. Consequently they emphasise that we have a responsibility towards caring for the environment and reducing unnecessary suffering in other species. Similarly a naturalisation of the goals of energy efficiency and risk reduction can appear appropriate today. For instance, the expansion of electricity generation, whether in terms of burning fossil fuels or nuclear power, is threatening to the environment. Better to reduce risk and use what we currently produce more efficiently. If archaeology does have an overt political role, as Shanks and Tilley claim, and this provides a criterion for choosing which type of prehistoric world to envisage, then evolutionary approaches appear very germane to our present context. They emphasise responsibilities that we face and our ability through creative thought and co-operative behaviour to face them and change our world for the better.

Finally I might ask what sort of archaeology this book has been. Is it processual? It certainly shares some elements with the processual archaeology of the 1970s: the preference for an ecological rather than a symbolic framework; the use of mathematical modelling; the belief that there is a past to explain, and in a pragmatic objectivity. But equally it shares some features of a post-processual idiom: the concentration on the individual; the emphasis on historical contexts; a rather anarchical approach to seeking explanation; a political awareness of the archaeologist's role. It is none of these. Indeed it refuses to recognise any significant value in the division, let alone be pigeon-holed into one or other camp. The work has been as critical of the processual cultural ecology of current Mesolithic studies as of the post-processual representation of evolutionary/ecological approaches. It has found inspiration from both Binford's call for methodology to translate 'statics into dynamics' and Hodder's call for a greater concern with 'active individuals', though both of these are eclipsed by Renfrew's (1981) essay, 'The Simulator as Demiurge'. But if this work is neither processual nor post-processual, then nor is it a compromise. This book has been an attempt to develop a robust theoretical framework and methodology. I have tried to use these to explain patterning and variation in the archaeological record. In the course of this I hope to have gained some insights into the nature of prehistoric society, culture change and the human condition. In short, this book has simply been my attempt at doing archaeology.

Aaris-Sørensen, K. 1980. Depauperation of the Mammalian Fauna of the Island of Zealand during the Atlantic Period. *Videnskabelige Meddelser fra Dansk naturhistorik Forening* 142: 131–8.

Abrahams, M. 1986. Patch Choice under Perceptual Constraints: A Cause for Departures from an Ideal Free Distribution. *Behavioural Ecology and Sociobiology* 19: 409–15.

Albon, S.D., T.H. Clutton-Brock and F.E. Guinness. 1987. Early Development and Population Dynamics in Red Deer II. Density Independent Effects and Cohort Variation. *Journal of Animal Ecology* 56: 69–81.

Albrethsen, S.E. and E.B. Petersen. 1976. Excavation of a Mesolithic Cemetery at Vedbaek, Denmark. *Acta Archaeologica* 47: 1–28.

Alexander, R.McN., V. Longman and A. Jayes. 1977. Fast Locomotion of some African Ungulates. *J. Zoology (London)* 183: 291–300.

Allen, P.M. and J.M. McGlade. 1987. Evolutionary Drive: The Effect of Microscopic Diversity, Error Making and Noise. *Foundations of Physics* 17(7): 723–38.

Alloy, L. and N. Tabachnik. 1984. Assessment of Covariation by Humans and Animals: The Joint Influence of Prior Expectations and Current Situational Information. *Psychological Review* 9(1): 112–49.

Altman, J.C. 1984. Hunter-Gatherer Subsistence Production in Arnhem Land: The Original Affluence Hypothesis Re-examined. *Mankind* 14(39): 179–90.

Altuna, J. 1983. On the Relationship between Archaeo-Faunas and Parietal Art in the Caves of the Cantabrian Region. In *Animals and Archaeology, 1: Hunters and their Prey*, J. Clutton-Brock and C. Grigson (eds.), pp. 227–38. Oxford: British Archaeological Reports Int. Series 163.

    1986. The Mammalian Faunas from the Prehistoric Site of La Riera. In *La Riera Cave: Stone Age Hunter-Gatherer Adaptations in Northern Spain*, L. Straus and G. Clark (eds.), pp. 737–74. Arizona State University, Anthropological Research Papers, No. 36.

Andersen, S.H. 1973. Ringkloster, en jysk indlandsboplads med Ertebøllekultur (with English summary). *KUML* 1973–4: 11–108.

    1985. Tybrind Vig: A Preliminary Report on a Submerged Ertebølle Settlement on the West Coast of Fyn. *Journal of Danish Archaeology* 4: 52–69.

Andersen, S.T. 1984. Forest at Løvenholm, Djursland, Denmark, at Present and in the Past. *Det Kongelige Danske Videnskabenes Selskab Biologiske Skrifter* 24:1.

Anderson, R. 1972. Hunt and Deceive: Information Management in Newfoundland Deep–Sea Trawler Fishing. In *North Atlantic Fishermen: Anthropological Essays on Modern Fishing*, R. Anderson and C. Wadel (eds.), pp. 120–41. *Newfoundland Social and Economic Papers No. 5*. Toronto: University of Toronto Press.

Baffier, D. 1984. Les caractères sexuels secondaires des mammifères dans l'art pariétal paléolithique franco-cantabrique. In *La contribution de la zoologie et de l'éthologie à l'interprétation de l'art de peuples chasseurs préhistoriques*, H. Bandi *et al.* (eds.), pp. 143–54. Editions Universitaires Fribourg, Suisse.

Bahn, P.G. 1977. Seasonal Migration in South West France during the Late Glacial Period. *Journal of Archaeological Science* 4: 245–57.

1979. La paléoéconomie magdalénienne du Bassin de Tarascon (Ariège). *Bulletin de la Société Préhistorique de l'Ariège* 34:37–46.

1982. Inter-site and Inter-regional Links During the Upper Palaeolithic: the Pyrenean Evidence. *Oxford Journal of Archaeology* 1: 247–68.

1983. Late Pleistocene Economies of the French Pyrenees. In *Hunter-Gatherer Economy in Prehistory*, G. Bailey (ed.), pp. 168–87. Cambridge: Cambridge University Press.

1984. *Pyrenean Prehistory*. Warminster: Aris and Phillips.

1986. No Sex, Please, We're Aurignacians. *Rock Art Research* 3: 99–120.

Bahn. P.G. and J. Vertut. 1988. *Images of the Ice Age*. London: Windward.

Bailey, G. 1978. Shell Middens as Indicators of Post-Glacial Economies: A Territorial Perspective. In *The Early Post-Glacial Settlement of Northern Europe*, P. Mellars (ed.), pp. 37–64. London: Duckworth.

1981a. Concepts of Resource Exploitation: Continuity and Discontinuity in Palaeoeconomy. *World Archaeology* 13: 1–15.

1981b. Concepts, Time Scales and Explanations in Economic Prehistory. In *Economic Archaeology*. G. Bailey and A. Sheridan (eds.), pp. 97–117. Oxford: British Archaeology Reports Int. Series 96.

1983. Economic Change in Late Pleistocene Cantabria. In *Hunter-Gatherer Economy in Prehistory*, G. Bailey (ed.), pp. 149–65. Cambridge: Cambridge University Press.

Bang, P. and P. Dahlstrom. 1974. *Animal Tracks and Signs*. London: Collins.

Barker, G. 1985. *Prehistoric Farming in Europe*. Cambridge: Cambridge University Press.

Barnard, C.J. and C.A.J. Brown. 1981. Prey Size Selection and Competition in the Common Shrew. *Behavioural Ecology and Sociobiology* 16: 161–4.

Barry, H., I. Child and M. Bacon. 1959. Relation of Child Training to Subsistence Economy. *American Anthropologist* 61: 51–63.

Bateson, P.P.G. 1983. Genes, Environment and the Development of Behaviour. In *Genes, Development and Learning*, T.R. Halliday and P.J.B. Slater (eds.), pp. 52–81. Oxford: Blackwell Scientific Publications.

Bay-Peterson, J.L. 1978. Animal Exploitation in Mesolithic Denmark. In *The Early Post Glacial Settlement of Northern Europe*, P. Mellars (ed.), pp. 115–46. London: Duckworth.

Beckerman, S. 1983. Carpe Diem: An Optimal Foraging Approach to Bari Fishing and Hunting. In *Adaptive Responses of Native Amazonians*, R. Hames and W. Vickers (eds.), pp. 269–99. New York: Academic Press.

Beddington, J. and R. May. 1977. Harvesting Natural Populations in a Randomly Fluctuating Environment. *Science* 197: 463–5.

Belovsky, G. 1987. Hunter-Gatherer Foraging: A Linear Programming Approach. *Journal of Anthropological Archaeology* 6: 29–76.

Bennet, L., D. English and R. McCain. 1940. A Study of Deer Populations by Use of Pellet Group Counts. *Journal of Wildlife Management* 4: 398–403.

Berger, J. 1960. *Permanent Red*. London: Methuen.

Bergerud, A.T. 1980. A Review of the Population Dynamics of Caribou and Wild Reindeer. In *Proceedings of the Second International Reindeer/Caribou Symposium, Roris, Norway*, E. Reimers (ed.), pp. 556–81. Direktorate fir Vilt og Ferkvannisfirsk.

Biesele, M. 1976. Aspects of !Kung Folklore. In *Kalahari Hunter-gatherers*, R. Lee and I. DeVore (ed.), pp. 302–25 Cambridge, Mass.: Harvard University Press.

Binford, L. 1968. Post-Pleistocene Adaptations. In *New Perspectives in Archaeology*,

S.R. Binford and L.R. Binford (eds.), pp. 313–41. Chicago: Aldine Publishing Company.

1978. *Nunamiut Ethnoarchaeology*. New York: Academic Press.

1980. Willow Smoke and Dogs' Tails: Hunter-Gatherer Settlement Systems and Archaeological Site Formation. *American Antiquity* 43: 330–61.

1983. *In Pursuit of the Past*. London: Thames and Hudson.

1984. *Faunal Remains from Klasies River Mouth*. New York: Academic Press.

1985a. Paper Presented at Prehistoric Society Conference, Norwich.

1985b. Human Ancestors: Changing Views of their Behaviour. *Journal of Anthropological Archaeology* 4: 292–327.

1988. Review of *Reading the Past* by I. Hodder, *American Antiquity* 53(4): 875–6.

Bion-Griffen, P. 1984. Forager Resource and Land Use in the Humid Tropics: The Agta of Northeastern Luzon, the Philippines. In *Past and Present in Hunter Gatherer Studies*, C. Schrire (ed.), pp. 95–118. London: Academic Press.

Birket-Smith, K. and F. De Laguna. 1938. *The Eyak Indians of the Copper River Delta, Alaska*. Copenhagen: Levin and Munksgaard.

Blankholm, H.P. 1987a. Late Mesolithic Hunter-gatherers and the Transition to Farming in South Scandinavia. In *Mesolithic Northwest Europe: Recent Trends*, P.A. Rowley-Conwy, M. Zvelebil and H.P. Blankholm (eds.), pp. 155–62. Sheffield Dept of Archaeology and Prehistory.

1987b. Maglemosian Hut Floors: An Analysis of the Dwelling Unit, Social Unit and Intra-Site Behaviour Patterns in Early Mesolithic South Scandinavia. In *Mesolithic Northwest Europe: Recent Trends*, P.A. Rowley-Conwy, M. Zvelebil and H.P. Blankholm (eds.), pp. 109–20, Sheffield: Dept of Archaeology and Prehistory.

Bleed, P. 1986. The Optimal Design of Hunting Weapons: Maintainability or Reliability. *American Antiquity* 51: 737–47.

Blumenschine, R. 1986. *Early Hominid Scavenging Opportunities*. Oxford: British Archaeological Reports Int. Series 283.

Blurton-Jones, N. and M.J. Konner. 1976. !Kung Knowlege of Animal Behaviour. In *Kalahari Hunter-Gatherers*, R. Lee and I. DeVore (eds.), pp. 326–48 Cambridge, Mass.: Harvard University Press.

Bonner, J.T. 1980. *The Evolution of Culture in Animals*. Princeton: Princeton University Press.

Bonsall, C. (ed.). 1989. *The Mesolithic in Europe:* Papers presented at the Third International Symposium. Edinburgh: John Donald.

Borgerhoff Mulder, M. 1987. Adaptation and Evolutionary Approaches to Anthropology. *Man (N.S.)* 22: 25–41.

Bouchner, M. 1982. *Animal Tracks and Traces*. London: Octopus Books.

Bourguignon, E. 1979. *Psychological Anthropology*. New York: Holt, Rinehart and Winston.

Boyd, R. and P.J. Richerson. 1985. *Culture and the Evolutionary Process*. Chicago: University of Chicago Press.

Brandstatter, H., J. Davis and H. Schuler (eds.). 1978. *Dynamics of Group Decisions*. Beverley Hills: Sage Publications.

Brandstatter, H., J. Davies and G. Stocker-Kreichgauer (eds.). 1982. *Group Decision Making*. London: Academic Press.

Breuil, H. 1952. *Quatre cents siècles d'art pariétal*. Montignac: Centre d'Etudes et de Documentation Préhistorique.

Breuil, H. and H. Obermaier. 1935. *The Cave of Altamira at Santillana del Mar, Spain*. Madrid: Tipografia de Archivos.

Brown, A. 1978. Knowing When, Where and How to Remember: A Problem of Meta-cognition. In *Advances in Instructional Psychology*, vol. 1. R. Glaser (ed.), pp. 77–165. New Jersey: Lawrence Erlbaum Associates.

Burch, E. 1972. The Caribou/Wild Reindeer as a Human Resource. *American Antiquity* 37: 339–68.

Campbell, V. 1978. Ethnohistorical Evidence on the Diet and Economy of the Aborigines of the Macleay River Valley. In *Records of Time Past: Ethnohistorical Essays on the Culture and Ecology of the New England Tribes*. I. McBryde (ed.), pp. 82–100. Canberra: Institute of Aboriginal Studies.

Camps, G. 1984. La Défécation dans l'art paléolithique. In *La Contribution de la zoologie et de l'éthologie à l'interprétation de l'art des peuples chasseurs préhistoriques*, H. Bandi *et al.* (eds.), pp. 251–62. Fribourg: Editions Universitaires.

Cancian, F. 1984. Risk and Uncertainty in Agricultural Decision Making. In *Agricultural Decision Making*, P. Barlett (ed.), pp. 161–75. London: Academic Press.

Cant, J.G.H. and L.A. Temerin. 1984. A Conceptual Approach to Foraging Adaptations in Primates. In *Adaptations for Foraging in Nonhuman Primates*, P. Rodman and J. Cant (eds.), pp. 304–42. New York: Columbia University Press.

Capitan, L., H. Breuil and D. Peyrony. 1910. *La Caverne de Font de Gaume*. Monaco: Imprimerie Vue A. Chene.

Carston, R. 1988. Language and Cognition. In *Linguistics: The Cambridge Survey*, Vol. III, *Language: Psychological and Biological Aspects*, F.J. Newmeyer (ed.), pp. 38–68. Cambridge: Cambridge University Press.

Chapman, A. 1982. *Drama and Power in a Hunting Society: The Selkn'am of Tierra del Fuego*. Cambridge: Cambridge University Press.

Charnov, E.L. 1976. Optimal Foraging: The Marginal Value Theorem. *Theoretical Population Biology* 9: 129–36.

Chase, P. 1986. *The Hunters of Combe Grenal*. Oxford: British Archaeological Reports, Int. Series 286.

Chibnik, M. 1981. The Evolution of Cultural Rules. *Journal of Anthropological Research* 37: 256–68

Chomsky, N. 1980. *Rules and Representations*. Oxford: Basil Blackwell.

Clark, C.W. and M. Mangel. 1984. Foraging and Flocking Strategies: Information in an Uncertain Environment. *American Naturalist* 123(5): 626–41.

Clark, G.A. 1983a. The Asturian of Cantabria: Early Holocene Hunter-Gatherers in Northern Spain. *Anthropological Papers of the University of Arizona 41*. Tucson: University of Arizona Press.

1983b. Boreal Phase Settlement-Subsistence Models for Cantabrian Spain. In *Hunter-Gatherer Economy in Prehistory*, G. Bailey (ed.), pp. 96–110. Cambridge: Cambridge University Press.

Clark, G.A. and M. Neeley. 1987. Social Differentiation in European Mesolithic Burial Data. In *Mesolithic Northwest Europe: Recent Trends*, P.A. Rowley-Conwy M. Zvelebil and H.P. Blankholm (eds.), pp. 121–7. Sheffield: Dept of Archaeology and Prehistory.

Clark, G.A. and L. Straus. 1983. Late Pleistocene Hunter-Gatherer Adaptations in Cantabrian Spain. In *Hunter-Gatherer Economy in Prehistory*, G. Bailey (ed.), pp. 131–49. Cambridge: Cambridge University Press.

Clark, J.G.D. 1954. *Excavations at Star Carr*. Cambridge: Cambridge University Press.

Clarke, D. 1976. Mesolithic Europe: The Economic Basis. In *Problems in Social and Economic Archaeology*, G. de G. Sieveking *et al.* (eds.), pp. 449–81. London: Duckworth.

Classon, A.T. 1977. Die Tierknochen. In Modderman 1977. pp. 101–20. *Analecta Praehistorica Leidensia* 10.

Clot, A. 1973. *L'Art graphique préhistorique des hautes Pyrénées*. Saragossa: Octavio Y Félez.

Clottes, J. 1984. Grotte de Niaux. In *L'Art des cavernes: atlas des grottes ornées paléolithiques françaises*, pp. 417–23. Paris: Imprimeries Nationale.

 1986. Comments on P.G. Bahn 'No Sex, Please, We're Aurignacians'. *Rock Art Research* 3: 99–120.

Clottes, J. and F. Rouzard. 1984. Grotte des Églises. In *L'Art des cavernes: atlas des grottes ornées paléolithiques françaises*, pp. 428–32. Paris: Imprimeries Nationale.

Clottes, J., F. Rouzard and L. Wahl. 1984. Grotte de Fontanet. In *L'Art des cavernes: atlas des grottes ornées paléolithiques françaises*, pp. 433–7. Paris: Imprimeries Nationale.

Clottes, J. and R. Simonnet, 1979. Le paléolithique final dans le bassin de Tarascon-sur-Ariège, d'après les gisements des Églises (Ussat) et de Rhodes II (Arignac). In *La Fin des temps glaciaires en Europe*. D. de Sonneville-Bordes (ed.), vol. 2: 647–59. Parsis: Centre Nationale de la Recherche Scientifique.

 1984. Le Réseau René Clastres. In *L'Art des cavernes: atlas des grottes ornées paléolithiques française*, pp. 424–7. Paris: Imprimeries Nationale.

Clutton-Brock, T.H., S.D. Albon and F. Guinness. 1983. *Red Deer: Behaviour and Ecology of Two Species*. Chicago: Chicago University Press.

Clutton-Brock, T.H. and P. Harvey. 1980. Primates, Brains and Ecology. *Journal of Zoology, London* 190: 309–23.

Clutton-Brock, T.H., M. Major, S.D. Albon and F.E. Guinness. 1986. Early Development and Population Dynamics in Red Deer I. Density Dependent Effects on Juvenile Survival. *Journal of Animal Ecology* 56: 53–67.

Coe, M.J. and R.D. Carr. 1983. The Relationship between Large Ungulate Body Size and Faecal Pellet Weight. *African Journal of Ecology* 21(3): 165–74.

Cohen, M. 1977. *The Food Crisis in Prehistory*. New Haven: Yale University Press.

Cole, M. and S. Scribner. 1974. *Culture and Thought: A Psychological Introduction*. New York: John Wiley and Sons.

Conkey, M. 1978. Style and Information in Cultural Evolution: Toward a Predictive Model for the Palaeolithic. In *Social Archaeology: Beyond Subsistence and Dating*, C. Redman *et al* (eds.), pp. 61–85. New York: Academic Press.

 1985. Ritual Communication, Social Elaboration and the Variable Trajectories of Paleolithic Material Culture. In *Prehistoric Hunter-Gatherers: The Emergence of Cultural Complexity*, T.D. Price and J.A. Brown (eds.), pp. 299–320. New York: Academic Press.

Damas, D. 1984. *Handbook of North American Indians, Vol. 5: Arctic*. Washington: Smithsonian Institution.

Dams, L. 1978. *L'Art paléolithique de la caverne de la Pileta*. Graz: Akademische Druck-U-Verlagsantalt.

 1980. *L'Art pariétal de la Grotte du Roc Saint-Cirq*. British Archaeological Reports, Int. Series 79, Oxford.

Damuth, J. 1981. Population Density and Body Size in Mammals. *Nature* 290: 699–700.

David, N.C. 1973. On Upper Palaeolithic Society, Ecology and Technological Change: The Noallian Case. In *The Explanation of Culture Change: Models in Prehistory*, C. Renfrew (ed.), pp. 277–303. London: Duckworth.

Davis, J.H. 1973. Group Decision and Social Interaction: A Theory of Social Decision Schemes. *Psychological Review* 80: 97–125.

 1982. Social Interaction as a Combinatorial Process in Group Decisions. In *Group Decision Making*, H. Brandstatter *et al.* (eds.), pp. 211–58. London: Academic Press.

Davis, J.H. and V.B. Hinsz. 1982. Current Research Problems in Group Performance and Group Dynamics. In *Group Decision Making*, H. Brandstatter *et al.* (eds.), pp. 1–20. London: Academic Press.

Dawkins, M. 1982. Evolutionary Ecology of Thinking: State of the Art Report. In *Animal Mind – Human Mind*, D. Griffin (ed.), pp. 355–73. Berlin: Springer-Verlag.

Dawkins, R. 1982. *The Extended Phenotype*. Oxford: Oxford University Press.

DeGroot, M.H. 1974. Reaching a Consensus. *Journal of the American Statistical Association* 69: 118–21.

De Groot, P. 1980. Information Transfer in a Socially Roosting Weaver Bird (*Quelea quelea*; *ploceiliae*): An Experimental Study. *Animal Behaviour* 28: 1,249–57.

De Laguna, F. 1972. *Under Mount Saint Elias: The History and Culture of the Yakutat Tlingit*. Washington: Smithsonian Institution Press.

Delluc, B. and G. Delluc. 1984. Grotte de Comarque. In *L'art des cavernes: atlas des grottes ornées*, pp. 119–22. Paris: Imprimerie Nationale.

1985. De l'empreinte au signe. In *Traces et messages de la préhistoire*. Dossiers de l'Arch 90: 56–62.

Delpech, F. 1983. *Les faunes du paléolithique supérieur dans le sud ouest de la France*. Paris: Centre National de la Recherche Scientifique.

Delpech, F. and O. Le Gall. 1983. La Faune magdalénienne de la Grotte des Églises (Ussat, Arièfe). *Bulletin de la Société Préhistorique de l'Ariège* 38: 91–118.

Delporte, H. 1984. L'Art mobilier et ses rapports avec la faune paléolithique. In *La Contribution de la zoologie et de l'éthologie à l'interpretation de l'art des peuples chasseurs préhistoriques*, H. Bandi *et al.* (eds.), pp. 111–42. Fribourg: Editions Universitaires.

Dennell, R. 1983. A New Chronology for the Mousterian. *Nature* 301: 199–201.

1985. *European Economic Prehistory: A New Approach*. London: Academic Press.

Dewalt, B. and K. Dewalt. 1984. Stratification and Decision Making in the Use of New Agricultural Technology. In *Agricultural Decision Making*, P. Bartlett (ed.), pp. 289–316. London: Academic Press.

Donner, J. 1975. Pollen Composition of the Abri Pataud Sediments. In *Excavations of the Abri Pataud, Les Eyzies (Dordogne)*, H.L. Movius (ed.), pp. 160–173. Cambridge, Mass: American School of Prehistoric Research, Bulletin 30.

Draper, P. 1976. Social and Economic Constraints on Child Life Among the !Kung. In *Kalahari Hunter-Gatherers: Studies of the !Kung and their Neighbours*, R. Lee and I. DeVore (eds.), pp. 199–218. Cambridge, Mass.: Harvard University Press.

Drent, R.H. 1982. Risk-Benefit Assessment in Animals. In *Animal Mind – Human Mind*, D. Griffin (ed.), pp. 75–94. Berlin: Springer-Verlag.

Dunbar, R. 1981. Sociobiology, Biosophy and Human Behaviour: A Review of 'Genes, Mind and Culture' by C.J. Lumsden and E.O. Wilson and 'The Evolution of Human Consciousness' by J.H. Crook. *Ethology and Sociobiology* 2: 187–90.

1982. Adaptation, Fitness and the Evolutionary Tautology. In *Current Problems in Sociobiology*, King's College Sociobiology Group (eds.), pp. 9–28. Cambridge: Cambridge University Press.

1984. *Reproductive Decisions*. Guildford Princeton: Princeton University Press.

Dunnell, R.C. 1980. Evolutionary Theory and Archaeology. In *Advances in Archaeological Method and Theory*, vol. 3, M. Schiffer (ed.), pp. 38–99. New York: Academic Press.

Earle, T.K. and R.W. Preucel. 1987. Processual Archaeology and the Radical Critique. *Current Anthropology* 28(4): 501–38.

Eisenberg, J.F. and D.E. Wilson. 1978. Relative Brain Size and Feeding Strategies in the Chiroptera. *Evolution* 32: 240–51.

Elmendorf, W. and A.L. Kroeber. 1960. *The Structure of Twana Culture with Comparative Notes on the Structure of the Yurok Culture*. Washington: Washington State University Press.

Elner, R. and R. Hughes. 1978. Energy Maximisation in the Diet of the Shore Crab, *Carcinus maenus*. *Journal of Animal Ecology* 47: 103–16.

Estes, W.K. 1984. Human Learning and Memory. In *The Biology of Learning*, P. Marler and H.S. Terrace (eds.), pp. 617–28. Berlin: Springer-Verlag.

Estioko-Griffen, A. 1986. Daughters of the Forest. *Natural History* 95(5): 36–42.

Falkus, H. 1978. *Nature Detective*. London: Victor Gollancz.

Fischer, A. 1982. Trade in Danubian Shaft-Hole Axes and the Introduction of Neolithic Economy in Denmark. *Journal of Danish Archaeology* 1: 7–12.

Fisher, B.A. 1980. *Small Group Decision Making*. New York: McGraw Hill.

Flannery, K. 1986a. Ecosystem Models and Information flows in the Tehuacán-Oaxaca Region. In *Guilá Narquitz: Archaic Foraging and Early Agriculture in Oaxaca, Mexico*, K. Flannery (ed.), pp. 439–507. London: Academic Press.

    1986b. Adaptation, Evolution and Archaeological Phases: Some Implications of Reynolds' Simulation. In *Guilá Narquitz: Archaic Foraging and Early Agriculture in Oaxaca, Mexico*, K. Flannery (ed.), pp. 501–7. London: Academic Press.

Flavell, J. 1976. Metacognitive Aspects of Problem solving. In *The Nature of Intelligence*, L.B. Resnick (ed.), pp. 231–235. Hillsdale, New Jersey: Lawrence Erlbaum Association.

Flood, J. 1980. *The Moth Hunters: Aboriginal Prehistory of the Australian Alps*. Canberra: Australian Institute of Aboriginal Studies.

Fodor, J.A. 1983. *The Modularity of Mind: an Essay on Faculty Psychology*. Cambridge, Mass: M.I.T. Press.

    1985. Précis of 'The Modularity of Mind'. *The Behavioural and Brain Sciences* 8: 1–42.

Foley, R. 1985. Optimality Theory in Anthropology. *Man* 20: 222–42.

    1987a. *Another Unique Species*. Harlow: Longman Scientific and Technical.

    1987b. Hominid Species and Stone-Tool Assemblages: How are they Related? *Antiquity* 61: 380–92.

Gailli, R., N. Pailhaugue and F. Rouzard. 1984. Grotte de Bédeilhac. In *L'Art des cavernes: atlas des grottes ornées paléolithiques françaises*, pp. 369–75. Paris: Imprimeries Nationales.

Gamble, C. 1982. Interaction and Alliance in Palaeolithic Society. *Man (N.S.)* 17: 92–107.

    1983. Caves and Faunas from Last Glacial Europe. In *Animals and Archaeology: 1 Hunters and their Prey*, J. Clutton-Brock and C. Grigson (eds.), pp. 163–72. Oxford: British Archaeological Reports, Int. Series 163.

    1984. Regional Variation in Hunter-Gatherer Strategy in the Upper Pleistocene of Europe. In *Hominid Evolution and Community Ecology*, R. Foley (ed.), pp. 237–55. London: Academic Press.

    1986. *The Palaeolithic Settlement of Europe*. Cambridge: Cambridge University Press.

Garber, P.A. 1987. Foraging Strategies among Living Primates. *Annual Review of Anthropology* 16: 339–64.

Gatty, H. 1958. *Nature is your Guide: How to Find your Way on Land and Sea*. London: Collins.

Gellner, E. 1987. *The Concept of Kinship and Other Essays*. Oxford: Basil Blackwell.

    1988. *Plough, Sword and Book: The Structure of Human History*. London: Collins Harvill.

Ghiglieri, M.P. 1984. Feeding Ecology and Sociality of Chimpanzees in Kibale forest,

Uganda. In *Adaptations for Foraging in Nonhuman Primates*, P. Rodman and J.G.H. Cant (eds.), pp. 161–94. New York: Columbia University Press.

Giddens, A. 1985. *The Constitution of Society: Outline of a Theory of Structuration.* Cambridge: Polity Press.

Gladwin, H. and M. Murtaugh. 1984. The Attentive – Preattentive Distinction in Agricultural Decision Making. In *Agricultural Decision Making*, P. Barlett (ed.), pp. 115–36. New York: Academic Press.

Goodale, J.C. 1971. *Tiwi Wives: A Study of the Women of Melville Island, North Australia.* Seattle: University of Washington Press.

Gordon, B. 1988. *Of Men and Reindeer Herds in French Magdalenian Prehistory.* Oxford: British Archaeological Reports, Int. Series 390.

Gould, J. and P. Marler. 1987. Learning by Instinct. *Scientific American* 256: 62–73.

Gould, J.P. 1974. Risk, Stochastic Preference, and the Value of Information. *Journal of Economic Theory* 8: 64–84.

Gould, P. and R. White. 1974. *Mental Maps.* New York: Penguin.

Gould, R.A. 1980. *Living Archaeology.* Cambridge: Cambridge University Press.

Graziosi, P. 1960. *Palaeolithic Art.* New York: McGraw Hill.

  1969. *Levanzo: Pitture e incisioni*, Florence: Sansoni.

Green, R.F. 1984. Stopping Rules for Optimal Foragers. *American Naturalist* 123: 30–40.

Greene, E. 1987. Individuals in an Osprey Colony Discriminate between High and Low Quality Information. *Nature* 329: 239–41.

Griffin, D. 1976. *The Question of Animal Awareness: Evolutionary Continuity of Mental Experience.* New York: Rockefeller University Press.

  1984. *Animal Thinking.* Cambridge, Mass.: Harvard University Press.

Gubser, N.J. 1965. *The Nunamiut Eskimos: Hunters of Caribou.* New Haven: Yale University Press.

Guthrie, R.D. 1984. Ethological Observations from Palaeolithic Art. In *La Contribution de la zoologie et de l'éthologie pour l'interprétation de l'art des peuples chasseurs préhistoriques*, H. Bandi *et al.* (eds.), pp. 35–74. Editions Universitaires Fribourg, Suisse.

Hallam, J.S., B.J.N. Edwards, B. Barnes, and A.J. Stuart. 1973. A Late Glacial Elk with Associated Barbed Points from High Furlong, Lancashire. *Proceedings of the Prehistoric Society* 39: 100–28.

Halverson, J. 1987. Art for Art's Sake in the Palaeolithic. *Current Anthropology* 28(1): 63–89.

Hames, R. and W.T. Vickers. 1982. Optimal Diet Breadth Theory as a Model to Explain Variability in Amazonian Hunting. *American Ethnologist* 9(2): 358–78.

Hammond, K., McClelland, G. and J. Mumpower. 1980. *Human Judgement and Decision Making; Theories, Methods and Procedures.* New York: Praeger.

Harley, C.B. 1981. Learning the Evolutionary Stable Strategy. *Journal of Theoretical Biology* 89: 611–33.

Harwood, J. 1981. Managing Gray Seal Populations for Optimum Stability. In *Dynamics of Large Mammal Populations*, C. Fowler and T. Smith (eds.), pp. 159–72. New York: John Wiley and Sons.

Hassrick, R.B. 1964. *The Sioux.* Norman: University of Oklahoma Press.

Hawkes, K., K. Hill and J. O'Connell. 1982. Why Hunters Gather: Optimal Foraging and the Áche of Eastern Paraguay. *American Ethologist* 9(2): 379–91.

Heffley, S. 1981. The Relationship Between Northern Athapaskan Settlement Patterns and Resource Distribution: An Application of Horn's Model. In *Hunter-Gatherer Foraging Strategies: Ethnographic and Archaeological Analysis*, B. Winterhalder and E.A. Smith (eds.) pp. 126–7. Chicago: University of Chicago Press.

Hewlett, B.S. and L.L. Cavalli-Sforza. 1986. Cultural Transmissions Among the Aka Pygmies. *American Anthropologist* 88: 922–34.

Higgs, E. 1972. *Papers in Economic Prehistory.* Cambridge: Cambridge University Press.

1975. *Palaeoeconomy.* Cambridge: Cambridge University Press.

Hill, J. 1984. Prestige and Reproductive Success in Man. *Ethology and Sociobiology* 5(2): 77–95.

Hill, J. and J. Gunn (eds.). 1977. *The Individual in Prehistory.* London: Academic Press.

Hill, K. and K. Hawkes. 1983. Neotropical Hunting among the Áche of Eastern Paraguay. In *Adaptive Responses of Native Amazonians,* R. Hames and W. Vickers (eds.), pp. 139–88. New York: Academic Press.

Hinde, R.A. 1987. *Individuals, Relationships and Culture.* Cambridge: Cambridge University Press.

Hodder, I. 1985. Post-Processual Archaeology. In *Advances in Method and Theory,* M. Schiffer (ed.), 8: 1–25.

1986. *Reading the Past: Current Approaches to Interpretation in Archaeology.* Cambridge: Cambridge University Press.

1987. Comments on 'Processual Archaeology and the Radical Critique' by T.K. Earle and R.W. Preucel. *Current Anthropology* 28(4): 501–38.

1988. The Creative Process in Long Term Perspective (Comments on 'The Creative Mind: Toward an Evolutionary Theory of Discovery and Innovation' by C.S. Findlay and C.J. Lumsden). *Journal of Social and Biological Structures* 11: 99–101.

Hodges, A. 1983. *Alan Turing: The Enigma of Intelligence.* London: Unwin.

Hooper, A. 1977. Note sur les oiseaux figures dans l'art paléolithique. *Bulletin de la Société Préhistorique de l'Ariège* 32: 85–7.

1980. Note sur l'interprétation des trois frises de têtes animales de Lascaux. *Bulletin de la Société Préhistorique de l'Ariège* 35: 111–13.

Horne, G. and G. Aiston. 1924. *Savage Life in Central Australia.* London: Macmillan.

Houston, A. 1983. Comments on 'Learning the Evolutionary Stable Strategy'. *Journal of Theoretical Biology* 105: 175–8.

Houston, A., A. Kacelnik and J.M. McNamara. 1982. Some Learning Rules for Acquiring Information. In *Functional Ontogeny,* D.J. McFarland (ed.), pp. 140–91. London: Pitman Books.

Humphrey, N. 1976. The Social Function of Intellect. In *Growing Points in Ethology,* P. Bateson and R. Hinde (eds.) pp. 303–17. Cambridge: Cambridge University Press.

1984. *Consciousness Regained.* Oxford: Oxford University Press.

Ingold, T. 1981. The Hunter and his Spear: Notes on the Cultural Mediation of Social and Ecological Systems. In *Economic Archaeology,* G. Bailey and A. Sheridan (eds.), pp. 119–30. Oxford: British Archaeological Reports, Int. Series 96.

1986. *The Appropriation of Nature: Essays on Human Ecology and Social Relations.* Manchester: Manchester University Press.

Iwasa, Y., M. Higashi and N. Yamamura. 1981. Prey Distribution as a Factor Determining the Choice of Optimal Foraging Strategies. *American Naturalist* 117(5): 710–23.

Jacobi, R. 1976. Britain Inside and Outside Mesolithic Europe. *Proceedings of the Prehistoric Society* 42: 67–84.

1978. Northern England in the Eighth Millennium bc: An Essay. In *The Early Post-Glacial Settlement of Northern Europe,* P. Mellars (ed.), pp. 295–332. London: Duckworth.

Janetos, A.C. and B.J. Cole. 1981. Imperfectly Optimal Animals. *Behavioural Ecology and Sociobiology* 9: 203–9.

Janis, I.L. 1972. *Victims of Group-Think*. Boston: Houghton Mifflin.

Jennes, D. 1977. *The Indians of Canada*. (Seventh edition). Ottawa: University of Toronto Press.

Jensen, H. 1983. A Micro-wear Analysis of Unretouched Blades from Ageröd V. In *Ageröd V: An Atlantic Bog Site in Central Scania*. Acta Archaeologica Lundensia 8, No. 12, pp. 144–52.

Jochim, M. 1976. *Hunter-gatherer Subsistence and Settlement: A Predictive Model*. New York: Academic Press.

1983a. Palaeolithic Cave Art in Ecological Perspective. In *Hunter-Gatherer Economy in Prehistory*, G. Bailey (ed.), pp. 212–19. Cambridge: Cambridge University Press.

1983b. Optimization Models in Context. In *Archaeological Hammers and Theories*, J.A. Moore and A.S. Keene (eds.), pp. 157–70. New York: Academic Press.

Johnson, G. 1978. Information Sources and the Development of Decision Making Organizations. In *Social Archaeology: Beyond Subsistence and Dating*, C. Redman *et al.* (eds.), pp. 87–112. New York: Academic Press.

Johnson, M.K. and C.R. Raye. 1981. Reality Monitoring. *Psychological Review* 88(1): 67–85.

Jonsson, L. 1986. Animal Bones from Bredasten – Preliminary Results. *Menddelanden från Lunds Universitets Historiska Museum* 1985–6: 50–1.

In press. The Vertebrate Faunal Remains from the Late Atlantic Settlement of Skateholm in Scania, S. Sweden. In *The Skateholm Project*, L. Larrson (ed.). Stockholm: Almquist and Wiksell International.

Kacelnik, A. and J.R. Krebs. 1985. Learning to Exploit Patchily Distributed Food. In *Behavioural Ecology: Ecological Consequences of Adaptive Behaviour*, R.M. Sibly and R.H. Smith (eds.), pp. 189–205. Oxford: Blackwell Scientific Publications.

Kamil, A.C. 1983. Optimal Foraging Theory and the Psychology of Learning. *American Zoologist* 23: 291–302.

1984. Adaption and Cognition: Knowing What Comes Naturally. In *Animal Cognition*, H.L. Roitblat *et al.* (eds.), pp. 533–44. Hillsdale, New Jersey: Lawrence Erlbaum Associates.

Kaplan, H. and K. Hill. 1985. Hunting Ability and Reproductive Success among Male Áche Foragers: Preliminary Results. *Current Anthropology* 26(1): 131–3.

Kearins, J.M. 1981. Visual Spatial Memory in Australian Aboriginal Children of Desert Regions. *Cognitive Psychology* 13: 434–60.

Keene, A.S. 1981. *Prehistoric Foraging in a Temperate Forest: A Linear Programming Model*. New York: Academic Press.

1983. Biology, Behaviour and Borrowing: A Critical Examination of Optimal Foraging Theory in Archaeology. In *Archaeological Hammers and Theories*, J.A. Moore and A.S. Keene (eds.), pp. 137–55. New York: Academic Press.

Klein, R., C. Wolf, L.G. Freeman and K. Allwarden. 1981. The Use of Dental Crown Heights for Constructing Age Profiles of Red Deer and Similar Species in Archaeological Samples. *Journal of Archaeological Science* 8: 1–32.

Klein, R., K. Allwarden and C. Wolf. 1983. The Calculation and Interpretation of Ungulate Age Profiles from Dental Crown Heights. In *Hunter-Gatherer Economy in Prehistory*, G. Bailey (ed.), pp. 47–57. Cambridge: Cambridge University Press.

Kozlowski, J.K. and S.K. Kozlowski. 1986. Foragers of Central Europe and their Acculturation. In *Hunters in Transition*, M. Zvelebil (ed.), pp. 95–108. Cambridge: Cambridge University Press.

Krause, A. 1956. *The Tlinglit Indians*. Seattle: University of Washington Press.

Krebs, J.R. 1978. Optimal Foraging: Decision Rules for Predators. In *Behavioural Ecology: An Evolutionary Approach*, J.R. Krebs and N.B. Davis (eds.), pp. 23–63. Oxford: Blackwell Scientific Publications.

Krebs, J.R., A. Kacelnik and P. Taylor. 1978. Test of Optimal Sampling by Great Tits. *Nature* 275: 27–31.

Krebs, J.R., D.W. Stephens and W.J. Sutherland. 1983. Perspectives in Optimal Foraging. In *Perspectives in Ornithology*, G.A. Clark and A.H. Brush (eds.), pp. 165–216. New York: Cambridge University Press.

Kurland, J.A. and S.J. Beckerman. 1985. Optimal Foraging and Hominid Evolution: Labour and Reciprocity. *American Anthropologist* 87(1): 73–93.

Laming-Emperaire, A. 1962. *La Signification de l'art rupestre paléolithique*. Paris: Picard.

Larsson, L. 1975. A Contribution to the Knowledge of Mesolithic Huts in Southern Scandinavia. *Meddelanden från Lunds Universitets Historiska Museum* 1973–4: 5–28.

   1977. Mesolithic Bone and Antler Artefacts from Central Scania. *Meddelanden från Lunds Universitets Historiska Museum* 1977–8: 28–67.

   1978. *Ageröd I:B – Ageröd I:D: A Study of Early Atlantic Settlement in Scania*, Acta Archaeologica Lundensia 4, No. 12.

   1980. Some Aspects of the Kongemose Culture of Southern Sweden. *Meddelanden från Lunds Universitets Historiska Museum* 1979–80: 5–22.

   1982. *Segebro: en tidigatlantisk Boplats vid sege ås mynning*. Malmöfynd 4, Utgiven av Malmö Museum.

   1983. *Ageröd V: An Atlantic Bog Site in Central Scania*. Acta Archaeologica Lundensia 8, No. 12.

   1984. The Skateholm Project – A Late Mesolithic Settlement and Cemetery Complex at a Southern Sweden Bay. *Meddelanden från Lunds Universitets Historiska Museum* 1983–4: 38.

   In press. *The Skateholm: Project*. Stockholm: Almquist and Wiksell International.

Larsson, M. 1986. Bredasten – An Early Ertebølle Site with Dwelling Structure in South Scandinavia. *Meddelanden från Lunds Universitets Historiska Museum* 1985–6: 25–49.

Laughlin, P.R. and J. Adamupoloulas. 1982. Social Decision Schemes as Intellective Tasks. In *Group Decision Making*, H. Bradstatter *et al.* (eds.), pp. 81–94. London: Academic Press.

Laviern, L. Van and J. Esser. 1979. Numbers, Distribution and Habitat Preference of Large Mammals in Bouba Ndjidu National Park, Cameroon. *African Journal of Ecology* 17: 141–53.

Lawrence, M.J. and R.W. Brown. 1967. *Mammals of Britain: Their Tracks, Trails and Signs*. London: Blandford Press.

Layton, R. 1985. The Cultural Context of Hunter-Gatherer Rock Art. *Man (N.S.)* 20: 434–53.

Leacock, E. 1969. The Montagnais-Naskapi Band. *National Museum of Canada Bulletin, No. 228, Anthropology Series* 84: 1–17.

Leavitt, H.J. 1951. Some Effects of Certain Communication Patterns on Group Performance. *Journal of Abnormal and Social Psychology* 46: 38–50.

Lee, R.B. 1976. !Kung Spatial Organization. In *Kalahari Hunter Gatherers: Studies of the !Kung and their Neighbours*, R. Lee and I. DeVore (eds.), pp. 73–98. Cambridge, Mass.: Harvard University Press.

   1979. *The !Kung San: Men, Women and Work in a Foraging Society*. Cambridge: Cambridge University Press.

Legge, A.J. and P.A. Rowley-Conwy. 1988. *Starr Carr Revisited*. The Archaeology Laboratory, Centre for Extra-Mural Studies, Birkbeck College, London.

Leroi-Gourhan, A. 1968. *The Art of Prehistoric Man in Western Europe*. London: Thames and Hudson.

   1984. Le Réalisme du comportement dans l'art paléolithique d'Europe de l'ouest. In

La Contribution de la zoologie et de l'éthologie à l'interprétation de l'art des peuples chasseurs préhistoriques, H. Bandi *et al.* (eds.), pp. 75–90, Fribourg: Editions Universitaires.

Leroi-Gourhan, A. and M. Brézillon. 1972. *Fouilles de Pincevent*. Paris: Recherche Scientifique.

Leslie, P.H. 1945. On the Use of Matrices in Certain Population Mathematics. *Biometrika* 33: 183–212.

Leuthold, W. and B. Leuthold. 1976. Density and Biomass of Ungulates in Tsaua East National Park, Kenya. *East African Wildlife Journal* 14: 49–58.

Levitt, D. 1981. *Plants and People; Aboriginal Uses of Plants on Groote Eylandt.* Canberra: Australian Institute of Aboriginal Studies.

Lewis, E.C. 1942. On the Generation and Growth of a Population. *Sankhya* 6: 93–6.

Lewthwaite, J. 1986. The Transition to Food Production: A Mediterranean Perspective. In *Hunters in Transition*, M. Zvelebil (ed.), pp. 53–66. Cambridge: Cambridge University Press.

Lima, S. 1983. Downy Woodpecker Foraging Behaviour: Efficient Sampling in Simple Stochastic Environments. *Ecology* 65, 166–74.

  1985. Sampling Behaviour of Starlings: Foraging in Simple Patchy Environments. *Behavioural Ecology and Sociobiology* 16: 135–42.

Lorblanchet, M. 1974. *L'Art préhistorique en Quercy: La Grotte des Escabasses (Thémines, Lot)*. Saint Jammes: PGP.

  1977. From Naturalism to Abstraction in European Prehistoric Rock Art. In *Form in Indigenous Art*, P. Ucko (ed.), pp. 44–56. London: Duckworth.

Lumsden, C. and E.O. Wilson. 1981. *Genes, Mind and Culture*. Cambridge, Mass.: Harvard University Press.

Lyons, J. 1985. The Origins of Language. In *Origins: The Darwin College Lectures*, C. Fabian (ed.), pp. 141–68. Cambridge: Cambridge University Press.

Mace, G.M., P.H. Harvey and T.H. Clutton-Brock. 1981. Brain Size and Ecology in Small Mammals. *Journal of Zoology, London* 193: 333–54.

Marks, S.A. 1976. *Large Mammals and a Brave People: Subsistence Hunters in Zambia.* Seattle: University of Washington Press.

  1977. Buffalo Movements and Accessibility to a Community of Hunters in Zambia. *East African Wildlife Journal* 15: 251–61.

Marshack, A. 1972. *The Roots of Civilization*. London: Weidenfeld and Nicholson.

Marshall, L. 1976. *The !Kung of Nyae Nyae*. Cambridge, Mass.: Harvard University Press.

Martin, C. 1978. *Keepers of the Game: Indian-Animal Relationships and the Fur Trade.* Berkeley: University of California Press.

Martin, J.K. 1983. Optimal Foraging Theory: A Review of Some Models and their Applications. *American Anthropologist* 85: 612–29.

May, R., J. Beddington, J. Horwood and J. Shepherd. 1978. Exploiting Populations in an Uncertain World. *Mathematical Biosciences* 42: 219–52.

Maynard-Smith, J. 1982. *Evolution and the Theory of Games*. Cambridge: Cambridge University Press.

  1984. Game Theory and the Evolution of Behaviour. *Behavioural and Brain Sciences* 7: 95–125.

McBryde, I. 1978. Some Documents Relating to the Aborigines of Northern New South Wales. In *Records of Times Past: Ethnohistorical Essays on the Culture and Ecology of the New England Tribes*, I. MacBryde (ed.), pp. 235–86. Canberra: Australian Institute of Aboriginal Studies.

McNair, J.N. 1982. Optimal Giving Up Times and the Marginal Value Theorem. *American Naturalist* 119: 511–29.

McNamara, J.M. and A.I. Houston. 1980. The Application of Statistical Decision

Theory to Animal Behaviour. *Journal of Theoretical Biology* 85: 673–90.

Mech, L.D. 1974. *The Wolf*. New York: The Natural History Press.

Meehan, B. 1982. *Shell Bed to Shell Midden*. Canberra: Australian Institute of Aboriginal Studies.

Meldgaard, M. 1983. Resource Fluctuations and Human Subsistence: A Zoo-archaeological and Ethnographic Investigation of a West Greenland Caribou Hunting Camp. In *Animals and Archaeology: Hunters and Their Prey*, J. Clutton-Brock and C. Grigson (eds.) BAR Int. Ser. 163, pp. 259–72.

Mellars, P. 1976. Settlement Patterns and Industrial Variability in the British Mesolithic. In *Problems in Economic and Social Archaeology*, G. de G. Sieveking *et al.* (eds.), pp. 375–400. London: Duckworth.

  1985. The Ecological Basis of Social Complexity in the Upper Palaeolithic of Southwestern France. In *Prehistoric Hunter Gatherers: The Emergence of Cultural Complexity*, T.D. Price and J.A. Brown (eds.), pp. 271–97. New York: Academic Press.

Menzel, E.W. Jr. 1978. Cognitive Mapping in Chimpanzees. In *Cognitive Processes in Animal Behaviour*, S.H. Hulse, H. Fowler and W.K. Honig (eds.), pp. 375–442. Hillsdale, New Jersey: Lawrence Erlbaum Associates.

Merton, R.K. 1936. The Unanticipated Consequences of Purposive Social Action. *American Sociological Review* 1: 894–904.

  1963. *Social Theory and Social Structure*. Glencoe: Free Press.

Midgley, M. 1980. *Beast and Man: The Roots of Human Nature*. London: Methuen.

Miller, D. and C. Tilley. 1984a. Ideology, Power and Long Term Social Change. In *Ideology, Power and Prehistory*, D. Miller and C. Tilley (eds.), pp. 147–52. Cambridge: Cambridge University Press.

  1984b. Ideology, Power and Prehistory: An Introduction. In *Ideology, Power and Prehistory*, D. Miller and C. Tilley (eds.), pp. 1–15. Cambridge: Cambridge University Press.

Milton, K. 1980. *The Foraging Strategies of Howler Monkeys: A Study in Primate Economics*. New York: Columbia University Press.

Minc, L.D. 1986. Scarcity and Survival: The Role of Oral Tradition in Mediating Subsistence Crisis. *Journal of Anthropological Archaeology* 5: 39–113.

Mithen, S.J. 1986a. The Application of Leslie Matrix Models in Archaeology. *Science in Archaeology* 28: 24–31.

  1986b. Review of 'Upper Palaeolithic Land Use and Settlement in the Perigord' by R. White. *Journal of Archaeological Science* 13: 601–3.

  1987. Prehistoric Red Deer Hunting: A Cost-Risk-Benefit Analysis with Reference to Upper Palaeolithic Spain and Mesolithic Denmark. In *Current Research in the Mesolithic of Northwest Europe*, P.A. Rowley-Conwy *et al.* (eds.), pp. 93–108. Sheffield: Dept of Archaeology and Prehistory.

  1988a. *Hunter-Gatherer Decision Making in Foraging Strategies: An Archaeological and Ethnographic Study*. Unpublished Ph.D Thesis, Cambridge University.

  1988b. Looking and Learning: Upper Palaeolithic Art and Information Gathering. *World Archaeology* 19(3): 297–327.

  1989a. Evolutionary Theory and Post-Processual Archaeology. *Antiquity* 63: 483-94.

  1989b. Modeling Hunter-Gatherer Decision Making: Complementing Optimal Foraging Theory. *Journal of Human Ecology* 17(1): 53–89 (in press).

Modderman, P.J.R. 1977. Die neolithische Besiedlung bei Hienheim, Ldkr. Kelheim I: Dei Ausgrabungen am weinberg 1965–1970. *Analecta Praehistorica Leidensia* 10.

Møhl, U. 1978a. Elsdyrskeltterne fra Skottemarke og Favrbo: Skik og Brug Ved Borealtidens Jagter (Finds of Elk Skeleton Yielding Evidence about Preboreal Hunting Methods). *Aarbøger fra Nordisk Oldkyndighed og Historie* 1978: 5–32.

1978b. Aggersund-bopladsen zoologisk belyst. Svanejagt sum årsag til bosaettelse? (with English summary) *KUML* 1978: 57–75.

Moore, D. 1979. *Islanders and Aborigines at Cape York*. Canberra: Australian Institute of Aboriginal Affairs.

Moore, J.A. 1981. The Effects of Information Networks in Hunter-Gatherer Societies. In *Hunter-Gatherer Foraging Strategies: Ethnographic and Archaeological Analysis*, B. Winterhalder and E.A. Smith (eds.), pp. 194–217. Chicago: University of Chicago Press.

1983. The Trouble of Know-It-Alls: Information as a Social and Ecological Resource. In *Achaeological Hammers and Theories*, J. Moore and A. Keene (eds.), pp. 173–191. New York: Academic Press.

Morphy, H. 1977. Schematisation, Meaning and Communication in Toas. In *Form in Indigenous Art*, P. Ucko (ed.), pp. 77–89. London: Duckworth.

Murie, O. 1954. *A Field Guide to Animal Tracks*. Cambridge, Mass.: The Riverside Press.

Nelson, R.K. 1973. *Hunters of the Northern Forest: Designs for Survival among the Alaskan Kutchin*. Chicago: University of Chicago Press.

1983. *Make Prayers to the Raven: A Koyukon View of the Northern Forest*. Chicago: University of Chicago Press.

Noe-Nygaard, N. 1973. The Vig Bull: New Information on the Final Hunt. *Bulletin of the Geological Society of Denmark* 22: 244–8.

1974. Mesolithic Hunting in Denmark Illustrated by Bone Injuries Caused by Human Weapons. *Journal of Archaeological Science* 1: 217–48.

Nougier, L-R. and R. Robert. 1965. Les Félins dans l'art quaternaire. *Bulletin de la Société Préhistorique de l'Ariège* 20: 17–84.

O'Connell, J. 1987. Alyawara Site Structure and its Archaeological Implications. *American Antiquity* 52(1): 74–108.

O'Connell, J. and K. Hawkes. 1981. Alyawara Plant Use and Optimal Foraging Theory. In *Hunter-Gatherer Foraging Strategies: Ethnographic and Archaeological Analysis*, B. Winterhalder and E.A. Smith (eds.), pp. 99–125. Chicago: Chicago University Press.

1984. Food Choice and Foraging Sites among the Alyawara. *Journal of Anthropological Research* 40: 504–35.

O'Connell, J., K. Hawkes and N. Blurton-Jones. 1988. Hadza Hunting, Butchering and Bone Transport and their Archaeological Implications. *Journal of Anthropological Research* 44(2): 113–61.

O'Frake, C. 1985. Cognitive Maps of Time and Tide among Medieval Seafarers. *Man* (N.S.) 20(2): 254–71.

Opler, M.E. 1941. *An Apache Life Way: The Economic, Social and Religious Institutions of the Chiricahua Indians*. Chicago: University of Chicago Press.

Orians, G.H. 1980. *Some Adaptations of Marsh-Nesting Blackbirds*. Princeton: Princeton University Press.

Orians, G.H. and N. Pearson. 1979. On the Theory of Central Place Foraging. In *Analysis of Ecological Systems*, D. Horn, G. Stairs and R. Mitchell (eds.), pp. 154–77. Columbus: Ohio State University Press.

O'Shea, J. and M. Zvelebil. 1984. Oleneostrovski Mogilnik: Reconstructing the Social and Economic Organisation of Prehistoric Foragers in Northern Russia. *Journal of Anthropological Archaeology* 3(1): 1–40.

Packer, C. 1977. Reciprocal Altruism in *Papio anubis*. *Nature* 265: 441–3.

Pálsson, G. and P. Durrenberger. 1982. To Dream of Fish: The Causes of Icelandic Skippers' Fishing Success. *Journal of Anthropological Research* 38: 227–42.

Paquerceau, M-M. 1976. La Végétation au pleistocène supérieur et au début de l'holocène dans le sud-ouest. In *La préhistoire française*, H. de Lumley (ed.), pp. 525–30. Paris: Centre de la Recherche Scientifique.

Patou, M. 1984. La Faune de la galerie rive droite du Mas d'Azil (Ariège), donnés paléoclimatiques et paléthnographiques. *Bulletin de la Société Préhistorique Française* 81: 311–19.

Petersen, E. Brinch. 1973. A Survey of the Late Palaeolithic and the Mesolithic of Denmark. In *The Mesolithic in Europe*, S.K. Kozlowski (ed.), pp. 71–121: Warsaw University Press.

Petersen, P. Vang. 1984. Chronological and Regional Variation in the Late Mesolithic of Eastern Denmark. *Journal of Danish Archaeology* 3: 7–18.

Pfeiffer, J. 1982. *The Creative Explosion: An Inquiry into the Origins of Art and Religion*. New York: Harper and Row.

Pielou, E. 1969. *An Introduction to Mathematical Ecology*. New York: John Wiley and Sons.

Piette, E. 1904. Etudes d'éthnographie préhistorique: V11(1) Classification des sédiments formées dans les cavernes pendant l'âge du renne. *L'Anthropologie* 15: 129–76.

1907. *L'Art pendant l'âge du renne*. Paris: Masson.

Pimlott, D. 1967. Wolf Predation and Ungulate Populations. *American Zoologist* 7: 267–78.

Price, T.D. 1978. Mesolithic Settlement Systems in the Netherlands. In *The Early Postglacial Settlement of Northern Europe*, P. Mellars (ed.), pp. 81–113. London: Duckworth.

1985. Affluent Foragers of Mesolithic Southern Scandinavia. In *Prehistoric Hunter Gatherers: The Emergence of Cultural Complexity*, T.D. Price and J.A. Brown (eds.), pp. 341–60. New York: Academic Press.

Pryor, F. 1986. The Adoption of Agriculture: Some Theoretical and Empirical Evidence. *American Anthropologist* 88: 879–97.

Pugh, G.E. 1977. *The Biological Origin of Human Values*. New York: Basic Books.

Pulliam, H.R. and C. Dunford. 1980. *Programmed to Learn: An Essay on the Evolution of Culture*. New York: Columbia University Press.

Pyke, G., R. Pulliam and E.L. Charnov. 1977. Optimal Foraging Theory: A Selective Review of Theory and Tests. *Quarterly Review of Biology* 52: 137–54.

Pyke, M. 1970. *Man and Food*. New York: McGraw Hill.

Quinn, N. 1978. Do Mfantse Fish Sellers Estimate Probabilities in their Heads? *American Ethnologist* 5: 206–26.

Radcliffe-Brown, A. 1929. Notes on Totemism in Eastern Australia. *Journal of the Royal Anthropological Institute* 59: 399–415.

Ray, V.F. 1963. *Primitive Pragmatists: The Modoc Indians of Northern California*. Seattle: University of Washington Press.

Reinach, S. 1913. *Répertoire de l'art quaternaire*. Paris: Leroux.

Renfrew, C. 1979. Transformations. In *Transformations: Mathematical Approaches to Culture Change*, C. Renfrew and K. Cooke (eds.), pp. 3–44. New York: Academic Press.

1981. The Simulator as Demiurge. In *Simulations in Archaeology*, J. Sabloff (ed.), pp. 283–306. Albuquerque: University of New Mexico Press.

1987. Problems in the Modelling of Socio-Cultural Systems. *European Journal of Operational Research* 30: 179–92.

Reynolds, R.G. 1986. An Adaptive Computer Model for the Evolution of Plant Collecting and Early Agriculture in the Eastern Valley of Oaxaca. In *Guilá Narquitz: Archaic Foraging and Early Agriculture in Oaxaca, Mexico*, K. Flannery (ed.), pp. 439–507. London: Academic Press.

Reynolds, R.G. and B.P. Zeigler. 1979. A Formal Mathematical Model for the Operation of Consensus Based Hunting-Gathering Bands. In *Transformations: Mathematical Approaches to Culture Change*, C. Renfrew and K. Cooke (eds.), pp. 405–18. New York: Academic Press.

Rice, P.C. and A.L. Paterson. 1985. Cave Art and Bones: Exploring the Inter-Relationships. *American Anthropologist* 87: 94–100.

1986. Validating the Cave Art – Archeofaunal Relationships in Cantabrian Spain. *American Anthropologist* 88: 658–67.

Rindos, D. 1984. *The Origins of Agriculture: An Evolutionary Perspective*. London: Academic Press.

Ristau, C.A. and D. Robbins. 1982. Language in the Great Apes: A Critical Review. *Advances in the Study of Behaviour* 12: 142–225.

Rivenq, C. 1984. Grotte de Ganties-Montespan. In *L'Art des cavernes: atlas des grottes ornées paléolithiques françaises*, pp. 438–45. Paris: Imprimerie Nationale.

Rogers, E.S. 1972. The Mistassini Cree. In *Hunter and Gatherers Today*, M. Bicchieri (ed.), pp. 90–137. New York: Holt, Rinehart and Winston.

Rowley-Conwy, P. 1983. Sedentary Hunters: The Ertebølle Example. In *Hunter Gatherer Economy in Prehistory*, G. Bailey (ed.), pp. 111–26. Cambridge: Cambridge University Press.

1984. The Laziness of the Short Distance Hunter: The Origins of Agriculture in Western Denmark. *Journal of Anthropological Archaeology* 3: 300–24.

1986. Between Cave Painters and Crop Planters: Aspects of the Temperate European Forest Mesolithic. In *Hunters in Transition*, M. Zvelebil (ed.), pp. 17–32. Cambridge: Cambridge University Press.

1987. Animal Bones in Mesolithic Studies: Recent Progress and Hopes for the Future. In *Mesolithic Northwest Europe: Recent Trends*, P. Rowley-Conwy. M. Zvelebil and H.P. Blankholm (eds.), pp. 74–89. Sheffeld: Dept of Archaeology and Prehistory.

Rowley-Conwy. P.A., M. Zvelebil and H.P. Blankholm (eds.). 1987. *Mesolithic Northwest Europe: Recent Trends*. Sheffield: Department of Archaeology and Prehistory.

Rozoy, J.G. 1978. Les Derniers chasseurs. *Bulletin de la Société Archéologique champenoise, numéro spécial*, 2 vols.

Ruddle, K. and R. Chesterfield. 1977. *Education for Traditional Food Procurement in the Orinoco Delta*. Berkeley: University of California Press.

Saachi, D. 1972. Une Curieuse gravure d'oiseau dans le gisement magdalénien de Belvis (Aude). *Zephyrus* 23–4: 189–92.

Sabine, N. 1978. The Paddymelon Stone: An Increase Centre of the Gumbaynggir Tribe, Nymboida. In *Records of Time Past: Ethnohistorical Essays on the Culture and Ecology of the New England Tribes*, I. McBryde (ed.), pp. 218–21. Canberra: Australian Institute of Aboriginal Studies.

Schimdt-Nielsen, K. 1984. *Scaling: Why is Animal Size so Important?* Cambridge: Cambridge University Press.

Seton, E.T. 1925. *Animal Tracks and Hunters' Signs*. New York: Doubleday.

Shanks, M. and C. Tilley. 1987a. *Re-constructing Archaeology: Theory and Practice*. Cambridge: Cambridge University Press.

1987b. *Social Theory and Archaeology*. Cambridge: Polity Press.

Shennan, S. 1986. Towards a Critical Archaeology. *Proceedings of the Prehistoric Society* 52: 327–33.

1989. Evolution, Adaptation and the Study of Prehistoric Change. In *What's New? A Closer Look at the Process of Innovation*, by S. van de Leeuw and R. Torrence (eds.), London: Hyman and Unwin.

Sherman, S.J. and E. Corty. 1984. Cognitive Heuristics. In *Handbook of Social Cognition, Vol. 1,* R. Wyer Jr and T. Srull (eds.), pp. 189–286. Hillsdale, New Jersey: Lawrence Erlbaum Associates.

Sieveking, A. 1979. *The Cave Artists.* London: Thames and Hudson.

1980. Style and Regional Grouping in Magdalenian Cave Art. *Institute of Archaeology Bulletin* 16–17: 95–109.

1984. Palaeolithic Art and Animal Behaviour. In *La contribution de la zoologie et de l'éthologie à l'interprétation de l'art des peuples chasseurs préhistoriques,* H. Bandi *et al.* (eds.), pp. 91–109. Fribourg: Editions Universitaires.

Sih, A. and K.A. Milton. 1985. Optimal Diet Theory: Should the !Kung Eat Mongongos. *American Anthropologist* 87: 396–401.

Silberbauer, G. 1981. *Hunter and Habitat in the Central Kalahari Desert.* New York: Cambridge University Press.

Simek, J. 1987. Spatial Order and Behavioural Change in the French Palaeolithic. *Antiquity* 61: 25–40.

Simmons, I.G., G.W. Dimbleby and C. Grigson. 1981. The Mesolithic. In *The Environment in British Prehistory,* I.G. Simmons and M. Tooley (eds.), pp. 82–124. London: Duckworth.

Simon, H.A. 1979. *Models of Thought.* New Haven: Yale University Press.

Simonnet, G., L. Simonnet and R. Simonnet. 1984. Grotte de Labastide. In *L'Art des cavernes: atlas des grottes ornées paléolithiques françaises.* Paris: Imprimerie Nationale.

Skogland, T. 1983. The Effect of Density Dependent Resource Limitation on the Size of Wild Reindeer. *Oecologica (Berlin)* 60: 156–68.

1985. The Effects of Density Dependent Resource Limitation on the Demography of Wild Reindeer *Journal of Animal Ecology* 54: 359–74.

Slobodin, R. 1969. Leadership and Participation in a Kutchin Trapping Party. *National Museum of Canada Bulletin No. 228, Anthropology Series* 84: 56–90.

Smith, E.A. 1983. Anthropological Applications of Optimal Foraging Theory: A Critical Review. *Current Anthropology* 24: 625–51.

Smith, E.A. and B. Winterhalder. 1985. On the Logic and Application of Optimal Foraging Theory: A Brief Reply to Martin. *American Anthropologist* 87: 645–8.

Spencer, R.F. 1969. *The North Alaskan Eskimo: A Study in Ecology and Society.* Washington: Smithsonian Institution Press.

Sperber D. and D. Wilson. 1986. *Relevance: Communication and Cognition.* Oxford: Blackwell.

Spier, L. 1933. *Yuman Tribes of the Gila River.* University of Chicago Publications in Anthropology, Ethnological Series.

Spiess, A.E. 1979. *Reindeer and Caribou Hunters: An Archaeological Study.* New York: Academic Press.

Stephens, D.W. and E.L. Charnov. 1982. Optimal Foraging: Some Simple Stochastic Models. *Behavioural Ecology and Sociobiology* 10: 251–63.

Stephens, D.W. and J.R. Krebs. 1986. *Foraging Theory.* Princeton: Princeton University Press.

Straus, L.G. 1979. Mesolithic Adaptations along the Northern Coast of Spain. *Quaternaria* 21: 305–27.

1982a. Observations on Upper Palaeolithic Art: Old Problems and New Directions *Zephyrus* 34–5: 71–80.

1982b. Carnivores and Cave Sites in Cantabrian Spain. *Journal of Anthropological Research* 38: 75–96.

1987a. The Palaeolithic Cave Art of Vasco-Cantabrian Spain. *Oxford Journal of Archaeology* 6(2): 149–63.

1987b. Upper Palaeolithic Ibex Hunting in Southwest Europe. *Journal of Archaeological Science* 14: 163–78.

Straus, L.G., J. Altuna, G.A. Clark, M. González Morales, H. Laville, A. Leroi-Gourhan, M. Menéndez de la Hoz and J. Ortea. 1981. Palaeoecology at La Riera. *Current Anthropology* 22: 655–82.

Straus, L.G. and G.A. Clark. 1986. *La Riera: Stone Age Hunter-Gatherer Adaptations in Cantabrian Spain*. Arizona State University Anthropological Research Papers No. 36. Tucson: University Arizona Press.

Sullivan. R.J. 1942. *The Ten'a Food Quest*. Washington: The Catholic University of America Press.

Tanaka, J. 1976. Subsistence Ecology of Central Kalahari San. In *Kalahari Hunter gatherers: Studies of the !Kung and their Neighbours*, R. Lee and I. DeVore (eds.), pp. 98–120. Cambridge, Mass.: Harvard University Press.

Tanner, A. 1978. Divinations and Decisions: Multiple Explanations for Algonkion Scapulimancy. In *The Yearbook of Symbolic Anthropology (1)*, E. Schwimmer (ed.), pp. 89–101. Montreal: McGill-Queens University Press.

1979. *Bringing Home Animals: Religious Ideology and Mode of Production of the Mistassini Cree Hunters*. London: C. Hurst.

Tauber, H. 1981. ^{13}C Evidence for Dietary Habits of Prehistoric Man in Denmark. *Nature* 292: 332–3.

Tinbergen, J. 1981. Foraging Decisions in Starlings (*Sturnus Vulgaris*). *Ardea* 69: 1–67.

Torrence, R. 1983. Time Budgeting and Hunter-Gatherer Technology In *Hunter-Gatherer Economy in Prehistory*, G. Bailey (ed.), pp. 11–22. Cambridge: Cambridge University Press.

1989a. (ed.) *Time, Energy and Stone Tools*. Cambridge: Cambridge University Press.

1989b. Tools and Optimal Solutions. In *Time, Energy and Stone Tools*, R. Torrence (ed.), pp. 1–6. Cambridge: Cambridge University Press.

1989c. Re-tooling. Towards a Behavioural Theory of Stone Tools. In *Time, Energy and Stone Tools*, R. Torrence (ed.), pp. 57–66. Cambridge: Cambridge University Press.

Tversky, A. and D. Kahneman. 1971. Belief in the Law of Small Numbers. *Psychological Bulletin* 76: 105–10.

1974. Judgement under Uncertainty: Heuristics and Biases. *Science* 185: 1,124–31.

Ucko P. and A. Rosenfeld. 1967. *Palaeolithic Cave Art*. London: World University Library.

Usher, M.B. 1972. Developments in the Leslie Matrix Model. In *Mathematical Models in Ecology*, J.N.R. Jeffers (ed.), pp. 29–60. Symposium of the British Ecology Society 12. Oxford: Blackwell.

1976. Extensions to Models used in Renewable Resource Management which Incorporate an Arbitrary Structure. *Journal of Environmental Management* 4: 123–46.

Vouvé, J., J. Brunet, P. Vidal and J. Marsal. 1982. *Lascaux en Périgord Noir: environment, art pariétal et conservation*. Périgeux: Pierre Fanlac.

Walker, S. 1983. *Animal Thought*. London: Routledge and Kegan Paul.

Watanabe, H. 1973. *The Ainu Ecosystem: Environment and Group Structure*. American Ethnological Society Monograph, No. 54. Seattle: University of Washington Press.

Watkins, J.W.N. 1952a. The Principle of Methodological Individualism. *British Journal for the Philosophy of Science* 3: 186–9.

1952b. Ideal Types and Historical Explanations. *British Journal of the Philosophy of Science* 3: 22–43.

Webster, D. and G. Webster. Optimal Hunting and Pleistocene Extinctions. *Human Ecology* 12: 275–84.

Welinder, S. 1977. *The Mesolithic Stone Age of Eastern Middle Sweden*. Stockholm: Almquist and Wiksell International.

Werner, D. 1983. Why do the Mekranti Trek. In *Adaptive Responses of Native Amazonians*, R. Hames and W. Vickers (eds.), pp. 225–38. New York: Academic Press.

White, R. 1985. *Upper Palaeolithic Land Use in the Perigord: A Topographic Approach to Subsistence and Settlement*. Oxford: British Archaeological Reports, S 253.

Whitelaw, T. 1986. Times of Feast, Times of Famine: Strategies for Coping with Temporal Variations in Subsistence Resources among Hunter Gatherers. Paper presented at the 1986 International Conference on Hunter-Gatherers, London School of Economics.

Wiessner, P. 1983. Style and Social Information in Kalahari San Projectile Points. *American Antiquity* 48: 253–76.

Winterhalder, B. 1981. Foraging Strategies in the Boreal Environment: An Analysis of Cree Hunting and Gathering. In *Hunter-Gatherer Foraging Strategies: Ethnographic and Archaeological Analysis*, B. Winterhalder and E.A. Smith (eds.), pp. 66–98. Chicago: University of Chicago Press.

   1986. Diet Choice, Risk and Food Sharing in a Stochastic Environment. *Journal of Anthropological Archaeology* 5: 369–92.

Winterhalder, B. and E.A. Smith. 1981. *Hunter-Gatherer Foraging Strategies: Ethnographic and Archaeological Analysis*. Chicago: University of Chicago Press.

Wobst, H.M. 1977. Stylistic Behaviour and Information Exchange. In *Papers for the Director: Research Essays in Honour of James B. Griffen*, C.E. Cleland (ed.), pp. 317–42. Anthropological Papers No. 61, Museum of Anthropology, University of Michigan.

Woodburn, J. 1968. An Introduction to Hazda Ecology. In *Man the Hunter*, R. Lee and I. DeVore (eds.), pp. 49–55. New York: Aldine Publishing Company.

Woodman, P.C. 1978. The Chronology and Economy of the Irish Mesolithic. In *The Early Post-Glacial Settlement of Northern Europe*, P. Mellars (ed.), pp. 333–70. London: Duckworth.

Wrangham, R.W. 1982. Mutualism, Kinship and Social Evolution. In *Current Problems in Sociobiology*, King's College Sociobiology Group (eds.), pp. 269–89. Cambridge: Cambridge University Press.

Wright, A. and Vlietstra, A. 1975. The Development of Selective Attention: From Perceptual Explanation to Logical Search. In *Infant Perception: From Sensation to Cognition*, L.B. Cohen and P. Salapatek (eds.), pp. 169–89. New York: Academic Press.

Wyszomirska, B. 1988. *Ekonomisk stabilitet vid kusten: Nymölla III. En tidigneolitisk bosättning med Fångstekonomi I nordöstra Skåne*. Acta Archaeologica Lundensia, Series 8, No. 17.

Yellen, J.E. 1976. Settlement Patterns of the !Kung. In *Kalahari Hunter-Gatherers: Studies of the !Kung and their Neighbours*, R. Lee and I. DeVore (eds.), pp. 47–72. Cambridge, Mass.: Harvard University Press.

Yost, J.A. and P.M. Kelley. 1983. Shotguns, Blowguns and Spears: The Analysis of Technological Efficiency. In *Adaptive Responses of Native Amazonians*, R. Hames and W. Vickers (eds.), pp. 189–224. New York: Academic Press.

Zvelebil, M. 1981. *From Forager to Farmer in the Boreal Zone*. Oxford: British Archaeological Reports, Int. Series 115(i & ii).

   1984. Clues to Recent Human Evolution from Specialised Technology. *Nature* 307: 314–15.

1986a. Postglacial Foraging in the Forests of Europe. *Scientific American* May, pp. 86–93.

1986b. *Hunters in Transition*. Cambridge: Cambridge Univerity Press.

1986c. Mesolithic Societies and the Transition to Farming: Problems of Time, Scale and Organisation. In *Hunters in Transition*, M. Zvelebil (ed.), pp. 167–88. Cambridge: Cambridge University Press.

Zvelebil, M. and P. Rowley-Conwy. 1986. Foragers and Farmers in Atlantic Europe. In *Hunters in Transition*, M. Zvelebil (ed.), pp. 67–94. Cambridge: Cambridge University Press.

INDEX